WESTERN SOCIETIES
Primary Sources in Social History

Volume I

WESTERN SOCIETIES
Primary Sources in Social History

*Volume I: From the Ancient Near East to
the Seventeenth Century*

RICHARD M. GOLDEN
Clemson University

THOMAS KUEHN
Clemson University

St. Martin's Press   New York

Acquisitions Editor: Louise H. Waller
Manager, publishing services: Emily Berleth
Project management: Denise Quirk
Cover design: Celine Brandes
Cover art: Peter Brueghel the Elder, *Peasant Dance*. Kunsthistorisches
        Museum, Vienna. Art Resource, NY.
Cover photo: © Erich Lessing.

For information, write:
St. Martin's Press, Inc.
175 Fifth Avenue
New York, NY 10010

ISBN: 0-312-08032-8

Acknowledgments

Acknowledgments and copyrights are continued at the back of the book on pages 329-30, which constitute an extension of the copyright page.

It is a violation of the law to reproduce these selections by any means whatsoever without the written permission of the copyright holder.

"The Atrahasis Story." From Victor H. Matthews and Don C. Benjamin, eds. *Old Testament Parallels: Stories and Laws from the Ancient Near East* (Mahwah, NJ: Paulist Press, 1991). Reprinted by permission of Lawrence Boadt.

"The Teachings of Ptah-Hotep." From Victor H. Matthews and Don C. Benjamin, eds. *Old Testament Parallels: Stories and Laws from the Ancient Near East* (Mahwah, NJ: Paulist Press, 1991). Reprinted by permission of Lawrence Boadt.

"The Farmer and the Courts." From Victor H. Matthews and Don C. Benjamin, eds. *Old Testament Parallels: Stories and Laws from the Ancient Near East* (Mahwah, NJ: Paulist Press, 1991). Reprinted by permission of Lawrence Boadt.

"Sexual Prohibitions and Violence in the Hebrew Bible." From the Revised Standard Version of the Bible, copyright 1946, 1952, 1971 by the Division of Christian Education of the National Council of the Churches of Christ in the U.S.A. and used by permission.

"On Marriage and the Education of a Wife." Xenophon. Reprinted from Leo Strauss, ed., *Xenophon's Socratic Discourse: An Interpretation of the Oeconomicus* (Ithaca: Cornell University Press, 1970). Translation of the *Oeconomicus* by Carnes Lord. Used by permission of the Publisher, Cornell University Press.

"On Household Management." Aristotle. From the *Oeconomica*, translated by E. S. Forster in *The Oxford Translation of Aristotle*, vol 10., edited by W. D. Ross. (Oxford: Clarendon Press, 1921). Reprinted by permission of Oxford University Press.

"An Action for Assault." Demosthenes. Reprinted by permission of the publishers and the

Preface

Western Societies is a two-volume primary-source reader for freshmen in Western civilization courses. In the years that we have taught Western civilization, we have used many books, texts, and readers designed specifically for introductory courses. We decided to compile this reader because we believe there is a need for an anthology centering on useful, readable primary sources with a social historical perspective. A related issue is the need for inclusion in source readers of materials discussing women, minorities, or simply the nonelite groups of the past.

A Western civilization reader cannot be all things to all instructors and students, but we have consciously tried to make these volumes useful for as many Western civilization courses as possible, despite the widely varying ways in which such courses are taught. The readings in these volumes cover many geographical areas and a broad range of topics in social history. Some historians argue that Western civilization began with the Greeks, but we have included in Volume One a section on the ancient Near East for the courses that begin there. Both volumes contain material on the seventeenth century. This chronological overlap is intentional because Western civilization courses break differently according to the policies of instructors and institutions.

To show how the vast majority of articles in *Western Societies* may be used in most Western civilization courses, there is a correlation chart at the beginning of each volume that relates each selection to a relevant chapter in major Western civilization textbooks currently on the market. Though the textbooks do not always offer discrete discussions on all the subjects covered in the selections, they touch upon many of them. As for the other texts, students will at least be able to place the selections in a historical context by reading the standard history of the period in the relevant textbook chapter and, more important, will gain fresh insight into that historical period.

We have also provided introductions to the major periods in history for each volume as well as an introduction to each selection, in which we have asked pertinent questions in order to direct students into the selections and to encourage them to think about the problems and issues the selections raise. These are not summaries and so may not be substituted for the selections themselves.

We have tried to define all proper names, identify all terms that may be unfamiliar to students, and translate all foreign expressions in notes to the selections. Unless indicated otherwise, all notes are ours. Dates given are of birth and death, except for rulers, where the years of the reign are indicated.

What we set out to construct was a different sort of primary-source anthology for use in standard college-level Western civilization courses, such as the one we teach at Clemson. Our most important criterion was to avoid the imbalances of traditional types of sources gathered in available anthologies. Intellectual, political, and religious readings, especially those culled from so-called great books (for example, Plato, Aquinas, Voltaire) dominate existing books. Textbooks, however, increasingly feature the findings of research in social history.

We have been careful to include selections that are readable and interesting, as well as valuable. We bear in mind that our audience will be composed mainly of freshmen, who are notoriously reluctant to read material they consider boring. Nevertheless, we have not pandered to students.

We have chosen selections not previously often used in existing anthologies of Western civilization sources. At the same time, we have chosen sources with an eye to consistency across the volumes. Legal sources, for example, have been included in several sections, thus allowing students to compare issues across time as they deepen their acquaintance with Western culture. The same is true for other topics, such as women's history.

The selections run roughly between five and ten pages—long enough to be substantive but not so long as to be repetitive or to present needless detail. Where possible, complete texts have been used. It must be recognized, however, that to a certain extent each text dictates its own treatment.

The preparation of this reader was more time-consuming than we had originally thought possible. We cannot begin to imagine how much more time it would have required of us if we had not had the generous help and suggestions of the following: Bruce Adams, William Allsbrook, Ove Andersen, Robert Bireley, S. J., Elizabeth Carney, Lawrence Estaville, Jonathan Fowler, Michael Galgano, Hilda Golden, Leonard Greenspoon, Alan Grubb, John Hurt, Bonnelyn Kunze, Donald McKale, Steven Marks, Victor Matthews, William Murnane, David Nicholas, Denis Paz, Julius Ruff, Jim Sack, Roy Vice. Finally, this book would not have been completed without the assistance of the staff at St. Martin's Press—editors Don Reisman and Louise Waller, and associate editors Randi Israelow and Huntley McNair Funsten.

We would also like to thank the following individuals who reviewed this edition for St. Martin's Press: Frederic Baumgartner, Virginia Polytechnic Institute and State University; Gary Cunningham, California State —Los Angeles; Albert Hamsher, Kansas State University; Paul Hanson, Butler University; Donna McCaffrey, Providence College; Gail Savage, Syracuse University; and Thomas Treadway, Augustana College.

Contents

Topical Table of Contents

SEXUALITY

SOCIAL GROUPS

WOMEN

WORK AND ECONOMIC LIFE

URBAN LIFE

Correlation Chart for Western Civilization Texts and Western Societies, Volume I

	The Atrahasis Story	The Teachings of Ptah-Hotep	The Farmer and the Courts	Sexual Prohibitions and Violence in the Hebrew Bible	Xenophon, On Marriage and the Education of a Wife	Aristotle, On Household Management
Winks et al., *A History of Civilization*, 7/e, (1989)	1	1	1	1	2	2
Willis, *Western Civilization*, 4/e (1985)	1	1	1	1	2	2
Wallbank et al., *Civilization Past and Present*, 6/e (1987)	1	1	1	1	2	2
Spielvogel, *Western Civilization* (1991)	1	1	1	2	3	3
Perry et al., *Western Civilization: Ideas, Politics & Society*, 4/e (1992)	1	1	1	2	3	3
Perry, *Western Civilization: A Brief Survey* (1990)	1	1	1	2	3	3
Palmer & Colton, *A History of the Modern World*, 7/e (1992)					1	1
McNeill, *History of Western Civilization*, 6/e (1986)	I,A	I,A	I,A	I,A	II,A	II,A
McKay, Hill, Buckler, *A History of Western Society*, 4/e (1991)	1	1	1	2	3	3
Lerner et al., *Western Civilizations* 11/e (1988)	3	3	3	4	5	5
Kishlansky et al., *Civilization in the West* (1991)	1	1	1	1	3	3
Kagan, Ozment, Turner, *The Western Heritage*, 4/e (1991)	1	1	1	1	3	3
Harrison, Sullivan, Sherman, *A Short History of Western Civilization*, 7/e (1990)	1	1	1	2	6	6
Greer, *A Brief History of the Western World*, 6/e (1992)	1	1	1	1	2	2
Greaves et al., *Civilization of the West* (1992)	1	1	1	1	2	2
Goff et al., *A Survey of Western Civilization* (1987)	1	1	1	1	4	4
Darst, *Western Civilization to 1648* (1990)	2	2	2	2	4	4
Chodorow, *The Mainstream of Civilization*, 5/e (1989)	1	1	1	1	2	2
Chambers et al., *The Western Experience*, 5/e (1991)	1	1	1	1	3	3
Bouchard, *Life and Society in the West* (1988)	1	1	1	1	2	2
Blackburn et al., *Western Civilization* (1991)	1	1	1	2,3	4	4

Reading	1	2	3	4	5	6	7	8	9	10	11	12	13	14	15	16	17	18	19	20
Demosthenes, An Action for Assault	4	2	3	2	4	5	2	2	6	3	3	5	3	II,A	1	3	3	2	2	2
Hellenistic Family Documents	4	2	3	2	4	5	3	2	7	3	3	6	4	II,B	1	3	4	2	3	3
The Twelve Tables	5	3	4	3	5	6	4	3	8,11	4	4	7	5	II,C	1	4	5	3	4	4
Columella, Management of a Large Estate	5	3	4	3	5	7	4	3	8	4	4	7	5	II,C	1	4	5	3	4	4
Marriage, Adultery, and Prostitution	5	3	5	4	6	7	4	3	9,10	5	5	7	6	II,D	1	4	6	3	5	4
Tacitus, Germany and Its Tribes	5,6	4	5,6	4	7	9,10	5	3	13	5	5	7,8	6	II,D,F	1	4	6	3	6,7	5
The Gospel of Bartholomew	5	3	5	4	7	8,9	5	4	12	5	6	8	6	II,D	1	5	8	4	6	5
The Martyrdom of Saints Agape, Irene, and Chione	5	3	5	4	7	9	5	4	12	5	6	8	6	II,D	1	5	8	4	6	5
The Life of Saint Germanus	5	4	5	4	9	9	5	4	12	5	6	8	6,7	II,D	1	5	8	5	6,7	5
The Burgundian Code	6,7	4	6	5	9	10	5	5	15	6	8	8	7	II,F	2	6	9	5	7	5
The Carolingian Capitulary concerning Estates	7	5	6	9	9	11	7	5	16,17	6	8	9	8	II,F	2	6	9	5	8	7
Peasant Landholding	7,9	6	6,8	10	9,10	12	7	5	17	8	9	10	8,10	III,A	3	6	9	6	9	8
The Memoirs of Abbot Guibert of Nogent	8,9	7	8	10	10	12	7	6	18	7	9	10	11	III,B	3	6	10	6	9	9
Marriage in Canon Law	8	7	8	11	11	13	8	6	22	7	9	11	11	III,B	4	7	10	7	10	11
Early Statutes of the Sorbonne	8	8	8	10	11	14	8	6	23	8	9	11	11	III,B	4	7	11	7	10	11

Correlation Chart for Western Civilization Texts and Western Societies, Volume I

Text	London Assize of Nuisance	Sentences against Heretics	The Annals of Ghent	Jean de Venette, The Black Death	The Testament of Michele di Vanni Castellani (c. 1370)	An Anonymous Merchant, How to Succeed in Business	The Goodman of Paris
Winks et al., *A History of Civilization*, 7/e, (1989)	7	8	7	10	10	11	11
Willis, *Western Civilization*, 4/e (1985)	9	8	9	10	11	11	10
Wallbank et al., *Civilization Past and Present*, 6/e (1987)	9	11	9	9	12	12	12
Spielvogel, *Western Civilization* (1991)	11	11	11	12	12	12	12
Perry et al., *Western Civilization: Ideas, Politics & Society*, 4/e (1992)	10	11	10	12	12	12	12
Perry, *Western Civilization: A Brief Survey* (1990)	6	7	7	7	7	7	7
Palmer & Colton, *A History of the Modern World*, 7/e (1992)	3	4	3	5	5	5	5
McNeill, *History of Western Civilization*, 6/e (1986)	III,B	III,B	III,B	III,B	III,B	III,B	III,B
McKay, Hill, Buckler, *A History of Western Society*, 4/e (1991)	11	11	11	12	12	12	12
Lerner et al., *Western Civilizations* 11/e (1988)	10	11	10	12	12	12	12
Kishlansky et al., *Civilization in the West* (1991)	9	9	9	10	10	10	10
Kagan, Ozment, Turner, *The Western Heritage*, 4/e (1991)	8	7	8	9	9	9	9
Harrison, Sullivan, Sherman, *A Short History of Western Civilization*, 7/e (1990)	18	22	24	24	24	24	24
Greer, *A Brief History of the Western World*, 6/e (1992)	6	6	7	7	7	7	7
Greaves et al., *Civilization of the West* (1992)	7	8	7	9	9	9	9
Goff et al., *A Survey of Western Civilization* (1987)	12	13	12	12	12	12	12
Darst, *Western Civilization to 1648* (1990)	10	10	10	12	13	12,13	12
Chodorow, *The Mainstream of Civilization*, 5/e (1989)	11	11	14	14	14	14	14
Chambers et al., *The Western Experience*, 5/e (1991)	9	9	9	11	12	12	12
Bouchard, *Life and Society in the West* (1988)	7	8	7	9	9	9	9
Blackburn et al., *Western Civilization* (1991)	9	8	9	10	10	10	10

Document																					
Florence: Catasto of 1427	10	10	12	16	13	18	9	8	26	10	11	13	13	III,B	6	8	13	13	13	11	11
Leon Battista Alberti, On the Family	10	10	12	16	13	18	10	8	26	10	11	13	13	III,B	6	8	13	13	13	11	11
The Trés Riches Heures of the Duc de Berry	9	10	12	16	12	13,14	10	8	23	10	10	13	13	III,B	7	8	13	13	13	10	11
Articles of the Peasants of Stühlingen and Lupfen	11	10	14	17	14	20	11	9	30	11	13	14	14	III,C-1	9	8	14	14	14	12	12
Martin Luther, On Marriage Matters	11		14	17	14	20	11	9	30	11	13	14	14	III,C-1	9	8	14	14	14	12	12
Giovanni della Casa, Galateo: A Book of Manners	11		14	16	13	18	10	8	26	10	12	13	13	III,B	6	8	13	13	13	11	11
Gianfrancesco Morosini, Spanish Society in the Reign of Philip II	11		15	18	15	21	13	9	31	12	14	15	15	III,C-1	14	9	15	15	15	13	13
Pierre de L'Estoile, Life in Paris during the French Civil Wars	11		15	18	15	21	13	9	31	12	14	15	15	III,C-1	15	9	14	15	15	12	13
Jacques Callot, The Miseries of War	11		15	19	15	21	13	9	31	12	15	15	15	III,C-1	15	9	15	15	15	14	13
The Witches of Huntingdon, Their Examinations and Confessions	11		16	18	15	21	11	9	30	12	14	15	15	III,C-1	—	10	15	15	15	12	15
The Trial of Diogo Henriques before the Portuguese Inquisition	11		16	19	15	20	13	9	31	12	14	15	15	III,C-1	14	10	15	15	15	13	13
Edict Establishing the General Hospital for the Confining of the Poor Beggars of Paris	11		16	19	15	21	14	9	31	13	15	16	16	III,C-1	13	9	15	15	15	14	15

WESTERN SOCIETIES
Primary Sources in Social History

Volume I

I

THE ANCIENT NEAR EAST

Where and when a distinctly Western civilization began are questions to which no certain answer will ever be possible. Some scholars argue that it began with the Greeks, because they initiated forms of thought—historical, humanistic, scientific—that are similar to ours. The Greeks invented forms of historical writing, drama, philosophy, and the study of nature as an entity with its own laws and processes. Yet a good argument also exists that the ancient Near East was the cradle of Western civilization. Somewhere in the fifth millennium B.C., possibly earlier according to some historians, inhabitants of the ancient Near East gave up their nomadic existence as herdsmen. Instead, they developed agriculture and took up settled life in towns, which were generally located near rivers. These people then devised the earliest forms of writing, astronomy and common elements of mathematics, law codes, and important religious notions (especially those of the Hebrews) that were seminal elements of Western civilization. These elements of Near Eastern civilizations developed in the millennia between 3000 B.C. and 500 B.C. They later combined with and influenced elements of so-called classical civilization, which was fostered in ancient Greece and transmitted to Rome.

The major centers of Near Eastern civilization were Mesopotamia, Egypt, and the eastern Mediterranean. In Mesopotamia, people were attracted to the comparatively fertile soils along the valleys of the Tigris and Euphrates rivers (in present-day Iraq). Any people in possession of such an important, yet scarce, resource would find itself the object of aggression from others. The history of this region, therefore, was turbulent. Over the centuries, different peoples invaded and conquered, only to be vanquished themselves by subsequent invaders. Unfortunately for them all, Mesopotamia was not an easily defended area, having few natural barriers to discourage attackers otherwise drawn by the area's undoubted wealth.

That wealth, based on agriculture, was deeply dependent on irrigation systems because the climate of the region was very dry, with little annual rainfall. These systems required cooperation, which in turn led to economic, legal, and political relationships. Extensive power accrued to the warrior-monarchs and the priests who controlled the irrigation systems and thereby the social and economic lives of the people.

Ancient Egypt was also a civilization based on a river—the Nile. Life in Egypt was concentrated in a narrow strip of fertile land along the river. The ease of communication and the relative homogeneity of life along the banks of the Nile facilitated the development of centralized political institutions around the figure of the ruler, the pharaoh. Unlike Mesopotamia, however, Egypt was relatively isolated

1

and defended by the natural barrier of hundreds of square miles of harsh and forbidding desert and the Mediterranean Sea. Egypt, therefore, did not face an endless succession of invasions. Egyptian civilization was free to develop largely on its own terms, in relative political tranquility.

The eastern Mediterranean was a more diverse area, home to many different groups of peoples. Many of these groups turned to trade as an important part of their livelihood because they were located along the shores of the Mediterranean Sea and because they were on the overland routes between Mesopotamia and Egypt. The Phoenicians, for example, lived in coastal cities in what is now southern Lebanon and took up seaborne commerce, journeying all across the Mediterranean. One of the smallest and weakest of peoples in this region was the Hebrews, the group of tribes that settled ultimately in the southeastern corner of the Mediterranean. The Hebrews were unlike their neighbors in several respects. They did not engage in large-scale commerce, opting instead for an essentially pastoral existence, while attempting to preserve their tribal traditions and integrity. Chief among those traditions was their worship of a single personal god and adherence to moral, dietary, and other rules they believed had been laid down for them by him through a succession of religious leaders and prophets.

The people who lived during these millennia had no sense of contributing to an enduring form of civilization that would eventually influence life across the globe. They made their living largely as farmers, herders, and agricultural laborers, some of whom were slaves. Only a relative handful were otherwise engaged in making a living as craftsmen, priests, or warriors. Monarchs, such as the pharaohs of ancient Egypt, dominated political and economic life. Especially where the climate and environment were harsh and forbidding—in Mesopotamia and the eastern Mediterranean—people felt themselves subject to stern and inscrutable forces, divine and human. After all, this was a time when people had little technological means to manage their environment. Gods dominated intellectual and cultural life and were responsible for natural phenomena. Sunlight and darkness, heat and cold, rain and drought—all occurred simply because the gods brought them, for reasons known only to themselves and their priests. The major problem facing any society is to reproduce itself, not just biologically and economically but also socially and culturally. Beliefs and behavior cannot coincide precisely, but neither are they separable from each other. Social structures and economic organization interact with cultural values, beliefs, and norms, and vice versa. The dependence of Egyptian civilization on the Nile River, for example, can help explain both why Egyptian religious views took the form they did and permit us to see how the Egyptians organized and explained to themselves their lives along the river's banks. Both the fact of the Nile in their environment and the way they thought of that river—as a god—had a bearing on Egyptian social life and, therefore, on our understanding of it.

The Atrahasis Story

Myths of human creation and of a universal flood were common to many Near Eastern cultures. Originally Sumerian, but transmitted to the Assyrians and Babylonians, the Atrahasis story describes the gods' creation of life and subsequent desire to reduce human overpopulation.

Originally, only gods populated the world, but the younger gods refused to do all the work themselves and revolted. (Here one thinks immediately of more familiar religious myths depicting divine uprisings, such as the Titans in Greek mythology and the fallen angels in certain Christian stories.) Accepted by the Divine Assembly of the older gods, an accommodation was reached with the younger gods by which humans would be created to do the world's work. By focusing on the birthing process and the role of a midwife, does the Atrahasis story evoke elements and conditions of Near Eastern societies? What can you say about the role of women from the evidence presented in the Atrahasis story?

How does the reason for the gods' wish to reduce the earth's population reflect the reality and precariousness of life in ancient Mesopotamia? How do the creation myth and flood scene differ from the analogous descriptions of creation (Genesis 2:40–3:20) and of Noah's ark (Genesis 6–8) in the Hebrew Bible? There are also interesting parallels between the Atrahasis story, Genesis, and the classic epic of Mesopotamia, the Gilgamesh story.

Summon Nintu, the divine midwife!
   Let her deliver a newborn to labor for The Gods.

The Divine Assembly summoned the divine midwife,
   . . . Mami the wise woman.

"Midwife the lullu![1]
   Deliver Aborigines to labor for The Gods!

"Let them bear the yoke,
   Let them work for Enlil,[2]
   Let them labor for The Gods."

Nintu spoke,
   She said to The Divine Assembly:

"I have no authority,
   I cannot do Enki's work.

"Only Enki[3] has the jurisdiction,
   Only he has the clay I need!"

[1]Humans.

[2]Sumerian storm god; head of the Divine Assembly.

[3]God who was the patron of King Atrahasis.

Enki spoke,
   He said to The Divine Assembly:

"At the new moon, on the seventh day, at the full moon
   I will bathe.

"Let The Divine Assembly sacrifice a god.
   Let them be baptized.

"Let Nintu thin the clay,
   . . . with flesh and blood.

"Let Nintu mix a human clay,
   . . . with flesh and blood divine.

"Let the drum mark off the days,
   . . . count down the time.

"Let this god's flesh make them live,
   Let the midwife command: Live!
   Let them have eternal life."

The Divine Assembly agreed,
   The Anunnaki[4] consented.

At the new moon, on the seventh day, at the full moon Enki bathed.

The Divine Assembly sacrificed We-ila the Wise.

   . . .

Nintu thinned the clay,
   . . . with his flesh and blood.

The drum marked off the days,
   . . . counted down the time.

This god's flesh made them live,
   The midwife commanded: "Live!
   They had eternal life."

   .   .   .

Mami[5] spoke,
   She said to The Divine Assembly:

"You gave me a task;
   I have completed it.

"You sacrificed a god,
   . . . We-ila the Wise.

"I have assigned the lullu,
   To do the work of the Igigi.[6]

---

[4]The old or inactive gods who made up the Divine Assembly.
[5]Nintu-Mami, the divine midwife.
[6]The younger gods.

"You demanded Aborigines,
   . . .

"I have loosened your yoke,
   I have set you free."

The Divine Assembly listened to Mami,
   The gods kissed her feet.

"Yesterday, we called you 'Mami,'
   Today, you are 'Mother of the living.'"

They entered the labor room,
   . . . Ea the Prince, Mami the Wise.

She summoned the midwives,
   He worked the clay.

She sang the sacred song,
   He prayed the special prayer.

She finished singing,
   She pulled off fourteen pieces of clay.

She divided them into rows of seven,
   She set up the birth stool between the rows.

She summoned the midwives,
   She mounted the birth stool.

            .   .   .

She counted ten months,
   They determined her date.

The tenth month came,
   She went into labor.

Her face was beaming,
   . . . full of joy.

She put on her cap,
   She began to midwife.

She donned her apron,
   She began to pray.

She scattered the flour,
   She set up the birth stool.

"I have created,
   My hands gave life.

"Let the midwife rejoice in the labor room,
   Where an expectant woman gives birth,
   Where a woman births her child.

"Erect the birth stool for nine days,
   Honor Nintu the Midwife . . . ,

"Celebrate Mami continually,
    Praise The Midwife,
    Praise Kesh.[7]

"Let husband and wife lie together,
    . . . in their wedding bed.

"Let husband and wife do what Ishtar[8] commands,
    . . . in the father-in-law's house.
Celebrate for nine days,
    Honor Ishtar as 'Ishara.'"

In less than twelve hundred years . . . ,

The land was overpopulated,
    The people multiplied.

The land bellowed like a bull,
    The uproar disturbed The Gods.

When Enlil heard the noise,
    He complained to The Divine Assembly.

"I cannot stand this human uproar,
    I cannot sleep!

        .   .   .

    Send a plague upon the earth!" . . . [9]

"Command your messengers to proclaim,
    . . . to shout throughout the land—

"Do not worship The Gods,
    Do not pray to The Goddesses.

"Go to the gate of Namtar's[10] temple,
    Place your finest loaf of bread on his threshold.

"Your gift of grain will please him,
    Your gift will shame him into withdrawing his hand."[11]

---

[7]A city in Sumer sacred to Nintur, the birth goddess.

[8]Sumerian goddess of love and war.

[9]King Atrahasis then prays to Enki, his patron, for help, and Enki teaches him how to end the plague. (Original editors' note.)

[10]Sumerian god of plague, sometimes identified as Fate.

[11]Atrahasis persuaded The Elders to follow Enki's advice. They renovated the temple of Namtar—The God of Fate, placed their offering at the gate and Namtar stopped the plague.

Over the next six years, Enlil and The Divine Assembly try other means of controlling the human population. There is a drought and a famine. Then the soil becomes so salty that crops fail. An epidemic of skin disease—like [psoriasis] or shingles—and then malnutrition cripples the human population. Each time, King Atrahasis appeals to Enki, who advises the people not to worship The Gods and The Goddesses and to make an offering only to the god responsible for their suffering. Each time, the strategy works and the god is shamed into sending the necessary relief which allows humanity to survive. (Original editors' note.)

"I cannot stand this human uproar,
   I cannot sleep!

"Reduce their food supply,
   Let plants become scarce.

"Adad![12] Withhold the rain!
   Do not allow springs to rise from the deep.

"Winds! Blow the earth dry!
   Clouds! Gather, but do not rain.

"Let harvests be reduced,
   Let Nisaba, The Goddess of Grain, retard growth.

"Let the joy of the harvest, be gone!"

                    .   .   .

In the third year . . . ,
   Every human face was drawn with hunger.

Every human face was crusted like malt.
   Every human lived on the brink of death.

                    .   .   .

In the fifth year . . . ,

A daughter stares while her mother goes into the house,
   . . . while her mother locks her out of the house.

A daughter stares while her mother is sold as a slave,
   A mother stares while her daughter is sold as a slave.

In the sixth year . . . ,

A daughter is cooked for dinner,
   A son is eaten for food.

The people are not diminished,
   They are more numerous than ever.[13]

"Listen to me, Wall!
   You Reed Mat, pay attention to me.

"Pull down your house,
   Build a barge.

---

[12]Sumerian god of rain; Assyrian and Syro-Palestinian storm god.

[13]Thus, every effort of The Divine Assembly to reduce the human population is obstructed by Enki's advice to King Atrahasis. In the face of Enki's opposition and aid to Atrahasis, The Divine Assembly determined that the only way to deal with the human population was a devastating flood. The Gods command Enki to take an oath that he will not reveal to Atrahasis how to save the humans from the flood. However, Atrahasis falls asleep in the temple of Enki. As the king begins to dream, Enki sits behind a lattice screen woven from reeds and begins to whisper his advice (1 Sam 3:3–4). Careful not to violate his oath, Enki does not speak to Atrahasis directly, but only to a wall, and Atrahasis thinks he has only dreamed of how to escape the flood. (Original editors' note.)

"Abandon all your possessions,
   Save only your life.
"The barge should be . . .
   . . . equal . . .
"Place a roof over it,
   Cover it like Apsu, The Heavens, covers The Earth.
"Do not let The Sun see inside,
   Enclose it completely.
"Make the joints strong,
   Caulk the timbers with pitch.
"I will gather flocks of birds for your food,
   . . . and schools of fish for you to eat."
Then, Enki filled the water clock,
   Set the time for the flood on the seventh night.
King Atrahasis addressed The Elders:
   "My god has had a dispute with your god.
"Enki and Enlil are at odds,
   So I must leave this place.
"Since I worship Enki,
   I am a partner in this conflict.
"I can no longer live here,
   I can no longer dwell in the House of Enlil."[14]
The weather began to change . . . ,
Adad roared within the clouds.
   Atrahasis heard Adad's voice,
He closed the door
   And sealed it with pitch.
Adad's roar filled the clouds,
   The winds blew fiercely.
Atrahasis cut the mooring rope,
   He let the barge float free.
The noise in the land ceased,
   Like the silence following the breaking of a pot.

The flood rushed forward,
   The flood charged the people like an army.
One person could not see the other,
   In the water no one was recognizable.

---

[14]With this as his explanation, Atrahasis proceeds to construct a barge and fill it with all sorts of animals. Once he has it loaded, he stages a banquet and sends his family on board. As he sits, saddened by the impending flood, it begins to rain. (Original editors' note.)

The flood bellowed like a bull,
  The winds howled like a wild ass braying.

          .   .   .

There was no sun,
  Only the darkness of the flood.

          .   .   .

The noise of the flood terrified The Gods.
Enki was furious,
  Seeing his children destroyed.
Nintu, The Lady,
  Bit her lips in anger.
The Anunnaki sat without food to eat,
  The Mighty went without wine to drink.
Mami The Wise wept at what she saw,
  The Divine Midwife broke into tears.
"How could I have agreed with The Divine Assembly?
  How could I have voted for a destruction so complete?
"Enlil's evil decree has gone too far,
  His words are worse than Tiruru.[15]

          .   .   .

"Where is Anu,[16] Our Leader, now?
  Where are the humans to carry out his commands?
"Where is he who so thoughtlessly decreed a flood?
  . . . who condemned his own people to destruction?"[17]

          .   .   .

The Gods smelled the aroma,
  They swarmed like flies around his sacrifice.
After The Gods had eaten their fill,
  Nintu indicted them all.
"Where is Anu, Our Leader, now?
  Why has this aroma not brought Enlil here?
"Where is he who so thoughtlessly decreed a flood?
  . . . who condemned his own people to destruction?
"You decreed complete destruction,
  You darkened every shining face on the earth."

          .   .   .

[15]Another name of the Sumerian goddess Ishtar.

[16]Sumerian god of the sky and winds; one of the primeval gods who shared power with Enlil.

[17]For seven days and seven nights the flood covered the earth. Nintu and The Divine Assembly wept. Because the temples were flooded and the humans were dead, there were no sacrifices for them to eat or drink. Although the text is broken at this point, it can be assumed that the flood subsided and Atrahasis disembarked to prepare a sacrificial meal for The Gods. (Original editors' note.)

Enlil The Warrior saw the barge,

Enlil was furious with The Igigi— The Younger Gods,
   "The Anunnaki, The Older Gods, all swore an oath!
"How could anyone survive that flood?
   How did this human escape destruction?"[18]
Let there be three new kinds of women . . .
Let some women be fertile,
   But let other women be sterile.
Let The Demon prey on the newborn,
   Let Pashittu steal infants from their mothers' laps.
Let there be women who are taboo,
   Let them be priestesses forbidden to have children.

The Teachings of Ptah-Hotep

An Egyptian teacher in the middle of the third millennium B.C., Ptah-Hotep wrote his teachings—his wisdom—for his students. In the ancient Near East, a teacher received much respect and was referred to as "father" or "mother" by a student who would be addressed as "child." The teacher aimed to prepare the student for life by teaching him—students were always male—right action and morality. Echoes of Ptah-Hotep's advice can be found not only in the Book of Proverbs in the Hebrew Bible but also in Mesopotamian literature and later in Greek works with Socrates and others. Indeed, the literary genre of dispensing advice echoes throughout Western civilization. Books of advice can be obtained in bookstores today that resemble in part the teachings of Ptah-Hotep.

   Ptah-Hotep offers advice for different occupations. How does he think a ruler should behave? A messenger (administrator)? A judge? A landowner? What is his counsel for house guests and heirs? For students? Is there some common assumption or quality to his advice for all occupations? Which pieces of advice do you find to be tied solely to ancient Egyptian civilization? What advice is still relevant today?

My students, in all things—
Be intelligent, not arrogant,
   Be wise, not over-confident.
Seek advice from the simple,
   As well as from the wise.

---

[18]Anu immediately accused Enki of once again interfering with the will of the gods. Enki defends himself, but the final solution to the human population explosion is achieved when Enki and Nintu create women who are sterile, whose newborns die from crib death and who become celibate priestesses. (Original editors' note.)

No one ever reaches full potential,
  There is always more to learn.

Wisdom hides like emeralds,
  But it can always be uncovered—

— in a poor man,
  —in a young woman grinding grain.

Now—

If you become *a ruler*,
  Do what is right,
  Stay above reproach.

Be just in your decisions,
  never ignoring the law.

Injustice brings punishment,
  Injustice brings all your work to nothing.

Injustice brings success for a moment,
  Injustice brings success for two generations. . . .

If you *work for someone* else,
  Take what your master offers.

Do not look about with envy,
  Do not always hope for more.

Stand humbly until your master speaks to you,
  Speak only when spoken to.

Laugh when your master laughs,
  Try to please your master in everything.

But remember this—
  No one knows what is in another's heart.

When masters are at the table,
  They may seem to dispense favors as they see fit,

—to favor those who are useful,
  —to favor those who think as they do.

But Ka, The Human Soul, is guided by The Gods,
  Therefore, do not complain about their choices.

If you become *a messenger* for the mighty,
  Be completely reliable on every assignment.

Carry out your orders to the letter.
  Withhold nothing,
  Forget nothing,
  Forge nothing,
  Repeat nothing,
  Embellish nothing.

Do not make harsh language worse,
   Vulgarity turns the mighty into enemies.

If you *work for the newly rich*,
   Ignore their former lack of wealth and distinction.

Do not be prejudiced against them,
   Do not detest them for once being lower class.

Respect them for their accomplishments,
   Acknowledge them for their acquisition of property.

Property does not come of itself,
   Property must be earned.

It is their law for those who wish it.
   As for those who overstep, they are feared.

It is The Gods who determine the quality of people.
   The Gods defend them even when they sleep. . . .

If you become *a judge*,
   Listen patiently to the plaintiff's suit.

Give plaintiffs time to air their cases,
   Plaintiffs want petitions heard more than granted.

If you interrupt plaintiffs,
   If you are rude to petitioners,
   People will complain: "Why does the judge do that?"

To grant every petition is unnecessary,
   To hear every petition calms passions, prevents violence.

If you become *the owner of a house* or are a *house guest*,
   Stay away from the women of the house!

Keep your mind on business, your eyes off pretty faces.
   Foolish dreamers become casualties of unwise actions.

Escape love sickness and lust,
   And succeed in everything else you do.

If you *inherit property*,
   Take only your own portion of the estate,
   Do not covet the portions of others.

Those who respect the property of others earn respect.
   Those who defraud others lose their own property.

To covet even a small thing,
   Is to convert peaceful neighbors into enemies!

If you become a *landowner*,
   Establish a household,
   Be faithful to your wife.

Feed her, clothe her, make her happy,
   And she will provide you with an heir.

Do not sue her in court,
   But do not let her dominate you.
To judge a woman's moods,
   Is to read a woman's eyes.
A wife who shares her husband's wealth,
   Is a wife who is faithful to her husband.
If you are *promoted*,
   Be generous with the wealth The Gods give you,
   Take care of your home town now that you can.
Finally, my students, remember—
The wise follow their teachers' advice,
   Consequently, their projects do not fail.
The wise rise to positions of trust,
   Guided by their teachers' instruction.
The wise rise early to begin the day's work,
   Fools rise early to worry about all there is to do.

The Farmer and the Courts

This selection presents the protest of a peasant in the courts of Egypt during the First Intermediate Period (2258–2052 B.C.). It was composed, however, during the subsequent Middle Kingdom (2134–1786 B.C.) and captured the sense prevailing then of the political and social chaos of the earlier era. Interesting parallels can be found in the biblical books of Judges and Job.

The text consists of prose narrative passages that serve to introduce exchanges between the farmer and various judges, which were rendered poetically. Poetic form conveys something of the very stilted and formal atmosphere of judicial proceedings. As you read, consider the following issues: Who was Tut-nakht in relation to the farmer? Why did he think he could get away with stealing the farmer's grain? Why did the pharaoh keep the farmer talking while sending food to his family? What was the concept of justice at work in this piece, and how does it compare to others with which you may be familiar or that are discussed in your Western civilization textbook, such as that of the Hebrews or of Hammurabi?

Once, there was a farmer named Khun-Anup, who lived in The Salt-Field District near Thebes. One day he said to Marye, his wife: "I am going down to the city for food. Go into the barn and see how much grain is left from last year's harvest." After determining that there were twenty-six measures of barley, the farmer took six with him to trade and left the rest to feed his family.

The farmer loaded the asses with salt, reeds, leopard skins, wolf hides, doves and other goods from his district to trade. Then he set out for the city. He traveled south toward Herakleopolis[1] through Per-fefi, north of Medenit. Tut-nakht, son of Isri—who was an official of The Chief Steward, Rensi, the son of Meru—was standing on the bank of the canal and saw the farmer coming.

As he watched the farmer approach, Tut-nakht said to himself: "I think I have a scheme I can use to steal this farmer's goods!"

At one point the public path along the embankment of the canal in front of Tut-nakht's house was no wider than a loincloth. One side of the path was flooded with water, and the other side was overgrown with barley from Tut-nakht's field. Tut-nakht told one of his slaves: "Get me some clothes from my house!" When the slave brought them, Tut-nakht laid the clothes down over the water.

Just then, the farmer came down the path. Tut-nakht shouted to him: "Be careful, you farmer! You are about to step on my garments."

The farmer answered: "I am being careful! I do not wish to offend you, but your garments are right in my way. I cannot climb the steep embankment along the canal on one side of them, nor do I want to trample the grain in your field on the other. Please give me permission to pass."

As he stood there talking, one of the asses bit off a stalk of barley. Then Tut-nakht said: "Now I am going to confiscate your ass for eating my grain. I will sentence it to the threshing floor for this offence."

But the farmer pleaded: "My intentions are good. Only one stalk has been damaged. If you do not let me pay for the damage done and buy back my donkey, I will appeal to Rensi, the son of Meru, who is The Chief Steward and Governor of this district. Is it likely that he will allow me to be robbed in his own district?"

Tut-nakht answered. "Why do the poor always want to speak to masters? You are speaking to me, not to The Chief Steward!" Then he took a stick and beat the farmer and confiscated his asses.

The farmer protested his painful sentence and the injustice done to him.

Tut-nakht tried to silence him in the name of Osiris, The God of Silence.

The farmer protested the attempt to silence him and swore by Osiris that he would not keep quiet until his property was returned.

For ten days, the farmer appealed to Tut-nakht without results. So, he went to Herakleopolis to appeal to Rensi, the son of Meru, who was The Chief Steward. As he was rushing off to board his barge, the official asked the farmer to file his protest with a lower court, which finally took his statement.

---

[1]Capital of one of the thirty-six nomes into which pharaonic Egypt was administratively divided. Modern town of Ahnas.

Eventually, Rensi and his council considered the case and decided that Tut-nakht was guilty only of harassing a farmer who no longer worked for him and should be sentenced only to return the farmer's goods. However, Rensi did not announce the verdict. So the farmer went to see about his appeal in person.

"You are The Chief Steward,
  You are my lord!

"You are my last hope,
  You are my only judge.

"When you sail The Lake of Justice,
  Fairness fills your sail!

"You father the orphan,
  You husband the widow.

"You brother the divorced,
  You mother the motherless.

"I will extol your name throughout the land,
  I will proclaim you a just judge!

". . . a ruler without greed,
  . . . a great man without fault.

". . . a destroyer of lies,
  . . . a just judge, who hears the cry of the poor.

"Hear me when I speak,
  Give me justice.

"Relieve me of this burden of poverty,
  . . . the care which weighs me down!"

The farmer appealed to Rensi in the name of Neb-kau-Ra, Pharaoh of Upper and Lower Egypt.

So, Rensi went to the Pharaoh and said: "My lord, I am hearing the case of a truly eloquent farmer. His goods have been stolen by a man in my service and he has come to me for justice."

The Pharaoh said: "I am ordering you to keep this man waiting without giving him any reply. Just keep him talking. You must write down each of his speeches and send them to me. Furthermore, without letting this farmer know, I want you to provide for his wife and children as well as for his own needs."

Each day, a friend of The Chief Steward delivered ten loaves of bread and two jars of beer to the farmer. Rensi also ordered the governor of The Field-of-Salt District to deliver three measures of grain to the farmer's wife every day.

The second time the farmer comes to see about his appeal, The Chief

Steward asks him whether these goods were really worth going to prison over.

The farmer replies.

"The Distributer puts more grain in his own pile,
    The Giver of Full Measure shorts his people.
"The Lawmaker approves of robbery,
    —who is left to punish the wrongdoer?—
    The Inspector condones corruption.

"One is publicly criminal,
    The other tolerates injustice.

"Do not learn from such as these!

"Punishment lasts for a moment,
    Injustice goes on forever.

"Good example is remembered forever,
    Follow this teaching—

" 'Do unto others,
    As you would have others do unto you.'

"Thank others for their work,
    Parry blows before they strike,
    Give jobs to the most qualified." . . .

The third time, the farmer said:

"Do justice,
    And live!

"Carry out sentences on convicts,
    And fulfill your duty beyond all others.

"Does the hand-scale lie?
    Is the stand-scale tilted?
    Is Thoth, God of The Scales, looking the other way?

"Do not be tempted by corruption . . .
    Do not return evil for good,
    Do not substitute lesser for better goods.

"Do not steal,
    Do not make deals with thieves,
    Greed is blind.

"Close your eyes to violence,
    And no one will punish criminals.

"Ferry only those who can pay,
    And you become an honest man gone bad,
    . . . a shopkeeper who gives no credit to the poor."

When the farmer made this appeal before The Chief Steward at the gate of the court, Rensi had two guards arrest him and flog him.

Nonetheless, the farmer said:

"The Son of Meru continues to do evil.
   He sees, but does not see,
   He hears, but does not hear;
   He ignores what he is told."[2]

"Since you will not grant my appeal,
   I will take it before Anubis himself."

Then, Rensi, the son of Meru and The Chief Steward, sent two guards to arrest the farmer. The farmer was frightened, thinking he was about to be sentenced to death.

"Death long-desired arrives like water for the thirsty,
   . . . like the first drop of milk on a baby's tongue."[3]

Sexual Prohibitions and Violence in the Hebrew Bible

One does not often think of the Hebrew Bible as a sourcebook for human sexuality, but it is replete with rich stories and laws relating to human sexual conduct, as the following six passages demonstrate.

In the first, a mob demanded that Lot release to them the male guests in his house in order to rape them. Instead, Lot offered his two daughters. Why would he do such a callous thing? Soon after, God destroyed the cities of Sodom and Gomorrah for their wickedness. A traditional interpretation is that all the inhabitants of the two cities were killed because of their sexual sins. Does the story support that view? And what are we to make of Lot's incestuous relations with his daughters?

In the second section, Shechem raped Dinah and then wished to marry her. Some

---

[2]The farmer eventually makes nine appeals to Rensi. In each appeal, the farmer recites all the wrongs done to him, describes Egypt as a topsy-turvy world where lawgivers become lawbreakers and appeals to Rensi and others in authority to take their responsibilities seriously and give him justice. In one final burst of frustration, the farmer decides that his only hope for justice will be in the afterlife where Anubis is The Divine Judge. (Original editors' note.)

[3]But Rensi reassures the farmer that no harm will come to him. Then he orders the transcripts of the farmer's appeals, which he had sent to Pharoah Neb-kau-Ra, to be read aloud and the Pharoah's judgment to be announced. Tut-nakht is summoned to the court and given an inventory of all the property which he is ordered to return to the farmer. (Original editors' note.)

of her family objected to the marriage and subsequently murdered all the males in She-chem's cities and took their property and wives. It could be argued that the punishment exceeded the crime, as innocent people suffered as a result of Shechem's deed. What does this episode tell us about Hebrew values of family and their attitudes toward crime?

The third passage recounts the famous sin of Onan, which Christian theologians later used as authority to prohibit masturbation and contraception (coitus interruptus). Why did God kill Onan for spilling "the semen on the ground"?

In the fourth excerpt, prohibitions against incest are listed. What other types of sexual behavior do these laws stigmatize?

The fifth selection pertains to virginity and adultery. Why was virginity prized? Why was a man who raped a virgin compelled to marry her rather than condemned? Why were adulterers punished so severely?

Finally, the story of the wandering Levite recalls Lot's experience. Once more a mob besieged a house demanding the guest inside; once more the host offered his virgin daughter. The guest, the Levite, tendered his concubine, whom the crowd raped repeatedly during the night. She died the next morning. Why did the Levite then cut his concubine—a woman deserving of some sympathy—into twelve pieces and proceed to send the body parts throughout Israel?

What do these stories taken together tell us about the beliefs and mores of the ancient Hebrews? What attitudes about women do these passages express?

GENESIS 19

The two angels came to Sodom in the evening; and Lot was sitting in the gate of Sodom. When Lot saw them, he rose to meet them, and bowed himself with his face to the earth, and said, "My lords, turn aside, I pray you, to your servant's house and spend the night, and wash your feet; then you may rise up early and go on your way." They said, "No; we will spend the night in the street." But he urged them strongly; so they turned aside to him and entered his house; and he made them a feast, and baked unleavened bread, and they ate. But before they lay down, the men of the city, the men of Sodom, both young and old, all the people to the last man, surrounded the house; and they called to Lot, "Where are the men who came to you tonight? Bring them out to us, that we may know them." Lot went out of the door to the men, shut the door after him, and said, "I beg you, my brothers, do not act so wickedly. Behold, I have two daughters who have not known man; let me bring them out to you, and do to them as you please; only do nothing to these men, for they have come under the shelter of my roof." But they said, "Stand back!" And they said, "This fellow came to sojourn, and he would play the judge! Now we will deal worse with you than with them." Then they pressed hard against the man Lot, and drew near to break the door. But the men put forth their hands and brought Lot into the house to them, and shut the door. And they struck with blindness the men who were at the door of the house, both small and great, so that they wearied themselves groping for the door.

Then the men said to Lot, "Have you any one else here? Sons-in-laws, sons, daughters, or any one you have in the city, bring them out of the place; for we are about to destroy this place, because the outcry against its people has become great before the LORD, and the LORD has sent us to destroy it." So Lot went out and said to his sons-in-law, who were to marry his daughters, "Up, get out of this place; for the LORD is about to destroy the city." But he seemed to his sons-in-law to be jesting.

When morning dawned, the angels urged Lot, saying, "Arise, take your wife and your two daughters who are here, lest you be consumed in the punishment of the city." But he lingered; so the men seized him and his wife and his two daughters by the hand, the LORD being merciful to him, and they brought him forth and set him outside the city. And when they had brought them forth, they said, "Flee for your life; do not look back or stop anywhere in the valley; flee to the hills, lest you be consumed." And Lot said to them, "Oh, no, my lords; behold, your servant has found favor in your sight, and you have shown me great kindness in saving my life; but I cannot flee to the hills, lest the disaster overtake me, and I die. Behold, yonder city is near enough to flee to, and it is a little one. Let me escape there—is it not a little one?—and my life will be saved!" He said to him, "Behold, I grant you this favor also, that I will not overthrow the city of which you have spoken. Make haste, escape there; for I can do nothing till you arrive there." Therefore the name of the city was called Zo'ar. The sun had risen on the earth when Lot came to Zo'ar.

Then the LORD rained on Sodom and Gomor'rah brimstone and fire from the LORD out of heaven; and he overthrew those cities, and all the valley, and all the inhabitants of the cities, and what grew on the ground. But Lot's wife behind him looked back, and she became a pillar of salt. And Abraham went early in the morning to the place where he had stood before the LORD; and he looked down toward Sodom and Gomor'rah and toward all the land of the valley, and beheld, and lo, the smoke of the land went up like the smoke of a furnace.

So it was that, when God destroyed the cities of the valley, God remembered Abraham, and sent Lot out of the midst of the overthrow, when he overthrew the cities in which Lot dwelt.

Now Lot went up out of Zo'ar, and dwelt in the hills with his two daughters, for he was afraid to dwell in Zo'ar; so he dwelt in a cave with his two daughters. And the first-born said to the younger, "Our father is old, and there is not a man on earth to come in to us after the manner of all the earth. Come, let us make our father drink wine, and we will lie with him, that we may preserve offspring through our father." So they made their father drink wine that night; and the first-born went in, and lay with her father; he did not know when she lay down or when she arose. And on the next day, the first-born said to the younger, "Behold, I lay last night with my father; let us make him drink wine tonight also; then you go in and lie with him, that we may preserve offspring through our father." So they made their father drink wine that night also; and the younger arose, and lay with him; and he did not know when she lay down or when she arose. Thus both the daughters of Lot were with child by their father. The first-born bore a son, and called his name Moab; he is the father of the Moabites to this day. The younger also bore a son, and called his name Ben-ammi; he is the father of the Ammonites to this day.

GENESIS 34

Now Dinah the daughter of Leah, whom she had borne to Jacob, went out to visit the women of the land; and when Shechem the son of Hamor the Hivite, the prince of the land, saw her, he seized her and lay with her and humbled her. And his soul was drawn to Dinah the daughter of Jacob; he loved the maiden and spoke tenderly to her. So Shechem spoke to his father Hamor, saying, "Get me this maiden for my wife." Now Jacob heard that he had defiled his daughter Dinah; but his sons were with his cattle in the field, so Jacob held his peace until they came. And Hamor the father of Shechem went out to Jacob to speak with him. The sons of Jacob came in from the field when they heard of it; and the men were indignant and very angry, because he had wrought folly in Israel by lying with Jacob's daughter, for such a thing ought not to be done.

But Hamor spoke with them, saying, "The soul of my son Shechem longs for your daughter; I pray you, give her to him in marriage. Make marriages with us; give your daughters to us, and take our daughters for yourselves. You shall dwell with us; and the land shall be open to you; dwell and trade in it, and get property in it." Shechem also said to her father and to her brothers, "Let me find favor in your eyes, and whatever you say to me I will give. Ask of me ever so much as marriage present and gift, and I will give according as you say to me; only give me the maiden to be my wife."

The sons of Jacob answered Shechem and his father Hamor deceitfully, because he had defiled their sister Dinah. They said to them, "We cannot do this thing, to give our sister to one who is uncircumcised, for that would be a disgrace to us. Only on this condition will we consent to you: that you will become as we are and every male of you be circumcised. Then we will give our daughters to you, and we will take your daughters to ourselves, and we will dwell with you and become one people. But if you will not listen to us and be circumcised, then we will take our daughter, and we will be gone."

Their words pleased Hamor and Hamor's son Shechem. And the young man did not delay to do the thing, because he had delight in Jacob's daughter. Now he was the most honored of all his family. So Hamor and his son Shechem came to the gate of their city and spoke to the men of their city, saying, "These men are friendly with us; let them dwell in the land and trade in it, for behold, the land is large enough for them; let us take their daughters in marriage, and let us give them our daughters. Only on this condition will the men agree to dwell with us, to become one people: that every male among us be circumcised as they are circumcised. Will not their cattle, their property and all their beasts be ours? Only let us agree with them, and they will dwell with us." And all who went out of the gate of his city hearkened to Hamor and his son Shechem; and every male was circumcised, all who went out of the gate of his city.

On the third day, when they were sore, two of the sons of Jacob, Simeon and Levi, Dinah's brothers, took their swords and came upon the city unawares, and killed all the males. They slew Hamor and his son Shechem with the sword, and took Dinah out of Shechem's house, and went away. And the sons of Jacob came upon the slain, and plundered the city, because their sister had been defiled; they took their flocks and their herds, their asses, and whatever was in the city and in the field; all their wealth, all their little ones and their wives, all that was in the houses, they captured and made their prey. Then Jacob said to Simeon and Levi, "You have brought trouble on me by making me odious to the inhabitants of the land, the Canaanites and the Per'izzites; my numbers are few, and if they gather themselves against me and attack me, I shall be destroyed, both I and my household." But they said, "Should he treat our sister as a harlot?"

GENESIS 38

It happened at that time that Judah went down from his brothers, and turned in to a certain Adullamite, whose name was Hirah. There Judah saw the daughter of a certain Canaanite whose name was Shua; he married her and went in to her, and she conceived and bore a son, and he called his name Er. Again she conceived and bore a son, and she called his name Onan. Yet again she bore a son, and she called his name Shelah. She was in Chezib when she bore him. And Judah took a wife for Er his first-born, and her name was Tamar. But Er, Judah's first-born, was wicked in the sight of the LORD; and the LORD slew him. Then Judah said to Onan, "Go in to your brother's wife, and perform the duty of a brother-in-law to her, and raise up offspring for your brother." But Onan knew that the offspring would not be his; so when he went in to his brother's wife he spilled the semen on the ground, lest he should give offspring to his brother. And what he did was displeasing in the sight of the LORD, and he slew him also. Then Judah said to Tamar his daughter-in-law, "Remain a widow in your father's house, till Shelah my son grows up"—for he feared that he would die, like his brothers. So Tamar went and dwelt in her father's house. . . .

LEVITICUS 18

And the LORD said to Moses, "Say to the people of Israel, I am the LORD your God. You shall not do as they do in the land of Egypt, where you dwelt, and you shall not do as they do in the land of Canaan, to which I am bringing you. You shall not walk in their statutes. You shall do my ordinances and keep my statutes and walk in them. I am the LORD your God. You shall therefore keep my statutes and my ordinances, by doing which a man shall live: I am the LORD.

"None of you shall approach any one near of kin to him to uncover nakedness. I am the LORD. You shall not uncover the nakedness of your father, which is the nakedness of your mother; she is your mother, you shall not uncover her nakedness. You shall not uncover the nakedness of your father's wife; it is your father's nakedness. You shall not uncover the nakedness of your sister, the daughter of your father or the daughter of your mother, whether born at home or born abroad. You shall not uncover the nakedness of your son's daughter or of your daughter's daughter, for their nakedness is your own nakedness. You shall not uncover the nakedness of your father's wife's daughter, begotten by your father, since she is your sister. You shall not uncover the nakedness of your father's sister; she is your father's near kinswoman. You shall not uncover the nakedness of your mother's sister, for she is your mother's near kinswoman. You shall not uncover the nakedness of your father's brother, that is, you shall not approach his wife; she is your aunt. You shall not uncover the nakedness of your daughter-in-law; she is your son's wife, you shall not uncover her nakedness. You shall not uncover the nakedness of your brother's wife; she is your brother's nakedness. You shall not uncover the nakedness of a woman and of her daughter, and you shall not take her son's daughter, and you shall not take her son's daughter or her daughter's daughter to uncover her nakedness; they are your near kinswomen; it is wickedness. And you shall not take a woman as a rival wife to her sister, uncovering her nakedness while her sister is yet alive.

"You shall not approach a woman to uncover her nakedness while she is in her menstrual uncleanness. And you shall not lie carnally with your neighbor's wife, and defile yourself with her. You shall not give any of your children to devote them by fire to Molech, and so profane the name of your God: I am the LORD. You shall not lie with a male as with a woman; it is an abomination. And you shall not lie with any beast and defile yourself with it, neither shall any woman give herself to a beast to lie with it: it is perversion.

"Do not defile yourselves by any of these things, for by all these the nations I am casting out before you defiled themselves; and the land became defiled, so that I punished its iniquity, and the land vomited out its inhabitants. But you shall keep my statutes and my ordinances and do none of these abominations, either the native or the stranger who sojourns among you (for all of these abominations the men of the land did, who were before you, so that the land became defiled); lest the land vomit you out, when you defile it, as it vomited out the nation that was before you. For whoever shall do any of these abominations, the persons that do them shall be cut off from among their people. So keep my charge never to practice any of these abominable customs which were practiced before you, and never to defile yourselves by them: I am the LORD your God."

DEUTERONOMY 22

. . ."If any man takes a wife, and goes in to her, and then spurns her, and charges her with shameful conduct, and brings an evil name upon her, saying, 'I took this woman, and when I came near her, I did not find in her the tokens of virginity,' then the father of the young woman and her mother shall take and bring out the tokens of her virginity to the elders of the city in the gate; and the father of the young woman shall say to the elders, 'I gave my daughter to this man to wife, and he spurns her; and lo, he has made shameful charges against her, saying, "I did not find in your daughter the tokens of virginity." And yet these are the tokens of my daughter's virginity.' And they shall spread the garment before the elders of the city. Then the elders of that city shall take the man and whip him; and they shall fine him a hundred shekels of silver, and give them to the father of the young woman, because he has brought an evil name upon a virgin of Israel; and she shall be his wife; he may not put her away all his days. But if the thing is true, that the tokens of virginity were not found in the young woman, then they shall bring out the young woman to the door of her father's house, and the men of her city shall stone her to death with stones, because she has wrought folly in Israel by playing the harlot in her father's house; so you shall purge the evil from the midst of you.

"If a man is found lying with the wife of another man, both of them shall die, the man who lay with the woman, and the woman; so you shall purge the evil from Israel.

"If there is a betrothed virgin, and a man meets her in the city and lies with her, then you shall bring them both out to the gate of that city, and you shall stone them to death with stones, the young woman because she did not cry for help though she was in the city, and the man because he violated his neighbor's wife; so you shall purge the evil from the midst of you.

"But if in the open country a man meets a young woman who is betrothed, and the man seizes her and lies with her, then only the man who lay with her shall die. But to the young woman you shall do nothing; in the young woman there is no offense punishable by death, for this case is like that of a man attacking and murdering his neighbor; because he came upon her in the open country, and though the betrothed young woman cried for help there was no one to rescue her.

"If a man meets a virgin who is not betrothed, and seizes her and lies with her, and they are found, then the man who lay with her shall give to the father of the young woman fifty shekels of silver, and she shall be his wife, because he has violated her; he may not put her away all his days.

"A man shall not take his father's wife, nor shall he uncover her who is his father's.

JUDGES 19–20
Judges 19

In those days, when there was no king in Israel, a certain Levite was sojourning in the remote parts of the hill country of E'phraim, who took to himself a concubine from Bethlehem in Judah. And his concubine became angry with him, and she went away from him to her father's house at Bethlehem in Judah, and was there some four months. Then her husband arose and went after her, to speak kindly to her and bring her back. He had with him his servant and a couple of asses. And he came to her father's house; and when the girl's father saw him, he came with joy to meet him. And his father-in-law, the girl's father, made him stay, and he remained with him three days; so they ate and drank, and lodged there. And on the fourth day they arose early in the morning, and he prepared to go; but the girl's father said to his son-in-law, "Strengthen your heart with a morsel of bread, and after that you may go." So the two men sat and ate and drank together; and the girl's father said to the man, "Be pleased to spend the night, and let your heart be merry." And when the man rose up to go, his father-in-law urged him, till he lodged there again. And on the fifth day he arose early in the morning to depart; and the girl's father said, "Strengthen your heart, and tarry until the day declines." So they ate, both of them. And when the man and his concubine and his servant rose up to depart, his father-in-law, the girl's father, said to him, "Behold, now the day has waned toward evening; pray tarry all night. Behold, the day draws to its close; lodge here and let your heart be merry; and tomorrow you shall arise early in the morning for your journey, and go home."

But the man would not spend the night; he rose up and departed, and arrived opposite Jebus (that is, Jerusalem). He had with him a couple of saddled asses, and his concubine was with him. When they were near Jebus, the day was far spent, and the servant said to his master, "Come now, let us turn aside to this city of the Jeb'usites, and spend the night in it." And his master said to him, "We will not turn aside into the city of foreigners, who do not belong to the people of Israel; but we will pass on to Gib'e-ah." And he said to his servant, "Come and let us draw near to one of these places, and spend the night at Gib'e-ah or at Ramah." So they passed on and went their way; and the sun went down on them near Gib'e-ah, which belongs to Benjamin, and they turned aside there, to go in and spend the night at Gib'e-ah. And he went in and sat down in the open square of the city; for no man took them into his house to spend the night.

And behold, an old man was coming from his work in the field at evening; the man was from the hill country of E'phraim, and he was sojourning in Gib'e-ah; the men of the place were Benjaminites. And he lifted up his eyes, and saw the wayfarer in the open square of the city; and the old man said, "Where are you going? and whence do you come?" And he said to him, "We are passing from Bethlehem in Judah to the remote parts of the hill country of E'phraim, from which I come. I went to Bethlehem in Judah; and I am going to my home, and nobody takes me into his house. We have straw and provender for our asses, with bread and wine for me and your maidservant and the young man with your servants; there is no lack of anything." And the old man said, "Peace be to you; I will care for all your wants; only, do not spend the night in the square." So he brought him into his house, and gave the asses provender; and they washed their feet, and ate and drank.

As they were making their hearts merry, behold, the men of the city, base fellows, beset the house round about, beating on the door; and they said to the old man, the master of the house, "Bring out the man who came into your house, that we may know him." And the man, the master of the house, went out to them and said to them, "No, my brethren, do not act so wickedly; seeing that this man has come into my house, do not do this vile thing. Behold, here are my virgin daughter and his concubine; let me bring them out now. Ravish them and do with them what seems good to you; but against this man do not do so vile a thing." But the men would not listen to him. So the man seized his concubine, and put her out to them; and they knew her, and abused her all night until the morning. And as the dawn began to break, they let her go. And as morning appeared, the woman came and fell down at the door of the man's house where her master was, till it was light.

And her master rose up in the morning, and when he opened the doors of the house and went out to go on his way, behold, there was his concubine lying at the door of the house, with her hands on the threshold. He said to her, "Get up, let us be going." But there was no answer. Then he put her upon the ass; and the man rose up and went away to his home. And when he entered his house, he took a knife, and laying hold of his concubine he divided her, limb by limb, into twelve pieces, and sent her throughout all the territory of Israel. And all who saw it said, "Such a thing has never happened or been seen from the day that the people of Israel came up out of the land of Egypt until this day; consider it, take counsel, and speak."

Judges 20

Then all the people of Israel came out, from Dan to Beer-sheba, including the land of Gilead, and the congregation assembled as one man to the LORD at Mizpah. And the chiefs of all the people, of all the tribes of Israel, presented themselves in the assembly of the people of God, four hundred thousand men on foot that drew the sword. (Now the Benjaminites heard that the people of Israel had gone up to Mizpah.) And the people of Israel said, "Tell us, how was this wickedness brought to pass?" And the Levite, the husband of the woman who was murdered, answered and said, "I came to Gib'e-ah that belongs to Benjamin, I and my concubine, to spend the night. And the men of Gib'e-ah rose against me, and beset the house round about me by night; they meant to kill me, and they ravished my concubine, and she is dead. And I took my concubine and cut her in pieces, and sent her throughout all the country of the inheritance of Israel; for they have committed abomination and wantonness in Israel. Behold, you people of Israel, all of you, give your advice and counsel here."

And all the people arose as one man, saying, "We will not any of us go to his tent, and none of us will return to his house. But now this is what we will do to Gib'e-ah: we will go up against it by lot, and we will take ten men of a hundred throughout all the tribes of Israel, and a hundred of a thousand, and a thousand of ten thousand, to bring provisions for the people, that when they come they may requite Gib'e-ah of Benjamin, for all the wanton crime which they have committed in Israel." So all the men of Israel gathered against the city, united as one man. . . .

II

GREECE AND ROME

Two imperial powers, the Assyrians and then the Persians, eventually controlled the ancient Near East. The Persians were a warlike people intent on expansion of their power through conquest. Their kings fell heir to the image of godlike political rulers that had arisen in the ancient Near East, and they needed to express their "divine" power through successful military activity. In the early fifth century B.C., the Persians began moving into Europe, where they encountered and were defeated by the Greeks. This victory in the Persian Wars by the numerically inferior but politically and militarily sophisticated Greeks preserved their cultural heritage and social life from absorption by the Persians. For the next century and a half, Greek poets, artists, and thinkers were able to celebrate and criticize the achievements and values of their people. The cultural legacy they left behind has inspired Western civilization ever since with ideas of political order and responsibility, artistic beauty, and rational speculation.

The people who espoused these ideals lived in a social world very different from that of the ancient Near East. The peninsula of Greece presented a varied environment and terrain, which encouraged the formation of discrete social and political units called city-states that included the city along with a rural hinterland. The Greek term for city-state was polis. Each polis was unique to a degree in its organization and culture. The polis was the center of political, social, cultural, and religious life for Greeks. It was so characteristic of their existence that as they came to colonize other areas around the Mediterranean (southern Italy and Sicily, parts of North Africa, and even parts of southern France and eastern Spain), they did so by establishing new independent poleis. By the fourth century B.C., it was possible for Aristotle, in his Politics, to insist that the male human was a political animal: a creature whose highest potential was to be realized in and through a polis. Women, who were excluded from active participation in the governance of a polis, were likewise excluded from consideration by Aristotle, except when he, or those influenced by him, came to discuss problems of household management.

Most people in the modern era have looked back on the world of the polis with admiration for the achievements of the Greeks. The largest polis of the classical era (fifth and fourth centuries B.C.), with a population of around 300,000 and a great deal of wealth, was Athens. Great poets, playwrights, historians, and philosophers graced that city, and their names sparkle in the pages of Western civilization textbooks to this day. Athens has also been admired in history for developing democratic political institutions, such as the assembly of citizens and juries.

More recently, however, attention has also been drawn to the contradictions, *problems, and ultimate failings that plagued Greek, especially Athenian, society. The achievements of these* poleis *also rested on slavery, on social intolerance for those who were not Greek and even those who were not of one's own* polis, *and on class and gender distinctions that greatly disadvantaged certain types of people. The basic unit within the* polis *was the citizen's household (oikos). It was as members of a household, not as individuals, that Greeks participated in political, social, economic, and ritual activities. Men and women did not participate equally in household affairs. Acquisition and preservation of the material resources and family prestige that were both crucial to the maintenance and well-being of the household fell in different measure to each gender. It was men who went forth in the public areas of their* polis *to see to their families' political fortunes, economic interests, and religious duties. Women were largely relegated to domestic activities. In Athens especially women's movements were carefully guarded; wives and daughters of wealthy citizens, especially, remained secluded within the home. Children too found their lives shaped to the needs of the family, including their choices of when and whom to marry. Most of the slaves found in Greek* poleis *also worked as domestic servants or on the farms and businesses of their owners. Greek families were the crucial center of social relationships in this first important civilization on the European continent.*

In the long term, the Greek polis *was a political failure. Intense loyalties to one's* polis *precluded the Greeks from ever forming enduring larger political units. The Greeks' competitiveness (these were the people who invented the Olympic games) prevented much cooperation. Even when faced with the massive outside threat of the Persians, the alliance of Greek cities almost disintegrated. Before the fifth century was over, the political disunity of Greece was manifest in the long and destructive Peloponnesian War (431–404 B.C.) between Athens and Sparta. Many Greek* poleis *feared Athenian economic and political expansion and sided with Sparta. The eventual defeat of the domineering and imperialistic power of Athens did not bring unity, however. Sparta's resulting supremacy proved ephemeral, as did that of Thebes, which arose to challenge Sparta in the mid-fourth century B.C. The proud city-states fell under the sway of the Macedonians to the north. After his father, Philip, had defeated the Greeks, the Macedonian king Alexander (known as "the Great"), who had been tutored by Aristotle, marshaled the united power of Greece to conquer Persia in a whirlwind campaign. His successors helped spread Greek ideas and artistic styles throughout the Near East during the period historians have labeled the Hellenistic Age. Yet under Alexander's successors, the fierce independence of the old Greek* poleis *again emerged. In the second century B.C., the growing power of Rome was drawn into the turmoil of Greek politics, and the independence of the* poleis *gave way once and for all before the conquering legions of this Italian city. It was Rome that succeeded in uniting the Mediterranean world through conquest and holding it together for several centuries.*

Rome began as a modest city on the banks of the Tiber River in central Italy. Throughout the fifth and fourth centuries B.C., by a pragmatic combination of alliances, conquests, and political maneuvers, Rome succeeded in drawing the entire peninsula of Italy under its influence or control. In the course of the third century B.C., Rome faced and resisted the opposition of the North African city of Carthage.

Once Carthage had been defeated and destroyed in the middle of the second century
B.C., Rome was free to expand its power on all sides of the Mediterranean.

During its conquests and expansion, Rome's power rested on its highly disci-
plined, professional army of citizen-soldiers. Roman notions of dedication to the
groups to which one owed allegiance, the city and one's family, were powerful
formative elements of Roman life. Roman society, like that of the Greek polis, rested
on family units. In Rome, all power and property ownership was nominally vested
in the male head of household, the paterfamilias. *His powers over his wife and*
children were extensive. Their loyalties to him were supposed to be unquestioned.
Betrayal of these loyalties, including by a wife's adultery, could be harshly dealt
with by the paterfamilias. *Roman law excluded women from politics and govern-*
ment. Wealthier Roman families, those that belonged to the patrician class, which
dominated the political offices of the city and constituted the membership of the
Roman Senate, maintained relations with a wider kindred, the gens. *The gens*
provided a patrician with political connections, allowing him to take positions of
responsibility in government and the military and thus giving him the opportunity
to gain prestige and fortune.

Those citizens who were not of the patrician class found themselves excluded
from politics in the early days of the Roman Republic, where deep social divisions
translated into political and legal differences. As early as the time of the first cod-
ification of Roman law, known as the Twelve Tables, in the mid fifth century B.C.
and later throughout the republic (to 30 B.C.), these social divisions among Roman
citizens were fought out and had their effect on Roman efforts to build everything
from bridges, roads, and aqueducts to a lasting political empire. Eventually, the
wealthier plebeians (the common people) gained full rights of political participation
and legal protection, but throughout Roman history, wealth and useful family and
political connections were the key ingredients in social and economic success.

Conquest brought problems for Rome. The wealthy accumulated large estates
and gangs of slaves, although they continued to pretend to an ideal life of the simple
small farmer and citizen. Marriage practices and family life were affected by the
pressures of mobile forms of wealth, political success and failure, and new ideas
garnered from peoples like the Greeks. Knowledge of Greek language, literature, and
philosophy came to be the hallmarks of a properly educated member of the Roman
elite. Those not in the elite did considerably less well. The citizen-soldier became
impoverished, and his loyalty was transferred to his commander, who could bring
him the spoils of victory. Powerful commanders led their armies not only against
outside enemies but against other Roman armies as well. Civil wars marked the first
century B.C. and the third century A.D.

The disappearance of the citizen-soldier and small landowner, the rise of a class
of newly wealthy people who exploited the economic opportunities provided by con-
quests, corruption in government administration, and the evolution of a complex
bureaucracy to fit the administration of a city-state to the much greater demands of a
complex empire, were all factors in the disintegration of the old republican system
and the emergence of the Roman Empire in the first century B.C. Law and civil
administration were truly Roman accomplishments that held the empire together for

centuries, despite the incompetence of some emperors and mounting pressures inside and out. Through the first two centuries of the Christian era, imperial power was consolidated and systematized with the aid of a cosmopolitan class of wealthy and educated Romans and provincials who staffed the judicial, administrative, and military offices. By the early third century, Roman citizenship was extended to all free inhabitants of the empire.

By the late third century, however, Roman ideas and institutions were crumbling or under attack from a variety of quarters. Migrating Germanic peoples were pressing against the empire's boundaries along the Rhine and Danube rivers and even taking a large role in the empire's defense. These people brought with them their own beliefs, customs, and practices. Other peoples within the empire, such as the Jews, the Copts of Egypt, and the Celtic peoples of western Europe, had maintained their cultural and religious beliefs beneath a veneer of Romanization. In time, the different offshoots of Judaism known to the Romans under the collective term Christian became increasingly prominent. The Christians themselves were not a single sect. They disagreed over what to believe, how to worship, and how to organize themselves. They shared, however, a belief in a divinity who was not necessarily tied to maintaining the existing social and political order, which had been the role of the Greek and Roman civic gods. Still, the Christians would find in Roman institutions an example of order. Bishops established themselves in the cities that were also centers of imperial administration, and church organization began to resemble imperial arrangements.

Worship of their god precluded the Christians from participating in the worship of imperial gods or divinized emperors. However, the maintenance of imperial order was held by Romans to rest on the performance of official acts of worship and prayer by all. The failure of the Christians to take part in the official cults thus subjected them to persecution at times through the first three centuries. The early Christian martyrs were heroic figures whose examples fed the faith of their coreligionists. With the conversion of Emperor Constantine, who reigned from 306 to 337, to Christianity, however, the religion became involved in the secular affairs of the empire. By the end of the fourth century, the Roman Empire had become a Christian empire. Churches became legal corporations, and bishops began to figure in imperial and local administration. Indeed, these ecclesiastical bodies would survive the disintegration of the civil administration of the empire to convert the Germanic invaders and keep select bits of classical culture alive.

On Marriage and the Education of a Wife

XENOPHON

Soldier, historian, and student of the Greek philosopher Socrates (470?–399 B.C.), Xenophon (430?–355? B.C.) in the Oeconomicus *relates the principles of household management. In the passage here, Socrates is talking with his student Ischomachos about the education Ischomachos has given his wife.*

In fifth- and fourth-century Athens, citizens confined their wives and female children to their homes, or even to certain parts of homes. Because fathers and husbands demanded that their daughters be virgins and their wives faithful—beyond any suspicion of impropriety—the women were rarely allowed outside the home and never unchaperoned. Males looked upon women as intellectually inferior, so fathers did not see to the education of their daughters, save for making sure that they knew how to perform household tasks such as the spinning of wool.

Soon after they began living together, Ischomachos felt it necessary to discuss with his young bride her role in the household. What presuppositions about the nature of women does Ischomachos reveal? In what ways does he feel women to be different than men? Are there any positive qualities that he believes women have that men do not share, or have to a greater degree than do men? What responsibilities within the household does Ischomachos delegate to his wife?

How does Ischomachos treat his wife? Was he content with her management of the household? Just what was she responsible for? There is one instance when Ischomachos rebuked his wife. What had she done? Are you able to reconstruct the interior space of the house from the instructions Ischomachos gives his wife?

Is it possible, from this source written by a man, to speculate about whether or not Ischomachos deceived himself about his wife's feelings toward him and toward her role in the management of the household?

"Seeing him then one day sitting in the colonnade of Zeus the Deliverer, I[1] went over to him, and as he seemed to be at leisure, I sat down with him and spoke. 'Why are you sitting like this, Ischomachos, you who are so unaccustomed to leisure? For I mostly see you either doing something or at least hardly at leisure in the market place.'

" 'Nor would you see me now, Socrates,' said Ischomachos, 'if I hadn't made an appointment to meet some foreigners here.'

" 'When you aren't doing this sort of thing,' I said, 'by the gods, how do you spend your time and what do you do? For I would like very much to inquire what it is you do in order to be called a gentleman, since you don't spend your time indoors, and the condition of your body hardly looks like that of one who does.'

---

[1]Socrates.

"And Ischomachos, laughing at my asking what he did to be called a gentleman and rather pleased, or so it seemed to me, spoke. 'I don't know whether some call me by that name when discussing me with you, but surely when they call me to an exchange[2] for the support of a trireme[3] or the training of a chorus, no one,' he said, 'goes looking for "the gentleman," but they summon me clearly,' he said, 'by the name Ischomachos and by my father's name. As to what you asked me, Socrates,' he said, 'I never spend time indoors. Indeed,' he said, 'my wife is quite able by herself to manage the things within the house.'

" 'It would please me very much, Ischomachos,' I said, 'if I might also inquire about this—whether you yourself educated your wife to be the way she ought to be, or whether, when you took her from her mother and father, she already knew how to manage the things that are appropriate to her.'[4]

" 'How, Socrates,' he said, 'could she have known anything when I took her, since she came to me when she was not yet fifteen, and had lived previously under diligent supervision in order that she might see and hear as little as possible and ask the fewest possible questions? Doesn't it seem to you that one should be content if she came knowing only how to take the wool and make clothes, and had seen how the spinning work is distributed among the female attendants? For as to matters of the stomach, Socrates,' he said, 'she came to me very finely educated; and to me, at any rate, that seems to be an education of the greatest importance both for a man and a woman.'

" 'And in other respects, Ischomachos,' I said, 'did you yourself educate your wife to be capable of concerning herself with what's appropriate to her?'

" 'By Zeus,' said Ischomachos, 'not until I had sacrificed and prayed that I might succeed in teaching, and she in learning, what is best for both of us.'

" 'Didn't your wife sacrifice with you and pray for these same things?' I said.

" 'Certainly,' said Ischomachos; 'she promised before the gods that she would become what she ought to be, and made it evident that she would not neglect the things she was being taught.'

" 'By the gods, Ischomachos,' I said, 'relate to me what you first began teaching her. I'd listen to you relating these things with more pleasure than if you were telling me about the finest contest in wrestling or horsemanship.'

---

[2]There was an Athenian law according to which a man charged with a public duty could challenge someone he believed richer than himself either to take on the duty or to exchange his property for that of the challenger. (Original editor's note.)

[3]A Greek galley with three banks of oars on each side.

[4]The expression can also mean "the things that belong to her." (Original editor's note.)

"And Ischomachos replied: 'Well, Socrates,' he said, 'when she had gotten accustomed to me and had been domesticated to the extent that we could have discussions, I questioned her somewhat as follows. "Tell me, woman, have you thought yet why it was that I took you and your parents gave you to me? That it was not for want of someone else to spend the night with—this is obvious, I know, to you too. Rather, when I considered for myself, and your parents for you, whom we might take as the best partner for the household and children, I chose you, and your parents, as it appears, from among the possibilities chose me. Should a god grant us children, we will then consider, with respect to them, how we may best educate them; for this too is a good common to us—to obtain the best allies and the best supporters in old age; but for the present this household is what is common to us. As to myself, everything of mine I declare to be in common, and as for you, everything you've brought you have deposited in common. It's not necessary to calculate which of us has contributed the greater number of things, but it is necessary to know this well, that whichever of us is the better partner will be the one to contribute the things of greater worth." To this, Socrates, my wife replied: "What can I do to help you?" she said. "What is my capacity? But everything depends on you: my work, my mother told me, is to be moderate." "By Zeus, woman," I said, "my father told me the same thing. But it's for moderate people—for man and woman alike—not only to keep their substance in the best condition but also to add as much as possible to it by fine and just means." "Then what do you see," said my wife, "that I might do to help in increasing the household?" "By Zeus," I said, "just try to do in the best manner possible what the gods have brought you forth to be capable of and what the law praises." "And what are these things?" she said. . . . "Since, then, work and diligence are needed both for the indoor and for the outdoor things, it seems to me,"' he had said, '"that the god directly prepared the woman's nature for indoor works and indoor concerns. For he equipped the man, in body and in soul, with a greater capacity to endure cold and heat, journeys and expeditions, and so has ordered him to the outdoor works; but in bringing forth, for the woman, a body that is less capable in these respects,"' he said that he had said, '"the god has, it seems to me, ordered her to the indoor works. But knowing that he had implanted in the woman, and ordered her to, the nourishment of newborn children, he also gave her a greater affection for the newborn infants than he gave to the man. Since he had also ordered the woman to the guarding of the things brought in, the god, understanding that a fearful soul is not worse at guarding, also gave the woman a greater share of fear than the man. And knowing too that the one who had the outdoor works would need to defend himself should someone act unjustly, to him he gave a greater share of boldness. But because it's necessary for both to give and to take, he endowed both with memory and diligence in like degree, so that you can't distinguish whether the male or the female kind has the greater share of these things. As for self-control in the necessary things, he endowed both with this too in like degree; and the god allowed the one who proved the better, whether the man or the woman, to derive more from this good. Since, then, the nature of each has not been brought forth to be naturally apt for all of the same things, each has need of the other, and their pairing is more beneficial to each, for where one falls short the other is capable. Now," I said, "O woman, as we know what has been ordered to each of us by the god, we must, separately, do what's appropriate to each. The law too praises these things,"' he said that he had said, '"in pairing man and woman; and as the god made them partners in children, so too does the law appoint them partners. . . . It will be necessary," I said, "for you to remain indoors and to send out those of the servants whose work is outside; as for those whose work is to be done inside, these are to be in your charge; you must receive what is brought in and distribute what needs to be expended, and as for what needs to be set aside, you must use forethought and guard against expending in a month what was intended to last a year. When wool is brought to you, it must be your concern that clothes be made for whoever needs them. And it must be your concern that the dry grain be fine and fit for eating. There is one thing, however," I said, "among the concerns appropriate to you, that will perhaps seem less agreeable: whenever any of the servants become ill, it must be your concern that all be attended." "By Zeus," said my wife, "that will be most agreeable, at least if those who have been well tended are going to be grateful and feel more good will than before." I admired her reply,' said Ischomachos, 'and spoke: "Isn't it through this kind of forethought that the leader of the hive so disposes the other bees to her that when she leaves the hive, not one of the bees supposes they must let her go, but rather they all follow? . . . But the most pleasant thing of all: if you look to be better than I and make me your servant, you will have no need to fear that with advancing age you will be honored any less in the household, and you may trust that as you grow older, the better a partner you prove to be for me, and for the children the better a guardian of the household, by so much more will you be honored in the household. . . ." I seem to remember saying such things to her, Socrates, at the time of our first discussion.'"

"'Did you notice, Ischomachos,' I said, 'that she was stirred to diligence by these things?'

"'Yes, by Zeus,' said Ischomachos. 'I know she once became very upset, and blushed deeply, when she was unable to give me one of the things I had brought in when I asked for it. Seeing she was irritated, I spoke. "Don't be discouraged, woman," I said, "because you can't give me what I happen to ask for. It is indeed clear poverty not to have a thing to use when it's needed; at the same time our present want—to look for something and be unable to find it—is certainly a less painful thing than not to look for it at all, knowing it's not there. But you aren't at fault in this," I said; "rather I am, since I handed over these things to you without giving orders as to where each kind of thing should be put, so that you would know where to put them and where to find them again. There is nothing, woman, so useful or fine for human beings as order. . . . That an ordered arrangement of implements is a good, then, and that it is easy to find in the house an advantageous place for each kind of thing, has been established. But how fine it looks, too, when shoes of any kind are set out in a regular manner; it is fine to see clothes of any kind when they are sorted, as also bedcovers, bronze kettles, and things pertaining to the table, and—what of all things would be most ridiculed, not indeed by the solemn man but by the wit— even pots have a graceful look when distinctly arranged."' "

"'What then, Ischomachos?' I said. 'Did your wife seem to listen at all to what you were trying so seriously to teach her?'

"'What else did she do if not promise to be diligent, manifest her very great pleasure, as though she had found some easy means out of a difficulty, and ask me to order things separately as quickly as possible in the way I had stated?'

"'How, then, Ischomachos,' I said, 'did you separately order them for her?'

"'What else seemed best to me if not to show her first the capacity of the house? For it is not adorned with decorations, Socrates; the rooms were planned and built simply with a view to their being the most advantageous receptacles for the things that would be in them, so that each calls for what is suitable to it. The bedroom, being in an interior part of the house, invites the most valuable bedcovers and implements; the dry parts of the dwelling, the grain; the cool places, the wine; and the well-lighted places, the works and implements that need light. And I displayed to her the areas for the daily use of human beings, furnished so as to be cool in summer and warm in winter. And I displayed to her the house as a whole, and how it lies open to the south—obviously, so as to be well exposed to the sun in winter and well shaded in summer. Then I pointed out to her the women's apartments, separated from the men's by a bolted door, so that nothing may be taken out that shouldn't be and so that the servants may not produce offspring without our knowledge. For the useful ones, for the most part, feel even more good will once they have had children, but when wicked ones are paired together, they become only more resourceful in their bad behavior. When we had gone through these things,' he said, 'we then proceeded to separate our belongings according to tribes. We began first,' he said, 'by collecting whatever we use for sacrifices. After this we distinguished the woman's ornaments for festivals, the man's dress for festivals and war, bedcovers for the women's apartments, bedcovers for the men's apartments, shoes for women, shoes for men. Another tribe consisted of arms, another of instruments for spinning, another of instruments for breadmaking, another of instruments for cooking, another of the things for bathing, another of the things for kneading bread, another of the things for the table; and all these things were further divided according to whether they were used every day or only for festivals. We also set apart the expenses for each month from the amount that had been calculated and reserved for the whole year; for in this way we could better see how things would come out at the end. And when we had sorted our belongings according to tribes, we took each kind of thing to its appropriate place. After this, as to the implements the servants use from day to day—those for the making of bread, for cooking, for spinning, and others of this sort—we pointed out to those who would be using them where each must go, handed them over, and gave orders that they be kept secure. Those we use for festivals, for entertaining foreigners, or only from time to time we handed over to the housekeeper, and after pointing out to her their places and counting and making lists of the various kinds of things, we told her to give each what he needed of them, to remember what she had given someone, and when she had got it back, to return it to the place she had taken it from. We chose as housekeeper the one who upon examination seemed to us the most self-controlled as regards food, wine, sleep, and intercourse with men, and who, in addition, seemed to have a good memory and the forethought to avoid punishment for negligence and to consider how, by gratifying us in some way, she might be honored by us in return. We taught her also to feel good will toward us, sharing our delights when we were delighted in some way, and when there was something painful, inviting her aid. We further educated her to be eager to increase the household, making her thoroughly acquainted with it and giving her a share in its prosperity. And we inspired justice in her, honoring the just more than the unjust and displaying to her that they live richer and freer lives than the unjust. We then installed her in the place. But in addition to all these things, Socrates,' he said, 'I told my wife that there would be no benefit in any of this unless she herself was diligent in seeing that the order is preserved in each thing. I taught her that in the cities subject to good laws the citizens do not think it enough merely to have fine laws, but in addition choose guardians of the laws to examine them, to praise the one who acts lawfully, and to punish the one who acts contrary to the laws. Then,' he said 'I suggested that my wife consider herself a guardian of the laws regarding the things in the house; that she inspect the implements whenever it seems best to her, just as a garrison commander inspects his guards; that she test the fitness of each thing, just as the council tests the fitness of horses and horsemen; and that, like a queen, she praise and honor the deserving, to the limit of her capacity, and rebuke and punish the one who needs such things. In addition,' he said, 'I taught her that she could not be justly annoyed if I gave her many more orders in regard to our possessions than I gave to the servants, displaying to her that the servants share in their master's wealth only to the extent that they carry it, attend to it, or guard it, and that no one of them is allowed to use it unless the lord gives it to him, whereas everything is the master's to use as he wishes. To the one deriving the greatest benefit from its preservation and the greatest harm from its destruction belongs the greatest concern for a thing—this I declared to her.'

"'What then?' I said. 'After your wife had heard these things, Ischomachos, did she at all obey you?'

"'What else did she do,' he said, 'if not tell me I didn't understand her correctly if I supposed that in teaching her to be concerned with our substance I had ordered her to do something hard. For as she told me,' he said, 'it would have been much harder if I had ordered her to neglect her own things than if she were required to concern herself with the goods of the household. For just as it seems natural,' he said, 'for a sensible woman to be concerned for her offspring rather than to neglect them, so, she said, it's more pleasant for a sensible woman to be concerned for those of the possessions that delight her because they are her own than to neglect them.'"

"On hearing that his wife had replied to him in this way," said Socrates, "I spoke. 'By Hera,[5] Ischomachos,' I said, 'you display your wife's manly understanding.'

"'There are other instances of her high-mindedness that I am willing to relate to you,' said Ischomachos, 'instances of her obeying me quickly in some matter after hearing it only once.'

"'In what sort of thing?' I said. 'Speak; for to me it is much more pleasant to learn of the virtue of a living woman than to have had Zeuxis display for me the fine likeness of a woman he had painted.'

"Ischomachos then speaks. 'And yet once, Socrates,' he said, 'I saw she had applied a good deal of white lead to her face, that she might seem to be fairer than she was, and some dye, so that she would look more flushed than was the truth, and she also wore high shoes, that she might seem taller than she naturally was. "Tell me, woman," I said, "would you judge me more worthy to be loved as a partner in wealth if I showed you our substance itself, didn't boast of having more substance than is really mine, and didn't hide any part of our substance, or if instead I tried to deceive you by saying I have more substance than is really mine and by displaying to you counterfeit money, necklaces of gilt wood, and purple robes that lose their color, and asserting they are genuine?" She broke in straightway. "Hush," she said; "don't you become like that; if you did, I

---

[5]The sister and wife of Zeus.

could never love you from my soul." "Haven't we also come together, woman," I said, "as partners in one another's bodies?" "Human beings say so, at least," she said. "Would I then seem more worthy to be loved," I said, "as a partner in the body, if I tried to offer you my body after concerning myself that it be healthy and strong, so that I would really be well complexioned, or if instead I smeared myself with vermilion, applied flesh color beneath the eyes, and then displayed myself to you and embraced you, all the while deceiving you and offering you vermilion to see and touch instead of my own skin?" "I wouldn't touch vermilion with as much pleasure as I would you," she said, "or see flesh color with as much pleasure as your own, or see painted eyes with as much pleasure as your healthy ones." "You must believe, woman,"' Ischomachos said that he had said, "'that I too am not more pleased by the color of white lead or dye than by your color, but just as the gods have made horses most pleasant to horses, oxen to oxen, and sheep to sheep, so human beings suppose the pure body of a human being is most pleasant. Such deceits may in some way deceive outsiders and go undetected, but when those who are always together try to deceive one another they are necessarily found out. For either they are found out when they rise from their beds and before they have prepared themselves, or they are detected by their sweat or exposed by tears, or they are genuinely revealed in bathing."'

"'By the gods,' I said, 'what did she reply to this?'

"'What else,' he said, 'was her reply, if not that she never did anything of the sort again and tried always to display herself suitably and in a pure state. At the same time she asked me if I could not advise her how she might really come to sight as fine and not merely seem to be. I advised her, Socrates,' he said, 'not always to sit about like a slave but to try, with the gods' help, to stand at the loom like a mistress, to teach others what she knew better than they, and to learn what she did not know as well; and also to examine the breadmaker, to watch over the housekeeper in her distribution of things, and to go about and investigate whether each kind of thing is in the place it should be. In this way, it seemed to me, she could both attend to her concerns and have the opportunity to walk about. And I said it would be good exercise to moisten and knead the bread and to shake out and fold the clothes and bedcovers. I said that if she exercised in this way, she would take more pleasure in eating, would become healthier, and so would come to sight as better complexioned in truth. And a wife's looks, when in contrast to a waiting maid she is purer and more suitably dressed, become attractive, especially when she gratifies her husband willingly instead of serving him under compulsion. On the other hand, women who always sit about in pretentious solemnity lend themselves to comparison with those who use adornments and deceit. And now, Socrates,' he said, 'know well, my wife still arranges her life as I taught her then and as I tell you now.'"

On Household Management

ARISTOTLE

The author of the Oeconomica, *long attributed to Aristotle (384–322* B.C.*), was, in fact, a Greek of the third century* B.C. *who was familiar both with the* Oeconomicus *of Xenophon and with the work of Aristotle. As you read this excerpt, compare it with the Xenophon selection. The major issue and point of departure here is the relation between the household and the city. In that connection, why are wife and property so important to the head of a household? More particularly, what are the most important possessions of a family? What tasks are assigned to slaves? Why is it so necessary to differentiate the roles of husband and wife? What does this selection say about the status of women in Greek society?*

The sciences of politics and economics differ not only as widely as a household and a city (the subject-matter with which they severally deal), but also in the fact that the science of politics involves a number of rulers, whereas the sphere of economics is a monarchy.

Now certain of the arts fall into sub-divisions, and it does not pertain to the same art to manufacture and to use the article manufactured, for instance, a lyre or pipes; but the function of political science is both to constitute a city in the beginning and also when it has come into being to make a right use of it. It is clear, therefore, that it must be the function of economic science too both to found a household and also to make use of it.

Now a city is an aggregate made up of households and land and property, possessing in itself the means to a happy life. This is clear from the fact that, if men cannot attain this end, the community is dissolved. Further, it is for this end that they associate together; and that for the sake of which any particular thing exists and has come into being is its essence. It is evident, therefore, that economics is prior in origin to politics; for its function is prior, since a household is part of a city. We must therefore examine economics and see what its function is.

The component parts of a household are man and property. But since the nature of any given thing is most quickly seen by taking its smallest parts, this would apply also to a household. So, according to Hesiod,[1] it would be necessary that there should be

First and foremost a house, then a wife . . . , for the former is the first condition of subsistence, the latter is the proper possession of all freemen. We should have, therefore, as a part of economics to make proper rules for

---

[1]Greek poet c. 700 B.C. whose *Works and Days* Aristotle cites here.

the association of husband and wife; and this involves providing what sort of a woman she ought to be.

In regard to property the first care is that which comes naturally. Now in the course of nature the art of agriculture is prior, and next come those arts which extract the products of the earth, mining and the like. Agriculture ranks first because of its justice; for it does not take anything away from men, either with their consent, as do retail trading and the mercenary arts, or against their will, as do the warlike arts. Further, agriculture is natural; for by nature all derive their sustenance from their mother, and so men derive it from the earth. In addition to this it also conduces greatly to bravery; for it does not make men's bodies unserviceable, as do the illiberal arts, but it renders them able to lead an open-air life and work hard; furthermore it makes them adventurous against the foe, for husbandmen are the only citizens whose property lies outside the fortifications.

As regards the human part of the household, the first care is concerning a wife; for a common life is above all things natural to the female and to the male. For we have elsewhere laid down the principle that nature aims at producing many such forms of association, just as also it produces the various kinds of animals. But it is impossible for the female to accomplish this without the male or the male without the female, so that their common life has necessarily arisen. Now in the other animals this intercourse is not based on reason, but depends on the amount of natural instinct which they possess and is entirely for the purpose of procreation. But in the civilized and more intelligent animals the bond of unity is more perfect (for in them we see more mutual help and goodwill and co-operation), above all in the case of man, because the female and the male co-operate to ensure not merely existence but a good life. And the production of children is not only a way of serving nature but also of securing a real advantage; for the trouble which parents bestow upon their helpless children when they are themselves vigorous is repaid to them in old age when they are helpless by their children, who are then in their full vigour. At the same time also nature thus periodically provides for the perpetuation of mankind as a species, since she cannot do so individually. Thus the nature both of the man and of the woman has been preordained by the will of heaven to live a common life. For they are distinguished in that the powers which they possess are not applicable to purposes in all cases identical, but in some respects their functions are opposed to one another though they all tend to the same end. For nature has made the one sex stronger, the other weaker, that the latter through fear may be the more cautious, while the former by its courage is better able to ward off attacks; and that the one may acquire possessions outside the house, the other preserve those within. In the performance of work, she made one sex able to lead a sedentary life and not strong enough to endure exposure, the other less adapted for quiet pursuits but well constituted for outdoor activities; and in relation to offspring she has made both share in the procreation of children, but each render its peculiar service towards them, the woman by nurturing, the man by educating them.

First, then, there are certain laws to be observed towards a wife, including the avoidance of doing her any wrong; for thus a man is less likely himself to be wronged. This is inculcated by the general law, as the Pythagoreans[2] say, that one least of all should injure a wife as being "a suppliant and seated at the hearth." Now wrong inflicted by a husband is the formation of connexions outside his own house. As regards sexual intercourse, a man ought not to accustom himself not to need it at all nor to be unable to rest when it is lacking, but so as to be content with or without it. The saying of Hesiod is a good one:

A man should marry a maiden, that habits discreet he may teach her.

For dissimilarity of habits tends more than anything to destroy affection. As regards adornment, husband and wife ought not to approach one another with false affection in their person any more than in their manners; for if the society of husband and wife requires such embellishment, it is no better than play-acting on the tragic stage.

Of possessions, that which is the best and the worthiest subject of economics comes first and is most essential—I mean, man. It is necessary therefore first to provide oneself with good slaves. Now slaves are of two kinds, the overseer and the worker. And since we see that methods of education produce a certain character in the young, it is necessary when one has procured slaves to bring up carefully those to whom the higher duties are to be entrusted. The intercourse of a master with his slaves should be such as not either to allow them to be insolent or to irritate them. To the higher class of slaves he ought to give some share of honour, and to the workers abundance of nourishment. And since the drinking of wine makes even freemen insolent, and many nations even of freemen abstain therefrom (the Carthaginians, for instance, when they are on military service), it is clear that wine ought never to be given to slaves, or at any rate very seldom. Three things make up the life of a slave, work, punishment, and food. To give them food but no punishment and no work makes them insolent; and that they should have work and punishment but no food is tyrannical and destroys their efficiency. It remains therefore to give them work and sufficient food; for it is impossible to rule over slaves without offering rewards, and a slave's reward is his food. And just as all other

[2]Followers of the Greek mathematician Pythagoras (sixth century B.C.) who formulated the theorem of right triangles that bears his name. They believed numbers held the key to the universe.

men become worse when they get no advantage by being better and there are no rewards for virtue and punishments for vice, so also is it with slaves. Therefore we must take careful notice and bestow or withhold everything, whether food or clothing or leisure or punishments, according to merit, in word and deed following the practice adopted by physicians in the matter of medicine, remembering at the same time that food is not medicine because it must be given continually.

The slave who is best suited for his work is the kind that is neither too cowardly nor too courageous. Slaves who have either of these characteristics are injurious to their owners; those who are too cowardly lack endurance, while the high-spirited are not easy to control. All ought to have a definite end in view; for it is just and beneficial to offer slaves their freedom as a prize, for they are willing to work when a prize is set before them and a limit of time is defined. One ought to bind slaves to one's service by the pledges of wife and children, and not to have many persons of the same race in a household, as is the case in a city. One ought to provide sacrifices and pleasures more for the sake of slaves than for freemen; for in the case of the former there are present more of the reasons why such things have been instituted.

The economist ought to possess four qualities in relation to wealth. He ought to be able to acquire it, and to guard it; otherwise there is no advantage in acquiring it, but it is a case of drawing water with a sieve, or the proverbial jar with a hole in it. Further, he ought to be able to order his possessions aright and make a proper use of them; for it is for these purposes that we require wealth. The various kinds of property ought to be distinguished, and those which are productive ought to be more numerous than the unproductive, and the sources of income ought to be so distributed that they may not run a risk with all their possessions at the same time. . . . Some things should be attended to by the master, others by his wife, according to the sphere allotted to each in the economy of the household. Inspections need only be made occasionally in small establishments, but should be frequent where overseers are employed. For perfect imitation is impossible unless a good example is set, especially when trust is delegated to others; for unless the master is careful, it is impossible for his overseers to be careful. And since it is good for the formation of character and useful in the interests of economy, masters ought to rise earlier than their slaves and retire to rest later, and a house should never be left unguarded any more than a city, and when anything needs doing it ought not to be left undone, whether it be day or night. There are occasions when a master should rise while it is still night; for this helps to make a man healthy and wealthy and wise. On small estates the Attic system of disposing of the produce is a useful one; but on large estates, where a distinction is made between yearly and monthly expenditure and likewise between the daily and the occasional use of household appliances, such matters must be entrusted to overseers. Furthermore, a periodical inspection should be made, in order to ascertain what is still existing and what is lacking.

The house must be arranged both with a view to one's possessions and for the health and well-being of its inhabitants. By possessions I mean the consideration of what is suitable for produce and clothing, and in the case of produce what is suitable for dry and what for moist produce, and amongst other possessions what is suitable for property whether animate or inanimate, for slaves and freemen, women and men, strangers and citizens. With a view to well-being and health, the house ought to be airy in summer and sunny in winter. This would be best secured if it faces north and is not as wide as it is long. In large establishments a man who is no use for other purposes seems to be usefully employed as a doorkeeper to safeguard what is brought into and out of the house. For the ready use of household appliances the Laconian method is a good one; for everything ought to have its own proper place and so be ready for use and not require to be searched for.

An Action for Assault

DEMOSTHENES

Oratory found a home and first flourished in classical Athens. Skillful oral presentation of arguments was useful in Athens both before the democratic political assemblies that deliberated policies and before the popular juries that heard legal cases. Delivering speeches became both an art form and entertainment in Athens. The Sophists arose in the fifth century B.C. as teachers of oratory. Their detractors complained that they were able to make weak arguments seem strong and twist truth into falsehood.

Demosthenes (384–322 B.C.) is most famous to later generations for his impassioned speeches intended to rouse his Athenian countrymen to the growing political danger they faced from the rising power of the Macedonian King Philip. But to his contemporaries, Demosthenes was best known as a brilliant forensic orator who could persuade juries to side with his clients. Indeed, the orator made his living from legal cases, where it was his knowledge of rhetorical devices, not any knowledge of law, that mattered most. The bulk of Demosthenes' surviving speeches come from legal cases. These cases allow us to see something of the problems and conflicts that arose in Greek city-states and how the Greeks saw these conflicts.

In this selection, Demosthenes speaks in place of the plaintiff, Ariston, in the first person. He attempts not only to present Ariston's story, complete with evidence and testimony, but also to anticipate and refute the defendant's arguments and strategies. What seems to have been the relationship between these parties prior to the assault? Why did the incident happen? What was at stake in the suit? In what sorts of delaying tactics and legal maneuvers did Ariston's opponents engage? What evidence does Demosthenes produce to impugn Conon's character? How does he build up his client's character? Does Athenian society appear especially contentious or violent? How do the legal proceedings and rules exhibited here compare with what you find in the Egyptian example of the farmer before the courts?

With gross outrage have I met, men of the jury, at the hands of the defendant, Conon, and have suffered such bodily injury that for a very long time neither my relatives nor any of the attending physicians thought that I should survive. Contrary to expectation, however, I did recover and regain my strength, and I then brought against him this action for the assault. All my friends and relatives, whose advice I asked, declared that for what he had done the defendant was liable to summary seizure as a highwayman, or to public indictments for criminal outrage; but they urged and advised me not to take upon myself matters which I should not be able to carry, or to appear to be bringing suit for the maltreatment I had received in a manner too ambitious for one so young. I took this course, therefore, and, in deference to their advice, have instituted a private suit, although I should have been very glad, men of Athens, to prosecute the defendant on a capital charge. And for this you will all pardon me, I am sure, when you hear what I have suffered. For, grievous as was the injury which at that time fell to my lot, it was no more so than the subsequent insults of the defendant. I ask as my right, therefore, and implore you all without distinction, to listen with goodwill, while I tell you what I have suffered, and then, if you think that I have been the victim of wrongful and lawless acts, to render me the aid which is my due. I shall state to you from the beginning each incident as it occurred in the fewest words I can.

Two years ago I went out to Panactum,[1] where we had been ordered to do garrison duty. The sons of the defendant, Conon, encamped near us, as I would to heaven they had not done; for our original enmity and our quarrels began in fact just there. How these came about, you shall hear. These men used always to spend the entire day after luncheon in drinking, and they kept this up continually as long as we were in the garrison. We, on our part, conducted ourselves while in the country just as we were wont to do here. Well, at whatever time the others might be having their dinner, these men were already drunk and abusive, at first toward our body-slaves, but in the end toward ourselves. For, alleging that the slaves annoyed them with smoke while getting dinner, or were impudent toward them, or whatever else they pleased, they used to beat them and empty their chamber-pots over them, or befoul them with urine; there was nothing in the way of brutality and outrage in which they did not indulge. When we saw this, we were annoyed and at first expostulated with them,

---

[1]Panactum was an Athenian fort on the borders of Boeotia. (Original editor's note.)

but they mocked at us, and would not desist, and so our whole mess in a body—not I alone apart from the rest—went to the general and told him what was going on. He rebuked them with stern words, not only for their brutal treatment of us, but for their whole behaviour in camp; yet so far from desisting, or being ashamed of their acts, they burst in upon us that very evening as soon as it grew dark, and, beginning with abusive language, they proceeded to beat me, and they made such a clamour and tumult about the tent, that both the general and the taxiarchs[2] came and some of the other soldiers, by whose coming we were prevented from suffering, or ourselves doing, some damage that could not be repaired, being victims as we were of their drunken violence. When matters had gone thus far, it was natural that after our return home there should exist between us feelings of anger and hatred. However, on my own part I swear by the gods I never saw fit to bring an action against them, or to pay any attention to what had happened. I simply made this resolve—in future to be on my guard, and to take care to have nothing to do with people of that sort.

I wish in the first place to bring before you depositions proving these statements, and then to show what I have suffered at the hands of the defendant himself, in order that you may see that Conon, who should have dealt rigorously with the first offences, has himself added to these far more outrageous acts of his own doing.

THE DEPOSITIONS [are read as evidence.]

These, then, are the acts of which I thought proper to take no account. Not long after this, however, one evening, when I was taking a walk, as my custom was, in the agora[3] with Phanostratus of Cephisia,[4] a man of my own age, Ctesias, the son of the defendant, passed by me in a drunken state opposite the Leocorion,[5] near the house of Pythodorus. At sight of us he uttered a yell, and, saying something to himself, as a drunken man does, in an unintelligible fashion, passed on up, toward Melite.[6] Gathered together there for a drinking bout, as we afterwards learned, at the house of Pamphilus the fuller, were the defendant Conon, a certain Theotimus, Archebiades, Spintharus, son of Eubulus, Theogenes, son of Andromenes, and a number of others. Ctesias made them all get up, and proceeded to the agora. It happened that we were turning back from the temple of Persephone, and on our walk were again about opposite the Leocorion when

[2]The taxiarchs were the commanders of the infantry detachments of the several tribes. (Original editor's note.)

[3]Marketplace.

[4]Cephisia, a deme of the tribe Erectheis. (Original editor's note.)

[5]This was a monument erected in honour of the three daughters of Leos, whom, in obedience to an oracle, their father had sacrificed for the safety of their country. (Original editor's note.)

[6]Melite was a hilly district in the western part of Athens. (Original editor's note.)

we met them. When we got close to them one of them, I don't know which, fell upon Phanostratus and pinned him, while the defendant Conon together with his son and the son of Andromenes threw themselves upon me. They first stripped me of my cloak, and then, tripping me up they thrust me into the mud and leapt upon me and beat me with such violence that my lip was split open and my eyes closed; and they left me in such a state that I could neither get up nor utter a sound. As I lay there I heard them utter much outrageous language, a great deal of which was such foul abuse that I should shrink from repeating some of it in your presence. One thing, however, which is an indication of the fellow's insolence and a proof that the whole affair has been of his doing, I will tell you. He began to crow, mimicking fighting cocks that have won a battle and his fellows bade him flap his elbows against his sides like wings. After this some people who happened to pass took me home stripped as I was, for these men had gone off taking my cloak with them. When my bearers got to my door, my mother and the women servants began shrieking and wailing, and it was with difficulty that I was at length carried to a bath. There I was thoroughly bathed, and shown to the surgeons.

To prove that these statements of mine are true, I shall call before you the witnesses who attest them. . . .

THE DEPOSITIONS [are read as evidence.]

That the wounds I received, then, were not slight or trifling, but that I was brought near to death by the outrage and brutality of these men, and that the action which I have entered is far more lenient than the case deserves, has been made clear to you, I think, on many grounds. I fancy, however, that some of you are wondering what in the world there can be that Conon will have the audacity to say in reply to these charges. I wish, therefore, to tell you in advance the defence which I hear he is prepared to make. He will try to divert your attention from the outrage and the actual facts, and will seek to turn the whole matter into mere jest and ridicule. He will tell you that there are many people in the city, sons of respectable persons, who in sport, after the manner of young men, have given themselves nicknames, such as Ithyphalli or Autolecythi,[7] and that some of them are infatuated with mistresses; that his own son is one of these and has often given and received blows on account of some girl; and that things of this sort are natural for young men. As for me and all my brothers, he will make out that we are not only drunken and insolent fellows, but also unfeeling and vindictive.

For myself, men of the jury, deeply indignant though I am at what I

---

[7]The former suggests gross licentiousness, and the latter . . . has been plausibly interpreted as indicating one who carried his own oil-flask. . . . He would thus dispense with the customary slave, and be freed from having even such an one as witness to his wanton doings. (Original editor's note.)

have suffered, I should feel no less indignation at this, and should count myself the victim of a fresh outrage, if you will pardon the strong expression, if this fellow Conon shall be deemed by you to be speaking the truth about us, and you are to be so misguided as to assume that a man bears the character which he claims for himself or which someone else accuses him of possessing, and respectable people are to derive no benefit from their daily life and conduct. No man in the world has ever seen us drunken or committing outrages, and I hold that I am doing nothing unfeeling in demanding to receive satisfaction according to the law for the wrongs I have suffered. . . .

But what has all this to do with me? Why, for my part, I am amazed if they have discovered any excuse or pretext which will make it possible in your court for any man, if convicted of assault and battery, to escape punishment. The laws take a far different view, and have provided that even pleas of necessity shall not be pressed too far. For example (you see I have had to inquire into these matters and inform myself about them because of the defendant), there are actions for evil-speaking; and I am told that these are instituted for this purpose—that men may not be led on, by using abusive language back and forth, to deal blows to one another. Again, there are actions for battery; and these, I hear, exist for this reason—that a man, finding himself the weaker party, may not defend himself with a stone or anything of that sort, but may await legal redress. Again, there are public prosecutions for wounding, to the end that wounds may not lead to murder. The least of these evils, namely abusive language, has, I think, been provided for to prevent the last and most grievous, that murder may not ensue, and that men be not led on step by step from vilification to blows, from blows to wounds, and from wounds to murder, but that in the laws its own penalty should be provided for each of these acts, and that the decision should not be left to the passion or the will of the person concerned.

This, then, is what is ordained in the laws; but if Conon says, "We belong to a club of Ithyphalli, and in our love-affairs we strike and throttle whom we please," are you, then, going to let him off with a laugh? I think not. No one of you would have been seized with a fit of laughter, if he had happened to be present when I was dragged and stripped and maltreated, when I was borne home on a litter to the house which I had left strong and well, and my mother rushed out, and the women set up such a wailing and screaming (as if someone had died in the house) that some of the neighbours sent to inquire what it was that had happened. Speaking broadly, men of the jury, I hold it right that no man should have any excuse or immunity to rely on, when he is brought before you, so valid that he is to be permitted to commit outrage; but if allowance is to be made for anyone, it should be for those only who commit an act of this sort in the folly of youth,—it is for these, I say, that such indulgence should be reserved, and even in their case it should not extend to the remission of the penalty, but to its mitigation. But when a man over fifty years of age in the company of younger men, and these his own sons, not only did not discourage or prevent their wantonness, but has proved himself the leader and the foremost and the vilest of all, what punishment could he suffer that would be commensurate with his deeds? For my part, I think that even death would be too mild. Why, if Conon had committed none of the acts himself, but had merely stood by while his son Ctesias did what he is himself proved to have done, you would regard him with loathing, and rightly. For if he has trained up his sons in such fashion that they feel no fear or shame while committing in his presence crimes for some of which the punishment of death is ordained, what punishment do you think too severe for him? I think these actions are a proof that he has no reverence for his own father; for if he had honoured and feared him, he would have exacted honour and fear from his own children. . . .

I wish now to tell you what they sought to do at the arbitration; for from this you will perceive their utter insolence. They spun out the time till past midnight, refusing to read the depositions or to put in copies; leading to the altar one at a time our witnesses who were present and putting them on oath; writing depositions which had nothing to do with the case (for instance "that Ctesias was the son of Conon by a mistress, and that he had been treated thus and so"[8]—a course of action, men of the jury, which I assure you by the gods roused resentment and disgust in the mind of every one present; and finally they were disgusted at themselves. Be that as it may, when they had had their fill and were tired of acting thus, they put in a challenge with a view to gaining time and preventing the boxes from being sealed, offering to deliver up certain slaves, whose names they wrote down, to be examined as to the assault. And I fancy that their defence will hinge chiefly upon this point. I think, however, that you should all note one thing—that if these men tendered the challenge in order that the inquiry by the torture should take place, and had confidence in this method of proof, they would not have tendered it when the award was now just being announced, when night had fallen and no further pretext was left them; no, before the action had been brought, while I was lying ill and not knowing whether I should recover, and was denouncing the defendant to all who came to see me as the one who dealt the first blow and was the perpetrator of most of the maltreatment I received,—it was then, I say, that he would have come to my house without delay, bringing with him a number of witnesses; it was then that he would have offered to deliver up his slaves for the torture, and would have invited some members of the Areopagus[9] to attend; for if I had died, the case would have come before them.

---

[8]If Ctesias were illegitimate, Conon could not be held responsible for his misdoings, and previous mistreatment by the plaintiff is alleged as justification of the assault made upon the latter by Ctesias. (Original editor's note.)

[9]The governing body of Athens.

But if he was unaware of this situation, and having this proof, as he will now say, made no preparation against so serious a danger, surely when I had left my sick bed and summoned him, he would at our first meeting before the arbitrator have shown himself ready to deliver up the slaves. But he did nothing of the kind.

To prove that I am speaking the truth, and that the challenge was tendered merely for the sake of gaining time, (*to the clerk*) read this deposition. I will be clear from this. . . .

THE DEPOSITIONS [are read as evidence.]

Well then, if people break into houses and beat those who come in their way, do you suppose they would scruple to swear falsely on a scrap of paper in the interest of one another—these men who are partners in such great and such reckless malignity and villainy and impudence and outrage? For I certainly think that all these terms fit the deeds they are in the habit of doing. And yet there are other deeds of theirs more dreadful even than these, though I should be unable to find out all who have suffered from them.

The thing, however, which is the most impudent of all that he is going to do, as I hear, I think it better to warn you of in advance. For they say that he will bring his children, and, placing them by his side, will swear by them, imprecating some dread and awful curses of such a nature that a person who heard them and reported them to me was amazed. Now, men of the jury, there is no way of withstanding such audacity; for, I take it, the most honourable men and those who would be the last to tell a falsehood themselves, are most apt to be deceived by such people—not but that they ought to look at their lives and characters before believing them. The contempt, however, which this fellow feels for all sacred things I must tell you about; for I have been forced to make inquiry. For I hear, then, men of the jury, that a certain Bacchius, who was condemned to death in your court, and Aristocrates, the man with the bad eyes, and certain others of the same stamp, and with them this man Conon, were intimates when they were youths, . . . and that these men used to devour the food set out for Hecate[10] and to gather up on each occasion for their dinner with one another the testicles of the pigs which are offered for purification when the assembly convenes, and that they thought less of swearing and perjuring themselves than of anything else in the world. Surely Conon, a man of that sort, is not to be believed on oath; far from it indeed. No; the man who would not swear by any object which your custom does not recognize even an oath which he intended to observe, and would not even think of doing so by the lives of his children, but would suffer anything rather than that; and who, if forced to swear, will take only a customary oath, imprecating de-

---

[10]Goddess of ghosts and sorcery identified with the underworld.

struction upon himself, his race, and his house, is more to be believed than one who swears by his children or is ready to pass through fire. I, then, who on every account am more worthy to be believed than you, Conon, offered to take the oath here cited, not that through readiness to do anything whatsoever I might avoid paying the penalty for crimes which I had committed, as is the case with you, but in the interest of truth, and in order that I might not be subjected to further outrage, and as one who will not allow his case to be lost through your perjury.

(*To the clerk.*) Read the challenge.

THE CHALLENGE [it is read at this point.]

This oath I was at that time ready to take, and now, to convince you and those who stand gathered about, I swear by all the gods and goddesses that I have in very truth suffered at the hands of Conon this wrong for which I am suing him; that I was beaten by him, and that my lip was cut open so that it had to be sewn up, and that it is because of gross maltreatment that I am prosecuting him. If I swear truly, may many blessings be mine, and may I never again suffer such an outrage; but, if I am forsworn, may I perish utterly, I and all I possess or ever may possess. But I am not forsworn; no, not though Conon should say so till he bursts. Therefore, men of the jury, since I have shown you all the just arguments which I have to present, and have furthermore added an oath, it is but right that you should feel toward Conon on my behalf the same resentment which each one of you, had he been the victim, would have felt toward the one who did the wrong, and not to regard an act of this sort as a private matter which might fall to the lot of any man. No; whoever may be the victim, bear him aid and give him the redress that is his due, and loathe those who in the face of their crimes are bold and reckless, but when they are brought to trial are impudent villains, caring nothing for reputation or character or anything else, provided only they can escape punishment. Of course Conon will entreat you and wail aloud. But consider, which of us is more deserving of pity, a man who has suffered such treatment as I have at the hands of the defendant, if I am to go forth having met with the further disgrace of losing my suit, or Conon, if he is to be punished? Is it to the advantage of each one of you that a man be permitted to indulge in battery and outrage, or that he be not permitted? I certainly think he should not be. Well then, if you let him off, there will be many such; if you punish him, fewer.

I might have much to say, men of the jury, about the services we have rendered you, I, and my father while he lived, both as trierarchs[11] and in the army, and in performing whatever duty was laid upon us, and I could show that neither the defendant nor any of his sons have rendered any

---

[11]One who provided to the Athenian navy a fully equipped trireme, a gallery that has three banks of oars on each side.

service; but the allowance of water is not sufficient nor is it at this time a question of such services. For, if it were indeed our lot to be by common consent regarded as more useless and more base than Conon, we are not, I suppose, to be beaten or maltreated.

I do not know what reason there is why I should say more; for I believe that nothing which I have said has escaped you.

Hellenistic Family Documents

Through the writings of Xenophon or the treatise attributed to Aristotle, we can gain an idea of how Greeks in the late classical period viewed family life. We know much less, however, about the actual conduct of life within Greek families. The conquest of the Near East by Alexander the Great, king of Macedon, 336–323 B.C., exported Greek culture and Greeks themselves to other areas of the empire. From Egypt, ruled by the Ptolemaic dynasty (305–30 B.C.), which was descended from one of Alexander's generals, papyrus fragments survive that give us a glimpse into Hellenistic family life.

Two documents are reproduced below: a marriage contract from 92 B.C. between two Persians living in Egypt, and a soldier's will from 126 B.C. Much of the marriage contract revolves around the dowry, the property brought by the wife from her family to the marriage. From what you see in the document, why was the dowry so important? What did it do for the wife? For the husband? What other agreements governed this marriage?

What sorts of property did the soldier Dryton own? To whom did he leave his property? What were his heirs' relations to him? Did he treat male and female heirs similarly? Finally, taken together, do these documents indicate that the family life of the Greek world as envisioned by Xenophon continued to exist? How, if at all, had things changed?

MARRIAGE CONTRACT

(Summary) Year 22, Mecheir 11.[1] Philiscus son of Apollonius, Persian of the Epigone,[2] acknowledges to Apollonia also called Kellauthis, daughter of Heraclides, Persian, having with her as guardian her brother Apollonius, that he has received from her in copper money 2 talents 4000 drachmae, the dowry for herself, Apollonia, agreed upon with him . . . Keeper of the contract: Dionysius.

(Text of contract) In the 22nd year of the reign of Ptolemy also called Alexander, the god Philometor, the priest of Alexander and the other priests being as written in Alexandria, the 11th of the month Xandicus, which is the 11th of Mecheir, at Kerkeosiris in the division of Polemon of

---

[1]Name of a month.

[2]Literally "Persian of the next generation," denoting a certain civil status; but it is hard to say what the term originally meant and what it eventually came to imply. (Original editors' note.)

the Arsinoite nome.[3] Philiscus son of Apollonius, Persian of the Epigone, acknowledges to Apollonia, also called Kellauthis, daughter of Heraclides, Persian, having with her as guardian her brother Apollonius that he has received from her in copper money 2 talents 4000 drachmae, the dowry for herself, Apollonia, agreed upon with him. Apollonia shall live with Philiscus, obeying him as a wife should her husband, owning their property in common with him. All necessaries and clothing and whatever else is proper for a wedded wife Philiscus shall supply to Apollonia, whether he is at home or abroad, in proportion to their means. It shall not be lawful for Philiscus to bring in another wife besides Apollonia, nor to keep a concubine or boy, nor to have children by another woman while Apollonia lives, nor to inhabit another house over which Apollonia is not mistress, nor to eject or insult or ill-treat her, nor to alienate any of their property to the detriment of Apollonia. If he is proved to be doing any of these things or fails to supply her with necessaries or clothing or other things as stated, Philiscus shall forthwith forfeit to Apollonia the dowry of 2 talents 4000 drachmae of copper. In like manner it shall not be lawful for Apollonia to spend the night or day away from the house of Philiscus without Philiscus's consent or to consort with another man or to dishonour the common home or to cause Philiscus to be shamed by any act that brings shame upon a husband. If Apollonia chooses of her own will to separate from Philiscus, Philiscus shall repay her the bare dowry within ten days from the date of the demand. If he does not repay as stated, he shall forthwith forfeit to her one and a half times the amount of the dowry which he has received. Witnesses: Dionysius son of Patron, Dionysius son of Hermaiscus, Theon son of Ptolemaeus, Didymus son of Ptolemaeus, Dionysius son of Dionysius, Heraclius son of Diocles, all six Macedonians of the Epigone. Keeper of the contract: Dionysius. (Acknowledgement) I, Philiscus son of Apollonius, Persian of the Epigone, acknowledge that I have received the dowry of 2 talents 4000 drachmae of copper as is stated above, and I have deposited the contract, being valid, with Dionysius. Dionysius son of Hermaiscus, the aforesaid, wrote for him, as he is illiterate. (Receipt) I, Dionysius, have received the contract, being valid. (Docketed) Deposited for registration on Mecheir 11 of year 22. (Endorsed) Marriage compact of Apollonia with Philiscus. . . .

WILL OF A SOLDIER

The 44th year, Pauni 9,[4] at Pathyris, before Asclepiades the agoranomus.[5] Dryton son of Pamphilus, Cretan, one of the *diadochi*[6] and belonging to the

---

[3]One of the administrative subdivisions of the Ptolemaic kingdom that had roots in pharaonic times.

[4]Name of a month.

[5]Official of the market who oversaw all transactions.

[6]An honorific title. (Original editors' note.)

reserve, hipparch[7] over men, being sound of body, sane and sensible, has made the following will. May it be mine to own my property in good health, but if I should suffer the lot of man, I bequeath and give my property in land and movable objects and cattle and whatever else I may have acquired, first my war-horse and all my armour to Esthladas my son by my former wife Sarapias daughter of Esthladas son of Theon, of civic rank,[8] in accordance with the laws and with the will which has been made through the record-office at Diospolis Parva before Dionysius the agoranomus in the 6th year of the reign of Philometor, which will besides the other matters which it sets forth appointed as his guardian (?) . . . being a kinsman, and of the household slaves I give him 4, whose names are Myrsine and her 3 children (?)—but the remaining two females, whose names are Irene and Ampelion, I give to Apollonia and her sisters, being 5 in all—also the vineyard site belonging to me at . . . in the Pathyrite nome and the wells therein of baked brick and the other appurtenances and the cart with the harness and the dove-cote and the other half-finished one and a yard of which the boundaries are, on the south waste grounds of the said Esthladas, on the north a vaulted room of Apollonia the younger, on the east waste ground of Petras . . . son of Esthladas, on the west waste ground of Esthladas up to the door opening to the west. The remaining rooms and fixtures and . . . and the waste ground assigned for a dove-cote down beyond the door of Esthladas and to the west of the vaulted chamber I give to Apollonia and Aristo and Aphrodisia and Nicarion and Apollonia the younger, being 5 in all, my daughters by my present wife Apollonia also called Semmonthis, in accordance with the laws, and they shall own the 2 female slaves and the cow in equal shares for their households, according to the division which I have made. Esthladas shall give up from the waste ground given to him opposite his door which opens to the west 4 square cubits[9] for the site of an oven. Of the remaining buildings and waste grounds at Diospolis Magna in the Ammonium[10] and in the potters' quarter Esthladas shall receive half and Apollonia and her sisters half, and of all my other property in corn and money contracts and all movable objects each party shall take half. Esthladas and Apollonia with her sisters shall provide funds in common for the building of a dove-cote on the site assigned until they finish it; and to my wife Apollonia also called Semmonthis, if she stays at home living irreproachably, they shall give every month for 4 years, for the maintenance of herself and for her 2 daughters, 2½ artabae of wheat, ¹⁄₁₂ of croton, and 200 copper drachmae; and after 4 years they shall give the same amounts in common to the two younger

---

[7]Commander of cavalry.

[8]That is, belonging to a family which possessed the citizenship in one of the Greek cities in Egypt. (Original editors' note.)

[9]A cubit, based on the length of the arm from elbow to finger tips, was about eighteen inches.

[10]At Thebes in the quarter of the temple of Ammon. (Original editors' note.)

daughters for 11 years. They shall give to Tachratis[11] for a dowry 12 copper talents out of the common funds. Whatever property Semmonthis may have manifestly acquired for herself while living with Dryton, she shall continue to own, and anyone who takes proceedings against her about this . . . Year 44, Pauni 9.

The Twelve Tables

A commission of patrician Roman magistrates issued the Twelve Tables in 449 B.C. They were originally inscribed on twelve bronze plaques placed in the Forum (hence the name). They were published in response to agitation by the common citizens of Rome (known as plebeians), who believed that a written statement of the city's laws would curb the arbitrary power of the magistrate class (the patricians) and contribute to a leveling of differences between the two classes of Roman citizens. Romans later told the story that a commission was sent to Athens to study the laws of that famous city and that the Twelve Tables resulted, but that was a fanciful fabrication designed to link Rome to Athenian philosophy and culture. These laws are entirely Roman in character.

Essentially, the Twelve Tables codified existing customs of what was, at the time, a predominantly agricultural and pastoral community of small landowners. The tables are our primary source for the social and economic conditions of the early Roman Republic. However, invading Gauls destroyed the Twelve Tables in 390 B.C.; thus, historians have had to piece together the text from fragmentary quotations in later Roman legal writings.

The Twelve Tables were mainly a code of private law, though there are some elements of public law and even of the sacral laws derived from Roman religious beliefs. The key to Roman private law lay in the family and in the authority of its male head, the paterfamilias. *How did Romans envision the family? How did they treat property? How did they conduct trials and other legal proceedings? How was public order maintained in Rome? What can we learn from a comparison of this code with earlier selections, such as the Egyptian farmer and the courts, Hebrew rules on sexuality, and the Hellenistic family documents?*

TABLE I: PRELIMINARIES TO AND RULES FOR A TRIAL

If plaintiff summons defendant to court, he shall go. If he does not go, plaintiff shall call witness thereto. Then only shall he take defendant by force.

If defendant shirks or takes to his heels, plaintiff shall lay hands on him.

If disease or age is an impediment, he [who summons defendant to

---

[11]The Egyptian name of Aphrodisia, the second daughter. (Original editors' note.)

court] shall grant him a team; he shall not spread with cushions the covered carriage if he does not so desire.

For a landowner, a landowner shall be surety; but for a proletarian person, let any one who is willing be his protector.[1] . . .

When parties make a settlement of the case, the judge[2] shall announce it. If they do not reach a settlement, they shall state the outline of their case in the meeting place or Forum before noon.

They shall plead it out together in person. After noon, the judge shall adjudge the case to the party present. If both be present, sunset shall be the time limit [of proceedings].

TABLE II: FURTHER ENACTMENTS ON TRIALS

Action under solemn deposit:[3] 500 *as* pieces[4] is the sum when the object of dispute under solemn deposit is valued at 1,000 in bronze or more, fifty pieces when less. Where the controversy concerns the liberty of a human being, fifty pieces shall be the solemn deposit under which the dispute should be undertaken.

If any of these be impediment for judge, referee, or party, on that account the day of trial shall be broken off.

Whoever is in need of evidence, he shall go on every third day to call out loudly before witness' doorway.

TABLE III: EXECUTION; LAW OF DEBT

When a debt has been acknowledged, or judgment about the matter has been pronounced in court, thirty days must be the legitimate time of grace. After that, the debtor may be arrested by laying on of hands. Bring him into court. If he does not satisfy the judgment, or no one in court offers himself as surety in his behalf, the creditor may take the defaulter with him. He may bind him either in stocks or in fetters; he may bind him with a weight no more than fifteen pounds, or with less if he shall so desire. The debtor, if he wishes, may live on his own. If he does not live on his own, the person [who shall hold him in bonds] shall give him one pound of grits for each day. He may give more if he so desires.

Unless they make a settlement, debtors shall be held in bonds for sixty

---

[1]The *vindex*, or "surety," was required to appear before the magistrate in place of the defendant at a preliminary trial before an action could begin. (Original editors' note.)

[2]The *iudex*, or "judge," agreed upon by the parties at the preliminary trial. (Original editors' note.)

[3]The *sacramentum*, or "solemn deposit," was a legal action in civil cases which involved the depositing by both parties to the litigation of a stake which was forfeited to the state by the loser. (Original editors' note.)

[4]The *as* was the Roman bronze monetary unit, originally pound ingots of copper divided into 12 *unciae*. (Original editors' note.)

days. During that time they shall be brought before the praetor's court in the meeting place on three successive market days, and the amount for which they are judged liable shall be announced; on the third market day they shall suffer capital punishment or be delivered up for sale abroad, across the Tiber.

On the third market day creditors shall cut pieces.[5] Should they have cut more or less than their due, it shall be with impunity.

Against a stranger, title of ownership shall hold good forever.

TABLE IV: PATRIA POTESTAS: RIGHTS OF HEAD OF FAMILY

Quickly kill . . . a dreadfully deformed child.

If a father thrice surrender a son for sale, the son shall be free from the father.

A child born ten months after the father's death will not be admitted into a legal inheritance.

TABLE V: GUARDIANSHIP; SUCCESSION

Females shall remain in guardianship even when they have attained their majority . . . except Vestal Virgins.

Conveyable possessions of a woman under guardianship of agnates cannot be rightfully acquired by *usucapio*,[6] save such possessions as have been delivered up by her with a guardian's sanction.

According as a person shall will regarding his [household], chattels, or guardianship of his estate, this shall be binding.

If a person dies intestate, and has no self-successor, the nearest agnate kinsman shall have possession of deceased's household.

If there is no agnate kinsman, deceased's clansmen shall have possession of his household.

To persons for whom a guardian has not been appointed by will, to them agnates are guardians.

If a man is raving mad, rightful authority over his person and chattels shall belong to his agnates or to his clansmen.

A spendthrift is forbidden to exercise administration over his own goods. . . . A person who, being insane or a spendthrift, is prohibited from administering his own goods shall be under trusteeship of agnates.

The inheritance of a Roman citizen-freedman shall be made over to his patron if the freedman has died intestate and without self-successor.

Items which are in the category of debts are not included in the divi-

---

[5]The majority of modern authorities agree with ancient commentators' literal interpretation that the Twelve Tables authorized actual cutting up of the debtor's body, though in customary practice the debtor's estate may have been divided. (Original editors' note.)

[6]*Usucapio* was a process by which one acquired title to goods if unclaimed by a previous owner after a certain time period (one or two years).

sion when they have with automatic right been divided into portions of an inheritance.

Debt bequeathed by inheritance is divided proportionally amongst each heir with automatic liability when the details have been investigated.

TABLE VI: ACQUISITION AND POSSESSION

When a party shall make bond or conveyance, the terms of the verbal declaration are to be held binding.

Articles which have been sold and handed over are not acquired by a buyer otherwise than when he has paid the price to the seller or has satisfied him in some other way, that is, by providing a guarantor or a security.

A person who has been ordained a free man [in a will, on condition] that he bestow a sum of 10,000 pieces on the heir, though he has been sold by the heir, shall win his freedom by giving the money to the purchaser.

It is sufficient to make good such faults as have been named by word of mouth, and that for any flaws which the vendor had expressly denied, he shall undergo penalty of double damage.

Usucapio of movable things requires one year's possession for its completion; but *usucapio* of an estate and buildings two years.

Any woman who does not wish to be subjected in this manner to the hand of her husband should be absent three nights in succession every year, and so interrupt the *usucapio* of each year.[7]

A person shall not dislodge from a framework a [stolen] beam which has been fixed in buildings or a vineyard. . . . Action [is granted] for double damages against a person found guilty of fixing such [stolen] beam.

TABLE VII: RIGHTS CONCERNING LAND

Ownership within a five-foot strip [between two pieces of land] shall not be acquired by long usage.

The width of a road [extends] to eight feet where it runs straight ahead, sixteen round a bend. . . .

Persons shall mend roadways. If they do not keep them laid with stone, a person may drive his beasts where he wishes.

If rainwater does damage . . . this must be restrained according to an arbitrator's order.

If a water course directed through a public place shall do damage to a private person, he shall have right of suit to the effect that damage shall be repaired for the owner.

Branches of a tree may be lopped off all round to a height of more than

---

[7]This limitation on the *patria potestas* [the father's legal power over legitimate children] introduced a form of civil marriage without *manus*, the legal power of a husband over his wife. (Original editors' note.)

15 feet. . . . Should a tree on a neighbor's farm be bent crooked by a wind and lean over your farm, action may be taken for removal of that tree.

It is permitted to gather up fruit falling down on another man's farm.

TABLE VIII: TORTS OR DELICTS

If any person has sung or composed against another person a song such as was causing slander or insult to another, he shall be clubbed to death.

If a person has maimed another's limb, let there be retaliation in kind unless he makes agreement for settlement with him.

If he has broken or bruised a freeman's bone with his hand or a club, he shall undergo penalty of 300 *as* pieces; if a slave's, 150.

If he has done simple harm [to another], penalties shall be 25 *as* pieces.

If a four-footed animal shall be said to have caused loss, legal action . . . shall be either the surrender of the thing which damaged, or else the offer of assessment for the damage.

For pasturing on, or cutting secretly by night, another's crops acquired by tillage, there shall be capital punishment in the case of an adult malefactor . . . he shall be hanged and put to death as a sacrifice to Ceres. In the case of a person under the age of puberty, at the discretion of the praetor either he shall be scourged or settlement shall be made for the harm done by paying double damages.

Any person who destroys by burning any building or heap of corn deposited alongside a house shall be bound, scourged, and put to death by burning at the stake, provided that he has committed the said misdeed with malice aforethought; but if he shall have committed it by accident, that is, by negligence, it is ordained that he repair the damage, or, if he be too poor to be competent for such punishment, he shall receive a lighter chastisement.

Any person who has cut down another person's trees with harmful intent shall pay 25 *as* pieces for every tree.

If theft has been done by night, if the owner kill the thief, the thief shall be held lawfully killed.

It is forbidden that a thief be killed by day . . . unless he defend himself with a weapon; even though he has come with a weapon, unless he use his weapon and fight back, you shall not kill him. And even if he resists, first call out.

In the case of all other thieves caught in the act, if they are freemen, they should be flogged and adjudged to the person against whom the theft has been committed, provided that the malefactors have committed it by day and have not defended themselves with a weapon; slaves caught in the act of theft should be flogged and thrown from the Rock;[8] boys under

---

[8]The Tarpeian Rock on the Capitoline Hill, commonly used as a place of execution in Rome. (Original editors' note.)

the age of puberty should, at the praetor's discretion, be flogged, and the damage done by them should be repaired.

If a person pleads on a case in theft in which the thief has not been caught in the act, the thief must compound for the loss by paying double damages.

A stolen thing is debarred from *usucapio*.

No person shall practice usury at a rate more than one twelfth . . . A usurer is condemned for quadruple amount.

Arising out of a case concerning an article deposited . . . action for double damages.

Guardians and trustees . . . the right to accuse on suspicion . . . action . . . against guardians for double damages.

If a patron shall have defrauded his client, he must be solemnly forfeited.[9]

Whosoever shall have allowed himself to be called as witness or shall have been scales-balancer, if he do not as witness pronounce his testimony, he must be deemed dishonored and incapable of acting as witness.

Penalty . . . for false witness . . . a person who has been found guilty of giving false witness shall be hurled down from the Tarpeian Rock. . . .

No person shall hold meetings by night in the city.

Members [of associations] . . . are granted . . . the right to pass any binding rule they like for themselves provided that they cause no violation of public law.

TABLE IX: PUBLIC LAW

Laws of personal exception [i.e., bills of attainder] must not be proposed; cases in which the penalty affects the person of a citizen must not be decided except through the greatest assembly and through those whom the censors[10] have placed upon the register of citizens.

The penalty shall be capital punishment for a judge or arbiter legally appointed who has been found guilty of receiving a bribe for giving a decision.

He who shall have roused up a public enemy, or handed over a citizen to a public enemy, must suffer capital punishment.

Putting to death . . . of any man who has not been convicted, whosoever he might be, is forbidden.

---

[9]The man thus adjudged *sacer* was placed outside human law by being dedicated to a divinity for destruction. This original death by sacrifice was later transformed into outlawry and confiscation of property. (Original editors' note.)

[10]Two censors held office for five-year terms and supervised the census of Roman citizens and their property.

TABLE X: SACRED LAW

A dead man shall not be buried or burned within the city.

One must not do more than this [at funerals]; one must not smooth the pyre with an axe.

. . . three veils, one small purple tunic, and ten flute-players. . . .

Women must not tear cheeks or hold chorus of "Alas!" on account of funeral.

When a man is dead one must not gather his bones in order to make a second funeral. An exception [in the case of] death in war or in a foreign land. . . .

Anointing by slaves is abolished, and every kind of drinking bout.

Let there be no costly sprinkling . . . no long garlands . . . no incense boxes. . . .

When a man wins a crown himself or through a chattel or by dint of valor, the crown bestowed on him . . . [may be laid in the grave] with impunity [on the man who won it] or on his father.

To make more than one funeral for one man and to make and spread more than one bier for him . . . this should not occur . . . and a person must not add gold. . . .

But him whose teeth shall have been fastened together with gold, if a person shall bury or burn him along with that gold, it shall be with impunity.

No new pyre or personal burning-mound must be erected nearer than sixty feet to another person's buildings without consent of the owner . . . the entrance chamber [of a tomb] and burning place cannot be acquired by *usucapio*.

TABLE XI: SUPPLEMENTARY LAWS

Intermarriage shall not take place between plebeians and patricians.

TABLE XII: SUPPLEMENTARY LAWS

Levying of distress [is granted] against a person who has bought an animal for sacrifice and is a defaulter by non-payment; likewise against a person who is a defaulter by non-payment of fee for yoke-beast which any one has hired out for the purpose of raising therefrom money to spend on a sacred banquet.

If a slave shall have committed theft or done damage . . . with his master's knowledge . . . the action for damages is in the slave's name.

Arising from delicts committed by children and slaves of a household establishment . . . actions for damages are appointed whereby the father or master could be allowed either to undergo "assessment for damages," or hand over the delinquent to punishment. . . .

If a person has taken a thing by false claim, if he should wish . . .

official must grant three arbitrators; by their arbitration . . . defendant must make good the damage by paying double the usufruct of the article.

It is prohibited to dedicate for consecrated use anything about which there is a controversy; otherwise the penalty is double the amount involved. . . .

Whatever the people has last ordained shall be held as binding by law.

Management of a Large Estate

COLUMELLA

Lucius Junius Moderatus Columella lived in the first century A.D. *He was a native of the region in Spain around Cádiz. His only extant writing is a treatise on agriculture, which provides insight into Roman agricultural techniques and farm life.*

*What sorts of buildings, tools, and animals does one find on the typical Roman estate (*villa*)? What crops does the estate produce? How is the work done and by whom? What is the relationship of the owner to the workers? How important is the Roman practice of slavery to successful agricultural enterprise?*

In comparison with the preceding selection, what are the particular powers and personal traits of a good householder in this system? Is Columella describing the life of the Roman household head as depicted in the Twelve Tables? Or have things changed significantly over the centuries since the early Roman Republic?

The size of the villa and the number of its parts should be proportioned to the whole enclosure, and it should be divided into three groups: the *villa urbana* (manor house), the *villa rustica* (farmhouse), and the *villa fructuaria* (storehouse). The manor house should be divided in turn into winter apartments and summer apartments, in such a way that the winter bedrooms face the southeast, and the winter dining room faces the west. The summer bedrooms, on the other hand, should look toward the south, but the dining rooms of that season should look toward the southeast. The baths should face the northwest, that they may be lighted from midday up to evening. The promenades should have a southern exposure, so as to receive both the maximum of sun in winter and the minimum in summer. But in the part devoted to farm uses there will be placed a spacious and high kitchen, that the rafters may be free from the danger of fire, and that it may offer a convenient place for the slave household to stop in at every season of the year. It will be best that cubicles for unfettered slaves be built facing the south; for those who are in chains there should be an underground prison, as wholesome as possible, receiving light through a number of narrow windows built so high from the ground that they cannot be reached with the hand.

For cattle there should be stables which will not be troubled by either heat or cold; for animals broken to work, two sets of stalls—one for winter, another for summer; and for the other animals which it is proper to keep within the farmstead there should be places partly covered, partly open to the sky, and surrounded with high walls so that the animals may rest in the one place in winter, in the other in summer, secure against attacks by wild animals. But stables should be roomy and so arranged that no moisture can flow in and that whatever is made there may run off quickly, to prevent the rotting of either the bases of the walls or the hoofs of the cattle. Ox stalls should be ten feet wide, or nine at least—a size which will allow room for the animal to lie down and for the oxherd to move around in it when performing his duties. The feedracks should not be too high for the ox or pack animal to feed from without inconvenience while standing. Quarters should be provided for the overseer alongside the entrance, so that he may have oversight of all who come in and go out; and for the steward over the entrance for the same reason, and also so that he may keep close watch on the overseer; and near both of these there should be a storehouse in which all farm gear may be collected, and within it a closet for the storing of the iron implements.

Cells for the herdsmen and shepherds should be adjacent to their animals, so that they may conveniently run out to care for them. And yet all should be quartered as close as possible to one another, so that the diligence of the overseer may not be overtaxed in making the rounds of the several places, and also that they may be witnesses of one another's industry and diligence.

The storehouse part is divided into rooms for oil, for presses, for wine, for the boiling down of must; lofts for hay and chaff; and storerooms and grain bins—in such a manner that those on the ground floor take care of liquid products, such as oil and wine for marketing, while dry products, such as grain, hay, leaves, chaff, and other fodder, should be stored in lofts. But the grain lofts, as I have said, should be reached by ladders and should receive ventilation through small openings on the north side; for that exposure is the coolest and the least humid, and both these factors contribute to the preservation of stored grain. The same reason holds true in the placing of the wine room on the ground floor; and it should be far removed from the baths, oven, dunghill, and other filthy places which give off a foul odor, and no less so from cisterns and running water, from which is derived a moisture that spoils the wine. . . .

The press rooms especially and the storerooms for oil should be warm, because every liquid is more readily thinned with heat and thickened by great cold; and if oil freezes, which seldom happens, it becomes rancid. But as it is natural heat that is wanted, arising from the climate and the exposure, there is no need of fire or flame, as the taste of oil is spoiled by smoke and soot. For this reason the pressing room should be lighted from the southern side, so that we may not find it necessary to employ fires and lamps when the olives are being pressed.

The cauldron room, in which boiled wine is made, should be neither narrow nor dark, so that the attendant who is boiling down the must may move around without inconvenience. The smoke room, too, in which timber not long cut may be seasoned quickly, can be built in a section of the farmhouse adjoining the farmhouse baths (it is important also that there be such places in which the household may bathe—but only on holidays; for the frequent use of baths is not conducive to physical vigor). Storerooms for wine will be situated to advantage over these places from which smoke is usually rising, for wines age more rapidly when they are brought to an early maturity by a certain kind of smoke. For this reason there should be another loft to which they may be removed, to keep them from becoming tainted, on the other hand, by too much smoking.

As for the situation of the farmhouse and the arrangement of its several parts, enough has been said. It will be necessary, next, that the farmhouse have the following near it: an oven and a mill, of such size as may be required by the number of tenant farmers; at least two ponds, one to serve for geese and cattle, the other in which we may soak lupines, elm withes, twigs, and other things suitable for our needs. There should also be two manure pits, one to receive the fresh dung and keep it for a year, and a second from which the old is hauled; but both of them should be built shelving with a gentle slope, in the manner of fish ponds, and built up and packed hard with earth, so as not to let the moisture drain away. . . .

The threshing floor is to be placed, if possible, in such manner that it can be viewed from above by the master, or at least by the farm manager. Such a floor is best when paved with hard stone, because the grain is thus threshed out quickly, since the ground does not give way under the beating of the hoofs and threshing sledges, and the winnowed grain is cleaner and is free from small stones and clods, which a dirt floor nearly always casts up during the threshing. . . .

The orchards, too, and the gardens should be fenced all around and should lie close by, in a place to which there may flow all manure-laden seepage from barnyard and baths, and the watery lees squeezed from olives; for both vegetables and trees thrive on nutriment of this sort, too.

After all these things have been obtained or constructed, the master must give special attention, among other things, to laborers; and these are either tenant farmers or slaves (unfettered or in chains). He should be civil in dealing with his tenant farmers, should show himself affable, and should be more exacting in the matter of work than of payments, as this gives less offense yet is, generally speaking, more profitable. For when land is carefully tilled, it usually brings a profit, and never a loss except when it is assailed by unusually severe weather or robbers; and therefore the tenant does not venture to ask for reduction of his rent. But the master should not be insistent on his rights in every particular to which he has bound his tenant, such as the exact day for payment of money, or the matter of demanding firewood and other trifling contributions; attention to such matters causes country folk more trouble than expense. . . . I myself remember having heard Publius Volusius, an old man who had been consul and was very wealthy, declare that estate to be most fortunate which had natives of the place as tenant farmers and which held them by reason of long association, even from the cradle, as if born on their own father's property. So I am decidedly of the opinion that repeated re-letting of a farm is a bad thing, but that a worse thing is the tenant farmer who lives in town and prefers to till the land through his slaves rather than by his own hand. Saserna[1] used to say that from a man of this sort the return was usually a lawsuit instead of income, and that for this reason we should take pains to keep with us tenants who are country-bred and at the same time diligent farmers, when we are not able to till the land ourselves or when it is not feasible to cultivate it with our own household; though this does not happen except in districts which are desolated by the severity of the climate and the barrenness of the soil. But when the climate is moderately healthful and the soil moderately good, a man's personal attention never fails to yield a larger return from his land than does that of a tenant. Even reliance on an overseer yields a larger return, except in the event of extreme carelessness or greed on the part of that slave. There is no doubt that in general both these offenses are either committed or fostered through the fault of the master, inasmuch as he has the authority to prevent such a person from being placed in charge of his affairs or to see to it that he is removed if so placed. On far-distant estates, however, which it is not easy for the owner to visit, it is better for every kind of land to be under free farmers than under slave overseers, but this is particularly true of grain land. To such land a tenant farmer can do no great harm, as he can to vineyards and trees, while slaves do it tremendous damage: they let out oxen for hire, and they keep them and other animals poorly fed; they do not plow the ground carefully, and they charge the account with far more seed than they have actually sown; what they have committed to the earth they do not foster so that it will make the proper growth; and when they have brought it to the threshing floor, every day during the threshing they lessen the quantity either by trickery or by carelessness. For they themselves steal it and do not guard against the thieving of others, and even when it is stored away, they do not enter it honestly in their accounts. The result is that both manager and hands are offenders, and the land pretty often gets a bad name. Therefore my opinion is that an estate of this sort should be leased if, as I have said, it cannot have the presence of the owner.

---

[1]Hostilius Saserna, a writer on agriculture of the late republican period. (Original editors' note.)

The next point is with regard to slaves—over what duty it is proper to place each, and to what sort of tasks to assign them. So my advice at the start is not to appoint an overseer from the sort of slaves who are physically attractive, and certainly not from that class which has been engaged in the voluptuous occupations of the city. This lazy and sleepy-headed class of slaves, accustomed to idling, to the Field of Mars, the circus and the theaters, to gambling, to taverns, to bawdy houses, never ceases to dream of these follies; and when they carry them over into their farming, the master suffers not so much loss in the slave himself as in his whole estate. A man should be chosen who has been hardened by farm work from his infancy, one who has been tested by experience. . . . He should be of middle age and of strong physique, skilled in farm operations or at least very painstaking, so that he may learn the more readily; for it is not in keeping with this business of ours for one man to give orders and another to give instruction, nor can a man properly exact work when he is being tutored by an underling as to what is to be done and in what way. Even an illiterate person, if only he have a retentive mind, can manage affairs well enough. Cornelius Celsus says that an overseer of this sort brings money to his master oftener than he does his book, because, being illiterate, he is either less able to falsify accounts or is afraid to do so through a second party, because that would make another aware of the deception.

But be the overseer what he may, he should be given a woman companion to keep him within bounds and moreover in certain matters to be a help to him. . . . He must be urged to take care of the equipment and the iron tools, and to keep in repair and stored away twice as many as the number of slaves requires, so that there will be no need of borrowing from a neighbor; for the loss in slave labor exceeds the cost of articles of this sort. In the care and clothing of the slave household he should have en eye to usefulness rather than appearance, taking care to keep them fortified against wind, cold, and rain, all of which are warded off with long-sleeved leather tunics, garments of patchwork, or hooded cloaks. If this be done, no weather is so unbearable but that some work may be done in the open. He should be not only skilled in the tasks of husbandry but should also be endowed, as far as the servile disposition allows, with such qualities of mind that he may exercise authority without laxness and without cruelty, and always humor some of the better hands, at the same time being forbearing even with those of lesser worth, so that they may rather fear his sternness than detest his cruelty. . . .

In the case of the other slaves, the following are, in general, the precepts to be observed, and I do not regret having held to them myself: to talk rather familiarly with the country slaves, provided only that they have not conducted themselves unbecomingly, more frequently than I would with town slaves; and when I perceived that their unending toil was lightened by such friendliness on the part of the master, I would even jest with them at times and allow them also to jest more freely. Nowadays I make it a practice to call them into consultation on any new work, as if they were more experienced, and to discover by this means what sort of ability is possessed by each of them and how intelligent he is. Furthermore, I observe that they are more willing to set about a piece of work on which they think that their opinions have been asked and their advice followed. Again, it is the established custom of all men of caution to inspect the slaves in the prison, to find out whether they are carefully chained, whether the places of confinement are quite safe and properly guarded, whether the overseer has put anyone in fetters or removed his shackles without the master's knowledge. . . . And the investigation of the householder should be the more painstaking in the interest of slaves of this sort, that they may not be treated unjustly in the matter of clothing or other allowances, inasmuch as, being subject to a greater number of people, such as overseers, taskmasters, and jailers, they are the more liable to unjust punishment, and again, when smarting under cruelty and greed, they are more to be feared. Accordingly, a careful master inquires not only of them, but also of those who are not in bonds, as being more worthy of belief, whether they are receiving what is due them under his instructions. He also tests the quality of their food and drink by tasting it himself and examines their clothing, mittens, and foot covering. In addition, he should give them frequent opportunities for making complaints against those persons who treat them cruelly or dishonestly. In fact, I now and then avenge those who have just cause for grievance, as well as punish those who incite the slaves to revolt or who slander their taskmasters; and, on the other hand, I reward those who conduct themselves with energy and diligence. Also, to women who are unusually prolific, and who ought to be rewarded for the bearing of a certain number of offspring, I have granted exemption from work and sometimes even freedom after they have reared many children: a mother of three children received exemption from work,[2] a mother of more, her freedom as well. Such justice and consideration on the part of the master contributes greatly to the increase of his estate. . . .

This, too, I believe: that the duties of the slaves should not be confused to the point where all take a hand in every task. For this is by no means to the advantage of the husbandman, either because no one regards any particular task as his own or because, when he does make an effort, he is performing a service that is not his own but common to all, and therefore shirks his work to a great extent; and yet fault cannot be fastened upon any one man because many have a hand in it. For this reason plowmen must be distinguished from vine dressers, and vine dressers from plowmen, and both of these from men of all work. Furthermore, squads should be

---

[2]During the Pax Romana slave owners turned more and more to breeding and rearing slaves in their homes and on their estates—practices they scorned in the heyday of their conquests, when huge supplies of war captives were dumped into the slave markets. (Original editors' note.)

formed, not to exceed ten men each, which the ancients called *decuriae* and approved of highly, because that limited number was most conveniently guarded while at work and the size was not disconcerting to the person in charge as he led the way. Therefore, if the field is of considerable extent, such squads should be distributed over sections of it and the work should be so apportioned that men will not be by ones or twos, because they are not easily watched when scattered; and yet they should not number more than ten, lest, on the other hand, when the band is too large, each individual may think that the work does not concern him. This arrangement not only stimulates rivalry, but also discloses the slothful; for, when a task is enlivened by competition, punishment inflicted on the laggards appears just and free from censure.

Marriage, Adultery, and Prostitution

Augustus, emperor, 27 B.C.–A.D. 14, was very concerned with the family life of the elite of Roman society. Increasingly, this elite was avoiding marriage or, if married, avoiding or limiting procreation. During his rule, Augustus enacted laws designed, among other things, to punish female adultery, while making it a crime subject to state prosecution rather than solely the matter of a wronged husband to pursue. He also drafted rules governing marriage and divorce procedures and giving certain legal rights and benefits to those couples who had more than three children. In all, Augustus issued three important pieces of legislation: the Julian law on adultery, the Julian law on the orders of marriage, and the Papia-Poppaean law (so named after the two consuls who were in power that year, A.D. 9). These laws became the basis of later Roman law on marriage and related matters.

In the centuries following Augustus, Roman law was developed in several different sources. Judicial officials, the practors, *published an annual decree stating what types of cases they would handle and what criteria of judgment they would apply. New elements entered the law through these decrees. The praetors or other judges, or the parties to a lawsuit, would also turn to experts in the law, the so-called jurisprudents, for advice. These men developed interpretation of all areas of law and instructed others as their students. Finally, later emperors continued to enact new laws and to handle legal questions submitted to them by imperial officials, to which they responded with imperial orders, known as rescripts.*

In the fourth decade of the sixth century, Justinian, emperor, 527–565, had these materials gathered into a single collection, which would be known later as the Corpus iuris civilis *(the "body of civil law"). The excerpts that follow come from those sections of the* Corpus *containing, first, the statements of famous jurisprudents (a section of the* Corpus *known as the Digest) and, second, the later rescripts of emperors (known as the Codex). All of these excerpts concern marriage law and the punishment of adultery. The author(s) of each piece of text were identified in the* Corpus *of Justinian, and their names remain here so you can see how different statements came from different people. Marcianus, Paulus, Terentius Clemens, Celsus, Mod-estinus, Gaius, Papinianus, Marcellus, Ulpianus, and Macer were all legal experts of the classical era of jurisprudence whose works, or parts thereof, were deemed important enough to preserve in the Digest. The most important of these figures were Papinianus (executed by the Emperor Caracalla in 212), who excelled at setting forth legal prob-lems arising from cases, and Ulpianus (d. 223), who wrote a commentary on Roman law in his era.*

How did Roman law view marriage and adultery? Had things changed much from the days of the Twelve Tables? Did the legal experts whose writings were ex-cerpted in the Digest view matters any differently from the emperors whose decrees were preserved in the Codex? Did the later rules of Constantine and other Christian emperors, at the end of this selection, greatly change this view? What sort of family life would result from Roman marriages? How did these families compare to the Greek families about which you have already read? What was the difference between a wife and a concubine? And what might this difference, as well as other facets of these laws, tell us about the roles and rights of women during the Roman Empire?

DIGEST

Book XXIII. Title II. On the Marriage Ceremony.

19. Marcianus, Institutes, Book XVI.

In the Thirty-fifth Section of the *Lex Julia*,[1] persons who wrongfully prevent their children, who are subject to their authority, to marry, or who refuse to endow them, are compelled by the proconsuls or governors of pro-vinces, under a Constitution of the Divine Severus and Antoninus,[2] to marry or endow their said children. They are also held to prevent their marriage where they do not seek to promote it.

20. Paulus, On the Rescript of the Divine Severus and Commodus.[3]

It must be remembered that it is not one of the functions of a curator[4] to see that his ward is married, or not; because his duties only relate to the trans-action of business. This Severus and Antoninus stated in a Rescript[5] in the following words: "It is the duty of a curator to manage the affairs of his ward, but the ward can marry, or not, as she pleases."

---

[1]Enactment by the Emperor Augustus in 18 B.C. that made marriage a duty for Roman patricians. The law's goal was to increase the population of elite educated Romans.

[2]Severus was emperor, 193–211; his son Antoninus (Caracalla) was co-ruler and then emperor, 212–217.

[3]Emperor, 180–192.

[4]Legal guardian for a minor or other person considered incapable of managing his or her own affairs.

[5]Emperor's answers to legal questions from individuals or officials.

21. Terentius Clemens, On the Lex Julia et Papia,[6] Book III.

A son under paternal control cannot be forced to marry.

22. Celsus, Digest, Book XV.

Where a son, being compelled by his father, marries a woman whom he would not have married if he had been left to the exercise of his own free will, the marriage will, nevertheless, legally be contracted; because it was not solemnized against the consent of the parties, and the son is held to have preferred to take this course.

23. The Same, Digest, Book XXX.

It is provided by the *Lex Papia* that all freeborn men, except senators and their children, can marry freedwomen.

24. Modestinus, Rules, Book I.

Where a man lives with a free woman, it is not considered concubinage but genuine matrimony, if she does not acquire gain by means of her body.

25. The Same, Rules, Book II.

A son who has been emancipated can marry without the consent of his father, and any son that he may have will be his heir. . . .

28. Marcianus, Institutes, Book X.

A patron cannot marry his freedwoman against her consent. . . .

30. Gaius, On the Lex Julia et Papia, Book II.

A pretended marriage is of no force or effect. . . .

34. Papinianus, Opinions, Book IV.

Where a general commission has been given to a man by someone to seek a husband for his daughter, this is not sufficient ground for the conclusion of a marriage. Therefore it is necessary that the person selected should be introduced to the father, and that he should consent to the marriage, in order for it to be legally contracted. . . .

(2) Marriage can be contracted between stepchildren, even though they have a common brother, the issue of the new marriage of their parents.

(3) Where the daughter of a senator marries a freedman, this unfortunate act of her father does not render her a wife, for children should not be deprived of their rank on account of an offence of their parent. . . .

---

[6]The *Lex Papia* was treated along with the *Lex Julia* (see note 1). Enacted in A.D. 9, it sought to make Romans marry within their social class.

41. Marcellus, Digest, Book XXVI.

It is understood that disgrace attaches to those women who live unchastely, and earn money by prostitution, even if they do not do so openly.

(1) If a woman should live in concubinage[7] with someone besides her patron, I say that she does not possess the virtue of the mother of a family.

42. Modestinus, On the Rite of Marriage.

In unions of the sexes, it should always be considered not only what is legal, but also what is decent.

(1) If the daughter, granddaughter, or great-granddaughter of a senator should marry a freedman, or a man who practices the profession of an actor, or whose father or mother did so, the marriage will be void.

43. Ulpianus, On the Lex Julia et Papia, Book I.

We hold that a woman openly practices prostitution, not only where she does so in a house of ill-fame, but also if she is accustomed to do this in taverns, or in other places where she manifests no regard for her modesty.

(1) We understand the word "openly" to mean indiscriminately, that is to say, without choice, and not if she commits adultery or fornication, but where she sustains the role of a prostitute.

(2) Moreover, where a woman, having accepted money, has intercourse with only one or two persons, she is not considered to have openly prostituted herself.

(3) Octavenus,[8] however, says very properly that where a woman publicly prostitutes herself without doing so for money, she should be classed as a harlot.

(4) The law brands with infamy[9] not only a woman who practices prostitution, but also one who has formerly done so, even though she has ceased to act in this manner; for the disgrace is not removed even if the practice is subsequently discontinued.

(5) A woman is not to be excused who leads a vicious life under the pretext of poverty.

(6) The occupation of a pander is not less disgraceful than the practice of prostitution.

(7) We designate those women as procuresses who prostitute other women for money. . . .

(9) Where one woman conducts a tavern, and keeps others in it who prostitute themselves, as many are accustomed to do under the pretext of

---

[7]A legally recognized state wherein a man and woman were regular sexual partners but were not officially married, and there was no dowry.

[8]An obscure Roman jurist.

[9]Not just a bad reputation but a legal condition that removed certain legal protections enjoyed by others.

employing women for the service of the house; it must be said that they are included in the class of procuresses. . . .

(12) Where a woman is caught in adultery, she is considered to have been convicted of a criminal offence. Hence if she is proved to have been guilty of adultery, she will be branded with infamy, not only because she was caught *flagrante delicto*,[10] but also because she was convicted of a criminal offence. If, however, she was not caught, but was, nevertheless, found guilty, she becomes infamous because she was convicted of a criminal offence; and, indeed, if she was caught but was not convicted, she would still be infamous. I think that even if she should be acquitted after having been caught, she will still remain infamous, because it is certain that she was taken in adultery, and the law renders the act infamous and does not make this dependent upon the judicial decision.

(13) It is not mentioned here, as in the *Lex Julia* on adultery, by whom or where the woman must be caught; hence she is considered infamous whether she was caught by her husband or by anyone else. She will also be infamous according to the terms of the law, even if she was not caught in the house of her husband or her father. . . .

45. *Ulpianus, On the Lex Julia et Papia, Book III.*

In that law which provides that where a freedwoman has been married to her patron, after separation from him she cannot marry another without his consent; we understand the patron to be one who has bought a female slave under the condition of manumitting her (as is stated in the Rescript of our Emperor and his father), because, after having been manumitted, she becomes the freedwoman of the purchaser. . . .

Book XXVI. Title VII. Concerning Concubines.

1. *Ulpianus, On the Lex Julia et Papia, Book II.*

Where a freedwoman is living in concubinage with her patron, she can leave him without his consent, and unite with another man, either in matrimony or in concubinage. I think, however, that a concubine should not have the right to marry if she leaves her patron without his consent, since it is more honorable for a freedwoman to be the concubine of a patron than to become the mother of a family.

(1) I hold with Atilicinus, that only those women who are not disgraced by such a connection can be kept in concubinage without the fear of committing a crime. . . .

(3) If a woman has lived in concubinage with her patron, and then maintains the same relation with his son or grandson, I do not think that she is acting properly, because a connection of this kind closely approaches one that is infamous, and therefore such scandalous conduct should be prohibited.

---

[10]In the act of committing an obvious wrong.

(4) It is clear that anyone can keep a concubine of any age unless she is less than twelve years old.

2. *Paulus, On the Lex Julia et Papia, Book XII.*

Where a patron, who has a freedwoman as his concubine, becomes insane, it is more equitable to hold that she remains in concubinage.

3. *Marcianus, Institutes, Book XII.*

The freedwoman of another can be kept in concubinage as well as a woman who is born free, and this is especially the case where she is of a low origin, or has lived by prostitution; otherwise if a man prefers to keep a woman of respectable character and who is free born in concubinage, it is evident that he can not be permitted to do so without openly stating the fact in the presence of witnesses; but it will be necessary for him either to marry her, or if he refuses, to subject her to disgrace.

(1) Adultery is not committed by a party who lives with a concubine because concubinage obtains its name from the law, and does not involve a legal penalty; as Marcellus states in the Seventh Book of the Digest.

4. *Paulus, Opinions, Book XIX.*

The woman must be considered a concubine even where only the intention to live with her is manifested.

5. *The Same, Opinions, Book II.*

An official who is a resident of the province where he administers the duties of his office can keep a concubine. . . .

Book XLVIII. Title V. Concerning the Julian Law for the Punishment of Adultery.

. . . (2) The crime of pandering is included in the Julian Law on Adultery, as a penalty has been prescribed against a husband who profits pecuniarily by the adultery of his wife; as well as against one who retains his wife after she has been taken in adultery.

(3) Moreover, he who permits his wife to commit this offence, holds his marriage in contempt; and where anyone who does not become indignant on account of such pollution, the penalty of adultery is not inflicted.

(4) Anyone who alleges that he has committed adultery with the assistance of the husband, desires, indeed, to lessen his crime, but an excuse of this kind is not admitted. Therefore, if the defendant should wish to denounce the husband for having acted as a pander, he shall not be heard, if he has once been accused. . . .

(6) Hence it may be asked whether he who has cognizance of the prosecution for adultery can decide against the husband because of his having acted as a pander? I think that he can do so. For Claudius Gorgus, a most

illustrious man, having accused his wife, and it having been ascertained that although he had caught her in adultery he still kept her, was condemned by the Divine Serverus for being guilty of pandering, without any accuser having appeared against him. . . .

(8) If the husband and the father of the woman appear at the same time for the purpose of accusing her, the question arises, which of them should be given the preference by the Praetor?[11] The better opinion is, that the husband should be entitled to the preference, for it may well be believed that he will prosecute the accusation with greater anger and vexation. This is so far true, that even where the father has already appeared, and filed the papers containing the accusation, if the husband has not been negligent or guilty of delay, but is himself prepared to bring the accusation, and introduce evidence, and fortify it, in order that the case may be the more easily proved before the judges, the same thing must be said. . . .

6. Papinianus, On Adultery, Book I.

The Julian Law only applies to free persons who have been the victims of adultery or debauchery. With reference to female slaves, recourse can easily be had to the action authorized by the Aquilian Law,[12] and that for injury will also lie, and the Praetorian action for the corruption of a slave will not be refused; so that the person guilty of this crime will not escape on account of the multiplicity of actions.[13]

(1) The law promiscuously and incorrectly designates the same crime by the terms debauchery and adultery. Properly speaking, adultery is only committed with a married woman; this name having been adopted on account of the child being begotten by another than the husband. Debauchery, which the Greeks call "corruption," is committed with a virgin, or a widow. . . .

8. Papinianus, On Adultery, Book II.

Anyone who knowingly lends his house to enable debauchery or adultery to be committed there with a matron who is not his wife, or with a male, or who pecuniarily profits by the adultery of his wife, no matter what may be his status, is punished as an adulterer.

(1) It is clear that by the term "house" every kind of habitation is meant. . . .

10. Papinianus, On Adultery, Book II.

A matron means not only a married woman, but also a widow.

(1) Women who lend their houses, or have received any compensation for debauchery which they have committed, are also liable under this Section of the law.

---

[11]One of the Roman magistrates who administered justice.

[12]Fundamental law of delict (torts) from the third century B.C.

[13]In Roman law, *action* is the term for a legal remedy and the procedures to pursue it.

(2) A woman who gratuitously acts as a bawd for the purpose of avoiding the penalty for adultery, or hires her services to appear in the theatre, can be accused and convicted of adultery under the Decree of the Senate. . . .

(11) Although a woman may be alleged to have married him with whom she is suspected of having committed adultery, she cannot be accused before the adulterer has been convicted. Otherwise, husbands desiring to have marriages, which have subsequently been contracted, annulled, would have recourse to this pretext, and say that their wives had married men with whom they had committed adultery.

(12) A woman, having heard that her absent husband was dead, married another, and her first husband afterwards returned. I ask, what should be decided with reference to this woman? The answer was that the question is one of law and not of fact; for if a long time had elapsed without any proof of debauchery having been made, and the woman, having been induced by false rumors, and, as it were, released from her former tie, married a second time in accordance with law, as it is probable that she was deceived, and she can be held to have done nothing deserving of punishment. If, however, it is established that the supposed death of her husband furnished an inducement for her marrying a second time, as her chastity is affected by this fact, she should be punished in proportion to the character of the offence.

(13) I married a woman accused of adultery, and, as soon as she was convicted, I repudiated her. I ask whether I should be considered to have furnished the cause of the separation. The answer was that, since by the Julian Law you are prohibited from keeping a wife of this kind, it is clear that you should not be considered to have furnished the cause for the separation. Therefore, the law will be applied just as if a divorce had taken place through the fault of the woman. . . .

13. Ulpianus, On Adultery, Book II.

Where a wife did not commit adultery, but a concubine did, the husband cannot accuse her as such, because she is not his wife; still, he is not prohibited by law from bringing an accusation as a stranger, provided that she, in giving herself as a concubine, did not forfeit the name of a matron, as, for instance, a woman who had been the concubine of her patron. . . .

(5) The judge who has jurisdiction of adultery must have before his eyes, and investigate whether the husband, living modestly, has afforded his wife the opportunity of having good morals; for it would be considered extremely unjust for the husband to require chastity for his wife, which he himself does not practice. This, indeed, may condemn the husband, but cannot afford a set-off for mutual crime when committed by both parties.

(6) If anyone wishes to accuse his wife, and alleges that she committed adultery before he married her, he cannot bring the accusation by his right as a husband, because she did not commit adultery while she was married to him.

This can also be said with reference to a concubine whom the man who kept her subsequently married; or with reference to a daughter under paternal control, to whose union her father afterwards gave his consent. . . .

20. *Papinianus, On Adultery, Book I.*

The right is granted to the father to kill a man who commits adultery with his daughter while she is under his control. Therefore no other relative can legally do this, nor can a son under paternal control, who is a father, do so with impunity.

21. *Ulpianus, On Adultery, Book I.*

Hence it happens that neither the father nor the grandfather can kill the adulterer. This is not unreasonable, for he cannot be considered to have anyone under his control who has not control of himself.

22. *Papinianus, On Adultery, Book I.*

In this law, the natural father is not distinguished from the adoptive father.

(1) In the accusation of his daughter, who is a widow, the father is not entitled to the preference.

(2) The right to kill the adulterer is granted to the father in his own house, even though his daughter does not live there, or in the house of his son-in-law. . . .

(4) Hence the father, and not the husband, has the right to kill the woman and every adulterer; for the reason that, in general, paternal affection is solicitous for the interests of the children, but the heat and impetuosity of the husband, who decides too quickly, should be restrained.

23. *Ulpianus, On Adultery, Book I.*

What the law says, that is, "If he finds a man committing adultery with his daughter," does not seem to be superfluous; for it signifies that the father shall have this power only when he surprises his daughter in the very act of adultery. Labeo[14] also adopts this opinion; and Pomponius says that the man must be killed while in the very performance of the sexual act. . . .

(1) It is sufficient for the father for his daughter to be subject to his authority at the time when he kills the adulterer, although she may not have been at the time when he gave her in marriage; for suppose that she had afterwards come under his control.

(2) Therefore the father shall not be permitted to kill the parties wherever he surprises them, but only in his own house, or in that of his son-in-law. The reason for this is, that the legislator thought that the injury was greater where the daughter caused the adulterer to be introduced into the house of her father or her husband.

---

[14]A jurist of the first century A.D. who founded the so-called Proculian school of jurisprudence that tended to a strict or literal interpretation.

(3) If, however, her father lives elsewhere, and has another house in which he does not reside, and surprises his daughter there, he cannot kill her.

(4) Where the law says, "He may kill his daughter at once;" this must be understood to mean that having to-day killed the adulterer he can not reserve his daughter to be killed subsequently; for he should kill both of them with one blow and one attack, and be inflamed by the same resentment against both. But if, without any connivance on his part, his daughter should take to flight, while he is killing the adulterer, and she should be caught and put to death some hours afterwards by her father, who pursued her, he will be considered to have killed her immediately.

24. Macer, Public Prosecutions, Book I.

A husband is also permitted to kill a man who commits adultery with his wife, but not everyone without distinction, as the father is; for it is provided by this law that the husband can kill the adulterer if he surprises him in his own house, but not if he surprises him in the house of his father-in-law; nor if he was formerly a pander; or had exercised the profession of a mountebank, by dancing or singing on the stage; or had been convicted in a criminal prosecution and not been restored to his civil rights; or is the freedman of the husband or the wife, or of the father or mother, or of the son or the daughter of any of them; nor does it make any difference whether he belonged exclusively to one of the persons above mentioned, or owed services to two patrons in common, or was a slave.

(1) It is also provided that a husband who has killed any one of these must dismiss his wife without delay.

(2) It is held by many authorities to make no difference whether the husband is his own master, or a son under paternal control.

(3) With reference to both parties, the question arises, in accordance with the spirit of the law, whether the father can kill a magistrate; and also where his daughter is of bad reputation, or has been illegally married, whether the father or the husband will still retain his right; and what should be done if the husband is a pander, or is branded with ignominy for some reason or other. It may properly be held that those have a right to kill who can bring an accusation as a father or a husband.

25. Ulpianus, On the Julian Law Relating to Adultery, Book II.

It is provided as follows in the Fifth Section of the Julian Law: "That where a husband has surprised an adulterer with his wife, and is either unwilling or unable to kill him, he can hold him for not more than twenty consecutive hours of the day and night, in order to obtain evidence of the crime, and make use of his right without endangering it." . . .

(5) The following clause, "In order to obtain evidence of the crime," means that he can introduce witnesses who will afterwards testify that the offender was taken in adultery.

26. The Same, Disputations, Book III.

A woman cannot be accused of adultery during marriage by anyone who, in addition to the husband, is permitted to bring the accusation; for a stranger should not annoy a wife who is approved by her husband, and disturb a quiet marriage, unless he has previously accused the husband of being a pander.

(1) When, however, the charge has been abandoned by the husband, it is proper for it to be prosecuted by another. . . .

CODEX

Book IX. Title IX. On the Lex Julia Relating to Adultery and Fornication.

1. The Emperors Severus and Antoninus to Cassia. [A.D. 198]

The *Lex Julia* declares that wives have no right to bring criminal accusations for adultery against their husbands, even though they may desire to complain of the violation of the marriage vow, for while the law grants this privilege to men it does not concede it to women. . . .

2. The Same Emperors to Cyrus. [A.D. 200]

Those are guilty of the crime of pimping who allow their wives taken in adultery to remain in marriage, and not those who merely suspect their wives of having committed adultery. . . .

3. The Emperor Antoninus to Julianus. [A.D. 214]

Not only the words of the *Lex Julia* concerning the repression of adultery, but also the spirit of the law, authorize a husband who desires to prove that his wife has been guilty of adultery to do so by torturing slaves of both sexes; and this applies only to the slaves of the persons specially mentioned in the law, that is to say, the woman, and her natural, not her adoptive father; and it forbids the said slaves to be either manumitted or sold within the term of sixty days, to be computed from the date of the dissolution of the marriage, and requires the husband to furnish a bond to the owners of said slaves to indemnify them, if the former should die under torture, or become deteriorated in value, and the woman be acquitted. . . .

4. The Emperor Alexander to Julian, Proconsul of the Province of Narbonne. [n.d.]

If Numerius, who killed Gracchus[15] at night in the act of adultery, did so under such circumstances that he could have taken his life with impunity by virtue of the *Lex Julia*, what was lawfully done will incur no penalty.

The same rule applies to sons who have obeyed the orders of their

---

[15]Numerius and Gracchus were two moderately wealthy Romans.

father, in a case of this kind. If, however, the husband, rendered insane by grief, killed the adulterer without being legally authorized to do so, even though the homicide may have been excusable, still, because it was committed at night, and his just grief diminished the criminality of the act, he can be sent into exile. . . .

7. The Same Emperor to Heruclanus. [A.D. 224]

The man who afterwards married her cannot be a lawful accuser, where an adult virgin was violated before her marriage; and therefore he cannot prosecute the crime as her husband, unless he was betrothed to the girl who was violated. If, however, she herself, with the assistance of her curators by whom her affairs were transacted, should prosecute for the injury committed upon her, the Governor of the province will impose a severe sentence in accordance with what is required by law for a crime of this kind, if its commission should be established. . . .

9. The Same Emperor to Proculus. [A.D. 225]

It is proper for the preservation of virtue during My reign that a woman convicted under the *Lex Julia* concerning chastity should suffer the legal penalty.

Moreover, anyone that knowingly marries, or takes back a woman convicted of adultery, who has in some way evaded the penalty prescribed for her crime, shall be punished by the same law as a procurer. . . .

10. The Same Emperor to Demetrianus. [A.D. 226]

It is not lawful to condone the crime of adultery, and he who is guilty of collusion is in the same position as one who refuses to reveal the truth. Moreover, he who accepts a sum of money to desist from prosecution, in a case where adultery has been discovered, is liable to the penalty imposed by the *Lex Julia*.

11. The Same Emperor to Narvanus.

No one doubts that a husband cannot accuse his wife of adultery if he continues to retain her in marriage. . . .

Extract from Novel 117, Chapter XVIII. Latin Text. [A.D. 542]

Under the new law, however, he can do so, and if the accusation is proved to be true, he can then repudiate her, and he should file a written accusation against her. If, however, the husband should not be able to establish the accusation of adultery which he brought, he will be liable to the same punishment which his wife would have undergone if the accusation had been proved.

12. The Same Emperor to Bassus. [A.D. 241]

Although, as you allege, he who was convicted of the crime of adultery was not restored to his civil rights; still, since your sister, with whom the adultery was said to have been committed, was not accused, she could not have been subjected to any penalty, or rendered infamous, especially as you state that the accuser afterwards died. . . .

18. The Same Emperors [Balerian and Gallienus] and the Caesar Valerian to Theodora. [A.D. 259]

There is no doubt that he who has two wives at once is branded with infamy, for, in a case of this kind, not the operation of the law by which Our citizens are forbidden to contract more than one marriage at a time, but the intention, should be considered; and therefore he who pretended to be unmarried, but had another wife in the province, and asked you to marry him, can lawfully be accused of the crime of fornification, for which you are not liable, for the reason that you thought that you were his wife. You can obtain from the Governor of the province the return of all your property of which you deplore the loss on account of the fraudulent marriage, and which should be restored to you without delay. But how can you recover what he promised to give you as his betrothed? . . .

20. The Same Emperors [Diocletian and Maximian] and Caesars to Didymus. [A.D. 290]

The laws punish the detestable wickedness of women who prostitute their chastity to the lusts of others, but does not hold those liable who are compelled to commit fornication through force, and against their will. And, moreover, it has very properly been decided that their reputations are not lost, and that their marriage with others should not be prohibited on this account. . . .

22. The Same Emperors and Caesars to Oblimosus. [A.D. 290]

If a woman whom you have carnally known indiscriminately sold herself for money, and prostituted herself everywhere as a harlot, you did not commit the crime of adultery with her. . . .

25. The Same Emperors and Caesars to Sossianus. [A.D. 291]

Although it is established by the contents of certain documents that you are consumed with the lust of immoderate desire, still, as it has been ascertained that you confined yourself to female slaves, and did not have intercourse with free women, it is clear that by a sentence of this kind your reputation suffers, rather than that you become infamous. . . .

27. The Same Emperors and Caesars to Phoebus. [A.D. 292]

Adultery committed with a man whom a woman afterwards married is not extinguished by the fact of the marriage. . . .

29. The Emperor Constantine to Africanus. [A.D. 326]

It should be ascertained whether the woman who committed adultery was the owner of the inn, or only a servant; and if, by employing herself in servile duties (which frequently happens), she gave occasion for intemperance, since if she were the mistress of the inn, she will not be exempt from liability under the law.

Where, however, she served liquor to the men who were drinking, she would not be liable to accusation as having committed the offense, on account of her inferior rank, and any freemen who have been accused shall be discharged, as the same degree of modesty is required of these women as of those who are legally married, and bear the name of mothers of families.

Those, also, are not subject to judicial severity who are guilty of fornication or adultery, and the vileness of whose lives does not render them worthy of the attention of the law. . . .

30. The Same Emperor to Evagrius. [A.D. 326]

Although the crime of adultery is included among public offenses, the accusation of which is granted to all persons without distinction, still, in order that those who inconsiderately wish to cause discord in households may not be allowed to do so, it is hereby decreed that only the nearest relatives of the guilty party shall have the power to bring the accusation; that is to say, the father, the brother, and the paternal and maternal uncles, whom genuine grief may impel to prosecute. We, however, also give the said persons permission to revoke the accusation, by withdrawing it, if they should so desire.

The husband, above all others, should be considered the avenger of the marriage bed, for he is permitted to accuse his wife on suspicion, and he is not forbidden to retain her, if he only suspects her; nor will he be liable if he files a written accusation when he accuses her as her husband, a privilege which was established by former Emperors. . . .

Extract from Novel 134, Chapter X. Latin Text. [A.D. 556]

At present, however, a woman convicted of adultery is placed in a monastery, from which her husband is permitted to remove her within the term of two years. After the two years have expired, without her husband having taken her back, or, before that, if he should have died, the adulteress, having had her head shaved, and assumed a religious habit, shall remain there during lifetime, and her property, if she has any, shall be divided into three parts, two of which should be given to her children, and the third to the monastery. When she has no children, and her parents are living and did not consent to her crime, they shall receive a third part of her property, and the monastery two-thirds of the same. If her aforesaid relatives are not living, all of her property shall be acquired by her monastery, and, in every instance, all rights under dotal agreements are reserved for the benefit of the husband. . . .

33. The Emperors Theodosius, Arcadius, and Honorius to Rufinus, Praetorian Prefect. [A.D. 392]

When a charge of adultery has been made, We order that all civil exceptions by means of which a dowry[16] may be claimed, or any other debt demanded, and which are ordinarily pleaded and examined, to be set aside, and that the progress of the case shall not be delayed through their inter-position. But when the accusation has been formulated, that is to say, when it has been regularly instituted, whether it was filed under the right of a husband, or under that of a stranger, the crime shall be investigated, the evidence produced, the more important matters in dispute settled, and all civil actions be subordinated to the criminal prosecution. The woman will afterwards have the right to begin any civil proceedings to which he is entitled, provided they do not interfere with the conduct of the criminal case. . . .

Germany and Its Tribes

TACITUS

Author of the Annals *and* Histories, *Publius Cornelius Tacitus (c. 55–c. 117) was one of the great historians of ancient Rome. Like many Greek and Roman historians, Tacitus believed history had a moral purpose to instruct, to disparage the evil and to praise the good that people have done. In the following selection, see if you can discern the lessons that Tacitus thought his Roman audience should learn from this description of German society. It is important to recognize that Tacitus came from a senatorial (patrician) background, admired the Roman Republic, and criticized the Roman emperors. Unfortunately, much of what we know about early German society comes solely from Roman authors, and their biases must be taken into account.*

According to Tacitus, how did geography influence the population of Germany? How did German religion reflect German culture? What does Tacitus say about the legal system? Was Germany a particularly violent society? What was done to limit violence? What type of government did the Germans have? What was the composition of the German elite? What human values and qualities did the Germans prize? Why does Tacitus admire German marriage, family life, and the treatment of children? How does this selection by Tacitus suggest that the Romans measure up to the Germans? What was right with the Germans and wrong with the Romans, by implication? Which was the more "civilized" people?

The Germans themselves I should regard as aboriginal, and not mixed at all with other races through immigration or intercourse. For, in former

---

[16]Property given by the bride's father or family to the groom or his father at the time of marriage.

times, it was not by land but on shipboard that those who sought to emi-
grate would arrive; and the boundless and, so to speak, hostile ocean beyond us, is seldom entered by a sail from our world. And, beside the perils
of rough and unknown seas, who would leave Asia, or Africa, or Italy for
Germany, with its wild country, its inclement skies, its sullen manners and
aspect, unless indeed it were his home? In their ancient songs, their only
way of remembering or recording the past, they celebrate an earth-born
god, Tuisco, and his son Mannus, as the origin of their race, as their founders. To Mannus they assign three sons, from whose names, they say, the
coast tribes are called Ingaevones; those of the interior, Herminones; all the
rest, Istaevones. Some, with the freedom of conjecture permitted by antiquity, assert that the god had several descendants, and the nation several
appellations, as Marsi, Gambrivii, Suevi, Vandilii, and that these are genuine old names. The name Germany, on the other hand, they say, is modern
and newly introduced, from the fact that the tribes which first crossed the
Rhine and drove out the Gauls, and are now called Tungrians, were then
called Germans. Thus what was the name of a tribe, and not of a race,
gradually prevailed, till all called themselves by this self-invented name of
Germans, which the conquerors had first employed to inspire terror.

They say that Hercules,[1] too, once visited them; and when going into
battle, they sing of him first of all heroes. They have also those songs of
theirs, by the recital of which ("baritus," they call it), they rouse their courage, while from the note they augur the result of the approaching conflict.
For, as their line shouts, they inspire or feel alarm. It is not so much an
articulate sound, as a general cry of valour. They aim chiefly at a harsh note
and a confused roar, putting their shields to their mouth, so that, by rever-
beration, it may swell into a fuller and deeper sound. . . .

For my own part, I agree with those who think that the tribes of Germany are free from all taint of intermarriages with foreign nations, and that
they appear as a distinct, unmixed race, like none but themselves. Hence,
too, the same physical peculiarities throughout so vast a population. All
have fierce blue eyes, red hair, huge frames, fit only for a sudden exertion.
They are less able to bear laborious work. Heat and thirst they cannot in
the least endure; to cold and hunger their climate and their soil inure them.

Their country, though somewhat various in appearance, yet generally
either bristles with forests or reeks with swamps; it is more rainy on the
side of Gaul, bleaker on that of Noricum[2] and Pannonia.[3] It is productive of
grain, but unfavourable to fruit-bearing trees; it is rich in flocks and herds,
but these are for the most part undersized, and even the cattle have not

[1]Mythological Greek hero who traveled widely to complete the twelve labors assigned
to him.

[2]Roman province in what is roughly Austria today.

[3]Roman province directly east of Noricum.

their usual beauty or noble head. It is number that is chiefly valued; they are in fact the most highly prized, indeed the only riches of the people. Silver and gold the gods have refused to them, whether in kindness or in anger I cannot say. I would not, however, affirm that no vein of German soil produces gold or silver, for who has ever made a search? They care but little to possess or use them. You may see among them vessels of silver, which have been presented to their envoys and chieftains, held as cheap as those of clay. The border population, however, value gold and silver for their commercial utility, and are familiar with, and show preference for, some of our coins. The tribes of the interior use the simpler and more ancient practice of the barter of commodities. They like the old and well-known money, coins milled, or showing a two-horse chariot. They likewise prefer silver and gold, not from any special liking, but because a large number of silver pieces is more convenient for use among dealers in cheap and common articles.

Even iron is not plentiful with them, as we infer from the character of their weapons. But few use swords or long lances. They carry a spear . . ., with a narrow and short head, but so sharp and easy to wield that the same weapon serves, according to circumstances, for close or distant conflict. As for the horse-soldier, he is satisfied with a shield and spear; the foot-soldiers also scatter showers of missiles, each man having several and hurling them to an immense distance, and being naked or lightly clad with a little cloak. There is no display about their equipment: their shields alone are marked with very choice colours. A few only have corslets, and just one or two here and there a metal or leathern helmet. Their horses are remarkable neither for beauty nor for fleetness. Nor are they taught various evolutions after our fashion, but are driven straight forward, or so as to make one wheel to the right in such a compact body that none is left behind another. On the whole, one would say that their chief strength is in their infantry, which fights along with the cavalry; admirably adapted to the action of the latter is the swiftness of certain foot-soldiers, who are picked from the entire youth of their country, and stationed in front of the line. Their number is fixed,—a hundred from each canton; and from this they take their name among their countrymen, so that what was originally a mere number has now become a title of distinction. Their line of battle is drawn up in a wedge-like formation. To give ground, provided you return to the attack, is considered prudence rather than cowardice. The bodies of their slain they carry off even in indecisive engagements. To abandon your shield is the basest of crimes; nor may a man thus disgraced be present at the sacred rites, or enter their council; many, indeed, after escaping from battle, have ended their infamy with the halter.

They choose their kings by birth, their generals for merit. These kings have not unlimited or arbitrary power, and the generals do more by example than by authority. If they are energetic, if they are conspicuous, if they fight in the front, they lead because they are admired. But to reprimand, to imprison, even to flog, is permitted to the priests alone, and that not as a punishment, or at the general's bidding, but, as it were, by the mandate of the god whom they believe to inspire the warrior. They also carry with them into battle certain figures and images taken from their sacred groves. And what most stimulates their courage is, that their squadrons or battalions, instead of being formed by chance or by a fortuitous gathering, are composed of families and clans. Close by them, too, are those dearest to them, so that they hear the shrieks of women, the cries of infants. *They* are to every man the most sacred witnesses of his bravery—*they* are his most generous applauders. The soldier brings his wounds to mother and wife, who shrink not from counting or even demanding them and who administer both food and encouragement to the combatants.

Tradition says that armies already wavering and giving way have been rallied by women who, with earnest entreaties and bosoms laid bare, have vividly represented the horrors of captivity, which the Germans fear with such extreme dread on behalf of their women, that the strongest tie by which a state can be bound is the being required to give, among the number of hostages, maidens of noble birth. They even believe that the sex has a certain sanctity and prescience, and they do not despise their counsels, or make light of their answers. In Vespasian's[4] days we saw Veleda,[5] long regarded by many as a divinity. In former times, too, they venerated Aurinia,[6] and many other women, but not with servile flatteries, or with sham deification.

Mercury[7] is the deity whom they chiefly worship, and on certain days they deem it right to sacrifice to him even with human victims. Hercules and Mars[8] they appease with more lawful offerings. Some of the Suevi[9] also sacrifice to Isis.[10] Of the occasion and origin of this foreign rite I have discovered nothing, but that the image, which is fashioned like a light galley, indicates an imported worship. The Germans, however, do not consider it consistent with the grandeur of celestial beings to confine the gods within walls, or to liken them to the form of any human countenance. They consecrate woods and groves, and they apply the names of deities to the abstraction which they see only in spiritual worship. . . .

About minor matters the chiefs deliberate, about the more important the whole tribe. Yet even when the final decision rests with the people, the affair is always thoroughly discussed by the chiefs. They assemble, except

---

[4]Roman emperor, 69–79.

[5]Prophetic virgin regarded as divine by many Germans.

[6]Prophetess venerated by some Germans.

[7]Messenger of the Roman gods.

[8]God of war.

[9]Tribe living between the Elbe and Oder rivers.

[10]Egyptian goddess of nature; her cult was a major religion in the Roman world.

in the case of a sudden emergency, on certain fixed days, either at new or at full moon; for this they consider the most auspicious season for the transaction of business. Instead of reckoning by days as we do, they reckon by nights, and in this manner fix both their ordinary and their legal appointments. Night they regard as bringing on day. Their freedom has this disadvantage, that they do not meet simultaneously or as they are bidden, but two or three days are wasted in the delays of assembling. When the multitude think proper, they sit down armed. Silence is proclaimed by the priests, who have on these occasions the right of keeping order. Then the king or the chief, according to age, birth, distinction in war, or eloquence, is heard, more because he has influence to persuade than because he has power to command. If his sentiments displease them, they reject them with murmurs; if they are satisfied, they brandish their spears. The most complimentary form of assent is to express approbation with their weapons.

In their councils an accusation may be preferred or a capital crime prosecuted. Penalties are distinguished according to the offence. Traitors and deserters are hanged on trees; the coward, the unwarlike, the man stained with abominable vices, is plunged into the mire of the morass, with a hurdle put over him. This distinction in punishment means that crime, they think, ought, in being punished, to be exposed, while infamy ought to be buried out of sight. Lighter offences, too, have penalties proportioned to them; he who is convicted, is fined in a certain number of horses or of cattle. Half of the fine is paid to the king or to the state, half to the person whose wrongs are avenged and to his relatives. In these same councils they also elect the chief magistrates, who administer law in the cantons and the towns. Each of these has a hundred associates chosen from the people, who support him with their advice and influence.

They transact no public or private business without being armed. It is not, however, usual for anyone to wear arms till the state has recognised his power to use them. Then in the presence of the council one of the chiefs, or the young man's father, or some kinsman, equips him with a shield and a spear. These arms are what the "toga" is with us, the first honour with which youth is invested. Up to this time he is regarded as a member of a household, afterwards as a member of the commonwealth. Very noble birth or great services rendered by the father secure for lads the rank of a chief; such lads attach themselves to men of mature strength and of long approved valour. It is no shame to be seen among a chief's followers. Even in his escort there are gradations of rank, dependent on the choice of the man to whom they are attached. These followers vie keenly with each other as to who shall rank first with his chief, the chiefs as to who shall have the most numerous and the bravest followers. It is an honour as well as a source of strength to be thus always surrounded by a large body of picked youths; it is an ornament in peace and a defence in war. And not only in his own tribe but also in the neighbouring states it is the renown and glory of a chief to be distinguished for the number and valour of his followers, for such a man is courted by embassies, is honoured with presents, and the very prestige of his name often settles a war.

When they go into battle, it is a disgrace for the chief to be surpassed in valour, a disgrace for his followers not to equal the valour of the chief. And it is an infamy and a reproach for life to have survived the chief, and re-turned from the field. To defend, to protect him, to ascribe one's own brave deeds to his renown, is the height of loyalty. The chief fights for victory; his vassals fight for their chief. If their native state sinks into the sloth of prolonged peace and repose, many of its noble youths voluntarily seek those tribes which are waging some war, both because inaction is odious to their race, and because they win renown more readily in the midst of peril, and cannot maintain a numerous following except by vio-lence and war. Indeed, men look to the liberality of their chief for their war-horse and their blood-stained and victorious lance. Feasts and entertain-ments, which, though inelegant, are plentifully furnished, are their only pay. The means of this bounty come from war and rapine. Nor are they as easily persuaded to plough the earth and to wait for the year's produce as to challenge an enemy and earn the honour of wounds. Nay, they actually think it tame and stupid to acquire by the sweat of toil what they might win by their blood.

Whenever they are not fighting, they pass much of their time in the chase, and still more in idleness, giving themselves up to sleep and to feasting, the bravest and the most warlike doing nothing, and surrender-ing the management of the household, of the home, and of the land, to the women, the old men, and all the weakest members of the family. They themselves lie buried in sloth, a strange combination in their nature that the same men should be so fond of idleness, so averse to peace. It is the custom of the states to bestow by voluntary and individual contribution on the chiefs a present of cattle or of grain, which while accepted as a compli-ment, supplies their wants. They are particularly delighted by gifts from neighbouring tribes, which are sent not only by individuals but also by the state, such as choice steeds, heavy armour, trappings, and neckchains. We have now taught them to accept money also.

It is well known that the nations of Germany have no cities, and that they do not even tolerate closely contiguous dwellings. They live scattered and apart, just as a spring, a meadow, or a wood has attracted them. Their villages they do not arrange in our fashion, with the buildings connected and joined together, but every person surrounds his dwelling with an open space, either as a precaution against the disasters of fire, or because they do not know how to build. No use is made by them of stone or tile; they employ timber for all purposes, rude masses without ornament or attractiveness. Some parts of their buildings they stain more carefully with a clay so clear and bright that it resembles painting, or a coloured design. They are wont also to dig out subterranean caves, and pile on them great heaps of dung, as a shelter from winter and as a receptacle for the year's produce, for by such places they mitigate the rigour of the cold. And should an enemy approach, he lays waste the open country, while what is hidden and buried is either not known to exist, or else escapes him from the very fact that it has to be searched for.

They all wrap themselves in a cloak which is fastened with a clasp, or, if this is not forthcoming, with a thorn, leaving the rest of their persons bare. They pass whole days on the hearth by the fire. The wealthiest are distinguished by a dress which is not flowing, . . . but is tight, and exhibits each limb. They also wear the skins of wild beasts; the tribes on the Rhine and Danube in a careless fashion, those of the interior with more elegance, as not obtaining other clothing by commerce. These select certain animals, the hides of which they strip off and vary them with the spotted skins of beasts, the produce of the outer ocean, and of seas unknown to us. The women have the same dress as the men, except that they generally wrap themselves in linen garments, which they embroider with purple, and do not lengthen out the upper part of their clothing into sleeves. The upper and lower arm is thus bare, and the nearest part of the bosom is also exposed.

Their marriage code, however, is strict, and indeed no part of their manners is more praiseworthy. Almost alone among barbarians they are content with one wife, except a very few among them, and these not from sensuality, but because their noble birth procures for them many offers of alliance. The wife does not bring a dower to the husband, but the husband to the wife. The parents and relatives are present, and pass judgment on the marriage-gifts, gifts not meant to suit a woman's taste, nor such as a bride would deck herself with, but oxen, a caparisoned steed, a shield, a lance, and a sword. With these presents the wife is espoused, and she herself in her turn brings her husband a gift of arms. This they count their strongest bond of union, these their sacred mysteries, these their gods of marriage. Lest the woman should think herself to stand apart from aspirations after noble deeds and from the perils of war, she is reminded by the ceremony which inaugurates marriage that she is her husband's partner in toil and danger, destined to suffer and to dare with him alike both in peace and in war. The yoked oxen, the harnessed steed, the gift of arms, proclaim this fact. She must live and die with the feeling that she is receiving what she must hand down to her children neither tarnished nor depreciated, what future daughters-in-law may receive, and may be so passed on to her grand-children.

Thus with their virtue protected they live uncorrupted by the allurements of public shows or the stimulant of feastings. Clandestine correspondence is equally unknown to men and women. Very rare for so numerous a population is adultery, the punishment for which is prompt, and in the husband's power. Having cut off the hair of the adulteress and stripped her naked, he expels her from the house in the presence of her kinsfolk, and then flogs her through the whole village. The loss of chastity meets with no indulgence; neither beauty, youth, nor wealth will procure the culprit a husband. No one in Germany laughs at vice, nor do they call it the fashion to corrupt and to be corrupted. Still better is the condition of those states in which only maidens are given in marriage, and where the hopes and expectations of a bride are then finally terminated. They receive one husband, as having one body and one life, that they may have no thoughts beyond, no further-reaching desires, that they may love not so much the husband as the married state. To limit the number of their children or to destroy any of their subsequent offspring is accounted infamous, and good habits are here more effectual than good laws elsewhere.

In every household the children, naked and filthy, grow up with those stout frames and limbs which we so much admire. Every mother suckles her own offspring, and never entrusts it to servants and nurses. The master is not distinguished from the slave by being brought up with greater delicacy. Both live amid the same flocks and lie on the ground till the freeborn are distinguished by age and recognised by merit. The young men marry late, and their vigour is thus unimpaired. Nor are the maidens hurried into marriage; the same age and a similar stature is required; well-matched and vigorous they wed, and the offspring reproduce the strength of the parents. Sister's sons are held in as much esteem by their uncles as by their fathers; indeed, some regard the relation as even more sacred and binding, and prefer it in receiving hostages, thinking thus to secure a stronger hold on the affections and a wider bond for the family. But every man's own children are his heirs and successors, and there are no wills. Should there be no issue, the next in succession to the property are his brothers and his uncles on either side. The more relatives he has, the more numerous his connections, the more honoured is his old age; nor are there any advantages in childlessness.

It is a duty among them to adopt the feuds as well as the friendships of a father or a kinsman. These feuds are not implacable; even homicide is expiated by the payment of a certain number of cattle and of sheep, and the satisfaction is accepted by the entire family, greatly to the advantage of the state, since feuds are dangerous in proportion to a people's freedom.

No nation indulges more profusely in entertainments and hospitality. To exclude any human being from their roof is thought impious; every German, according to his means, receives his guest with a well-furnished table. When his supplies are exhausted, he who was but now the host becomes the guide and companion to further hospitality, and without invitation they go to the next house. It matters not; they are entertained with like cordiality. No one distinguishes between an acquaintance and a stranger, as regards the rights of hospitality. It is usual to give the departing guest whatever he may ask for, and a present in return is asked with as little hesitation. They are greatly charmed with gifts, but they expect no return for what they give, nor feel any obligation for what they receive.

On waking from sleep, which they generally prolong to a late hour of the day, they take a bath, oftenest of warm water, which suits a country where winter is the longest of the seasons. After their bath they take their meal, each having a separate seat and table of his own. Then they go armed to business, or no less often to their festal meetings. To pass an entire day and night in drinking disgraces no one. Their quarrels, as might be expected with intoxicated people, are seldom fought out with mere abuse, but commonly with wounds and bloodshed. Yet it is at their feasts that they generally consult on the reconciliation of enemies, on the forming of matrimonial alliances, on the choice of chiefs, finally even on peace and war, for they think that at no time is the mind more open to simplicity of purpose or more warmed to noble aspirations. A race without either natural or acquired cunning, they disclose their hidden thoughts in the freedom of the festivity. Thus the sentiments of all having been discovered and laid bare, the discussion is renewed on the following day, and from each occasion its own peculiar advantage is derived. They deliberate when they have no power to dissemble; they resolve when error is impossible.

A liquor for drinking is made out of barley or other grain, and fermented into a certain resemblance to wine. The dwellers on the river-bank also buy wine. Their food is of a simple kind, consisting of wild-fruit, fresh game, and curdled milk. They satisfy their hunger without elaborate preparation and without delicacies. In quenching their thirst they are not equally moderate. If you indulge their love of drinking by supplying them with as much as they desire, they will be overcome by their own vices as easily as by the arms of an enemy. . . .

Of lending money on interest and increasing it by compound interest they know nothing,—a more effectual safeguard than if it were prohibited.

Land proportioned to the number of inhabitants is occupied by the whole community in turn, and afterwards divided among them according to rank. A wide expanse of plains makes the partition easy. They till fresh fields every year, and they have still more land than enough; with the richness and extent of their soil, they do not laboriously exert themselves in planting orchards, inclosing meadows, and watering gardens. Corn is the only produce required from the earth; hence even the year itself is not divided by them into as many seasons as with us. Winter, spring, and summer have both a meaning and a name; the name and blessings of autumn are alike unknown.

The Gospel of Bartholomew

In December 1945 at Nag Hammadi in Egypt, a peasant discovered a number of manuscripts written in Coptic, a language of ancient Egypt. The manuscripts were, in fact, translations of earlier Greek texts of the sacred books of the Gnostics, one of the earliest Christian sects. Orthodox Christians denounced the Gnostics as heretics begin-

ning in the middle of the second century, and consequently most Gnostic writings had disappeared or been destroyed. The Nag Hammadi discovery revealed that the Gnostics had treasured a range of gospels attributed to Apostles—a Gospel of Thomas, a Gospel of Philip, and a Gospel of Truth, among others. Other texts were attributed, in the manner of epistles among the orthodox, to other followers of Jesus—the Secret Book of James, the Apocalypse of Paul, and so forth.

Of course, those who wrote and circulated these texts did not regard themselves as heretics. They saw themselves engaged in debate with others over the nature of God, the means of human salvation, and the nature of good and evil. They sought a form of insight (gnosis in Greek) into divinity. The existence of the Gnostic texts shows that Christianity was not a unified faith from the beginning; rather, uniformity, such as was known, was more a product of factors of institutionalization that operated in the course of the second century and later. What we now identify as Christian tradition is only a selection of sources from among a much greater number. And some of the Gnostic texts continued to be read even in the Middle Ages.

Certainly, some ideas embraced by the Gnostics were abhorred by the orthodox. Gnostics saw suffering and death imposed on humans by an evil force rather than as the consequence of human sin. They spoke of God as both male and female. But in other ways they were like orthodox Christians. They accepted Jesus as the Son of God. They too saw themselves in line with the Apostles. Their writings too were "gospels" ("glad tidings").

The Gospel of Bartholomew has survived not only in Coptic versions but in Greek and Latin copies. The lost original dates from the third century. As with many of the Gnostic gospels, it deals not with the life of Jesus but with the sayings and deeds of the risen Christ, who has returned to his followers to bring them insight (knowledge/enlightenment). According to this text, it is Bartholomew, of all the Apostles, who takes the lead in questioning Christ. Mary is also prominent, notably by explaining how it was that God came to be contained in her body. The questions posed to the risen Jesus seem to indicate that this text spoke to a popular audience, less learned in the philosophical and theological intricacies of the definitions of sin and evil. Rather, the gospel offers direct and graphic images of evil and the power of good.

In this gospel, the Apostles are shown both heaven and the abyss. How are they depicted? What makes heaven good? Bartholomew also speaks with the "adversary of men." What did Satan represent to the third-century readers of this text? How many spirits were in the world and what could they do? What is the contrast drawn between Eve and Mary? How does this gospel compare with others of which you are aware? How do the views in this text compare with the ancient Egyptian religious views you have read in earlier selections?

Now the apostles were in the place Chritir with Mary. And Bartholomew came to Peter and Andrew and John, and said to them: Let us ask Mary, her who is highly favoured, how she conceived the incomprehensible or how she carried him who cannot be carried or how she bore so much greatness. But they hesitated to ask her. Therefore Bartholomew said to Peter: Father Peter, do you as the chief one go to her and ask her. But Peter said to John: You are a chaste youth and blameless; you must ask her. And as they all were doubtful and pondered the matter to and fro, Bartholomew came to her with a cheerful countenance and said: You who were highly favoured, tabernacle of the Most High, unblemished, we, all the apostles ask you, but they have sent me to you. Tell us how you conceived the incomprehensible, or how you carried him who cannot be carried or how you bore so much greatness. But Mary answered: Do not ask me concerning this mystery. If I begin to tell you, fire will come out of my mouth and consume the whole earth. But they asked her still more urgently. And since she did not wish to deny the apostles a hearing, she said: Let us stand up in prayer. And the apostles stood behind Mary. And she said to Peter: Peter, chief of the apostles, the greatest pillar, do you stand behind me? Did not our Lord say: *The head of the man is Christ, but the head of the woman is the man?* Therefore stand in front of me to pray. But they said to her: In you the Lord set his tabernacle and was pleased to be contained by you. Therefore you now have more right than we to lead in the prayer. But she answered them: You are shining stars, as the prophet said: *I lifted up my eyes to the hills, from which comes my help* (Ps. 120:1 LXX). You, then, are the hills and you must pray. The apostles said to her: You ought to pray as the mother of the heavenly king. Mary said to them: In your likeness God formed the sparrows and sent them to the four corners of the world. But they answered her: He whom the seven heavens scarcely contain was pleased to be contained in you.

Then Mary stood up before them, and spread out her hands to heaven and began to pray thus: O God exceeding great and all-wise, king of the ages, indescribable, ineffable, who didst create the breadths of the heavens by thy word and arrange the vault of heaven in harmony, who didst give form to disorderly matter and didst bring together that which was separated, who didst part the gloom of the darkness from the light, who didst make the waters to flow from the same source, before whom the beings of the air tremble and the creatures of the earth fear, who didst give to the earth its place and didst not wish it to perish, in bestowing upon it abundant rain and caring for the nourishment of all things, the eternal Word (Logos)[1] of the Father. The seven heavens could scarcely contain thee, but thou wast pleased to be contained in me, without causing me pain, thou who art the perfect Word (Logos) of the Father, through whom everything was created. Glorify thine exceedingly great name, and allow me to speak before thy holy apostles. And when she had ended the prayer, she began to say to them: Let us sit down on the ground. Come, Peter, chief of the apostles, sit on my right hand and put your left hand under my shoulder. And you, Andrew, do the same on my left hand. And you, chaste John, hold my breast. And you, Bartholomew, place your knees on my shoulders and press close my back so that, when I begin to speak, my limbs are not loosed.

---

[1]In Christian theology, the *Word* is Christ as God. To Gnostics, the term also meant "saving wisdom from God."

And when they had done that, she began: When I lived in the temple of God and received my food from the hand of an angel, one day there appeared to me one in the form of an angel; but his face was indescribable and in his hand he had neither bread nor cup, as had the angel who came to me before. And immediately the veil of the temple was rent and there was a violent earthquake, and I fell to the earth, for I could not bear the sight of him. But he took me with his hand and raised me up. And I looked toward heaven; and there came a cloud of dew on my face and sprinkled me from head to foot, and he wiped me with his robe. Then he said to me: Hail, you who are highly favoured, the chosen vessel. And then he struck the right side of his garment and there came forth an exceedingly large loaf, and he placed it upon the altar of the temple, and first ate of it himself and then gave to me also. And again he struck his garment, on the left side, and I looked and saw a cup full of wine. And he placed it upon the altar of the temple, and drank from it first himself and gave it also to me. And I looked and saw that the bread did not diminish and the cup was full as before. Then he said: Three years more, and I will send my word and you shall conceive my son, and through him the whole world shall be saved. But you will bring salvation to the world. Peace be with you, favoured one, and my peace shall be with you for ever. And when he had said this, he vanished from my eyes and the temple was as before.

As she was saying this, fire came from her mouth, and the world was on the point of being burned up. Then came Jesus quickly and said to Mary: Say no more, or today my whole creation will come to an end. And the apostles were seized with fear lest God should be angry with them.

And he went with them to the mountain Mauria and sat down in their midst. But they hesitated to question him, because they were afraid. And Jesus answered and said: Ask me what you wish, so that I can teach you and show you. For there are still seven days, and then I ascend to my Father and shall no more appear to you in this form. But they, hesitating, said to him: Lord, show us the abyss, as you promised us. He answered: It is not good for you to see the abyss. But if you wish it, I will keep my promise. Come, follow me and see. And he led them to a place called Cherubim, that is, place of truth. And he beckoned to the angels of the west. And the earth was rolled up like a papyrus roll, and the abyss was exposed to their eyes. When the apostles saw it, they fell on their faces. But Jesus said to them: Did I not say to you that it was not good for you to see the abyss? And he again beckoned to the angels, and the abyss was covered up.

And he took them and brought them to the mount of Olives. And Peter said to Mary: You who are favoured, ask the Lord to reveal to us all that is in the heavens. And Mary answered Peter: O rock hewn above, did not the Lord build his church upon you? You therefore should be the first to go and ask him. Peter said again: You were made the tabernacle of the most high God. You ask him. Mary said: You are the image of Adam. Was not he formed first and then Eve? Look at the sun. It shines like Adam. Look at the moon. It is full of clay, because Eve transgressed the commandment. For God placed Adam in the east and Eve in the west, and he commanded the two lights to shine, so that the sun with its fiery chariot should shine on Adam in the east, and the moon in the west should shed on Eve its milk-white light. But she defiled the commandment of the Lord, and therefore the moon became soiled, and its light does not gleam. Since, therefore, you are the likeness of Adam, you ought to ask him. But in me the Lord took up his abode, that I might restore the dignity of women.

Now when they came to the top of the mountain, the Lord parted from them for a little while. Then Peter said to Mary: You made good the transgression of Eve, changing her shame into joy. So you ought to ask. But when Jesus appeared again, Bartholomew said to him: Lord, show us the adversary of men, that we may see his form, or what his work is, or where he comes from, or what power he has that he did not even spare you, but caused you to be hanged on the cross. And Jesus looked at him and said: O bold heart! You ask for that which you cannot look upon. But Bartholomew was frightened, and he fell at Jesus' feet and began to say: O lamp never extinguished, Lord Jesus Christ, everlasting one, who gave grace for the whole world to those who love you, and gave everlasting light through your appearing on earth, who at the command of the Father gave up your life above and completed your work, who changed the dejection of Adam into joy and overcame the sorrow of Eve with gracious countenance by your birth from a virgin mother, do not be angry with me, and grant me the right to ask. When he said this, Jesus raised him up and asked him: Bartholomew, do you wish to see the adversary of men? I tell you that, when you see him, not only you, but the apostles with you, and Mary will fall on your faces and will be like the dead. But they all said to him: Lord, we wish to see him. And he led them down from the mount of Olives, and threatened the angels of the underworld, and beckoned to Michael to sound his mighty trumpet in the height of heaven. Then the earth was shaken and Beliar came up, held by 660 angels and bound with fiery chains.

He was 1600 yards long and 40 yards broad. His face was like a lightning of fire, and his eyes like sparks, and from his nostrils came a stinking smoke. His mouth was like a cleft of rock and a single one of his wings was 80 yards long. As soon as the apostles saw him, they fell to the ground on their faces and became like dead men. But Jesus came near and raised up the apostles, and gave them the spirit of power. Then he said to Bartholomew: Come near to him, Bartholomew, and place your feet on his neck; then he will tell you what his work is, and how he deceives men. And Jesus stood at a distance with the apostles. And Bartholomew raised his voice and said: O womb more spacious than a city! O womb wider than the span of heaven! O womb that contained him whom the seven heavens do not contain. You contained him without pain and held in your bosom him who changed his being into the smallest of things. O womb that bare, concealed in (your) body, the Christ who has been made visible to many. O womb that became more spacious than the whole creation. And Bartholomew was afraid, and said: Lord Jesus, give me a hem of your garment, that I may venture to approach him. Jesus answered him: You cannot have a hem of my garment, for it is not the garment which I wore before I was crucified. And Bartholomew said: Lord, I fear lest, as he did not spare your angels, he will swallow me up also. Jesus answered: Were not all things made by my word and according to the plan of my Father? The spirits were made subject to Solomon himself. Go therefore, since you have been commanded to do so in my name, and ask him what you wish.

And Bartholomew went and trod upon his neck, and pressed down his face to the earth as far as his ears. And Bartholomew asked him: Tell me who you are and what is your name. He replied: Ease me a little, and I will tell you who I am and how I came into this condition and what my work is and how great my power is. Bartholomew eased him and asked him: Tell me all you have done and all you do. Beliar answered and said: If you wish to know my name, I was first called Satanael, which means "angel of God." But when I rejected the image of God, I was called Satan, which means "angel of hell." And again Bartholomew asked him: Reveal everything to me, and conceal nothing from me. And he replied: I swear to you by the mightly glory of God that even if I wished, I can conceal nothing from you; for he who can convict me stands near me. For if I had the power, I would destroy you as I hurled one of you to destruction. I was the first angel to be created. For when God made the heavens, he took a handful of fire and formed me first, Michael second, the captain of the hosts above, Gabriel third, Uriel fourth, Raphael fifth, Nathanael sixth and 6,000 other angels, whose names I cannot tell. There are rod-bearers (lictors) of God, and these scourge me seven times a day and seven times a night and never leave me alone and break in pieces all my power. These are the avenging angels, who stand by God's throne. All these belong to the first-created angels. And after them was the whole number of the angels created: 100 myriads for the first heaven, and the same number for the second, third, fourth, fifth, sixth and seventh heavens. Outside the seven heavens there is the first sphere (the firmament); and there dwell the angels of power who influence men. There are also four angels who are set over the winds. The first rules over Boreas. He is called Chairum, and he has in his hand a fiery rod, and restrains the great moisture which this wind has, so that the earth should not dry up. And the angel who rules over Aparktias[2] is called

---

[2]Aparktis is also a north wind. (Original editor's note.)

Oertha. He has a torch of fire in his hand, and holds it to him and to his sides and warms his coldness so that he does not freeze the earth. And the angel of the south wind is called Kerkutha, and he breaks his violence so as not to shake the earth. And the angel who is set over the south-west wind is called Naoutha. He has a rod of ice in his hand and puts it at his mouth, and quenches the fire which comes from his mouth. And if the angel did not quench it at his mouth, it would set the whole world on fire. And another angel rules over the sea, and makes it rough with the waves. I will not tell you more, for he who stands near me does not permit it.

Then Bartholomew asked him: How do you chastise the souls of men? Beliar answered: Am I to describe to you the punishment of the hypocrites, the slanderers, the jesters, the covetous, and adulterers, the sorcerers, the soothsayers, and of those who believe in us, and of all behind whom I stand? Bartholomew said to him: I wish you to be brief. And he gnashed his teeth together, and there came up from the abyss a wheel with a sword flashing fire, which had pipes. And I asked him: What is the sword? He answered: It is the sword for the gluttonous. They are put into this pipe, because in their gluttony they turn to every kind of sin. Into the second pipe come the slanderers, because they secretly slander their neighbours. Into the third pipe come the hypocrites and the rest whom I trip up with my machinations. And Bartholomew said: Do you do this by yourself? Satan replied: If I were able to go out by myself, I would destroy the whole world in three days, but neither I nor any of the 600 goes out. We have other swift servants whom we command. We equip them with a many-barbed hook, and send them out to hunt, and they catch men's souls for us, enticing them with the sweetness of various allurements, that is, drunkenness, laughter, slandering, hypocrisy, pleasures, fornications, and the other devices in their treasury which weaken men. I will tell you also the rest of the names of the angels. The angel of the hail is called Mermeoth. He holds the hail on his head, and my servants adjure him and send him wherever they wish. And other angels rule over the snow, and others over the thunder, and others over the lightning, and when a spirit wishes to go forth from among us, either over land or over water, these angels send out fiery stones and set our limbs on fire. Bartholomew said: Be silent, dragon of the abyss. And Beliar said: I will tell you much about the angels. Those who run together through the heavenly and earthly regions are Mermeoth, Onomatath, Duth, Melioth, Charuth, Graphathas, Hoethra, Nephonos, and Chalkatura. Together they fly through the regions of heaven, of earth, and the underworld . . .

Bartholomew interrupted him and said: Be silent and powerless, so that I can entreat my Lord. And Bartholomew fell on his face, and scattered earth on his head, and began: O Lord Jesus Christ, the great and glorious name. All the choirs of the angels praise you, Lord; and I also, who am unworthy in my lips, praise you, Lord. Hear me, your servant, and as you called me from the custom-house and did not allow me to remain to the end in my former manner of life, hear me, Lord Jesus Christ, and have mercy on the sinners. When he had so prayed, the Lord said to him: Stand up, turn to him that groans. I will declare the rest to you. And Bartholomew raised up Satan, and said to him: Go to your place with your angels, but the Lord has mercy on all his world. But the devil said: Allow me to tell you how I was cast down here, and how God made man. I wandered to and fro in the world, and God said to Michael: Bring me earth from the four ends of the world and water out of the four rivers of paradise. And when Michael had brought them to him, he formed Adam in the east, and gave form to the shapeless earth, and stretched sinews and veins, and united everything into a harmonious whole. And he showed him reverence for his own sake, because he was his image. And Michael also worshipped him. And when I came from the ends of the world, Michael said to me: Worship the image of God which he has made in his own likeness. But I said: I am fire of fire, I was the first angel to be formed, and shall I worship clay and matter? And Michael said to me: Worship, lest God be angry with you. I answered: God will not be angry with me, but I will set up my throne over against his throne, and shall be as he is (Isa. 14:14f.). Then God was angry with me and cast me down, after he had commanded the windows of heaven to be opened.

When I was thrown down, he asked the 600 angels that stood under me, whether they would worship (Adam). They replied: As we saw our leader do, we also will not worship him who is less than ourselves. After our fall upon the earth we lay for forty years in deep sleep, and when the sun shone seven times more brightly than fire, I awoke. And when I looked around, I saw the 600 under me overcome by deep sleep. And I awoke my son Salpsan, and took counsel with him how I could deceive the man on whose account I had been cast out of heaven. And I devised the following plan. I took a bowl in my hand, and scraped the sweat from my breast and my armpits, and washed myself in the spring of water from which the four rivers flow. And Eve drank of it, and desire came upon her. For if she had not drunk of that water, I should not have been able to deceive her. Then Bartholomew commanded him to go into Hades. And he came to Jesus, and fell at his feet, and began with tears to speak thus: Abba, Father, who cannot be discovered by us, Word of the Father, whom the seven heavens hardly contained, but who were pleased to be contained easily and without pain in the body of the Virgin, without the Virgin knowing that she carried you, while you by your thought ordained everything as it should be, you who give us our daily bread without our asking for it. You who wore a crown of thorns, in order to prepare for us repentant sinners the precious heavenly crown, who hung upon the cross (and were given gall and vinegar to drink), in order to give us to drink the wine of contrition, and were pierced in the side with the spear, in order to satisfy us with your body and blood. . . .

When Bartholomew had uttered this prayer, Jesus said to him: Bartholomew, the Father named me Christ, that I might come down on earth and anoint with the oil of life everyone who came to me. And he called me Jesus, that I might heal every sin of the ignorant and give to men the truth of God. And again Bartholomew said to him: Lord, may I reveal these mysteries to every man? Jesus answered him: Bartholomew, my beloved, entrust them to all who are faithful and can keep them for themselves. For there are some who are worthy of them; but there are also others to whom they ought not to be entrusted, for they are boasters, drunkards, proud, merciless, idolaters, seducers to fornication, slanderers, teachers of falsehood, and doers of all the works of the devil, and therefore they are not worthy that they should be entrusted to them. These things are also to be kept secret because of those who cannot contain them. For all who can contain them shall have a share in them. As regards this, therefore, my beloved, I have spoken to you, for you are blessed and all who are akin to you in having this message entrusted to them, for all who contain it shall receive all they wish in all times of my judgment. At that time, I, Bartholomew, wrote this in my heart, and I took the hand of the friend of men, and began joyfully to speak thus: Glory be to thee, O Lord Jesus Christ, who givest to all thy grace which we have all perceived. Alleluia. Glory be to thee, O Lord, the life of sinners. Glory be to thee, O Lord, through whom death is put to shame. Glory be to thee, O Lord, the treasure of righteousness. We praise thee as God. And when Bartholomew spoke thus, Jesus put off his mantle, and took the kerchief from Bartholomew's neck and began joyfully to say: I am good to you. Alleluia. I am meek and kind to you. Alleluia. Glory be to thee, O Lord. For I give myself to all who desire me. Alleluia. Glory be to Thee, O Lord, world without end. Amen. Alleluia. And when he had finished, the apostles kissed him, and he gave them the peace of love.

Bartholomew said to him: Tell us, Lord, which sin is more grievous than all other sins. Jesus replied: Truly, I say to you that hypocrisy and slander are more grievous than all other sins. For because of them the prophet said in the Psalm (1:5): *The ungodly shall not stand in the judgment nor sinners in the congregation of the righteous,* nor the godless in the judgment of my Father. *Truly, truly, I say to you, that every sin shall be forgiven every man, but the sin against the Holy Spirit shall not be forgiven* (Mt. 12:31). And Bartholomew said: What is the sin against the Holy Spirit? Jesus answered: Everyone who decrees against any man who serves my Father has blasphemed against the Holy Spirit. For every man who serves God with reverence is worthy of the Holy Spirit, and he who speaks any evil against him shall not be forgiven. Woe to him who swears by the head of God, even if he does not commit perjury, but speaks the truth. For God, the Most High, has twelve heads. He is the truth, and in him is no lie and perjury. Go, therefore, and preach to the whole world the word of truth, and you, Bartholomew, preach this (secret) word to everyone who wishes it, and all who believe in it shall have eternal life. Bartholomew said: If any sins with lust of the flesh, how is he recompensed? Jesus answered: It is good if he who is baptized preserves his baptism without blame. But the lust of the flesh will practise its allurement. A single marriage belongs to chaste living. For truly I say to you: He who sins after the third marriage is unworthy of God. But do you preach to all, that they must guard themselves from such things. For I do not depart from you and I give you the Holy Spirit. And Bartholomew with the apostles glorified God before him exceedingly, saying: Glory be to thee, Holy Father, inextinguishable sun, incomprehensible, full of light. To thee be honour, to thee glory and worship world without end. Amen.

The Martyrdom of Saints Agape, Irene, and Chione

Although the Roman government persecuted Christians only sporadically and usually only when pressured to do so by the populace, there was a final, great persecution in the early fourth century during the reign of the Emperor Diocletian, 284–305. In 303, Diocletian issued an edict ordering Christians to relinquish their sacred books. A year later, an edict required that Christians sacrifice to Roman gods; the penalty for not doing so was death.

A few months after the promulgation of the 304 edict, seven young women were arrested in Thessalonika in Greece. It appears from the selection, which consists of three hearings before a Roman tribunal as well as explanations of the events, that the women may have been hiding in the mountains after the first of Diocletian's edicts.

What is the attitude of Dulcitius, the Roman judge? Did he understand why the women would not accede to the court's demands? In the first hearing, Dulcitius sentenced Agape and Chione to be burned and Eutychia to be sent back to jail because of her pregnancy. In the second hearing, Dulcitius questioned Irene about her possession of Christian writings and proposed to release her. Why did Irene refuse his offer of mercy? Irate at Irene's stubborness, the judge condemned her to a public brothel frequented by soldiers. According to this account, no one approaches Irene in the brothel, and Dulcitius ordered her back for a final hearing. She still would not obey the law and so followed her coreligionists to the flames.

The story of these martyrdoms contains material that might be considered improbable. Why were such stories written? Did the writer approve of the women's martyrdom? Their martyrdom was, after all, voluntary, for Dulcitius would have set them free had they but sacrificed to the gods. Does this selection suggest advice to other Christians as to how they should face persecution? What does this account further reveal about Roman attitudes about gender? How do they differ from those found in the selection on sexual prohibitions and violence in the Hebrew Bible and in the selections concerning the Greeks?

Since the advent and the presence on earth of our Lord and Saviour Jesus Christ, the greater the grace of the men of old, so much the greater was the victory of holy men. For instead of those visible enemies, we have now begun to crush enemies that cannot be seen with bodily eyes, and the invisible substance of the demons has been handed over to the flames by pure and holy women who were full of the Holy Spirit. Such were the three saintly women who came from the city of Thessalonica, the city that the inspired Paul celebrated when he praised its faith and love, saying, *Your faith in God has gone out to every place.*[1] And elsewhere he says, *Of charity for your brothers I have no need to write to you; for you yourselves have learned from God to love one another.*[2]

When the persecution was raging under the Emperor Maximian,[3] these women, who had adorned themselves with virtue, following the precepts of the Gospel, abandoned their native city, their family, property, and possessions because of their love of God and their expectation of heavenly things, performing deeds worthy of their father Abraham. They fled the persecutors, according to the commandment,[4] and took refuge on a high mountain. There they gave themselves to prayer: though their bodies resided on a mountain top, their souls lived in heaven.

At any rate, they were here captured and brought to the official who was conducting the persecution, that, by thus fulfilling the rest of the divine commands and loving their Master even unto death, they might weave for themselves the chaplet of immortality.[5] Of these girls one had preserved the shining purity of her baptism according to the holy prophet who said: *You will wash me and I shall be whiter than snow,*[6] and she was called Chione. The second girl possessed the gift of our God and Saviour within herself and manifested it to everyone according to the word, *My peace I give you,*[7] and she was called Irene by everyone. The third girl possessed the perfection of the Gospel, loving God with her whole heart and her neighbour as herself, in accord with the holy Apostle who says, *The aim of our charge is love,*[8] and she was appropriately named Agape. When these three girls were brought before the magistrate and refused to sacrifice, he sen-

[1] 1Thessalonians 1:8.
[2] 1 Thessalonians 4:9
[3] Emperor, 286–305, with Diocletian.
[4] Compare Matthew 10:23.
[5] Psalms 51:7.
[6] John 14:27.
[7] 1 Timothy 1:5.
[8] Greek word meaning "love."

tenced them to the fire, in order that thus by a short time in the fire they might overcome those that are devoted to fire, that is, the Devil and all his heavenly host of demons, and, attaining the incorruptible crown of glory, they might endlessly praise along with the angels the God who had showered this grace upon them. The record that was taken down in their case is the material of our account.

The prefect Dulcitius was sitting on the tribunal, and the court clerk Artemisius spoke: "With your permission, I shall read the charge which was sent to your Genius[9] by the [guard] here present in connection with the parties in court."

"You may read it," said the prefect Dulcitius. And the charge was duly read: "To you, my lord, greetings from Cassander, [staff-officer]. This is to inform you, Sir, that Agatho, Irene, Agape, Chione, Cassia, Philippa, and Eutychia refuse to eat sacrificial food, and so I have referred them to your Genius."

"What is this insanity," said the prefect Dulcitius, "that you refuse to obey the order of our most religious emperors and Caesars?" And turning to Agatho, he said: "When you came to the sacrifices, why did you not perform the cult practices like other religious people?"

"Because I am a Christian," said Agatho.

The prefect Dulcitius said: "Do you still remain in the same mind today?"

"Yes," said Agatho.

The prefect Dulcitius said: "What do you say, Agape?"

"I believe in the living God," replied Agape, "and I refuse to destroy my conscience."

"What do you say, Irene?" asked the prefect Dulcitius. "Why did you disobey the command of our lords the emperors and Caesars?"

"Because of my fear of God," said Irene.

"What do you say, Chione?" asked the prefect.

"I believe in the living God," replied Chione, "and I refuse to do this."

The prefect said: "And how about you, Cassia?"

"I wish to save my soul," said Cassia.

The prefect said: "Are you willing to partake of the sacrificial meat?"

"I am not," said Cassia.

"The prefect said: "And what say you, Philippa?"

"I say the same," said Philippa.

"What do you mean, the same?" said the prefect.

Said Philippa: "I mean, I would rather die than partake."

"Eutychia," said the prefect, "what do you say?"

"I say the same," said Eutychia; "I would rather die."

---

[9]Much like "your Majesty" or "your Grace." As an exhalted invocation of one in power, *Genius* refers not just to the emperor's intelligence or insight, but also to his spirit guiding the empire.

The prefect said. "Do you have a husband?"

"He is dead," said Eutychia.

"When did he die?" asked the prefect.

"About seven months ago," said Eutychia.

The prefect said, "How is it then that you are pregnant?" Eutychia said: "By the man whom God gave me."

The prefect said: "But how can you be pregnant when you say your husband is dead?"

Eutychia said: "No one can know the will of almighty God. So God willed it."

The prefect said: "I urge Eutychia to cease this madness and to return to sound reason. What do you say? Will you obey the imperial command?"

"No, I will not," said Eutychia. "I am a Christian, a servant of almighty God."

The prefect said: "Since Eutychia is pregnant, she shall be kept meanwhile in gaol." Then he added: "What say you, Agape? Will you perform all the actions which religious persons perform in honour of our lords the emperors and Caesars?"

Agape replied: "It is not at all in Satan's power. He cannot move my reason; it is invincible."

The prefect said: "What say you, Chione?"

Chione said: "No one can change my mind."

The prefect said: "Do you have in your possession any writings, parchments, or books of the impious Christians?"

Chione said: "We do not, Sir. Our present emperors have taken these from us."

"Who was it who gave you this idea?" asked the prefect.

"God almighty," said Chione.

The prefect said: "Who was it who counselled you to commit such folly?"

"It was almighty God", answered Chione, "and his only begotten Son, our Lord Jesus Christ."

The prefect Dulcitius said: "It is clear to all that you are all liable to the crime of treason against our lords the emperors and Caesars. But seeing that you have persisted in this folly for such a long time, in spite of strong warnings and so many decrees, sanctioned by stern threats, and have despised the command of our lords the emperors and Caesars, remaining in this impious name of Christian, and seeing that even today when you were ordered by the soldiers and officials to deny your belief and signify this in writing, you refused—therefore you shall receive the punishment appropriate for you."

Then he read the sentence written on a sheet: "Whereas Agape and Chione have with malicious intent acted against the divine decree of our lords the Augusti and Caesars, and whereas they adhere to the worthless and obsolete worship of the Christians which is hateful to all religious men, I sentence them to be burned." Then he added: "Agatho, Irene, Cassia, Philippa, and Eutychia, because of their youth are to be put in prison in the meanwhile."

After the most holy women were consumed in the flames, the saintly girl Irene was once again brought before the court on the following day. Dulcitius said to her: "It is clear from what we have seen that you are determined in your folly, for you have deliberately kept even till now so many tablets, books, parchments, codices, and pages of the writings of the former Christians of unholy name; even now, though you denied each time that you possessed such writings, you did show a sign of recognition when they were mentioned. You are not satisfied with the punishment of your sisters, nor do you keep before your eyes the terror of death. Therefore you must be punished.

"It would not, however, seem out of place to show you some measure of mercy: if even now you would be willing to recognize the gods you will be released from all danger and punishment. Now what do you say? Will you do the bidding of our emperors and Caesars? Are you prepared to eat the sacrificial meats and to sacrifice to the gods?"

"No," said Irene, "I am not prepared, for the sake of the God almighty who *has created heaven and earth and the seas and all that is in them.*[10] For those who transgress the word of God there awaits the great judgement of eternal punishment."

The prefect Dulcitius said: "Who was it that advised you to retain those parchments and writings up to the present time?"

"It was almighty God," said Irene, "who bade us to love him unto death. For this reason we did not dare to be traitors, but we chose to be burned alive or suffer anything else that might happen to us rather than betray the writings."

The prefect said: "Was anyone else aware that the documents were in the house where you lived?"

"No one else," said Irene, "saw them, save almighty God who knows all things. But no stranger. As for our own relatives, we considered them worse than our enemies, in fear that they would denounce us. Hence we told no one."

"Last year," said the prefect, "when this edict of our lords the emperors and Caesars was first promulgated, where did you hide?"

"Wherever God willed," said Irene. "We lived on the mountains, in the open air, as God is my witness."

"Whom were you living with?" asked the prefect.

Irene answered: "We lived out of doors in different places among the mountains."

The prefect said: "Who supplied you with bread?"

---

[10]Acts 4:24.

Irene answered: "God, who supplies all men."

"Was your father aware of this?" asked the prefect.

Irene answered: "I swear by almighty God, he was not aware; he knew nothing at all about it."

"Were any of your neighbours aware of this?" asked the prefect.

Irene answered: "Go and question our neighbours, and inquire about the area to see whether anyone knew where we were."

The prefect said: "Now after you returned from the mountain where you had been, as you say, were any persons present at the reading of these books?"

Irene answered: "They were in our house and we did not dare to bring them out. In fact, it caused us much distress that we could not devote ourselves to them night and day as we had done from the beginning until that day last year when we hid them."

Dulcitius the prefect said: "Your sisters, in accordance with my commands in their regard, have received their sentence. Now you have been guilty even before you ran away and before you concealed these writings and parchments, and hence I do not wish you to die immediately in the same way. Instead I sentence you to be placed naked in the brothel with the help of the public notaries of this city and of Zosimus the executioner; and you will receive merely one loaf of bread from our residence, and the notaries will not allow you to leave."

And so, after the notaries and the slave Zosimus, the executioner, were brought in, the prefect said: "Be it known to you that if ever I find out from the troops that this girl was removed from the spot where I have ordered her to be even for a single instant, you will immediately be punished with the most extreme penalties. The writings we have referred to, in the cabinets and chests belonging to Irene, are to be publicly burned."

After those who were put in charge had taken the girl off to the public brothel in accordance with the prefect's order, by the grace of the Holy Spirit which preserved and guarded her pure and inviolate for the God who is the lord of all things, no man dared to approach her, or so much as tried to insult her in speech. Hence the prefect Dulcitius called back this most saintly girl, had her stand before the tribunal, and said to her: "Do you still persist in the same folly?"

But Irene said to him: "It is not folly, but piety."

"It was abundantly clear from your earlier testimony," said the prefect Dulcitius, "that you did not wish to submit religiously to the bidding of the emperors; and now I perceive that you are persisting in the same foolishness. Therefore you shall pay the appropriate penalty."

He then asked for a sheet of papyrus and wrote the sentence against her as follows: "Whereas Irene has refused to obey the command of the emperors and to offer sacrifice, and still adheres to a sect called the Christians, I therefore sentence her to be burned alive, as I did her two sisters before her."

After this sentence had been pronounced by the prefect, the soldiers took the girl and brought her to a high place, where her sisters had been martyred before her. They ignited a huge pyre and ordered her to climb up on it. And the holy woman Irene, singing and praising God, threw herself upon it and so died. It was in the ninth consulship of Diocletian Augustus, in the eighth of Maximian Augustus, on the first day of April,[11] in the kingship of our Lord Christ Jesus, who reigns for ever, with whom there is glory to the Father with the Holy Spirit for ever. Amen.

[11]That is, 1 April 304.

III

⟡

THE MIDDLE AGES
(FIFTH TO FOURTEENTH
CENTURIES)

From the ruins and remains of classical civilization and the Roman imperial system, a European culture and forms of social order began to emerge in the early Middle Ages. Certain basic stable elements marked the period between 400 and 1400. For most people, life was locally or regionally focused. They seldom traveled far from their place of birth. Rather, their entire lives were spent in one area, subsumed in the customs and dialect they shared with those around them. In the centuries up to the year 1000, economic activity remained essentially agricultural, centered on estates that gathered peasant (serf) households under the protection of a landlord. Serfs could not leave the land without permission, but they also could not be forced off it or have their rents or labor obligations arbitrarily increased. They had a social status superior to that of a slave (though the word serf is derived from the Latin word for slave, servus). The landlords were ecclesiastical institutions and lay families. The lay landlords were bound up in a world of violence and military valor, with all the honor and plunder it provided. The Church, with its ceremonies and saints, with its scriptures and clergy, provided other forms of protection and of spiritual reassurance. A legacy of ideas and texts from the classical period, marked by the persistence of Latin as the language of learning, also knit together the interests and outlooks of medieval scholars and rulers.

Following the collapse of Roman political power in western Europe, rule passed to Germanic kings and nobles and to some bishops and abbots of monasteries. Roman law persisted as the legal customs of the indigenous Roman population, while the Germanic peoples introduced their very different rules and procedures. The Frankish empire of the Carolingians, which reached its fullest extent under Charlemagne's reign, 768–814, attempted to bring together Christian, Germanic, and classical cultural currents under the guise of a revived Roman Empire. The empire itself soon succumbed in the ninth and tenth centuries to internal disorder and invasions by Norsemen (Vikings), Magyars (Hungarians), and Moors (Moslems); but, not only did the ideal of empire endure through the Middle Ages, but administrative measures taken by Charlemagne served as the basis of the distinctive medieval feudal order.

Feudalism was a means of governing that incorporated a structure to define the

*position of those in the class of noble warriors. The core of feudalism was the rela-
tionship of vassalage between two men, one of whom (the vassal) swore to be the
other's "man," to support his lord with military service against enemies, to protect
him and his family in need, and to serve on his lord's court when summoned. For
his part, the lord swore to defend and protect his vassal and furnished him with the
use of lands, termed a* fief. *In this way, feudalism rested on a sort of contractual
obligation that bound lord and vassal in mutual interest. Their interests had much
to do, in fact, with ideals of heroic glory and desire for plunder—ideals celebrated in
early medieval Germanic epics like* Beowulf *and throughout the Middle Ages in
literary monuments like the* Song of Roland *and the Arthurian romances.*

*Relations between lords and vassals were notoriously problem-ridden. Vassals
dodged obligations, at times by pledging fidelity to a second lord. Lords were able in
certain circumstances to circumvent their vassals, not always with their consent.
When King John of England too frequently took advantage of vassals' young heirs
and exploited his guardianship of their daughters, his vassals compelled him to seal
the Magna Carta in 1215, defining his and their mutual rights and obligations.*

*Feudalism was a source of both order and disorder in the medieval world. It
defined and sustained a knightly class of warriors, whose social purpose was to
fight. The Church attempted to restrict fighting in the Peace and Truce of God
movements that arose around the year 1000. Later, the Crusades offered an outlet
for fighting against non-Christians in distant lands. For nobles, warfare had its
own meanings and rewards, as they sought plunder and glory on the fields of battle.*

*The Middle Ages were also an era of kaleidoscopic variety and change. Major
developments in Western civilization occurred during those centuries. The Church
in late antiquity and the early Middle Ages saw the rise of monasteries, where
monks pursued an ideal of ascetic holiness. This ascetic ideal was marked by the
renunciation of material and sexual pleasures and the consequent disciplining of the
body and mind. Ascetic ideals also inspired later religious movements, including
both the mendicant friars founded in the thirteenth century by St. Dominic and St.
Francis and the heretics whom the mendicants were intent on combatting. The
clergy as a whole were to remain celibate in accord with this vision of sanctity,
which would come under debate in the later Reformation and which was not even a
formal rule of the Church (though long an encouraged practice) until 1123.*

*The Church itself underwent momentous changes. Christianity spread with the
conversion of the Germanic peoples, and in doing so, it acquired some different
customs and practices. The desire of lay people to attach themselves in a tangible
way to the sanctity of the Church led to the accumulation of lands and other wealth
in the hands of bishops and monasteries. Rulers and nobles sought to appropriate or
control such wealth, especially those Church lands that had originated from their
ancestors. Tensions arose between lay and clerical prerogatives and between the
demands of secular existence and the ideals of ascetic spirituality. These tensions
came to a head in the Investiture Controversy of the eleventh century. The bishops of
Rome solidified their claims to administrative and doctrinal control of the Church by
excluding emperors, kings, and other secular figures from selecting the holders of
clerical offices, while the other bishops of the Church were also excluded from choos-*

ing the holders of clerical positions outside their dioceses. At the same time, theological positions were staked out defining all aspects of Christian belief and worship and the sacramental function of the Church in the salvation of all. A distinctive body of law governing the Church, the clergy, and Church functions was drawn together from the decrees of Church councils and synods of bishops, papal letters, fragments of Scripture, and the writings of the authoritative fathers of the early Church. This canon law had an important influence on lay people in its rules concerning marriage and inheritance, while it gave the Church a judicial structure of its own that rivaled the courts of the lay rulers and cities. The medieval universities arose to teach and to elaborate on the elements of Church doctrine and the principles of canon law, as well as Roman civil law, which was revived as an object of study in the late eleventh century. Majestic Romanesque cathedrals and those in the later hauntingly beautiful soaring style known as Gothic survive as monuments to the power of the faith and the Church's sacraments and clergy in medieval life.

There were other points of stress in the medieval world. Efforts to reconcile such divergent interests, however, were to furnish some of the most creative moments in medieval history. During the eleventh and twelfth centuries, European population grew, agriculture expanded, trade increased enormously, and merchants settled in cities. These growing and wealthy cities, however, ill fit into a world where nobles thought of war and plunder, where birth and inheritance were the means of access to wealth and power, and where the Church saw the more mobile forms of wealth used in trade in terms of the vice of greed and the sinful device of usury (lending at interest). Ingenious solutions to these problems were tried. The communal form of government arose in cities, whereby an oath of common allegiance among the more powerful residents to protect their shared interests and prerogatives, established a counterweight to feudal and ecclesiastical power. The resulting communes acquired "liberties" for their members, giving them rights of personal freedom and property. Somewhat later, in a closely related development, merchants operating in the same market or those engaged in the same craft formed guilds to regulate labor and professional standards and control the sources of food and industrial raw materials. They would thus ensure that there was enough for all, that a monopoly would reside with the group as a whole and not with one individual who would throw the others into poverty, while they also tried to keep outsiders from interfering in their trade. At the same time, these artisans and merchants faced the Church's concerns about usury and a "just price" for goods. While some people looked askance at the accumulation of money and material goods, others tried to find ways of accommodating the needs of commerce and the moral demands of religion.

Even within the family such stresses were to be found. Kinship was calculated bilaterally—that is, through both parents. But after 1000, especially among the landed nobility and some urban elites, patrilineal kinship (calculated through males) gained pride of place for purposes of inheritance. Marriage was another important moment in family life, uniting sets of kin. The Church came to take the position that consent of the spouses was the fundamental requirement for a valid marriage, but actually parents among the propertied classes arranged their children's marriages. Finally, there was death. That was the moment when one had to look to the state of one's soul and to the disposition of one's material goods. Among the landed nobility and the urban patriciate, the dying head of a household faced difficult choices—what to leave to the Church for the good of his soul, what to leave to his widow and children, what to do if he had no children. In Mediterranean regions, women frequently were excluded by law from inheriting from their fathers and husbands, especially land, by a variety of means; although in many areas there was also a return to the Roman custom of a dowry paid from the woman's family to her husband at the time of marriage. If there were no sons, women could inherit in some areas of Europe, despite the claims of more distant male kin.

In the late Middle Ages, the period between about 1300 and 1500, these and other tensions were barely contained. This era was marked by economic depression, prolonged wars (most notably the Hundred Years' War between the kings of England and France), and rebellions by peasants and urban lower classes. The universal pretensions of the papacy to supremacy over Christendom became entangled with the interests of the French and English kings during the removal of the papacy from Rome to Avignon (1306–1378). The pope's return to Rome only exacerbated conditions, as the resulting Great Schism (1378–1417) meant that allegiances of Christians were divided between two and sometimes three popes. Intellectual developments in the philosophical movement known as nominalism in the universities and in the Conciliar Movement, which aimed to reunify the Church under one pope through the mechanisms of a council representative of all the Church clergy and laity, attacked the bases of the papal claim to universal supremacy.

The development that came to touch or threaten more lives than any other was the series of plagues that began in 1348 and continued intermittently through 1720. The first outbreak of plague between 1348 and 1351, known colloquially as the Black Death, killed between 25 and 45 percent of Europe's population. The plague may have been a blessing in disguise for the survivors, at least for a while, in that wages and standards of living for workers and peasants improved. Yet the elites, whose standard of living could have been hurt by these developments, found ways to react against economic and social changes, using legislation, taxation, and bloody repression. And the plague remained endemic in Europe, recurring every few decades—a constant threat to life and prosperity for individuals and families. It became all the more important to prepare for death. Concern with death also led, in some quarters, to renewed reflection on life. Historians have pointed to an increase of secularism, which means perhaps not so much a forsaking of spiritual concerns for material ones as an elevation of material things to a level of concern and self-consciousness parallel to the spiritual. Certainly spiritual and material were intricately intertwined in the late Middle Ages.

The Life of Saint Germanus

Saint Germanus (c. 378–448) was bishop of Auxerre in east central France. This area experienced the decline of Roman imperial power in a marked way and was in the forefront of the migrations of barbarian peoples. The events in the life of Germanus provide evidence of the chaotic conditions along the Roman frontiers. Germanus's popularly acknowledged sanctity and the miracles attributed to him are indicative of the needs and concerns of people at the time. What was Germanus's background? How did it equip him for his role as bishop and saint? What sorts of miracles did he perform? Why might these happenings have seemed miraculous to the author of the life and his audience?

A monk named Constantius of Lyon (b. c. 415) wrote this life of Germanus around 480. He says it was written at the insistence of Patiens, a bishop of Lyon, though it is evident that the saint's life was circulated in Auxerre by the bishop Censurius. Why were bishops so interested in propagating the life of this saint? What do Germanus's actions as bishop tell us about the nature of the Church in the fifth century?

Most people are drawn to writing by an abundance of materials, and wits are supposed to be enriched where there is much to say; but for myself, as I begin to recount, far from completely, the life and deeds of that most illustrious man, Bishop Germanus, I am filled with trepidation at the number of his miracles. Just as the brightness of the sun brought to bear upon stupefied humans blunts the keenness of the eyes, and light throws light into confusion, so my feeble mind shrinks from so much to praise, heaped up before its impotence. Thus, within my breast, two courses are in conflict. On the one side, my knowledge of my impotence says "No"; on the other side, the sight of such piety, and the witness borne by countless miracles, drive me to record and bring to light matters that it would be impious to hide under a veil of silence from those who might profit by a knowledge of them. I have chosen, therefore, to shut my eyes to my own shame rather than allow the works of God to grow old in a prolonged oblivion. The materials must excuse the narrator. Those who are displeased by my rustic idiom will at least find pleasure in the beauty of the deeds it recounts. . . .

Germanus, then, was a native of the town of Auxerre, born of parents of the highest ranks, and was from earliest childhood given a liberal education. In this, the instruction he received was matched by the abundance of his talent and together these gave him learning doubly assured, by nature and by industry. Moreover, that nothing should be lacking to complete his education, when he had done with the lecture-rooms of Gaul he added in Rome a knowledge of law to the completeness he had already attained.

Next, practising as a barrister he became the ornament of the law-courts. While he was thus engaged and dazzling all by the praises he drew upon himself, he took a wife, whose birth, wealth and character were all of the highest. Then, when he was at the height of his reputation in the legal profession, the state promoted him to official rank by conferring on him the supreme office of *dux*[1] and the rule over more than one Province.[2] Assuredly his training was being directed by the hidden wisdom of God so that nothing should be lacking to the completeness of the apostolic pontiff-to-be. Eloquence was provided to equip the preacher, legal learning as an aid to justice, and the society of a wife to witness to his chastity.

Suddenly divine authority intervened and universal consent executed its decrees. For all the clergy, the whole nobility, the townsfolk and the countryfolk, with one accord demanded Germanus for their bishop. A war was declared by the people against their magistrate, who was easily overcome, since even his own staff turned against him. Thus he received the fulness of the priesthood under compulsion, as a conscript; but, this done, immediately he made the change complete. He deserted the earthly militia to be enrolled in the heavenly; the pomps of this world were trodden underfoot; a lowly way of life was adopted, his wife was turned into a sister, his riches were distributed among the poor and poverty became his ambition.

But no words can describe the fierceness with which he did violence to himself and the crucifixions and penances with which he persecuted his own body. I will summarise them briefly, with strict fidelity to the truth. From the day upon which he entered upon the fulness of the priesthood until the end of his life, he persisted in nourishing his soul by starving his body, even to the extent of never taking wheaten bread, nor wine, nor vinegar, nor oil nor pulse nor even salt for seasoning. (It is true that on Easter and Christmas Day a drink was served in which there would have been a taste of wine if it had not been destroyed by excessive dilution in the way one tempers with quantities of water the harshness of vinegar!) At meals he first took a taste of ashes, then bread made of barley which he himself had pounded and ground. And this food, acknowledged to be more trying than fasting, was never served until evening, except sometimes on a Wednesday and generally on Saturdays.

His clothing was a cloak and tunic, regardless of the seasons, for winter brought no addition to it nor was summer allowed to lighten it. These two garments continued to be used, unless one was given away, until they fell to pieces from hard wear. Under them there was always a hair-shirt. Narrow rough-hewn planks formed a framework for his bed, the space be-

---

[1]The rank of *dux* (afterwards "duke") was at this period strictly military and, by a rule made by the Emperor Diocletian a century earlier, might not be combined with civil office. (Original editor's note.)

[2]Armorica and Nervica, roughly Brittany, Normandy and Hainault, all of them districts liable to be raided either by sea or by land. (Original editor's note.)

tween them being filled to the brim with ashes. These, by being constantly compressed by his weight, became as hard as unbroken earth. His only bedclothes were a piece of sacking spread beneath him and a single military cape over him; there was nothing in the way of a pillow to place under his neck to support his head.

Lying flat like this, he condemned his limbs to be stretched out along the ground. He never removed his clothes at night and seldom either his girdle or his shoes, and he always had round his neck a leather strap with a box containing relics. His groans were continual and prayer unceasing, for he could get little sleep in such acute discomfort. Everyone must have his own opinion; mine is quite definitely that the blessed Germanus, amid all these crucifixions, endured a drawn-out martyrdom. But how wonderful is the power and goodness of our God! for He gave His servant, travelling faithfully along the true road, a two-fold recompense. Such errors as he may formerly have committed were purged away and in the process a refined sanctity was rapidly acquired; and, though he may have been a debtor by reason of past sins, he was presently able to draw for the benefit of others upon a stock of accumulated virtues. . . .

There was at that time a man of high character named Januarius who was in the Governor's service as head of his office staff and used to bring him the gold collected in taxes from the Province. One day he broke his journey to visit the Bishop and mislaid his handbag. It was accidentally found, when no one was looking, by a man who was frequently the victim of demoniacal possession. Presently the traveller resumed his journey and discovered his loss. He filled the city with his lamentations and demanded the money back from the holy Bishop just as if he had entrusted it to him. The latter, as if he had really been his debtor, promised in the name of God that it should be restored.

Now, the day on which the man had rushed all over the city in his frantic search had been a Saturday. The next day, when there was still no trace of the gold, the man who was looking for it clasped the Bishop's knees with tears in his eyes, assuring him that it would mean the death penalty for him if the state's money were not found. The Bishop enjoined patience, promising that all would be well. Soon afterwards, before setting out for Mass, he gave orders for one of the sufferers from demoniacal possession to be brought before him privately; and who should be brought to him but the man responsible for the theft.

He put him through a strict examination, saying that it was impossible for a crime on his conscience to remain concealed. Then he ordered the enemy of souls who had been prompting these evil deeds to admit the truth of the matter without delay. But the wicked spirit, from sheer malice, denied having committed the crime. At this the Bishop, in righteous anger, ordered the liar to be produced in front of the congregation and, without further delay, set out to celebrate Mass.

He gave the solemn salutation to the people, then prostrated him at full length in prayer. All at once the unhappy man, the captive and at the same time the servant of the demon, was lifted high into the air. The church was filled with his screams, the whole congregation was in confusion and the man himself, yelling out the Bishop's name as if he were in the midst of flames, confessed his crime.

Then at last the man of blessings rose from his prayer and came down to the steps of the sanctuary. He called up the raving man, cross-examined him and learnt the whole truth. The coins were brought out of their hiding-place, the acclamations of the people resounded, and with one accord they proclaimed the sanctity of Germanus and the power of God. By one and the same miracle the man who had been robbed had got back his money and the demoniac his sanity. Germanus had, indeed, cured many before this, but always under a veil of secrecy. What made this occasion so notable was its publicity.

At one time there was a fearful conspiracy of demons to wage a kind of war on the man of blessings himself. When they found him immune, thanks to the breastplate of faith, to all their assaults, they contrived a device for the destruction of his flock. First the children, then their elders, began to succumb to a swelling in their throats which brought death after an illness of less than three days. His congregation was being wiped out as if they were being slaughtered by the sword. No human measures brought any relief and, when it was almost too late, the panic-stricken people appealed to their Bishop for divine aid.

Immediately he blessed some oil and, at its touch, the internal swelling went down and a passage was thereby opened for breathing and swallowing. The heavenly remedy effected a cure as rapidly as the onslaught of the disease had brought death. One of those who had been possessed bawled out when he was being exorcised that all this had been brought about by the entry of demons, and acknowledged that they had been put to flight by the holy man's prayer.

The man of blessings made it his practice, as general of the soldiers of God, to stay alternately at the monastery and the church, to set the goal of perfection before each of the rivals in this warfare. On one occasion, when he had been invited to the monastery, he was detained by business and excused himself from coming. A little later, however, when the cause of the delay had been disposed of, he set off to give the brethren a surprise. Now, some of them were troubled by demons and it happened that just then one of the sufferers was in the grip of one. Suddenly he announced at the top of his voice: "Germanus is at the river but cannot cross because he has no boat."

For a long time the abbot gave no credence to this assertion, supposing the evil spirit to be lying, since the Bishop had excused himself and would not be coming. But he persisted in his cries and one of the brethren was sent and reported that the demon was right. A boat was sent and the Bishop crossed and was received with the usual fervour. He fell at once to praying and the community knelt with him.

Suddenly the demoniac rose in the empty air, held by invisible cords. There was no more delay than was necessary for the Bishop to rise from prayer, and all that he required of the demon was that it should go out of the man with some bodily weakness of his. Thus adjured it departed, leaving filth behind it and a stench worthy of it.

Meanwhile the Saxons and the Picts had joined forces to make war upon the Britons. The latter had been compelled to withdraw their forces within their camp and, judging their resources to be utterly unequal to the contest, asked the help of the holy prelates. The latter sent back a promise to come, and hastened to follow it. Their coming brought such a sense of security that you might have thought that a great army had arrived; to have such apostles for leaders was to have Christ Himself fighting in the camp.

It was the season of Lent and the presence of the bishops made the sacred forty days still more sacred; so much so that the soldiers, who received instruction in daily sermons, flew eagerly to the grace of baptism; indeed, great numbers of this pious army sought the waters of salvation. A church was built of leafy branches in readiness for Easter Day, on the plan of a city church, though set in a camp on active service. The soldiers paraded still wet from baptism, faith was fervid, the aid of weapons was thought little of, and all looked for help from heaven.

Meanwhile the enemy had learnt of the practices and appearance of the camp. They promised themselves an easy victory over practically disarmed troops and pressed on in haste. But their approach was discovered by scouts and, when the Easter solemnities had been celebrated, the army—the greater part of it fresh from the font—began to take up their weapons and prepare for battle and Germanus announced that he would be their general. He chose some light-armed troops and made a tour of the outworks. In the direction from which the enemy were expected he saw a valley enclosed by steep mountains. Here he stationed an army on a new model, under his own command.

By now the savage host of the enemy was close at hand and Germanus rapidly circulated an order that all should repeat in unison the call he would give as a battle-cry. Then, while the enemy were still secure in the belief that their approach was unexpected, the bishops three times chanted the Alleluia. All, as one man, repeated it and the shout they raised rang through the air and was repeated many times in the confined space between the mountains.

The enemy were panic-stricken, thinking that the surrounding rocks and the very sky itself were falling on them. Such was their terror that no effort of their feet seemed enough to save them. They fled in every direction, throwing away their weapons and thankful if they could save at least their skins. Many threw themselves into the river which they had just crossed at their ease, and were drowned in it.

Thus the British army looked on at its revenge without striking a blow, idle spectators of the victory achieved. The booty strewn everywhere was collected; the pious soldiery obtained the spoils of a victory from heaven. The bishops were elated at the rout of the enemy without bloodshed and a victory gained by faith and not by force.

Thus this most wealthy island, with the defeat both of its spiritual and of its human foes, was rendered secure in every sense. And now, to the great grief of the whole country, those who had won the victories over both Pelagians and Saxons made preparations for their return. Their own merits and the intercession of Alban the Martyr secured for them a calm voyage; and a good ship brought them back in peace to their expectant people.

All Gaul rejoiced at the return of the revered priests; the Churches were gladdened, the demons trembled. The return of Germanus, in particular, had been prayed for by his diocese with a double intention, since he was looked to as its protector both in the court of heaven and in the tempests of this world. A burden of taxes beyond the ordinary and countless other exactions had crushed the spirit of his people who, without him, had felt like orphaned children. So he took the destitute under his protection, en-quired into complaints, condoled with the sorrowing. And, when he might have claimed quiet and repose after the dangers of the sea, he incurred the toil of a long journey by land, by undertaking to seek remedies for the distresses of his diocese. But, though about to travel right across Gaul, he contented himself with the smallest possible retinue and the poorest of mounts. Better than the amplest riches, he carried Christ in his breast.

. . . A eunuch named Acolus, at that time Imperial Chamberlain, had an adopted son to whom he had given an excellent education but who was now plagued by a demon. It was the kind that strikes down its victims every month at the new moon, by causing them to keep falling to the ground. The Empress through her courtiers arranged for him to be taken to the holy man and put into his charge.

After a long examination of him, Germanus put off the exorcism to the next day, although he ordinarily expelled even the most rabid demons at the first laying on of hands. He did this because this demon had entered so deeply into the very inmost parts of the wretched youth that during the periods of possession it practically made his body its own. That night he arranged for the boy to occupy the same room as himself. Then, indeed, the demon burst out openly from its inner lair. As if in torture it revealed how it had first taken possession of its victim in the innocence of early childhood. Now at the Bishop's order it went out of him, and the next day the youth was back in the palace, purged.

It had been the affairs of Armorica that had made this long journey necessary and Germanus would undoubtedly have had them settled as he wished, by obtaining for the Armoricans pardon and security for the future, if it had not been for the treachery of Tibatto, who persuaded that fickle and undisciplined people to rebel again.[3] After that, not even the intercession of the Bishop could do anything for them, for common prudence made it impossible for the Imperial government to trust them; and their many times perjured leader before long paid the penalty of his reckless treason. . . .

An illness did in fact follow, a few days later [following Germanus's dream of death]. As it grew more serious, the whole city was in consternation. But He who was calling him to glory hastened his journey; the Lord was inviting the tired hero to receive the reward of his laborious days.

The Empress laid aside the haughtiness of royalty and went visiting the pauper; she sought out the sick man and promised him anything he asked. But he had only one request to make, and to this she consented most unwillingly, that his dust should return to his native soil. Day and night the crowd of visitors was as much as the house and the forecourt could hold. The chanting of the psalms was kept up continuously; and the seventh day of the illness saw the passing of his faithful and blessed soul to heaven.[4]

Then came the division of what he had left behind him. The Empire and the Church each claimed a share; and over his scanty possessions there arose a dispute such as we associate with great riches—there was so little for them to seize, poor heirs of a mere benediction! The Empress took the reliquary; Bishop Peter annexed the cloak with the hairshirt inside it. The six prelates, to make sure of having something associated with the saint, were glad to tear to pieces what remained. One had his pallium,[5] the second his girdle, two divided his tunic and two his soldier's cape.[6]

Next came an eager rivalry over his funeral, everyone insisting that no expense should be spared. Acolius had the body embalmed in spices; the Empress saw to its vestments. When all this was duly accomplished, the

[3] . . . Tibatto had been the leader of the Armoricans in an earlier rebellion and been captured. But he may have escaped or been released. (Original editor's note.)

[4] Probably on 31 July 448. (Original editor's note.)

[5] A kind of stole sometimes given by the Pope to bishops (more usually to archbishops) as a mark of special favour and authority. (Original editor's note.)

[6] His bed-covering. (Original editor's note.)

Emperor provided the bier and the equipage for the journey and a large body of his own servants to attend them. The clergy were in charge of the chanting of the liturgy, at each stage arranging for it to be carried on by those of the next town—there was one long procession all the way to Gaul.

The body reached Piacenza on its journey when it was quite dark. It was placed in the church, and, while the liturgical prayers were being recited, a lady of the town who was so badly paralysed that she could use none of her limbs asked as a favour to be placed under the bier. There she remained stretched out till dawn. When, early in the morning, the corpse was taken up again, the woman rose too and astonished everybody by following in the procession on her own feet.

Even greater was the devotion manifested in Gaul to its own protector, for there was personal affection as well as reverence. Every kind of person hastened to perform every kind of service. Some smoothed the roads by clearing away stones, others linked them by restoring bridges. Some contributed to the expenses, others chanted the psalms, others again took the bier on to their shoulders. The profusion of torches ousted the sun's rays and provided light for the day. Such were the services of love with which he was brought back to his own see, where his body is buried but he himself lives on in his daily miracles and his glory.

The Burgundian Code

The Burgundians were one of the Germanic tribes that migrated into the Roman Empire after 406. By 413, they had established themselves in the area of the modern German city of Worms, on the west bank of the Rhine River, and had been accepted into the empire as an allied people (foederati). The ferocious Huns overthrew this first Burgundian kingdom in 436, however, and the remnants of the Burgundians moved south to an area north of Lake Geneva. Under the reign of King Gundobad, 474–516, the second Burgundian kingdom achieved its furthest extent, stretching from the Alps west to the Rhône and Loire rivers, reaching Langres on the north and Provence to the south. The sons of the Frankish King Clovis, who reigned from 481 to 511, eventually defeated the sons of Gundobad, and Burgundy was absorbed into the Frankish domains in 534.

The Roman subjects of the Burgundians continued to cling to their law, which was very different from the customs prevailing among a Germanic people like the Burgundians. In order for the two peoples to interact under the same ruler, and under the influence of the model of written Roman law (the Theodosian Code of the fifth century), Gundobad undertook a compilation of laws for both Burgundians and Romans between 483 and 501. The selection here is from the laws for the Burgundians. It shows a set of rules that combine old elements of tribal custom and new rules enacted on royal authority.

Compare this selection as a form of law with the selections from the Roman law of the Twelve Tables and from the later marriage laws. How are these laws stated? What can you tell about legal procedures and how courts operated? How are penalties set and of what do they consist? Germanic law codes embraced a system of compensation for offenses and damages, laid out by values of persons (wergeld) and things. These forms of compensation were offered judicially as an alternative to a wronged party avenging his own grievance through self-help, even to the point of blood feud. How, then, are we to understand the section dealing with murder? What concerns are evident in the various rules involving offenses against women? Is the concern with rape or sexual assault, for example, the same as that in modern U.S. law? What was at stake in a divorce?

PREFACE

First Constitution

2. For the love of justice, through which God is pleased and the power of earthly kingdoms acquired, we have obtained the consent of our counts . . . and leaders . . . , and have desired to establish such laws that the integrity and equity of those judging may exclude all rewards and corruptions from themselves.

3. Therefore all administrators . . . and judges must judge from the present time on between Burgundians and Romans according to our laws which have been set forth and corrected by a common method, to the end that no one may hope or presume to receive anything by way of reward or emolument from any party as the result of the suits or decisions; but let him whose case is deserving obtain justice and let the integrity of the judge alone suffice to accomplish this.

4. We believe the condition of this law should be imposed on us that no one may presume to tempt our integrity in any kind of case with favors or rewards; first, since our zeal for equity repudiates from ourselves those things which we forbid to all judges under our rule, let our treasury accept nothing more than has been established in the laws concerning the payment of fines.

5. Therefore let all nobles . . . , counsellors . . . , bailiffs . . . , mayors of our palace . . . , chancellors . . . , counts . . . of the cities or villages, Burgundian as well as Roman, and all appointed judges and military judges . . . know that nothing can be accepted in connection with those suits which have been acted upon or decided, and that nothing can be sought in the name of promise or reward from those litigating; nor can the parties (to the suit) be compelled by the judge to make a payment in order that they may receive anything (from their suit).

6. But if any of those mentioned, corrupted against our laws, or even judging justly, has been convicted of receiving rewards from suits or decisions, and the crime has been proved, let him be punished capitally as an example to all: with the further provision that the penalty which has been

imposed shall not cause any loss of property to the sons or legitimate heirs of him whose dishonesty was punished.

7. Indeed for the payments given to the scribes . . . of our appointed judges in rendering decisions in suits exceeding ten solidi,[1] we give the opinion that a single tremissis should suffice; in suits involving less than ten solidi, let smaller payments be sought.

8. Since a similar condition has been forbidden among Romans in cases of the crime of venality, we command that Romans be judged by the Roman laws just as has been established by our predecessors; let them know that they must follow the form and statement of the written law when they render decisions so that no one may be excused on grounds of ignorance.

9. In the case of unjust decisions rendered before this time, let the conditions of the earlier law be followed. But we add this also, that if perchance a judge has been accused of corruption and has been convicted without sufficient reason, let the accuser be compelled to receive a punishment similar to that which we ordered the corrupted judge to receive.

10. If indeed anything is not covered by the statement of our laws, we order those judging to refer such matters to us. . . .

OF MURDERS.

1. If anyone presumes with boldness or rashness bent on injury to kill a native freeman of our people of any nation[2] or a servant of the king, in any case a man of barbarian tribe, let him make restitution for the committed crime not otherwise than by the shedding of his own blood.

2. We decree that this rule be added to the law by a reasonable provision, that if violence shall have been done by anyone to any person, so that he is injured by blows of lashes or by wounds, and if he pursues his persecutor and overcome by grief and indignation kills him, proof of the deed shall be afforded by the act itself or by suitable witnesses who can be believed. Then the guilty party shall be compelled to pay to the relatives of the person killed half his wergeld according to the status of the person: that is, if he shall have killed a noble of the highest class . . . , we decree that the payment be set at one hundred fifty solidi, i.e., half his wergeld; if a person of middle class . . . , one hundred solidi; if a person of the lowest class . . . , seventy-five solidi.

---

[1]There are three Roman coins named in the Burgundian Code: the solidus, the semissis, and the tremissis. The solidus was a gold coin which under Constantine succeeded the aureus and continued to be coined until the fall of the Byzantine Empire. . . . Originally, the solidus was worth about 25 denarii, although in the later empire it was reduced to about half that amount; as a medieval money of account it was equal to 12 denarii. The semissis was a coin minted under the later emperors worth half a solidus and said to contain 59.8 grains of gold. The tremissis was worth a third of a solidus. However, it is hard to give any comprehensible value to these moneys, even in purchasing power, since it would seem almost impossible for the Burgundians of the lower classes to raise the sums which might be levied against them under the terms of the laws. (Original editor's note.)

[2]Nation, i.e., barbarian nation or tribe. (Original editor's note.)

3. If a slave unknown to his master presumes to kill a native freeman, let the slave be handed over to death, and let the master not be made liable for damages.

4. If the master knows of the deed, let both be handed over to death.

5. If the slave himself flees . . . after the deed, let his master be compelled to pay thirty solidi to the relatives of the man killed for the value (wergeld) of the slave.

6. Similarly in the case of royal slaves, in accordance with the status of such persons, let the same condition about murderers be observed.

7. In such cases let all know this must be observed carefully, that the relatives of the man killed must recognize that no one can be pursued except the killer; because just as we have ordered the criminals to be destroyed, so we will suffer the innocent to sustain no injury. . . .

OF THE STEALING OF GIRLS.

1. If anyone shall steal a girl, let him be compelled to pay the price set for such a girl ninefold, and let him pay a fine to the amount of twelve solidi.

2. If a girl who has been seized returns uncorrupted to her parents, let the abductor compound six times the wergeld of the girl; moreover, let the fine be set at twelve solidi.

3. But if the abductor does not have the means to make the above-mentioned payment, let him be given over to the parents of the girl that they may have the power of doing to him whatever they choose.

4. If indeed, the girl seeks the man of her own will and comes to his house, and he has intercourse with her, let him pay her marriage price threefold; if moreover, she returns uncorrupted to her home, let her return with all blame removed from him.

5. If indeed a Roman girl, without the consent or knowledge of her parents, unites in marriage with a Burgundian, let her know she will have none of the property of her parents.

OF THOSE COMMITTING ASSAULT AND BREACH OF THE PEACE.

1. If anyone in an act of assault or robbery kills a merchant or anyone else, let him be killed; with the further condition that if those things which he took cannot be found, let them be compensated in fee simple[3] from his property.

2. But if a man committing an assault shall have been killed by those whom he intended to rob, let no suit be brought for this reason against the killers by the master or relatives of the man killed.

3. We order all lawbreakers who plunder houses or treasure chests to be killed.

---

[3]That is, given full ownership of the guilty party's property.

OF WOMEN VIOLATED.

1. Whatever native freeman does violence to a maidservant, and force can be proved, let him pay twelve solidi to him to whom the maidservant belongs.

2. If a slave does this, let him receive a hundred fifty blows.

OF INJURIES WHICH ARE SUFFERED BY WOMEN.

1. If any native freewoman has her hair cut off and is humiliated without cause (when innocent) by any native freeman in her home or on the road, and this can be proved with witnesses, let the doer of the deed pay her twelve solidi, and let the amount of the fine be twelve solidi.

2. If this was done to a freedwoman, let him pay her six solidi.

3. If this was done to a maidservant, let him pay her three solidi, and let the amount of the fine be three solidi.

4. If this injury (shame, disgrace) is inflicted by a slave on a native freewoman, let him receive two hundred blows; if a freedwoman, let him receive a hundred blows; if a maidservant, let him receive seventy-five blows.

5. If indeed the woman whose injury we have ordered to be punished in this manner commits fornication voluntarily (i.e., if she yields), let nothing be sought for the injury suffered.

OF DIVORCES.

1. If any woman leaves (puts aside) her husband to whom she is legally married, let her be smothered in mire.

2. If anyone wishes to put away his wife without cause, let him give her another payment such as he gave for her marriage price, and let the amount of the fine be twelve solidi.

3. If by chance a man wishes to put away his wife, and is able to prove one of these three crimes against her, that is, adultery, witchcraft, or violation of graves, let him have full right to put her away: and let the judge pronounce the sentence of the law against her, just as should be done against criminals.

4. But if she admits none of these three crimes, let no man be permitted to put away his wife for any other crime. But if he chooses, he may go away from the home, leaving all household property behind, and his wife with their children may possess the property of her husband.

OF THE PUNISHMENT OF SLAVES WHO COMMIT A CRIMINAL ASSAULT ON FREEBORN WOMEN.

1. If any slave does violence to a native freewoman, and if she complains and is clearly able to prove this, let the slave be killed for the crime committed.

2. If indeed a native free girl unites voluntarily with a slave, we order both to be killed.

3. But if the relatives of the girl do not wish to punish their own relative, let the girl be deprived of her free status and delivered into servitude to the king.

OF INCESTUOUS ADULTERY.

If anyone has been taken in adultery with his relative or with his wife's sister, let him be compelled to pay her wergeld, according to her status, to him who is the nearest relative of the woman with whom he committed adultery; and let the amount of the fine be twelve solidi. Further, we order the adulteress to be placed into servitude to the king.

OF THE INHERITANCE OF THOSE WHO DIE WITHOUT CHILDREN.

1. Although we have ordered many things in former laws concerning the inheritance of those who die without children, nevertheless after considering the matter thoroughly, we perceive it to be just that some of those things which were ordered before should be corrected. Therefore we decree in the present constitution that if a woman whose husband has died without children has not taken her vows a second time, let her possess securely a third of all the property of her husband to the day of her death; with the further provision that after her death, all will revert to the legitimate heirs of her husband.

2. Let that remain in effect which has been stated previously concerning the morning gift.[4] . . . For if she wishes to marry within a year from the time of the death of her first husband, let her have full right to do so, but let her give up that third part of the property which she had been permitted to possess. However, if she wishes to take a husband after a year or two have passed, let her give up all as has been stated above which she received from her first husband, and let the heirs in whose portion the inheritance of her former husband belongs receive the price which must be paid for her (second) marriage.

OF THE ADULTERY OF GIRLS AND WIDOWS.

1. If the daughter of any native Burgundian before she is given in marriage unites herself secretly and disgracefully in adultery with either barbarian or Roman, and if afterward she brings a complaint, and the act is established as charged, let him who has been accused of her corruption, and as has been said, is convicted with certain proof, suffer no defamation of charac-

[4] A gift from the groom to the bride on the wedding day.

ter . . . upon payment of fifteen solidi. She indeed, defeated in her purpose by the vileness of her conduct, shall sustain the disgrace of lost chastity.

2. But if a widow who has not been sought, but rather overcome by desire, unites with anyone, and she bursts forth in an accusing voice, let her not receive the stated number of solidi, and we order that she, demanding marriage thus, be not awarded to him in whom she joined herself in such a disgraceful manner, because it is just that she, defeated by her vile conduct, is worthy of neither matrimony nor reward.

OF THOSE WHO DENY THOSE THINGS CHARGED AGAINST THEM, AND OFFER OATHS.

We know that many of our people are corrupted through inability to establish a case and because of instinct of greed, so that they do not hesitate frequently to offer oaths about uncertain matters and likewise to perjure themselves about known matters. To break up this criminal practice, we decree by the present law that as often as a case shall arise among our people and he who has been accused denies by offering oaths that that which is sought is owed by him, and that that has been done which is charged, it is fitting that an end be made to their litigation in this manner: if the party to whom oath has been offered does not wish to receive the oath, but shall say that the truthfulness of his adversary can be demonstrated only by resort to arms, and the second party (the one accused) shall not yield (the case charged), let the right of combat not be refused; with the further provision that one of the same witnesses who came to give oath shall fight, God being the judge. For it is just that if anyone shall say without delay that he knows the truth of the matter and shall offer to take oath, he should not hesitate to fight. But if the witness of him who offered oath was overcome in that combat, let all witnesses who promised that they would take oath be compelled to pay a fine of three hundred solidi without any grant of delay. But if he who refused to receive the oath (the accuser) shall have been killed, let the victorious party be repaid ninefold the sum (debt) involved taken from his property (i.e., from the property of the dead man) as damages, so that as a result, one may delight in truth rather than falsehood.

OF WOMEN WHO GO TO THEIR HUSBANDS VOLUNTARILY.

If any woman, Burgundian or Roman, gives herself voluntarily in marriage to a husband, we order that the husband have the property of that woman; just as he has power over her, so also over her property and all her possessions.

OF THE MARRIAGE PRICE. . . .[5]

1. If any Burgundian of the highest . . . or middle class . . . unites with the daughter of another (probably of the same class) without her father's consent, we order that such a noble make a triple payment of one hundred fifty solidi to the father whose daughter he took, if he took her without stating his intentions in advance or seeking his consent; and let the fine be thirty-six solidi.

2. Indeed if one of the lower class . . . has presumed to do this (i.e., has married one of his own class without her father's consent), let him likewise make a triple payment, that is, forty-five solidi; and let the fine be twelve solidi.

The Carolingian Capitulary concerning Estates

Charlemagne himself probably issued this capitulary (directive) on the management of royal estates sometime before 800. It was meant to apply broadly throughout the Frankish and German lands of his empire. Stewards (literally called "judges") were given instructions regarding a range of responsibilities—economic, judicial, military. From such a document, historians can reconstruct the conditions of early medieval agriculture.

The estate, or manor, was designed to be as self-sufficient as possible, though that was an impossible goal in practice. What the estates produced was available for royal consumption, but generally the king and his entourage had to come to the estate to use its products. Kings moved among their far-flung estates in the early Middle Ages. There were no permanent capital cities and palaces as would appear centuries later. What sorts of agricultural activities occurred on these estates? What commodities were produced? What were the obligations of the serfs to their lord? How was the steward to collect these obligations for the lord? Where were the serfs supposed to take their grievances?

One abiding concern was to maintain some sort of control over the steward. From what you can see here, how might a steward have taken advantage of his position? What types of control (other than being physically present on the estate) could the king hope to exercise? Finally, how does estate management depicted here differ from that described by Columella for Roman estates?

1. We wish that our estates, which we have established to serve our needs, shall serve entirely for our benefit and not for that of other men.

---

[5]The husband's payment to the father of the bride, almost a form of compensation for taking his daughter.

2. That the people on our estates be well taken care of, and that they be reduced to poverty by no one.

3. That the stewards do not dare to enlist our people in their own service. They should not force them to perform agricultural labors, to cut wood or to do other work for them. Nor should the stewards accept any gifts from them, neither a horse nor an ox nor cow nor pig nor sheep nor piglet nor lamb nor anything else, excepting bottles of wine, garden produce, fruits, chickens and eggs.

4. If any of our people commit against our interests the crime of robbery or other offense, let him make good the damage, and further, let him be punished by whipping in satisfaction of the law, except in cases of murder and arson, for which fines may be collected. The stewards should strive to render to other men the justice which they may deserve, according to the law. Our people, as we have said, instead of paying fines, are to be whipped. Freemen, however, who reside on our properties and estates, should strive to make good whatever injuries they may commit according to their law. Whatever they give in fines, whether in cattle or other payments, should be collected for our use.

5. Whenever our stewards are to see that our work is performed—sowing, plowing, harvesting, cutting of hay or gathering of grapes—let each of them at the proper time and place supervise and give directions how the work is to be done, so that it may be done well. If the steward is not within his district and cannot come to a particular place, let him send a good messenger from among our people or another reliable man, in order to supervise our affairs and conduct them to a good end. The steward should diligently see to it that he sends a faithful man to take care of this matter.

6. We wish that our stewards pay a full tenth of all produce to the churches which are on our property, and do not let our tenth be given to the church of another [lord], unless in places where this is an ancient custom. Other clerics should not hold these churches, but only our own or those from our people or from our chapel.

7. That every steward should perform his full service as he has been directed. And if necessity requires that he should serve additional time, he should determine whether he should increase the [day] service or the night service.

8. That our stewards take care of our vineyards which are in their territory, and make sure that they are worked well. Let them place the wine in good containers and let them diligently see to it that nothing is lost in shipping it. Let them acquire through purchase special kinds of wine, in order to send it to the royal estates. And when more of this wine has been purchased than is needed for the provisioning of our estates, they should inform us of this, so that we may command whatever may be our will. They should have vine slips from our vineyards sent for our use. The rents from our estates which are paid in wine are to be stored in our cellars.

9. We wish that every steward keep in his territory measures of *modia*, *sextaria*,[1] containers of eight *sextaria*, and baskets, of the same type as we have in our palace.

10. That our mayors, foresters, stablemen, cellarers, deans, toll collectors and other servants do regular services and pay pigs for their farms [*mansi*]. In place of manual labor let them perform their offices well. And whatever mayor may have a benefice, let him send a substitute, who may perform for him the manual labor and other service.

11. That no steward take lodging for himself or for his dogs from our men or from those living outside our estates.

12. That no steward should commend [with a benefice] any hostage on our estates.

13. That the stewards should take good care of our stallions and not allow them to remain too long in one place, lest the pasturage be damaged. And if a stallion should be unhealthy or old so as to be likely to die soon, they should inform us of this at the proper time, before the season comes when they are to be placed with the mares.

14. That they should watch our mares well, and segregate the colts at the proper time. And if the fillies should increase in number, they should be separated so as to form a new herd by themselves.

15. Let them have our foals sent to our winter palace at the feast of St. Martin [November 11].

16. We wish that whatever we or the queen should command to any steward, or whatever our servants, the seneschal[2] or the butler,[3] should order, the stewards in our name or that of the queen, they should perform as was told them. Whoever should fail to do so through negligence, let him abstain from drink from the time he has been told until he appears in our presence or that of the queen and requests pardon from us. And if the steward was in the army or on guard duty or on a mission or elsewhere, and ordered his subordinates to perform something and they did not do so, then they should come on foot to the palace. They should abstain from drink and meat while they give the reasons why they were negligent. Then they should accept their punishment, either in whipping or however else it may please us or the queen.

17. The steward should appoint as many men as there are estates in his territory, to keep bees for our needs.

18. At our mills the stewards should keep chickens and geese according to the quality of the mill and as many more as can be maintained.

19. The stewards should keep in the barns of our principal estates no

---

[1]*Modius* was a grain measure divided into sixteen *sextaria*. It was a bit less than two gallons.

[2]A household official in charge of the servants and domestic arrangements.

[3]Chief male servant.

fewer than 100 chickens and 30 geese; on smaller farms let them have no fewer than 50 chickens and 12 geese.

20. Every steward should always send the produce [of the fowls] to our court abundantly throughout the year, except when they make visits three or four or more times.

21. Every steward should keep fish ponds on our estates where they were in the past. He should enlarge them if possible. And if they were not there in times past but can now be made, let them be made.

22. Those who hold our vineyards should keep for our use no fewer than three or four crowns of grapes.

23. The stewards should maintain in each of our estates cow barns, pig pens, folds for sheep and goats, as many as possible. No estate should be without them. Moreover, let them have cows delivered by our serfs in fulfillment of their service, so that our cow barns or plow teams are not diminished by service on our demesne. Let them also obtain, in order to supply meat, lame but healthy oxen and cows, horses which are not mangy, or other healthy beasts. As we have said, our cow barns or plow teams should not be diminished for this.

24. Every steward should see to it that whatever is provided for our table be good and of highest quality, and that whatever they deliver has been prepared carefully and cleanly. And whenever someone serves at our table, he should receive for his service two meals of wheat every day. The other provisions, whether in flour or in meat, should similarly be of good quality.

25. The stewards should report on the first of September whether or not there is pasturage for the hogs.

26. Mayors[4] should not administer a territory which is too large for them to ride through and inspect in a single day.

27. Our manor houses should have continuous watch fires and guards so that they may be secure. When our *missi* or a legation come to or from the palace, they should not take lodging in the royal manor houses, unless by our special permission or that of the queen. The count in his district or those men who have been traditionally accustomed to care for the *missi* or legations should continue to provide pack horses in the usual fashion and all things needed by them. Thus they may journey to and from our palace with ease and dignity.

28. We wish that every year, on Palm Sunday in Lent, which is called "Hosanna Sunday," the stewards should deliver to us at our command the monetary part of our revenue, after we find out for the present year how great our revenue is.

29. Every steward should see to it that those of our men who wish to

---

[4]Latin *maior* means "greater." Here it designates an important noble to whom administrative and military functions had been assigned.

plead cases are not required to come into our presence to plead. He should not through negligence allow those days to be lost which the man should serve. If our serf should have to seek justice outside our estates, his master should expend every effort to gain justice for him. If the serf is unable to obtain justice in a particular locale, the master should not allow our serf to suffer for this, but through himself or his messenger he should inform us of this.

30. We wish that our stewards separate from the entire revenue that which is needed in our service. Similarly, let them take out supplies needed to fill the carts sent into the army, both those of householders and those of shepherds. And let them know how much they send for this purpose.

31. That they should similarly deduct each year what is to be given to the household servants or to the women working in the women's quarters. Let them give it fully at the proper time and let them inform us how they have done so and from where it was taken.

32. That every steward should see to it that he always has good seed of highest quality, by purchase or otherwise.

33. After all these parts of our revenue have been allocated or sown or consumed, whatever is left from the produce should be kept in expectation of our order, so that it may be sold or stored according to our command.

34. Whatever is made by hand should be closely supervised with all diligence, so that they are made or prepared with the maximum cleanliness: that is, lard, smoked meat, sausage, newly salted meat, wine, vinegar, mulberry wine, boiled wine, garn, mustard, cheese, butter, malt, beer, mead, honey, wax, and flour.

35. We wish that tallow be made from fat sheep and also from pigs. Furthermore, let them keep in each estate no less than two fattened oxen, whether to be fattened there or to be delivered to us.

36. That our woods and forests be well protected. And where there is room for clearing, let the stewards clear it, and they should not allow fields to become overgrown with woods. And where woods should be, they should not allow them to be excessively stripped and damaged. Let them guard well our wild beasts within the forests. Similarly, let them take care of our falcons and hawks for our use, and collect our rents diligently. If our stewards or mayors or their men let their hogs forage in our forest for fattening, let them be the first to pay a tenth, in order to set a good example, so that in the future other men will pay their tenth fully.

37. That our stewards maintain our fields and cultivated lands well, and let them guard our meadows in season.

38. That they should always keep fat geese and chickens for our needs, when they ought to provide them for us or deliver them to us.

39. Let them receive the chickens and eggs which serfs or residents of farms return every year; when they are not needed, they should sell them.

40. Let every steward always keep for the sake of ornament on every

estate swans, peacocks, pheasants, ducks, pigeons, partridges and turtle-doves.

41. Let the buildings within our manors and the fences about them be well cared for, and let stables, kitchens, bakeries or wine presses be carefully constructed, so that our servants can perform their tasks properly and cleanly.

42. Let every estate have within its hall beds, mattresses, pillows, bed linens, table cloths, seat covers, vessels of bronze, lead, iron and wood, andirons, chains, pot hangers, planes, axes, hatchets, knives and all sorts of tools, so that it will not be necessary to seek them elsewhere or to borrow them. Let the stewards also have the responsibility of seeing to it that the iron tools which they provide for the army are good and that when they are returned they are sent to the manor hall.

43. To the workshop of the women they should provide material to work at suitable times, as has been commanded: that is, linen, wool, woàd, red dye, madder, carding implements, combs, soap, oil, containers, and other small things which are needed there.

44. Concerning Lenten food, let two-thirds be sent every year for our use, in vegetables, fish or cheese, butter, honey, mustard, vinegar, millet, panic, dry or green herbs, roots, turnips and wax or soap or other small items. Let them inform us by letter what is left over. They should by no means fail to do this, as they have in the past, because through those two parts we wish to learn about the third part which remains.

45. That every steward should have in his territory good artisans; that is, smiths, blacksmiths, gold- and silversmiths, tailors, turners, carpenters, shield makers, fishermen, falconers (that is, those who look after the birds), soap makers, brewers (that is, those who know how to make beer or cider, perry or other liquid fit to drink), bakers who can make bread for our need, net makers who know how to make nets for hunting, fishing or fowling, and other servants. It would be too long to name them all.

46. That the stewards should take good care of our woods, which the people call *brogilos* [walled parks], and let them always repair them in good time, and not delay until it should be necessary to rebuild them entirely. Let them take similar care of every building.

47. That our hunters and falconers and other servants, who serve us zealously in the palace, should receive help in our villages, as we or the queen may command through our letters, when we send them forth for any errand, or when the seneschal and butler should command them to do anything on our behalf.

48. The wine presses on our estates should be kept ready for use, and let the stewards take care that no one dare crush our grape harvest with his feet, but everything should be clean and orderly.

49. That our women's workshops be well arranged, that is, their houses, heated rooms, and living rooms. Let them have good fences throughout and strong doors, in order that they may perform our work well.

50. That every steward should determine how many horses should remain in one stable and how many grooms should stay with the horses. And those grooms who are freemen and have benefices for their service should support themselves by their benefices; freemen too, who have farms [*mansas*] on our public property which feed them. Whoever does not have this, should be given support from the demesne.

51. Every steward should take care lest wicked men conceal our seed under the ground or elsewhere. This makes our harvest grow sparser. Similarly, they should beware of other wicked deeds, to make sure that they never happen.

52. We wish that serfs on the public lands or our own serfs or freemen who are settled on our properties or estates give full and complete justice, whatever is fitting to men [from other estates].

53. That every steward should see to it that the men of their territory in no wise become thiefs or criminals.

54. That every steward should see to it that our people work well at their tasks and do not go about wasting time at markets.

55. We wish that the stewards write in one document whatever income they have been given or provided or received in our service, and in another whatever they have spent. They should inform us by letter what is left over.

56. That every steward in his territory hold frequent hearings, dispense justice and see to it that our people live law abiding lives.

57. If any of our serfs should wish to inform us of anything which is to our interest concerning his master, he should not be prevented from coming to us. And if the steward knows that those under his charge wish to come to the palace to complain against him, then the steward should deliver to us at the palace arguments against them, why their complaint should not cause resentment in our ears. And thus we wish to know, whether the subordinates are coming from necessity or under pretense.

58. When our puppies are given to stewards to be raised, the steward should feed them at his own expense or commend them to his subordinates, that is, the mayors, deans or cellarers, in order that they should feed them from their own property, unless by our own order or that of the queen they are to be raised on our estate. Then the steward should send a man to feed them, and should set aside that from which they are to be fed. It will not be necessary for the man to go daily to the kennels.

59. Every steward, during the time that he is on service, should give each day three pounds of wax, and eight *sextaria* of soap. Furthermore, at the feast of St. Andrew [November 30], he should give six pounds of wax, wherever we may be with our people. He should give the same in mid-Lent.

60. Mayors should never be chosen from powerful men, but from those of moderate station who are faithful.

61. During the time the steward performs his service, he should have

his malt delivered to the palace. Similarly, let masters come who know how to make good beer there.

62. That every steward should make known to us yearly on Christmas, with everything arranged in the proper order, what we have received by way of income, so that we may learn what and how much we possess of all things; what land our plowmen work with their cattle; what holdings they ought to plow; what taxes, rents, judgment costs, fees, fines for taking animals in our forests without our permission, and payments for other reasons; what income from mills, forests, fields, bridges or ships; what payments from freemen and from hundreds who serve our fisc; what revenues from markets, vineyards and those who pay in wine; what revenue from hay, wood, torches, planks or other lumber; what from wastelands, vegetables, millet and panic, wool, linen or hemp, fruits of trees, large or small nuts and graftings of various trees, gardens, turnips, fish ponds, skins, furs, horns, honey and wax; what from mulberry wine, cooked wine, mead and vinegar; what from beer, new and old wine, new and old grain, chickens, eggs and geese; what from fishermen, smiths, shield makers or tailors; what from kneading troughs, boxes or cases; what from turners or saddlers; what from forges and mines, that is, iron diggings or other lead diggings; what from persons liable to tribute payments; what from colts and fillies.

63. Concerning the above mentioned things, it should not disturb our stewards if we make inquiry, for we wish that they in like fashion require all these things from their subordinates without causing resentment. And all things whatsoever that a man ought to have in his house or estates, our stewards should have on our estates.

64. That our carts which go to the army, that is, the war carts, be well constructed, and that their coverings be well made of skins. They should be so sewn together that, if it is necessary to cross water, they can go across the rivers with their provisions inside and no water can enter. It should be possible to cross, as we have said, with our provisions protected. We wish that flour be placed in each cart at our expense, that is, twelve *modia* of farina. In those carts which carry wine let them put twelve *modia* according to our measurement. And let them supply for each cart a shield, lance, quiver and bow.

65. That the fish from our ponds be sold and others put in their place, so that there will always be a supply of fish. However, when we do not visit the estates, then they should be sold and the stewards should make profit from them to our advantage.

66. Let the stewards give us an accounting of the male and female goats and of their horns and skins; and let them bring to us yearly newly salted meat of fat goats.

67. Concerning deserted farms and newly acquired slaves, the stewards should inform us if they have any surplus [of slaves] and cannot find a place for them.

68. We wish that all stewards have always ready good barrels bound with iron, which they can send to the army and to the palace. They should not make containers of skins.

69. They should at all times keep us informed concerning wolves, how many each one has caught, and they should send us the skins. In May, they should hunt wolf cubs and catch them, both with poison and with hooks, as well as with traps and dogs.

70. We wish that they should have in the garden all kinds of plants. . . .

Peasant Landholding

The following documents all deal with aspects of peasant life and their rights with respect to their lords during the heyday of the medieval manors in the eleventh, twelfth, and thirteenth centuries. In the manorial regime, lords gained economic benefits from the labor of a subservient peasantry. The peasants were assured their rights to land and protection. The more prosperous peasants possessed a household unit, known as a manse in French regions, which consisted of a house with a small garden, strips or blocks sown with grain in the large common fields, and rights to use other resources, such as woods, streams, and meadows. Beyond that basic component, each manor was organized differently and managed more or less closely, depending in good part on who or what (individual or ecclesiastical institution) the landlord was. In most areas, the manse system had disintegrated by the eleventh century.

The documents that follow detail various transactions. Some are gifts or other forms of transfer. Some are judicial or quasi-judicial in that they assert rights held by one party. Others are administrative records from manors. In these selections, most of the lands were in the hands of churchmen, which is largely why these records have survived. The first group of documents concern conditions of landholding. What sorts of services and products did landlords expect? The second set of texts presents evidence on the personal status and dependency of peasants. How were they treated? What sorts of changes produced an improvement in their status or conditions? The third group of documents describes the manorial stewards and the powers they had over peasants and even the sorts of frauds they might perpetrate against their employers. What were the relations of stewards to their lords? What tasks were stewards expected to do?

The final document is a survey of the manor of Broughton in Huntingdonshire, England, which belonged to Ramsey Abbey. The monks commissioned the survey in order to learn what their peasants owed them. Can you say something about the material conditions of the peasants from this survey? What did the monks expect from this manor? How do their expectations in the mid-thirteenth century compare with those of the king as seen in the "Carolingian Capitulary concerning Estates"?

CONDITIONS OF LANDHOLDING
(1096–1127)

May all the sons of the church at Mâcon, as well as all other faithful Christians, know that canon Etienne de Chaumont, in the presence of sire Bérard, bishop of Mâcon, and of his clerks, has given a *manse*[1] situated in the region of Lyons, in the parish of la Chapelle, which belongs to the regular canons of St Peter, and in the village of *Brutoria*, with its appurtenances. In this *manse* Guichard, a good peasant, lives, who owes service:

> at Easter, a lamb;
> at haymaking, six pieces of money;
> at harvest, a meal (with several associates) and a *setier* of oats;
> at the grape harvest, twelve deniers;
> at Christmas, twelve deniers, three loaves, and a half-*setier* of wine;
> at the beginning of Lent, a capon;
> at Mid-Lent, six pieces of money. . . .

Etienne has confirmed this charter and has had it confirmed. . . .

(1108–1139)

. . . Alard, called the Apostle, owned for many years a *manse* near the walls of the city of Mâcon, near the church of St John, in the peasant way and for an annual service, but by negligence he left the *manse* a wilderness open to animals, for he did not dig the vineyard nor cause it to be dug. Because of that Archdeacon Bernard from whom Alard held the *manse* became angered and addressed repeated and renewed reproaches to him and summoned him many times to render him his rights. Alard constantly refused to do so or to start working again, relying on vague replies, and holding to no account what Bernard said to him. Finally, through the good offices of Etienne Bourse and Pierre called Lemoine, agreeing of his own free will to what the archdeacon demanded, he claimed [a price] for giving up to the latter in peace all [that he had] in the manse.

The said Bernard, seeing the *manse* a wilderness and, further, wishing to establish something in favour of St Vincent for the profit of his soul, agreed and promised to give his acquiescence to this proposition. . . . Alard and his wife Grausa came [in the presence] of Sir Bernard the archdeacon and received from him four livres of deniers. They sold and granted all that they had and held in this *manse* and vineyard, they abandoned it in perpetuity and promised to maintain in peace this agreement. For her approval, the wife of Alard, Grausa, received five sous. . . .

(ca. 1160)

May all those who profess the Christian faith, present and future, know that Robert Barbarot has abandoned to Notre-Dame and to the monks of la Ferté, withholding nothing, all that he claimed, justly or unjustly, in the

---

[1]House and enough land to support one household.

land which Guichard Morel gave to the house of la Ferté at the time of his conversion. This land is cultivated by the Brutinanges of Laives who must give for it twenty sous of rent annually.

It shall be noted that they may not give this land as a dowry to the daughters, nor remove it in any manner from the right of la Ferté. They may cultivate it as long as they shall acquit the rent promptly. But if they do not wish to render the rent the land must revert to the house of la Ferté. If, by reason of this land, they suffer any wrong from their neighbours they must bring their case before the monks, exclusively.

For this, Robert has received four *bichets*[2] of wheat and two cheeses, and he has sworn on the altar of St Martin, Julien, chaplain of Sennecé holding his hand, to keep the peace firmly. His sons have sworn the same thing. . . .

In the name of God. The year of His birth 1103, the third of the nones[3] of February, the twelfth of the proclamation. I, Martin, priest, rector of the church and monastery of the Blessed Mary, in the name of this church and according to the terms of our agreement, have decided to give in order to have, hold and work them, to enjoy and to improve them, to thee, Rainier, son of Bonand, all the parcels, lands, vineyards and property of which thou, Rainier, hast made a charter of gift in favour of the church and monastery of the Blessed Mary, which is situated in Campisitoli. The said properties are situated at Casi and other places. Giving and confirming these properties entirely with all the buildings which shall be found thereon to thee, Rainier, and to thy heirs. Thou, Rainier, and thy heirs must give for these lands and goods to us and to the said church and monastery, each year in the octave of Christmas, to us or to our envoy by you or your envoy for rent or customary dues, four good and shining deniers in money of Lucca, a shoulder of mutton and two peacocks, nothing more, and four sous for the renewal. And if, the agreement being kept by you, I, the prior, or my successors, either through the person we shall send or by a deed we shall have made previously, should come to oppose thee Rainier, or thy heirs and descendants on account of these lands and properties, lessening them in movables or immovables, taking them back or wishing to impose more than what has been read above, we must then pay them back or wishing to impose more than what has been read above, we must then pay a fine of 20 sous in good Lucca deniers. And I, Rainier, declare that if I or my heirs and descendants, neglect to pay each year to the said church and monastery this fixed rent, as it has been read above,

[2]Measure of grain ranging in size from approximately twenty to forty liters in different regions.

[3]That is, 3 February. By the Roman calendar, *Nones* fell on the fifth day of the month, except in March, May, July, and October, when it fell on the seventh.

then we must pay to the church and monastery the said fine of twenty sous.

Quinto (Tuscany), May 1121

. . . Florent, son of the late Andrea Kyscio, and Martino Bastacaro, and Pietro, son of the late Guidolo de Runco, and Guidolo, son of the late Stefano, and Pietro de Rio and Giovanni de Colle, and Pietro and Florent, brothers, sons of the late Rustico, and Guiglielmo, son of the late Guinizo, and Guiducio de Gerrard, and Azolino, son of the late Pietro Giovanni, and Giovanni, son of the late Pietro Fucola, and Giovanni Brittoli, by the staff which they held in their hands, have invested Giovanni, priest and archpriest of the chapter of Santa Reparata and Benedetto abbot of San Miniato. If in some way they or their heirs wished to alienate the lands or the vineyards which they hold from the said churches and their rectors, they shall give them to one of those who also hold lands and vineyards from the churches and their rectors if they wish and are able to take them, for the same price that they would have been able to obtain elsewhere without falsehood. And if such men cannot or do not wish to take them, they shall give them to the church of Santa Reparata and San Miniato, in a similar way, for the same price that they would have been able to obtain elsewhere without falsehood. And if one of them gives these lands to another and does not keep to what is read above, he shall lose this land and everything which he holds from these churches with all the rights which belong to them, and he shall pay besides to these churches sixty sous in good deniers of Lucca.

The year 1181, 14th October. . . . Marro, son of the late Guifredo, and Poisia, spouse, living under the Lombard law (and I, Poisia, with the consent of my husband Marro), in the presence of Jacopo, judge and representative of the lord Emperor Frederick,[4] have together received from thee, the priest Uberto, in the name of lord Pietro, archpriest of Santa Maria di Monte Velate, eight livres in Milanese deniers for three pieces of land situated at Velate. The first is a vineyard and lies in the place called *a Croso* (in the morning, the land of Ambrogio, at noon, that of Lanfranco, son of Ugo de Pocheria, in the evening, the same, to the north, the road). The second is a field which is called *a Braria* (in the morning the land of Guiglielmo de Cosgiago, at noon and in the north, that of Botto Ramberto, of Velate, in the evening, the road). The third is a chestnut wood and lies in the place called *a Cassaria* (in the morning, the land of the heirs of Guidrado, at noon, that of the said Botto, to the north, the same, in the evening, that of Sant'

---

[4]Frederick I (called "Barbarossa"), Holy Roman Emperor, 1152–1190.

Ambrogio). We promise to defend these lands. If we cannot do so then we promise to pay you double as a fine. Given at Velate. . . .

Marro and Pisa, spouses, have undertaken to defend these said parcels and they have given as surety Bertaroto, son of the late Girardo Ramberto of Velate, who has made a perpetual recognizance of all his goods to the value of the double fine. . . . And immediately, the said priest Uberto has invested the said Marro hereditarily with the said parcels for an annual fixed rent, payable to the said church at the wine harvest of Velate, of a waggon of unfermented wine; and if there is not enough unfermented wine, he will give what he has and will replace with cash, in the measure of eight Milanese sous for a waggon of unfermented wine. If it should happen that the tenant does not pay the rent during the year, he shall lose the said parcels. And there, the said Marro has bestowed on his wife Posia a field at *Braria* (in the morning the land of Botto, in the evening the road) and his field at Pisori (in the morning the land of Botto, in the evening the road) and his field at Pisori (in the morning the land of the heirs of Lanfranco ser Girardo, in the evening that of Guifredo de Otino) and his wood of Crivi (in the morning and the evening the land of Santa Maria di Monte) and with his field of Traversiana (in the morning the land of the heirs of Viviano Garzolana, in the evening that of Guifredo de Otino) and the house in which he lives at Velate, for fifteen livres in Milanese deniers, which is her dowry. . . .

STATUS OF PEASANTS

(1144)

Louis,[5] by the grace of God, king of France and Acquitaine, to all and for ever. We make known to all, present and future, that we have granted to the church of the Holy Father at Chartres, Havissa daughter of Renaud de Dambron, wife of Gilon Lemaire, mayor of Germignonville, who was ours in servile status, and we have given her to be owned in person and perpetually, with all the fruit of her womb. The abbot and the monks of the said church have given us in exchange another woman of their *familia*, with the approval of Pierre Lemaire and Renaux de Rebrechien. . . .

(1153–1160)

Peter Boterel, to William, by the grace of God bishop of Norwich, to Goscelin, archdeacon, and to Earl Conan, his lord, greeting. Know ye that for the souls of my father, my mother, my ancestors, and for my own soul, I have given to the church of St Melaine at Rennes, Godwin, reeve of Net-

[5]Louis VII, king of France, 1137–1180.

tlestead (Suffolk), and his heirs, with all that they hold of me. I have given it in perpetual alms, free and quit of all service, exaction and custom and released from all charge towards me, that he may leave my authority except for the service of the King and the Earl. I grant that the said Godwin and his heirs continue to enjoy in my village of Nettlestead the same rights in the commons that they held previously, in the woods, plains, pastures, waters, roads, paths and in all places. Furthermore, I give to the same rights in the commons that they held previously, in the woods, plains, pastures, waters, roads, paths and in all places. Furthermore, I give to the same church 12 acres of my demesne . . . quit and free of everything due to me and to the King and the Earl. And if Godwin or one of his heirs is guilty of default for the service which he owes me, he shall be judged for this by the monks in the court of the said church. The same Godwin and his heirs shall not be forced by me or my bailiffs to go to the Hundred or the Shire,[6] but after having paid the customary tax they may remain in peace. Furthermore I desire the said Church to hold this gift from me and my heirs, freely and in peace, for ever. The witnesses are: Maxilde, my wife, who joins me in this gift and agrees to it; Adam the priest of the village . . . Godric of the fountain, William, son of Lifrum . . . and the whole village of Nettlestead. . . .

I, Frederick, second of the name, by the grace of God archbishop of Cologne, wish to uphold by the authority which God has given us the excellent intention . . . of the servant of God Adelaide, abbess of the church of the Blessed Mary in Capitol at Cologne. . . . Formerly the said church rejoiced in very great possessions, but today, because of the evil times and the negligence of the officials, some of the manors have almost fallen in ruins and devastation. Amongst these, Efferen and Fischenich would have gone to ruin and certain abandon if they had not received help from the said abbess and a better statute. The male and female dependents attached to these manors, who paid the entire rent, that is ten deniers of annual *chevage*,[7] fled because of this excessive charge, and they became so few and so poor that the fixed rents of the church could not be levied in these manors and from this *familia*. The dependants having become too few on each demesne, the tenants who cultivated the *manses* there were forced in conformity with the rights of the advocate and the abbess to pay all the fixed rents of the church with their own dues. They decided to flee and to abandon their *manses*. Thus the injury to the church was double: on the dependent men and on the *manses*.

Before such a grave and injurious wrong Adelaide, the servant of God, on the counsel of the sisters and brothers of the same church, and also of

---

[6]Administrative divisions in Anglo-Saxon England kept after 1066 by the Normans.
[7]Head tax.

Guillaume, the illustrious count of Juliers, and of the priors of Cologne, provosts as well as abbots, caused a return to their ancient status and profit in the following manner. To all dependants of each manor who formerly paid the entire rent, that is, ten deniers of *chevage*, she gave the right to be *censuales*,[8] and to pay henceforth two deniers each per year. On the death of the man, the steward of the manor shall take the best of his animals, and if he has none, the best of his clothes and six deniers; the same on the death of the wife, the *Schultheiss*[9] of the manor shall take her best garment and six deniers. For permission to marry, the man, like the woman shall pay six deniers.

In exchange for this improvement of their condition, the dependants attached to the said manor have sworn to help with their own labour and with their property the said servant of God to restore the manor of Efferen, in buildings as much as in agricultural work and in the firm establishment of her right: in such manner that each year this manor shall deliver eight marks of silver, thirty *muids*[10] of wheat and seven *muids* of barley, for the maintenance of the sisters and brothers, and by the manor of Fischenich fifteens sous. Each hall shall receive complete equipment both in animals and tools and other necessities, according to the evidence given under oath by the *familia* of the hall. Furthermore so that the said manor of Fischenich can serve to the full, the abbess will allocate each year for purchases one mark of her own revenues.

Given in the year of the birth of Our Lord 1158. . . .

MANORIAL STEWARDS
(1113–1129)

I, Guillaume, abbot of St Père at Chartres, make known that I grant to Geoffroy d'Arrou the mayoralty of the land of Bois-Ruffin, which the lord Urson has given us in alms, and that I have invested him with this mayoralty in our chapter on the following conditions. I have bestowed on him in a suitable place on this same land, a piece of land for a plough, on condition however that he renders the half of the share of the crops (*terrage*) from the produce of this plough to the lord Urson. He shall have his profits and his rights (*droitures*) on this land, on condition, however, that his rights never exceed twenty deniers. He shall introduce before the monk who shall be appointed to this land all the pleas and the discussions of cases, and all the pleas shall be prorogued or remitted, discussed or terminated at the will of the monk and by his decision, save in all things his rights. As soon as the monk shall have established a house there, the pleas

---

[8]Subject to a rent (*census*).

[9]Manager or mayor of a manor.

[10]Measure of grain equal to a large barrel or hogshead.

shall be held on the land; while waiting, at Arrou. If Geoffroy believes that the provost of the monks' land tries to annul pleas through over long delays, he may complain to the prior of Brou or to the lord abbot, and be recompensed by them. Should he have a wood on the land, he shall, as much for himself as for his men of Arrou, have the use of the wood only for the house, and the free pasture for his pigs but without pannage. If, while he has the wood, he takes a wild goat, fox, wild cat or a hive of bees in the trees, they shall be his; if it is one of the settlers who takes them, he shall have a half. If one of the settlers conceals any one of the animals which have been caught, and if Geoffroy can seize any of them and prove it, he shall take it and confiscate it, without a fine.

According to these covenants, I, Guillaume, abbot have invested Geoffroy d'Arrou with the mayoralty of Bois-Ruffin; as for him, he has paid homage to me and lawful faith due to all our chapter. To be noted that Geoffroy shall have on this same land the steward whom he desires. For all offences that Geoffroy's steward shall commit, and after three summonses, if he does not pay the fine, the steward shall be removed from his office. . . .

(1103)

In the name of the Holy and undivided Trinity, may all know, present and future, that Duran, provost of Berzé, has given all his free holding and abandoned all the fief with all the lands which he has into the hand of the lord Hugues, abbot, and into our hands, to wit Josseran, Dom Seguin, Serge, Humbert the dean, and other brothers of ours, under the testimony also of these laymen, Guichard Nasu, Hugues de Meulin, Artaud de la Bruyère, Humbert, nephew of another Humbert, provost, Robert le Chauve, Guillaume, servant of Hardi, and many others. He has thus had to give up his possessions and our fief because he has not been able to deny that he and his relations have committed usurpations in divers things. But the lord abbot, wishing to remain within bounds, chooses to keep in demesne a *manse* with all the lands which depend on it and which Duran held because of this *manse*, that is, vineyards, fields and meadows. Furthermore he has held that land which was once belonging to the cook of Viscount Guigues, with a curtilage in another village, on which Hugues de Meulin had attempted to make a claim, although unjustly. Together with this all the meals which are due from the peasants for the wine harvest, with one measure of unfermented wine for each cutting, which measure is called *brazaige*. These things are transferred into our demesne rights in such a way that Duran has no subsequent claim there, nor anyone else on his behalf. Nevertheless, as long as he shall remain faithful to us, to him has been remitted, not as his due but by grace, half the income of all the rest, be it free holding or be it fief, and of all the resources which he claimed, be it in free holding, or be it in fief, for his, and which he assigns to himself. This share was given out of mercy to him who has lost all by the verdict of the law. But being said that it is on his behalf rather than on ours that are assigned all the goods which he had alienated of his possessions or of ours, and which he pledged to others. Taking for himself all the ill assured things, he left to us in our share the safest, until he had established the whole in an untroubled state. On each of the *manses* which Robert and Guigue held in their demesne when they gave them to us, had been granted to Duran two loaves with a *setier*[11] of wine, and for four deniers of meat. And, the measure of mercy being filled to overflowing, in order that all occasion for recrimination or recantation should be removed, he has been given sixty sous by the dean of the said obedientiary of Berzé. The same Duran, with his sons, has taken an oath and has sworn on the holy altar in the tower that he would in good faith keep this agreement inviolate; if he violates it, within fourteen days after the dean's complaint he shall restore what he has taken, or else he shall go on bail where he shall be told and shall not leave. . . .

(1096–1127)

Plea between the canons of Mâcon and Landry de Monceau on the subject of the wood of Chevignes and the assarts of this wood which is an allod of St Vincent.

The canons have granted to Landry the care of the wood on condition that henceforth it shall not be cleared neither to make a meadow nor to make arable. But when the wood contains acorns, Landry will faithfully perform his service in order that neither he nor any other harvests them until the canons give the order to introduce their pigs to eat the acorns; at this moment Landry shall introduce his herd. It has been agreed also here and there (the neighbours having, under pain of excommunication, borne witness that it was thus from ancient times) that the canons may take what they like in the wood for the use of the kitchen or refectory or for the work of their cloister. And the obedientiary of St Clement shall take in the same wood what he wishes for the work which he shall desire to do in the parish of St Clement. Similarly Landry shall take in this wood for the use of his own house and to make his *manses*; but he shall keep watch that, apart from the parishioners of St Clement, no man shall have access to the wood. He shall have for the guardianship one denier a year from each of the houses of the said parishioners having access to the wood. It has been decided on the subject of the meadow that Landry has made next to the wood that, each year, the hay being made, Laudry shall pay the *none*[12] to the canons, that he shall not protect the meadow save against the depreda-

---

[11] Unit of liquid measure of approximately one pint.

[12] A second tithe; the first was a tenth, so the second was a ninth (*none*).

tions of the swine, until the other meadows which are in the neighbour-
hood are also protected. From the crops of the other assarts which he has
or which others have for him, he shall render all the tithes and half the
nones to the canons. In exchange for this benefaction, granted to him by the
canons, Landry has paid homage and sworn fidelity to Sir Artaud, dean,
and it is included in the agreement that whoever of his successors shall
hold this benefaction from the canons shall pay homage and swear fidelity
to the dean of the church of Mâcon. Given with the assent of the whole of
the chapter, in the presence of Sir Béraud, venerable bishop. . . .

(27th May 1176)

I, Conrad, abbot of the church of Corvey, to all my successors in perpetuity. . . .

A certain Bruno, official of our church, who has received the "hall" of
Haversford in the capacity of *Schultheiss* with the agreement and consent of
our dear brother Henry, then prior and guardian, having died, Bernard,
his son, having obtained the grant of the said "hall" as a result of prayers,
with the agreement and consent of the said brother Henry, prior and
guardian, the same prior Henry requested that, by a deed established to
us, we should take measures henceforth to ensure, in order that the rights
of the guardian should not suffer prejudice, that this "hall" should be administered by knights, for these kind of men are rarely satisfied with what
they have, and have the habit of appropriating more than is granted to
them. Herenfrid, in fact, father of the said Bruno, had been the first of the
knightly condition to administer this "hall," which up till then had always
been administered by peasants. Which is why, in consideration of this request, pious and full of love towards St Vit, and for the sake also of our
patron himself, for the possessions of his altar must be defended like the
apple of our eye, we recognize, decide and decree that the whole village of
Haversford with all its possessions, its dependencies and its limits and
with all that is attached to it, that is the houses and other buildings, lands,
meadows, woods, fields, waters, cultivated and waste places, must be
within the *ban* of the guardian: to him are owed all the revenues of the
village, the fixed rent of the village, the fixed rent of the "hall," the fixed
rent of the *manses*, the inheritance of deceased men, the rent of the *lites*,[13]
the marriage of the girls, which is commonly called *beddemunt*. The revenues also of the adjacent forest (which is commonly called *sundere*), as well
as the dependencies of the village, belong to the guardian, although we
have sometimes put our pigs to fatten in this village, what we have done is by
grace of this same guardian. It is the guardian who, every time that it is
necessary, shall judge with the *lites* concerning the village affairs since it is

---

[13]Dependent peasants.

free of jurisdiction of the advocate. It is evident, then, from all this that the *villicus*[14] of the "hall" may not have any power over the *lites* and that he may not levy on them by prayers, any manorial right, he can only levy the profits of the "hall" which is leased to him, but all the rest . . . remains in the hands of the guardian. . . .

SURVEY OF BROUGHTON MANOR
(1252)

The custom of the village is estimated at 2½ ploughs per year.

These are the names of the meadows belonging to the manor. . . .

And if the abbot's demesne is sown in some part of these meadows, the said meadows may be prohibited; after the cutting and carrying of the hay nobody has the usage of these meadows with the lord, save 4 akermen who will have the right of pasture for 4 beasts with those of the master.

A wood belongs to the said manor, called Broughton wood; one part belongs to Little Raveley; all the men of Broughton and Little Raveley, free as well as villein[15] have common usage in this wood for their cattle, save goats and swine in the prohibited time; outside this wood on the Ripton side a green place remains in the demesne for reserved pasture. Nobody may take green or dry in this wood without permission.

In the marshes of Ramsey, Warboys and Wistow, the abbot may, because of his manor at Broughton, take peat, cut hay and graze his cattle at his pleasure, and give his men permission to cut hay and to graze. Freemen and villeins, however, give the manor of Warboys one goose per load for permission to enter the marshes.

The manor may keep two bulls, 20 cows with their progeny, 200 sheep, 100 pigs and 3 boars.

The sheep of cottars[16] and strangers must be folded for the manure of the demesne land and not elsewhere. . . .

. . . In the village of Broughton there are 7 hides and half a virgate of land outside the abbot's demesne which are held by freemen and villeins.

6½ virgates make a hide and 32 acres make a virgate.

Ralf de Broughton holds a quarter of a virgate for which he does homage to the abbot and follows the court of Broughton, and he gives 12d. per annum and ploughs 2 roods per year. He gives hidage[17] each time that service of the lord king is claimed from the abbey, pontage, sheriff's aid, and wodehac.[18] He holds also a portion of land which belonged to Mat-

[14]The steward.

[15]A peasant tied to the manor.

[16]Peasants who occupied cottages and labored on the lord's demesne.

[17]Tax due the royal treasury on each hide of land.

[18]An obligation for cutting wood.

thew, son of Nicolas, for which he gives 2d. to the lord abbot. This rent and the lordship of this land was brought by the lord abbot of Ramsey from the said Matthew. At the first autumn boon-work[19] he comes with two men. . . .

. . . Thomas, son of Henry, holds one virgate of land for which he gives 12d., six on St Andrew's Day, and 6 on St Benedict's Day; for the sherriff's aid 2d. at Martinmas and 2d. on the Nativity of St John the Baptist; he makes one measure of malt or gives 6d. at the lord's will, to wit 2 at martinmas, 2 at the Annunciation of the Blessed Virgin, and 2 on the Nativity of St John the Baptist. He shall give after Christmas one bushel of oats for foddercorn, at Christmas a hen and at Easter 10 eggs. He gives tallage, merchet, leyrwit, gersum, heriot, the view of frankpledge, hidage, pontage and wodehac, and also pannage,[20] to wit 2d. for a pig per year, one penny for a six-month-old pig, a half-penny for a three-month-old pig, and he does it at the acorn harvest whether he sends them to the wood or not. After Michaelmas he may not sell his pig without having paid pannage. At the view of the frankpledge he gives a halfpenny of custom. He does the same thing for each male child of 12 years old who is in his keeping.

He shall mow rushes in the marsh at Warboys when it shall be required of him, 40 good sheaves in the view of the bailliff, the reeve and others for the day's task, but shall not cart them. For a task he shall mow, bind and carry 20 sheaves. And if the lord causes rushes to be mown for a task, he shall take a good cartload with 2 horses for two days task.

From Michaelmas until August he shall work three days a week, Monday, Tuesday and Wednesday; Friday he shall plough with all the beasts which he has in his plough half an acre, save at Christmas and Easter. If he must dig in the "hall," dig a ditch, make a wall, cover or spread manure, he shall work from morning until evening. If he must dig a ditch outside the "hall," he shall in open country do a perch of 16½ feet long with a depth of 2 "spadegraff" and a width of three feet. For putting old ditches in order he shall do two perches of the same length and width for a task. When he must thresh, he shall thresh 24 sheaves of wheat; 30 of barley, oats, beans and peas. He shall gather in Broughton wood 2 faggots of thorn or a faggot of sticks which he shall bring to the "hall" for a task. In Wistow wood one faggot only for a task. He shall make an enclosure all day either inside or outside the "hall." In winter cultivation he shall harrow all day without stopping. In Lent, he shall harrow but with a halt for dinner but shall come back quickly afterwards. If he must cut or weed, he shall work all day. Each time that he mows in the village of Broughton he shall have a sheaf of hay in the evening, as much as he can lift on the handle of his scythe when it does

---

[19]A day's ploughing done without compensation.

[20]Various payments and services due from peasants to landlords for different occasions or purposes.

not touch the ground; if it breaks or falls to the ground he shall lose the grass. The day when he shall mow the meadow at Houghton he shall with his companion have 18d. from the abbot's purse, according to custom, and one of the best cheeses in the "hall" and a bowl of salt.

He shall make journeys in the hundred when he receives the order to do so, he shall do so alone for Elsworth; for Ellington, he and two other virgaters shall provide the horse. If it is for London, Shillington or other distant places, he and five virgaters shall make the journey with a horse, and they shall be free of all task until their return. And the load shall be a "ringa" of wheat, barley or oats.

At each ploughing boon-work he shall come with his plough if he has a whole plough or if he is associated with another; and in that way each week he shall plough on the land of the master one day as on his own land. If the ploughing is put off because of bad weather or other reasonable cause he shall come the following week at the demand of the steward.

Every week from August to Michaelmas he shall work every day, except Saturday, from morning to night wherever the master wishes to assign him work for the task. At all the autumn boon-works he himself or his wife shall come, with all the manpower at his disposal; if he has less than three labourers one only shall work; if he has more he shall bring his labourers, but not his wife; if he is ill his wife shall stay at home to look after him, but he shall send all his labourers to the boon-work. At the first boon-work he shall have with his companion two loaves, one of which shall suffice for two; if bread is bought, he and his companion shall have a loaf worth three farthings; barley beer, soup, fresh or salt meat and a slice of cheese. At the second, fish. At the third, meat. At the fourth, if it should be necessary, fish. And at each boon-work he shall have bread, barley beer, soup and cheese, as at the first. The day after each boon-work, he shall provide two labourers whom he shall feed, for the days of boon-work are not counted as tasks.

He shall convoy a cart of corn when he shall receive the order, and this shall not be counted as a task. He shall convoy two carts of corn or straw for a day's task; he shall mow and gather straw all day.

If he wishes to sell a horse, an ox or a colt, he shall inform the bailiff so that the lord can exercise his right of pre-emption.

Every time he shall be ill, he shall be quit of all task, save the ploughing. And if his illness lasts a year and a day, he shall be quit during all this time of every task, save ploughing. After a year and a day he shall not be exempted of task for any illness.

If his wife survives him she shall give 5s. for heriot for which she shall be quit during 30 days of all task.

The lord may put all the tasks to rent if he wishes. They are valued in winter and in summer at one penny per day, and in autumn at 2d. save for the work which is put to task and which is valued at a halfpenny a day.

He shall gather a faggot of sticks in Warboys and Wistow woods or St Ives wood and shall carry them to St Ives, and shall make a trellis or a hurdle for a task; another day he shall make there another work which shall not be allowed for him as a task. He shall provide a man to mount guard for one night for a task. The day of his wedding the servants of the "hall" shall receive bread, barley beer and meat according to his honour and his competence.

And if he becomes reeve,[21] he shall have for two horses, 4 oxen and 2 cows, if he possesses them, the right of pasture with the beasts of the master, and he shall be quit of all task in exchange for his office for as long as he shall hold the reeveship. And he shall be fed at the "hall" in the autumn. . . .

The Memoirs of Abbot Guibert of Nogent

Guibert (ca. 1064–ca. 1125) was from a minor noble family that furnished vassals to the counts of Clermont in Picardy (northern France). As abbot of the small monastery of Nogent, Guibert was able to exercise his literary talents. He wrote a treatise on relics and an account of the First Crusade, but he is best known for his memoirs, a combination of personal reminiscences and a chronicle of events during his lifetime. The following text contains evidence of three notable developments.

The first section is Guibert's record of the local implications of the campaign by Church reformers in the eleventh century to abolish clerical marriage and make celibacy the rule for all priests. Guibert's unscrupulous cousin tried to use the new rules to force a married cleric out of office and secure the position for Guibert, showing that more was at stake in these reforms than religious motivations. What does Guibert think of this married priest?

Guibert also writes about his mother, a devout lady, who raised him (his father died when Guibert was eight months old). What does his account of her marriage reveal about the fate of noble women in this period? Why was his parents' sexual life so difficult?

The third and longest section concerns the revolt in the town of Laon in 1112. Guibert's account is one of the best sources for the beginnings of urban life and the formation of the commune, a type of economic and political association by which townspeople sought to protect themselves and their economic interests from the demands of town lords, especially ecclesiastical lords. How does Guibert, as a noble by birth and a monk by vocation, view the aspirations and actions of urban lay people? How were the bishop and the nobles treating the folk of the town? Why did the townspeople resist the

[21]Steward of the manor.

bishop and the nobles? What sorts of activities and interests did the townspeople not share with their nominal rulers?

At length my mother tried by every means to get me into a church living. Now, the first opportunity for placing me was not only badly but abominably chosen. My adolescent brother, a knight and defender of the castle of Clermont (which, I should say, is situated between Compiègne and Beauvais), was expecting some money from the lord of that stronghold, either as largess or as a moneyfief,[1] I do not know which.[2] And when he deferred payment, probably through want of ready money, by the advice of some of my kinsmen it was suggested to him that he should give me a canonry, called a prebend, in the church of that place (which, contrary to canon law, was subject to his authority) and that he should then cease to be troubled for what he owed.

At that time the Apostolic See was making a fresh attack on married priests; this led to an outburst of rage against them by people who were so zealous about the clergy that they angrily demanded that married priests should either be deprived of their benefices or should cease to perform their priestly duties.[3] Thereupon a certain nephew of my father, a man conspicuous for his power and knowledge but so bestial in his debauchery that he had no respect for any woman's conjugal ties, now violently inveighed against the clergy because of this canon, as if exceptional purity of heart drove him to horror of such practices. A layman himself, he refused to be bound by a layman's laws, their very laxity making his abuse of them more shameful. The marriage net could not hold him; he never allowed himself to be entangled in its folds. Being everywhere in the worst odor through such conduct, but protected by the rank which his worldly power gave him, he was never prevented by the reproach of his own unchastity from thundering persistently against the holy clergy.

Having found a pretext by which I might profit at the expense of a priest with a benefice, he begged the lord of the castle, with whom, as one of his intimates, he had more than sufficient influence, to summon me and invest me with that canonry,[4] on the ground that the cleric was an absentee and utterly unsuitable for the office. For, contrary to all ecclesiastical law

[1]As largess, the money would be a gift; as fief, it would be given only in return for a vassal's oath of fealty (loyalty).

[2]The lord of Clermont-en-Beauvaisis was Renaud I, who fought at the battle of Mortemer in 1054 and was still alive in 1084. Guibert refers to his brother as *municeps*, an ambiguous word which probably means that he was one of the nobles of the castle. (Original editor's note.)

[3]Probably a reference to the disturbances which followed the program Gregory VII began in 1074 to suppress clerical marriage north of the Alps. (Original editor's note.)

[4]A benefice as a canon—a monk attached to the cathedral.

and right, he held the office of abbot by permission of the bishop, and, not being under rule himself, he demanded obedience to rule from those who were.[5] At this time not only was it treated as a serious offense for the members of the higher orders[6] and the canons to be married, but it was also considered a crime to purchase ecclesiastical offices involving pastoral care, such as prebends[7] and the offices of precentor,[8] provost,[9] etc., not to speak of the higher dignities. Consequently, those who were empowered to transact the affairs of the church, those who favored the side of the cleric who had lost his prebend, and many of my contemporaries began to stir up a whispering campaign about simony and excommunication, which recently the cleric had talked of publicly.

Now, married priest as he was, although he would not be separated from his wife by the suspension of his office, at least he had given up celebrating mass. Because he treated the divine mysteries as of less importance than his own body, he was rightly caught in that punishment which he thought to escape by the renunciation of the Sacrifice. And so, being stripped of his canonry, because there was no longer anything to restrain him, he now began freely to celebrate mass, while keeping his wife. Then a rumor grew that at this service he was daily repeating the excommunication of my mother and her family. My mother, always fearful in religious matters, dreading the punishment of her sins and therefore the giving of offense, thereupon surrendered the prebend which had been wickedly granted, and, in the expectation of some cleric's death, bargained with the lord of the castle for another for me. Thus "we flee from weapons of iron and fall before a bow of brass,"[10] for to grant something in anticipation of another's death is nothing else than a daily incentive to murder. . . .

After these lengthy accounts I return to Thee, my God, to speak of the conversion of that good woman, my mother. When hardly of marriageable age, she was given to my father, a mere youth, by the provision of my grandfather, since she was of the nobility, had a very pretty face, and was naturally and most becomingly of sober mein. She had, however, conceived a fear of God's name at the very beginning of her childhood. She had learned to be terrified of sin, not from experience but from dread of some sort of blow from on high, and—as she often told me herself—this dread had so possessed her mind with the terror of sudden death that in

---

[5]That is, with the authorization of the bishop of Beauvais the lord of Clermont had the right of presentation and oversight over the canons of the church in his castle. (Original editor's note.)

[6]Priest, deacon, and subdeacon. (Original editor's note.)

[7]A stipend granted to a priest of the cathedral.

[8]Director of the cathedral choir.

[9]Highest official among the cathedral clergy.

[10]Job 20:24.

later years she grieved because she no longer felt in her maturity the same stings of righteous fear as she had in her unformed and ignorant youth.

Now, it so happened that at the very beginning of that lawful union conjugal intercourse was made ineffective through the bewitchments of certain persons. It was said that their marriage drew upon them the envy of a stepmother, who had some nieces of great beauty and nobility and who was plotting to slip one of them into my father's bed. Meeting with no success in her designs, she is said to have used magical arts to prevent entirely the consummation of the marriage. His wife's virginity thus remained intact for three years, during which he endured his great misfortune in silence; at last, driven to it by those close to him, my father was the first to reveal the facts. In all sorts of ways, his kinsmen endeavored to bring about a divorce, and by their constant pressure upon my father, who was then young and dull-witted, they tried to induce him to become a monk, although at that time there was little talk of this order. They did not do this for his soul's good, however, but with the purpose of getting possession of his property.

When their suggestion produced no effect, they began to hound the girl herself, far away as she was from her kinsfolk and harrased by the violence of strangers, into voluntary flight out of sheer exhaustion under their insults, and without waiting for divorce. She endured all this, bearing with calmness the abuse that was aimed at her, and if out of this rose any strife, she pretended ignorance of it. Besides this, certain rich men, perceiving that she was not in fact a wife, began to assail the heart of the young girl; but Thou, O Lord, the builder of inward chastity, didst inspire her with purity stronger than her nature or her youth. . . .The desire of my mother, Thy servant, O Lord God, was to do nothing to hurt her worldly honor, yet following Thy Gregory,[11] whom, however, she had never read or heard read, she did not maintain that desire, for afterward she surrendered all her desires into Thy sole keeping. It was therefore good for her at that time to be attached to her worldly reputation.

Since the bewitchment by which the bond of natural and lawful intercourse was broken lasted seven years and more, it is all too easy to believe that, just as by prestidigitation the faculty of sight may be deceived so that conjurers seem to produce something out of nothing, so to speak, and to make certain things out of others, so reproductive power and effort may be inhibited by much less art; and indeed it is now a common practice, understood even by ignorant people. When that bewitchment was broken by a certain old woman, my mother submitted to the duties of a wife as faithfully as she had kept her virginity when she was assailed by so many attacks. In other ways she was truly fortunate, but she laid herself open not so much to endless misery as to mourning when she, whose goodness was

---

[11]Gregory I (called "the Great"), bishop of Rome, 590–604.

ever growing, gave birth to an evil son who (in my own person) grew worse and worse. Yet Thou knowest, Almighty One, with what purity and holiness in obedience to Thee she raised me, how greatly she provided me with the care of nurses in infancy and of masters and teachers in boyhood, with no lack even of fine clothes for my little body, so that I seemed to equal the sons of kings and counts in indulgence. . . .

Some time after the bishop[12] had set out for England to extract money from the English king,[13] whom he had served and who had been his friend, the archdeacons[14] Gautier and Guy and the nobles of the city devised the following plan. Since ancient times it had been the misfortune of the city of Laon that neither God nor any lord was feared there, but, according to each man's power and desire, the public authority was involved in rapine and murder. To begin with the source of the plague, whenever the king,[15] who ought to have exacted respect for himself with royal severity, happened to visit the city, he was himself first shamefully fined on his own property. When his horses were led out to water in the morning or evening, his grooms were beaten and the horses seized.[16] Also, it was known that the clergy themselves were held in such contempt that neither their persons nor their goods were spared, but the situation then followed the text "As it is with the people, so with the priest."[17] What then shall I say about the lower classes? None of the peasants came into the city (no one who did not have the best guaranteed safe-conduct even approached it) who was not thrown into prison and held for ransom, or, if the opportunity occurred, was not drawn into some lawless lawsuit.

As an example, let me adduce one practice which would be judged as the greatest violation of good faith if it occurred among the barbarians or Scythians, people who have no laws. On Saturdays when the countrypeople from different parts came there to buy and sell, the burghers carried round for sale vegetables, wheat, or other produce in cups and platters or other kinds of measures. When they had offered them for sale in the market place to the peasants seeking such things and the purchaser had settled on a price and agreed to buy, the merchant said, "Follow me to my house

---

[12]Gaudry, chancellor to Henry I of England before becoming bishop of Laon in 1106.

[13]Henry I, king of England, 1100–1135.

[14]Cathedral officials in charge of lands and money.

[15]Louis VI, king of France, 1108–1137.

[16]Since Laon was a *royal city* and the king had the right of compulsory lodging there . . . , Guibert's statement that the king had to pay a "fine" and that his horses were seized is probably distorted reporting of some more comprehensible practice. Herman of Laon states that when the king of France was crowned at Laon at the major festivals, he carried a gold crown to the church of Saint-Jean, and that the king and anyone else was required to leave his horses outside the walls of the abbey. . . . (Original editor's note.)

[17]Isaiah 24:2.

to see there the rest of the produce which I am selling you, and to take away what you have seen." The buyer would follow, but when he came to the bin, the honest seller would raise the lid and hold it up, saying, "Bend your head and shoulders over the bin to see that the rest does not differ from the sample which I showed you in the market place." And when the buyer got up on the edge of the bin and leaned his belly over it, the worthy seller standing behind lifted up his feet and pushed the unwary man into the bin, and, putting the lid down on him as he fell, kept him in a safe prison until he ransomed himself. These things and others like them were done in the city. The leaders and their servants openly committed theft and even armed robbery. No one was safe going out at night, for he would surely be either robbed or captured or killed.

The clergy and the archdeacons and the nobles, taking account of these conditions and looking out for ways of exacting money from the people, offered them through their agents the opportunity to have authorization to create a commune, if they would offer an appropriate sum of money. Now, "commune" is a new and evil name for an arrangement for them all to pay the customary head tax, which they owe their lords as a servile due, in a lump sum once a year, and if anyone commits a crime, he shall pay a fine set by law, and all other financial exactions which are customarily imposed on serfs are completely abolished. Seizing on this opportunity for commuting their dues, the people gathered huge sums of money to fill the gaping purses of so many greedy men. Pleased with the shower of income poured upon them, those men established their good faith by proffering oaths that they would keep their word in this matter.

After this sworn association of mutual aid among the clergy, nobles, and people had been established, the bishop returned with much wealth from England. Angered at those responsible for this innovation, for a long time he kept away from the city. But at last a quarrel full of honor and glory began between him and Gautier the archdeacon, his accomplice. The archdeacon made very unbecoming remarks about his bishop concerning the death of Gérard.[18] I do not know what the bishop did with others on this matter, but I do know that he complained to me about Gautier, saying, "Lord abbot, if Gautier should happen to bring up any charges against me at some council, would you take it without offense? At the time when you left your monks and retired to Fly, didn't he openly flatter you but secretly raise up discord against you, publicly taking your side but privately stirring me up against you?" Talking like this, he inveigled me to oppose that dangerous man, conscious of the very great weight of the charges against him, and fearful and suspicious of universal condemnation.

Although he said that he was moved by relentless wrath against those

---

[18]Gérard of Quierzy, guardian of the Benedictine convent of Saint-Jean of Laon, murdered in church by the bishop's people.

who had sworn an oath to the association and those who were the principals in the transaction, in the end his high-sounding words were suddenly quieted by the offer of a great heap of silver and gold. Then he swore that he would maintain the rights of the commune, following the terms of the charters of the city of Noyon and the town of Saint-Quentin. The king, too, was induced to confirm the same thing by oath with a bribe from the people.

O my God, who can describe the controversy that broke out when, after accepting so many gifts from the people, they then took oaths to overturn what they had sworn; that is, when they tried to return the serfs to their former condition after once freeing them from the yoke of their exactions? The hatred of the bishop and the nobles for the burghers was indeed implacable, and as he was not strong enough to crush the freedom of the French, following the fashion of Normandy and England, the pastor remained inactive, forgetful of his sacred calling through his insatiable greed. Whenever one of the people was brought into a court of law, he was judged not on his condition in the eyes of God but, if I may put it this way, on his bargaining power, and he was drained of his substance to the last penny.

Since the taking of gifts is commonly attended by the subversion of all justice, the coiners of the currency, knowing that if they did wrong in their office they could save themselves by paying money, corrupted the coinage with so much base metal that because of this many people were reduced to poverty. As they made their coins of the cheapest bronze, which in a moment by certain dishonest practices they made brighter than silver, the attention of the foolish people was shamefully deceived, and, giving up their goods of great or little value, they got in exchange nothing but the most debased dross. The lord bishop's acceptance of this practice was well rewarded, and thus not only within the diocese of Laon but in all directions the ruin of many was hastened. When he was deservedly powerless to uphold or improve the value of his own currency, which he had wickedly debased, he instituted halfpence of Amiens, also very debased, to be current in the city for some time. And when he could by no means keep them going, he struck a contemporary impression on which he had stamped a pastoral staff to represent himself. This was received with such secret laughter and scorn that it had even less value than the debased coinage. . . .

And so, seeing that masters and subjects were by act and will partners in wickedness, God could no longer restrain his judgment and at last permitted the malice that had been conceived to break out into open rage. When one is driven headlong by pride, through the vengeance of God he is completely shattered by a dreadful fall.

Calling together the nobles and certain of the clergy in the last days of Lent in the most holy Passiontide of Our Lord, the bishop determined to attack the commune, to which he had sworn and had with presents induced the king to swear. He had summoned the king to that pious duty, and on the day before Good Friday—that is, on Maundy Thursday—he instructed the king and all his people to break their oaths, after first placing his own neck in that noose.[19] As I said before, this was the day on which his predecessor Bishop Ascelin had betrayed his king. On the very day when he should have performed that most glorious of all episcopal duties, the consecration of the oil and the absolution of the people from their sins, he was not even seen to enter the church. He was intriguing with the king's courtiers so that after the sworn association was destroyed the king would restore the laws of the city to their former state. But the burghers, fearing their overthrow, promised the king and his courtiers four hundred pounds, and possibly more. In reply, the bishop begged the nobles to go with him to interview the king, and they promised on their part seven hundred pounds. King Louis, Philippe's son,[20] was a remarkable person who seemed well-suited for royal majesty, mighty in arms, intolerant toward sloth in business, of dauntless courage in adversity; although in other respects he was a good man, in this matter he was most unjust and paid too much attention to worthless persons debased by greed. This redounded to his own great loss and blame and the ruin of many, which certainly happened here and elsewhere.

When the king's desire was turned, as I said, toward the larger promise and he ruled against God, the oaths of the bishop and the nobles were voided without any regard for honor or the sacred season. Because of the turmoil with which he had so unjustly struck the people, that night the king was afraid to sleep outside the bishop's palace, although he had the right to compulsory lodging elsewhere. Very early the next morning the king departed, and the bishop promised the nobles they need have no fear about the agreement to pay so much money, informing them that he would himself pay whatever they had promised. "And if I do not fulfill my promise," he said, "hand me over to the king's prison until I pay it off."

After the bonds of the association were broken, such rage, such amazement seized the burghers that all the craftsmen abandoned their jobs, and the stalls of the tanners and cobblers were closed and nothing was exposed for sale by the innkeepers and chapmen, who expected to have nothing left when the lords began plundering. For at once the property of such individuals was calculated by the bishop and nobles, and the amount any man was known to have given to establish the commune was demanded of him to pay for its annulment. . . .

On Holy Saturday, when they should have been preparing to receive the Body and Blood of the Lord, they were actually preparing only for

---

[19]Maundy Thursday fell on April 18th in 1112. The proper "pious duty" for that day was for the king to wash the feet of the poor. (Original editor's note.)

[20]Philippe I, king of France, 1060–1108.

murder and perjury. To be brief, all the efforts of the bishop and the nobles in these days were reserved for fleecing their inferiors. But those inferiors were no longer merely angry, but were goaded into an animal rage. Binding themselves by mutual oaths, they conspired for the death, or rather the murder, of the bishop and his accomplices. They say that forty took the oath. Their great undertaking could not be kept completely secret, and when it came to the attention of Master Anselm[21] toward evening of Holy Saturday, he sent word to the bishop, who was retiring to rest, not to go out to the service of matins,[22] knowing that if he did he would be killed. With excessive pride the bishop stupidly said, "Nonsense, I'm not likely to die at the hands of such people." But although he scorned them orally, he did not dare to go out for matins and to enter the church.

The next day, as he followed the clergy in procession, he ordered the people of his household and all the knights to come behind him carrying short swords under their garments. During this procession when a little disorder began to arise, as often happens in a crowd, one of the burghers came out of the church and thought the time had come for the murder to which they were sworn. He then began to cry out in a loud voice, as if he were signaling, "Commune, Commune!" over and over again. Because it was a feast day, this was easily stopped, yet it brought suspicion on the opposition. And so, when the service of the mass was over, the bishop summoned a great number of peasants from the episcopal manors and manned the towers of the cathedral and ordered them to guard his palace, although they hated him almost as much, since they knew that the piles of money which he had promised the king must be drained from their own purses.

On Easter Monday, it is the custom for the clergy to assemble at the abbey of Saint-Vincent. Since the conspirators knew they had been anticipated the day before, they had decided to act on this day, and they would have done so if they had not seen that all the nobles were with the bishop. They did find one of the nobles in the outskirts of the city, a harmless man who had recently married a young cousin of mine, a girl of modest character. But they were unwilling to attack him, fearing to put others on their guard. Coming through to Tuesday and feeling more secure, the bishop dismissed those men whom he had put in the towers and palace to protect him and whom he had to feed there from his own resources. On Wednesday, I went to him because through his disorders he had robbed me of my grain supply and of some legs of pork, called *bacons* in French. When I requested him to relieve the city of these great disturbances, he replied, "What do you think they can do with their riots? If Jean, my moor, were to take by the nose the most powerful man among them, he would not even

---

[21]Dean of the clergy of Laon.

[22]First of the morning prayers in the seven canonical hours ending with vespers.

dare to grunt. For just now I have compelled them to renounce what they call their commune for as long as I live." I said something, and then, seeing the man was overcome with arrogance, I stopped. But before I left the city, because of his instability we quarreled with mutual recriminations. Although he was warned by many of the imminent peril, he took no notice of anyone.

The next day—that is, on Thursday—when the bishop and Archdeacon Gautier were engaged after the noon offices in collecting money, suddenly there arose throughout the city the tumult of men shouting, "Commune!" Then through the nave of the cathedral of Notre-Dame, and through the very door by which Gérard's killers had come and gone, a great crowd of burghers attacked the episcopal palace, armed with rapiers, double-edged swords, bows, and axes, and carrying clubs and lances. As soon as this sudden attack was discovered, the nobles rallied from all sides to the bishop, having sworn to give him aid against such an assault if it should occur. In this rally Guimar the castellan,[23] an older nobleman of handsome presence and guiltless character, armed only with a shield and spear, ran through the church. Just as he entered the bishop's hall, he was the first to fall, struck on the back of the head with a sword by a man named Raimbert, who had been his close friend. . . . Adon the *vidame*,[24] sharp in small matters and even keener in important ones, separated from the rest and able to do little by himself among so many, encountered the full force of the attack as he was striving to reach the bishop's palace. With his spear and sword he made such a stand that in a moment he struck down three of those who rushed to him. Then he mounted the dining table in the hall, where he was wounded in the knees and other parts of the body. At last, falling on his knees and striking at his assailants all round him, he kept them off for a long time, until someone pierced his exhausted body with a javelin. After a little he was burned to ashes by the fire in that house.

While the insolent mob was attacking the bishop and howling before the walls of his palace, the bishop and the people who were aiding him fought them off as best they could by hurling stones and shooting arrows. Now, as at all times, he showed great spirit as a fighter; but because he had wrongly and in vain taken up that other sword, he perished by the sword. Unable to resist the reckless assaults of the people, he put on the clothes of one of his servants and fled into the warehouse of the church, where he hid himself in a container. When the cover had been fastened on by a faithful follower, he thought himself safely hidden. As those looking for him ran hither and thither, they did not call out for the bishop but for a

[23]Noble in charge of the fortifications of Laon.

[24]A *vidame* (*vicedominus*) was a lay lord who was responsible for protecting and administering ecclesiastical property. . . . (Original editor's note.)

felon. They seized one of his pages, but he remained faithful and they could get nothing out of him. Laying hands on another, they learned from the traitor's nod where to look for him. Entering the warehouse and searching everywhere, at last they found him. . . .

As they sought for him in every vessel, Thiégaud[25] halted in front of the cask where the man was hiding, and after breaking in the head he asked again and again who was there. Hardly able to move his frozen lips under the blows, the bishop said, "A prisoner.". . . Sinner though he was and yet the Lord's anointed,[26] he was dragged out of the cask by the hair, beaten with many blows, and brought out in the open air in the narrow lane of the cloister before the house of the chaplain Godfrey. As he implored them piteously, ready to swear that he would cease to be their bishop, that he would give them unlimited riches, that he would leave the country, with hardened hearts they jeered at him. Then a man named Bernard of Bruyères raised his sword and brutally dashed out that sinner's brains from his holy head. Slipping between the hands of those who held him, before he died he was struck by someone else with a blow running under his eye sockets and across the middle of his nose. Brought to his end there, his legs were hacked off and many other wounds inflicted. Seeing the ring on the finger of the former bishop and not being able to draw it off easily, Thiégaud cut off the dead man's finger with his sword and took the ring. Stripped naked, he was thrown into a corner in front of his chaplain's house. My God, who shall recount the mocking words that were thrown at him by passers-by as he lay there, and with what clods and stones and dirt his corpse was pelted?

Marriage in Canon Law

One of the momentous changes of the Middle Ages that had enormous social consequences was the Church's propounding a doctrine of lifelong monogamous marriage. This view of marriage ran contrary to that of the Romans and the Germanic invaders of the early Middle Ages, for whom marriage was always a social alliance as well as a means of propagating children. In the laws of those peoples, divorce had been allowed, and the property arrangements accompanying marriage had been prominent concerns. One goal of this selection is to allow you to compare these ecclesiastical rules of marriage with those of the Burgundians and Romans that you have already encountered.

Church law truly began to take shape with the collection of textual fragments and the systematic exposition of legal problems undertaken by the monk Gratian working in Bologna between 1139 and 1150. Gratian borrowed from Roman law and other

---

[25]A serf in the abbey of Saint-Vincent.

[26]The Lord's injunction in I Paralipomenon 16:22, "Touch not my anointed," was a principle of fundamental importance to the priesthood. (Original editor's note.)

sources to assemble rules under different headings. The work he produced, The Concord of Discordant Canons, *known also as the* Decretum, *attempted to harmonize contradictions in diverse customs and rules emanating from within the Church over the preceding centuries. What follows consists of his general definition of the sources of law and his discussion of two sets of legal problems (or "causes"): the problems of social misalliance and of incest. How does Gratian resolve these problems? On what basis?*

The Decretum *became the essential textbook of canon law (the law of the Church) in the medieval universities. However, it was also immediately and continually supplemented by rules and judgments framed by the popes and their judges. These judgments, known as decretals, were assembled in various unofficial collections, until Pope Gregory IX, who was in office from 1227 to 1241, published an official collection. Several of the texts included in this collection also appear below. They all concern the issue of consent and the validity of marriage. Is marriage valid without the consent of the parties? Is anything else necessary for a valid marriage in the eyes of the church? What sorts of things about marriage do you* not *find discussed in these texts?*

The Church's rules, like any set of rules, raised difficulties that were treated in courts—in these cases, Church courts. An example from the English diocese of Canterbury in 1293 concludes this selection. How did that court reach a judgment? Did it impose the rules of canon law?

FIRST PART. OF DIVINE AND HUMAN LAW

GRATIAN: Mankind is ruled by two things—that is, natural law and customs. Natural law is that which is contained in the law and the Gospel, by which anyone is ordered to do to another that which he desires to have done to himself, and is prohibited from doing to others what he does not want done to himself. Whence Christ says in the Gospel: "Therefore all things whatsoever ye would that men should do to you, do ye even to them, for this is the law and the prophets."

Isidore[1] in the *Etymologies*, Book V, Chapter 2, says: Divine laws are established in the laws of nature; human laws, in custom.

All laws are either divine or human. Those of nature make up the divine; those of custom, the human: these latter differ among themselves, because each set seems good to a certain people.

Divine law is called *fas* [literally, "what is permitted"] human law *jus* [literally, "what is right"]. To cross another's field is acceptable to divine law, but not to human.

GRATIAN: From the words of this author, we are evidently given to understand how divine and human law differ, since everything which is *fas* goes by the name of divine or natural law, by "human law," customs, written law and tradition are understood. . . .

---

[1]Scholar of Visigothic Spain (seventh century) who compiled an encyclopedia of human knowledge in his *Etymologies*.

What law is.
Law is the written constitution.
What custom is.
Custom is long use; we must now deal with custom.
What use is.
Custom is a certain practice which becomes usual, which is accepted as
    law, when there is no written law. It makes no difference whether it
    depends on writing or reason, for reason commends the written law. . . .
    That which is in common use is called custom.

GRATIAN: Therefore we read: "they do not differ, whether custom depends
on writing or depends on reason." It appears that custom is partly put into
written form, partly remaining in the form of the usual practice. That
which has not been put in written form is called by the general term custom. . . .

There is, moreover, another division of the law, as Isidore says in Book V,
    Chapter 4:
What the kinds of law are.
Law, then, is either natural, or civil, or the law of peoples.
What natural law is.

GRATIAN: Natural law is common to all nations, that which prevails everywhere by natural instinct, not by formal legislation, as in the case of the
union of man and woman, the inheritance and education of children, possession of all goods in common and the existence of one freedom for all,
the taking of goods from the heavens, earth and sea; also the restitution of
property that has been deposited or of money commended to another's
care, the repulsing of violence by force.

For in these, or any similar cases, there is no injustice—it is merely that
    natural equity prevails.
What civil law is.
Civil law is that which a certain people or city made to govern itself, at the
    instigation of God and man.
What the law of nations [*jus gentium*] is.
The law of nations concerns the seizing of dwellings, building, arming,
    making war, captives, slaves, the restoration of civil privileges, pacts,
    peace treaties, armistices, the non-violation of the rights of ambas-
    sadors, prohibition of marriage between persons of different races.
These things are called the law of nations; almost every race keeps them. . . .

CAUSE XXIX

GRATIAN: A certain noblewoman was informed that she was sought in marriage by the son of a certain noble. She gave her consent. But one who was
not a noble and who was of slave condition offered himself in the name of
the first man and took her as a wife. The one who had first pleased her

finally came and sought her in marriage. She complained that she was deceived and wanted to be joined to the first man. It is first asked here: was there marriage between them? Secondly, if she first thought that he was a free man and afterwards learned that he was a slave, is it lawful for her to withdraw at once from him?

Question I

GRATIAN: That there is marriage between them is proved in this way. Marriage or matrimony is a union of man and woman keeping an undivided way of life. The consent of both makes the marriage. Those, therefore, who are joined in order to keep an undivided way of life, each consenting to the other, are called married.

To the foregoing, it will be responded as follows: Consent is the perception of two or more as to the same thing. He who is in error, however, does not perceive: so he does not consent—that is, sense the same thing with others. He has made an error, and does not consent. Thus she is not to be called married, because there was not the consent of each one, without which there can be no marriage. Just as one errs who is ordained by a man he thinks to be a bishop and who is still a layman; and just as such one is not called ordained, but is still to be ordained by a bishop; so she erred and is not coupled in marriage, but is still to be coupled.

Against this: Not every error eliminates consent. One who takes as a wife her whom he thinks to be a virgin, or one who takes a prostitute whom he thinks to be chaste, errs because he thinks she who has been corrupted is a virgin, or he accounts a prostitute to be chaste. Are they then to be said not to consent to these women? Or is either man to be given the option of sending away the woman and taking another? True it is that not every error excludes consent. But an error as to person is one thing; error as to fortune is another; error as to condition is another; error as to quality is another. An error as to person is when one is thought to be Virgil and he is Plato. An error as to fortune is when one is thought to be rich when he is poor, or conversely. An error as to condition is when one is thought to be free who is a slave. An error as to quality is when one is thought to be good who is bad. An error as to fortune and as to quality does not exclude consent to marriage. But an error as to person and as to condition does not allow consent to marriage. If one agrees that he will sell a field to Marcellus and later Paul comes saying that he is Marcellus and buys the field from him, did he agree with Paul about the price or is it to be said that he sold the field to him? Again, if one promises that he will sell me gold and in place of gold offers me yellow ore and so deceives me, am I to be said to consent to the yellow ore? I never wished to buy yellow ore, and I did not at some time consent to it, because there is no consent unless it is of the will. Just as error as to the matter here excludes consent, so does error of person in marriage. He does not consent to this one but to that one whom he thinks to be this one. . . .

An error as to fortune and quality does not exclude consent. When one consents to be the prelate of some church which he thinks is rich and it is less well off, although deceived by the error as to fortune, he still cannot renounce the prelacy accepted. Similarly, one who marries a poor man thinking he is rich cannot renounce this condition although she erred. Similarly an error as to quality does not exclude consent. When one buys a field or a vineyard which he thinks is very fruitful and errs as to the quality of the property and buys one less fertile, he still cannot rescind the sale. Similarly, one who takes as a wife a prostitute or one who has been corrupted whom he thinks to be chaste or a virgin cannot send her away and take another. . . .

Chapter I
It Is Lawful for Slaves to Contract Marriages

Again, Pope Julius:[2]

> There is one Father in heaven for all of us; and each one of us, rich and poor, free and slave, will equally render an account for himself and his soul. Therefore we do not doubt that all, whatever their condition, have one law as to the Lord. If, however, all have one law, then a free man cannot be sent away nor can a slave once coupled in marriage be sent away. . . .

GRATIAN: To the foregoing it will be answered in this way: It is not denied that a free woman can marry a slave, but it is said that if his slave condition is not known he can be freely sent away when his slavery is discovered. What is said by the Apostle[3] and Pope Julius is to be understood about those whose condition was known to both, but the condition of this man was unknown to the woman. Therefore, she is not compelled by the said authorities to stay with him; but she is shown to be free to stay with him or to withdraw. . . .

CAUSE XXXV

GRATIAN: A certain man, after the death of his wife, married a woman related to his deceased wife in the fourth degree, and to himself in the sixth. After three years, when she had presented him with children, he was accused before the church; he pleaded ignorance. (Question I) First this must be resolved, whether a man may marry a woman who is his blood relation? (Question 2) Secondly, whether a man may marry a woman who is his wife's blood relation? (Question 3) Thirdly, up to what degree of consanguinity ought anyone to refrain from taking a wife from among his own or his wife's relatives? (Question 4) Why is consanguinity calculated

[2]Julius I, bishop of Rome, 337–352.
[3]That is, St. Paul.

up to the seventh degree only—neither continued beyond it nor stopped before it? (Question 5) Fifthly, how are the degrees of consanguinity computed? (Question 6) Who ought to affirm the relationship by oath? (Question 7) Are the sons born of incestuous parents considered legitimate? (Question 8) If she is ignorant of the consanguinity or affinity to the man she marries, may she remain his wife by a dispensation? (Question 9) If the church should have mistakenly separated a woman from her husband because of supposed consanguinity, and after forty days she marries again, if it is subsequently discovered that she was not related to her first husband, ought the second marriage to be declared null, and the first reinstated? (Question 10) If a widow marries for a second time outside her affinity, can the children born of the second marriage attempt to marry anyone who has affinity to the mother's former husband? . . .

Questions 2 and 3

GRATIAN: Since, therefore, it has been shown that one ought to abstain from marrying blood relatives, it is now to be seen to what degree of consanguinity one ought to abstain, and whether or not a man may take in marriage a woman related to one's own wife.

> Concerning this, Pope Gregory[4] wrote at the Council of Meaux:
> No one may marry a woman related to him within seven generations. It is decreed that one ought to observe [the laws concerning] the blood-relationship by degrees of lineage up to the seventh generation. Inheritance, hallowed by the legal limits of testaments, extends hereditary succession to the seventh degree. For none succeed to their inheritances unless they ought to by virtue of descent.
> Let those who marry women related to them by blood be marked with infamy.

> Also Pope Calixtus[5] in his second letter to the bishops of Gaul:
> Prohibit related persons to marry, because both divine and secular laws prohibit them. By divine law, those who do this, and their children, are not only to be cursed, but called evildoers. Secular law calls them infamous, and denies them their inheritance. We, also, following our fathers and cleaving to their footsteps, mark them with infamy, and judge them to be infamous because they are spotted with blotches of infamy, and we ought not to harbor them nor accept the accusations of those whom secular law rejects. . . . We call those blood relatives who are related within the bounds of consanguinity, whom divine law, and imperial and Roman law, and even Greek law recognize as such, and whom those laws accept as heirs, and cannot reject.

---

[4]This dictum is traceable neither to Gregory [I, pope, 590–604] nor to the Council of Meaux. (Original editor's note.)

[5]In fact, not from Calixtus but from the pseudo-Isidorean decretals, a ninth-century collection of letters and decrees falsely attributed to popes and councils from the fourth century.

In-laws may unite in the fifth generation; in the fourth, if they have already done so, they are not to be separated.

Also, Pope Fabian:[6]
As to near relatives, related through their wife or husband, if the wife or husband dies, they may unite if related in the fifth generation; if related in the fourth, if they are discovered to be already united, they are not to be separated. If in the third degree, he cannot take another wife after his wife's death. It is the same when a man marries a woman who is related to him, and if, after his wife's death, he marries a female relative of hers. . . .

The same:[7]
Those who marry women related to them by blood, and then put them away, may not, as long as both still live, marry other women [here Gratian adds: "unless they are excused through a plea of ignorance"].
Whence in the council at Verberie:
A man who has consciously committed incest is not prohibited from marrying.

The same again:
If a man shall have fornicated with a woman, and his brother, unwittingly, marries her, the brother ought to do penance for seven years because he concealed the crime from his brother, and after his penance he may marry.
The woman, however, ought to do penance until her death, and remain without hope of ever having a husband.

GRATIAN: Concerning those who marry unwittingly, other authorities are to be consulted.

Pope Julius:[8]
No one may marry a woman related within seven degrees to him or to his wife. We do not permit anyone of either sex to marry someone related to him by blood or to his spouse up to the seventh degree of lineage, or to be united under the stigma of incest. . . .
No couple, incestuously united, is worthy of the name of married persons.

Also, from the Council of St. Agatha, Chapter 61:
As to spouses incestously united, we reserve no indulgence for them at all, unless their adultery be healed through separation. Incestuous spouses ought not to be called by the name of spouse, since even to designate them as such is horrible.
For we judge it to be incestuous if the man shall have defiled a woman, the widow of his brother (who heretofore was almost a sister to him), through a

---

[6]In fact, taken from a penitential book, often kept by abbots of monasteries between the sixth and eleventh centuries, that set specific penances for various sins.

[7]The reference to "Pope Fabian" is again a fiction, but the actual source of this dictum is unknown. (Original editor's note.)

[8]Actually from the Council of Orléans, 538. (Original editor's note.)

carnal union; or if the man should take his half brother's wife; or if a man shall have married his stepmother. . . .

DECRETALS

IV. 1.14

Alexander III to the Bishop of Pavia:

Because consent cannot occur where fear or force come into play, in instances where someone's assent is required, it is necessary to remove the source of the force. Marriage is contracted solely by consent and, where inquiry is made about consent the one making inquiry should enjoy full certainty, lest through fear he should say he likes what he really hates, and the result should follow that is usual for involuntary marriages. Wherefore instructing your brotherhood by apostolic writings we order that as far as the girl, the question of whose marriage is arisen between your citizens Siderios and Canes, have her kept honestly in the house where you placed her, so she should not have fear, until the aforesaid case will have reached a canonical conclusion and a sentence without contradiction from anyone can be executed.

IV. 1.22

Innocent III to the Bishop of Ferento:[9]

According to what we have received from you, your parishoner L affirmed by his own oath to her father that he would take P as his wife. Nor was it the husband's faith but rather the wife's that the marriage between them was not celebrated. Four or five years later the same L engaged E through words in the present tense, as her kinsmen claim, as a result of which P's brother has initiated legal proceedings with you. Because you have requested our response as to what should be done here, we respond to your request such that, if you are certain that L engaged P by words in the future tense but E by words in the present tense, first impose a suitable penance on him, because he broke faith with the first, unless in his oath he had set a fixed term within which he would take P as his wife and it was not his fault that he did not consummate the marriage within the stated period. Judge the marriage contracted in second place to be legitimate and to be kept and if necessary compel him by ecclesiastical constraint, unless there is some other impediment that would preclude the marriage. But if he contracted with both women by words in the future tense, you should make him keep the first engagement, as it was licitly made, and a penance should be inflicted for the second. If you are not fully satisfied on these matters, so long as you have cognizance of the case, then you are suffi-

[9]A town in the Etruria region of Italy.

ciently instructed on this. What is contained in the evidence concerning kinship which you sent to the apostolic See does not bear on the case, as that person by means of whom kinship is contracted between their parents is neutral to the contracting parties.

IV. 1.25

Innocent III to the Bishop of Brescia:

To your Brotherhood: You requested to be instructed whether by words alone and by what words marriage is contracted, since some persons doubt that spiritual matters can be contracted by words alone. We therefore respond to your request such that marriage in truth is contracted by legitimate consent of husband and wife; but as far as the church is concerned words of the present tense expressing consent are necessary. The deaf and mute can contract marriage by mutual consent without words, and children before legal age cannot contract it by words alone because they are understood to have not enough consent.

A MARRIAGE CASE, 1293

Osbert Crotehele, sworn and diligently examined on the consanguinity which is said to exist between John son of Simon Twyford and Alice widow of William Tannator, says that he does not know how to determine grades of consanguinity. He has heard it said, however, by old and trustworthy men that the said John and Alice are related in the fourth and fifth degree of consanguinity. This he heard after the start of the law suit. There is public voice and fame of it in the neighborhood of Bennington, and he firmly believes that it is true. He deposes neither corrupted nor instructed, and he is not related by consanguinity to either John or Alice.

Galfred Lillysdenne, sworn and questioned on the said consanguinity, says that there was a certain Richard Henxdenne, the ancestor, from whom was born Matilda, from whom Cecilia, from whom Alice, from whom John about whom the suit deals. Also from the ancestor was born Emma, from whom Muriel, from whom Alice about whom the suit deals. Asked if he has seen all those he names, the witness says no, except Alice and John on one side, and on the other Emma and Muriel and Alice. Asked if they conducted themselves as relations, he says that he does not know. Asked from whom he learned to determine grades of consanguinity, he says from several old and trustworthy men, and this after the start of the suit. Asked what the fame of the country is on the said consanguinity, he says that some say they are related by consanguinity, some say they are not. There was no fame on the consanguinity between them until after the publication of the banns. And he believes that they are related as he deposed above. And he is related by consanguinity to the woman about whom the suit deals.

John Ydenne, sworn and questioned on the said consanguinity, says that he does not himself know of any consanguinity between the aforesaid parties. He says, however, that some say they are related in the fourth and fifth degree, and some the third and fourth degree. And in what degree they are related, he does not know. Asked as to his belief, he replies that he does not know, but he says that the elders of the whole country say that they are related in the fourth and fifth degree of consanguinity. He is not related.

In the name of God, Amen. Having heard and fully understood the merits of the cause of marriage and divorce before us, brother R de Clyve commissary general of Canterbury *sede vacante*,[10]. . . having invoked the grace of the Holy Spirit and by the counsel of experts in the law assisting us, having pondered those things which are to be pondered, because we find that the said impediment of consanguinity is in no way proved, and the marriage between John and Alice was legitimately contracted, we pronounce that John and Alice may be coupled in marriage, and adjudge John to Alice as her man and husband and Alice to the said John as his legitimate wife by the same sentence.

Early Statutes of the Sorbonne

The expansion of the population, the growth of towns, and a measure of political stability were factors during the High Middle Ages that contributed to the development of universities, which joined monasteries and cathedral schools as centers of learning. The Church required learned clergymen to minister to the increased numbers of people, townspeople wanted their sons educated in order to conduct business better, and governments desired accomplished bureaucrats.

The most famous and the most cosmopolitan university in Europe was the University of Paris. It took shape gradually in the twelfth century before obtaining a charter from the French king in 1200. Unlike universities today, those in the Middle Ages originally did not possess any buildings. Professors (masters) rented rooms in which to lecture, and students found housing accommodations as best they could in the towns. Eventually, however, universities began to acquire physical plants, and residence halls (colleges) provided lodging and meals for poorer students in exchange for a modest fee. Students at the University of Paris were all male, they were all clerics, and they came from a variety of social groups (from peasnts to nobles). In 1258, Robert de Sorbon, a chaplain to the French king, established a college, whose name, the Sorbonne, later came to be attached to the Faculty of Theology and often to the University of Paris itself.

[10]*Sede vacante* means that the bishop had died and no successor had been installed, so the bishop's chair (*sede*) was vacant.

The statutes of the Sorbonne are very specific and allow us to appreciate the daily lives of the students who resided there. Medieval students were notorious for being rambunctious. What statutes attempted to curb the freedom of the students, that is, their ability to be rowdy? To what extent did religion permeate the students' lives? Was there any privacy? How did the statues regulate the students' clothes? Their table manners? Their food and drink?

The statutes also explain the offices of proctors and janitors. What functions and duties did they have? How did the proctors and janitors influence the lives of the fellows (the residents)?

Historians have argued that residence halls such as the Sorbonne acted in loco parentis *("in the place of a parent"), that is, had responsibility for the care of the students. In that case, society began to look upon students as minors needing direction and control. This contrasts with the situation before the creation of residence halls, when students were left to themselves to fend for housing, food, and their other needs.*

I wish that the custom which was instituted from the beginning in this house by the counsel of good men may be kept, and if anyone ever has transgressed it, that henceforth he shall not presume to do so.

No one therefore shall eat meat in the house on Advent, nor on Monday or Tuesday of Lent, nor from Ascension day to Pentecost.

Also, I will that the community be not charged for meals taken in rooms. If there cannot be equality, it is better that the fellow eating in his room be charged than the entire community.

Also, no one shall eat in his room except for cause. If anyone has a guest, he shall eat in hall. If, moreover, it shall not seem expedient to the fellow to bring that guest to hall, let him eat in his room and he shall have the usual portion for himself, not for the guest. If, moreover, he wants more for himself or his guest, he should pay for it himself. But if in the judgment of the fellow who introduces him the guest be a person of consequence or one through whom the house might be aided or the fellow promoted, then the said fellow may invite one or two others to entertain the guest and do him honor. These shall similarly have the portions due them from the community but always without loss to the community.

Also, no one resident in town shall eat in the house except in hall, and if he eats in a private room for cause, he shall scrupulously give his excuse before the bearer of the roll.

Also, if three or less were bled, they may have one associate who has not been bled. If they number more than three and less than eight, they may have two who have not been bled. If eight or more have been bled, then they may have three who have not been bled and who shall have their portions. If, however, more were not bled than as has been said, they shall have nothing from the common table.

Also, those who have been bled may eat in a private room for three days if they will, for as is said in the thirty-third chapter of *Genesis*, "On the third day the pain of a sound is worse."

Also, when fellows eat in private rooms, the fragments are collected lest they be lost and are returned to the dispenser who puts them in the common repository for poor clerks.

Also, the fellows should be warned by the bearer of the roll that those eating in private rooms conduct themselves quietly and abstain from too much noise, lest those passing through the court and street be scandalized and lest the fellows in rooms adjoining be hindered in their studies.

Also, those eating in private rooms shall provide themselves with what they need in season as best they can, so that the service of the community may be disturbed as little as possible. But if there are any infringers of this statute who are accustomed to eat in private rooms without cause, they shall be warned by the bearer of the roll to desist, which if they will not do, he shall report it to the master. If, moreover, other reasons arise for which anyone can eat in a private room, it shall be left to the discretion of the roll-bearer and proctors until otherwise ordered.

Also, the rule does not apply to the sick. If anyone eats in a private room because of sickness, he may have a fellow with him, if he wishes, to entertain and wait on him, who also shall have his due portion. What shall be the portion of a fellow, shall be left to the discretion of the dispenser. If a fellow shall come late to lunch, if he comes from classes or a sermon or business of the community, he shall have his full portion, but if from his own affairs, he shall have bread only.

Also, if a fellow eats in pension five days or less, he shall be a guest; but if he eats in town, he shall pay no less than if he had eaten in the house.

Also, whenever a fellow eats in town, whether he informs the household or not, he shall pay the whole pension and extras, and this in order that fellows may be discouraged from frequent eating in town.

Also, all shall wear closed outer garments, nor shall they have trimmings of vair or grise or of red or green silk on the outer garment or hood.

Also, no one shall have loud shoes or clothing by which scandal might be generated in any way.

Also, no one shall be received in the house unless he shall be willing to leave off such and to observe the aforesaid rules.

Also, no one shall be received in the house unless he pledges faith that, if he happens to receive books from the common store, he will treat them carefully as if his own and on no condition remove or lend them out of the house, and return them in good condition whenever required or whenever he leaves town.

Also, let every fellow have his own mark on his clothes and one only and different from the others. And let all the marks be written on a schedule and over each mark the name of whose it is. And let that schedule be given to the servant so that he may learn to recognize the mark of each one. And the servant shall not receive clothes from any fellow unless he sees the mark. And then the servant can return his clothes to each fellow.

Also, no outsider shall be placed on pension without permission of the master, nor shall he eat or sleep in the house as a guest more than three or four days without his permission.

Also, it is ordained that those who have lived in the house at the expense of the house until they could provide for themselves shall within a short time prepare and dispose themselves to progress in public sermons through the parishes, in disputations and lectures in the schools; otherwise they shall be totally deprived of the benefits of the house. And it may be they were able to do this by virtue of privilege: nevertheless I give them warning in all charity. Moreover, concerning those who are newly received or about to be admitted it is ordained that unless they have made progress in sermons, disputations and lectures as aforesaid within seven years from the time of their admission, they shall similarly be deprived. And if it should by chance happen that someone from fear of losing his pension should try to undertake to lecture on some text incautiously, unprepared, incompetent or unworthy, that he shall not be permitted to do so because of the scandal to others, unless by the judgment and testimony of the more advanced students in the house he be deemed competent and fitted to lecture.

Also, I wish, counsel, and decree that on fast days from All Saints to Lent those on pension in the house shall not eat except at Vespers and after all the day's lectures are over.

Also, for peace and utility we propound that no secular person living in town—scribe, corrector[1] or anyone else—unless for great cause eat, sleep in a room, or remain with the fellows when they eat, or have frequent conversation in the gardens or hall or other parts of the house, lest the secrets of the house and the remarks of the fellows be spread abroad.

Also, no outsider shall come to accountings or the special meetings of the fellows, and he whose guest he is shall see to this.

Also, no fellow shall bring in outsiders frequently to drink at commons, and if he does, he shall pay according to the estimate of the dispenser.

Also, no fellow shall have a key to the kitchen.

Also, no fellow shall presume to sleep outside the house in town, and if he did so for reason, he shall take pains to submit his excuse to the bearer of the roll.

Also, no fellow in the presence of outsiders shall propose in hall anything pertaining to the society except the word of God, which no one shall presume to impede but all shall hear in silence him who proposes it.

Also, no women of any worth shall eat in the private rooms. If anyone violates this rule, he shall pay the assessed penalty, namely, sixpence.

---

[1]One who goes over a manuscript and corrects scribal errors.

Also, no fellow shall send any dish outside the house, except by the consent of the person who has charge of them.

Also, if anyone has spoken opprobrious words or shameful to a fellow, provided it is established by two fellows of the house, he shall pay a purse which ought to belong to the society.

Also, if one of the fellows shall have insulted, jostled or severely beaten one of the servants, he shall pay a sexatarium of wine to the fellows, and this wine ought to be *vin superieur*[2] to boot.

Also, no one shall presume to take a dish or tray either at lunch or dinner except as it is passed to him by the provost and his helpers or the servants. Moreover, he who has done otherwise shall be penalized two quarts of wine. And therefore each provost should be diligent in serving the fellows well.

Also, at the deliberations of the fellows each shall peacefully remain silent until he has been called upon by the prior, and after he has had his say, he shall listen to the others calmly.

Also, no one shall form the habit of talking too loudly at table. Whoever after he has been warned about this by the prior shall have offended by speaking too loudly, provided this is established afterwards by testimony of several fellows to the prior, shall be held to the usual house penalty, namely, two quarts of wine.

The penalty for transgression of statutes which do not fall under an oath is twopence, if the offenders are not reported by someone, or if they were, the penalty becomes sixpence in the case of fines. I understand not reported to mean that, if before the matter has come to the attention of the prior, the offender accuses himself to the prior or has told the clerk to write down twopence against him for such an offense, for it is not enough to say to the fellows, "I accuse myself."

In all these and other good customs let the roll-bearer of the house be careful; but if he shall be remiss, he shall be held to the penalty assessed in the house which transgressors incur.

For the peace and utility of the community we ordain thus as to electing petty proctors and concerning those things which pertain to the exercise of their office. First, that each fellow in entering the office of proctor be required to swear according to the form of oath which fellows usually take on their admission, namely, that he will exercise the office well and faithfully and diligently.

Also, that before they leave office they ought to choose and nominate proctors to succeed themselves a fortnight before the times hitherto observed. The times are these: feast of St. Bartholomew, Christmas, and Eas-

[2]Superior wine.

ter. Those named are required to answer to the society the same day, if they were named at dinner; if in the afternoon, next day at dinner under penalty of twelve pence so far as answering is concerned, if they have received notice of their election which ought to be given them by the electors. Moreover, if they have accepted at that time, they may straightway receive accounts, if they wish, and their predecessors shall be prepared to render accounts. But if they wish, they may wait till the limit, unless they or one of them wishes or intends to leave the house.

Concerning those leaving we ordain as follows, that if any one of those elected wishes to leave the house within the fortnight mentioned, if he shall have accepted office he shall receive account before he leaves and his co-elect shall be required to receive the account with him and to exercise the functions pertaining to the office. Nor after they have accepted the office can they refuse it except because of a complete withdrawal from the house, without prospect of return within the term of the proctorship, or on account of grave infirmity or a lectureship, so that it cannot be fulfilled by themselves or by a suitable substitute. Because if one should allege complete withdrawal and then return within the term of the proctorship, he would be held to pay the same penalty as if he had not accepted the office. If, moreover, those chosen and nominated shall have refused the office, they shall pay the specified penalty, namely, ten solidi within a day after their nomination, which, if they fail to pay, for each day of delinquency each shall be charged sixpence and the proctors-electors shall keep choosing others until new proctors are had, in order that the utility of the society may not be retarded.

Moreover, this arrangement shall be observed in those who have held office before, that those shall be first chosen who are farthest removed from the time of office-holding, unless by the society or a majority thereof they be deemed unfit. If, moreover, of those older ones two held office before or paid the fine at the same time, it shall be at the discretion of the electors to choose this or that. Those, moreover, who were not proctors before, if they performed minor offices, namely, reading in hall, provostship, and office in chapel, can be elected indifferently at the electors' will and discretion.

To these functions, moreover, are held generally all petty proctors, forsooth to correct servants and to conduct themselves as follows: that they at any time with the persons here named, namely, the weekly reader, provost, clerk of the chapel and priest, without further deliberation of the other fellows can, or the majority of the said persons can, expel servants with or without salary on their conscience for the good of the fellows. And the proctors shall be held to provide other fit servants.

Also, all petty proctors generally shall be required at the beginning of their proctorship to receive and record a complete number of vessels and furniture from the preceding proctors and servants and to hand on to their successors a similar inventory. But if any are broken or lost, they ought first to repair these in order that the number of vessels may always remain certain and complete.

Besides, all vessels which are brought to table they should return clear, pure and whole at the end of their proctorship.

Also, they should attend to cleaning the chapel, hall, and court and cutting the grass at due seasons, and about all matters appertaining thereto.

Also, they should provide sufficiently concerning napkins and towels that the napkins be washed fresh and clean at least twice a week and the towels thrice.

Once a month they should propose what need to be provided for the fellows and, after deliberation by the greater and better part of the fellows who have remained in congregation, they should proceed in accordance with their deliberation. If no deliberation could be held, they should nevertheless provide for the needs of the society as shall seem to them expedient.

Also, they shall provide enough wine so that at least two hogsheads full are left at the close of their proctorship.

Also, the wines bought shall not be appraised by themselves but together with three or four fellows summoned for this and so precisely appraised according to the market where they are bought that equality shall be observed so far as possible.

Also, they shall call their rolls during octave in the accustomed manner and, when the time is up, they shall name the deficient for fines unless they wish to pay for them with their own money. But if they wish to pay for them, they should expunge them from the roll before the time expires. If they do not, they or the others shall be held to fines. The accustomed fine in the house is this, sixpence for absence for one day and a penny for each succeeding day of absence.

Also, they may use the money of the society for the personal utility of no one that results in damage or grievance to the society. Nay more, at the close of their proctorship they shall refund it all in cold cash or exchange, which if they do not do, they shall be charged ten solidi a day. But if they do not pay both fine and principal, for each day's delinquency each shall be penalized sixpence. If, moreover, they contumaciously delay in the said payments for a fortnight, then they shall be deprived of the fare of the society, the service of the domestics, and everything else in our power, without holding any further deliberation.

Moreover, if in some makings of change something has been lost and in others granted, the gain shall not be taken to distribute, unless first the loss has been restored.

Also, if any bad investment has been made in any debts through some unexpected cause and in some exchanges something has been made which ought to be distributed, let that bad debt be reckoned in the distribution and made up from the gain which was taken from the money of the society, and this in order that the fellows to whom the distribution ought to be made shall be more concerned about the recovery of the debt and that the money which is designated for the use of the society may always remain intact.

Along with these general requirements for all petty proctors are some special ones for certain of them, namely those who were elected at Easter: to provide concerning servants at the feast of St. John or concerning the preceding if they were fit, and to receive pledges anew, and to inquire into, to reduce to writing, and to leave to their successors the names of their sureties, the streets in which they dwell, and their standing. If they bring in new ones, they are required to do the same. And before they are hired outright and in full, they are tested for eight or fifteen days as is customary and those approved by the whole society or at least a majority are kept. Moreover, in accordance with the custom of Paris their sureties go surety for them with this added or specified that, if the servants for whom they swear contract debts which were credited to them from reverence for the house and society without the consent or knowledge of the fellows, if the servants should leave the house without paying, the sureties will be held for those debts. Moreover, those servants who are engaged shall take oath according to the form given them.

Also, the said proctors should provide wood for the hall and kitchen for a year, unless by vote of the fellows the time shall be extended after the feast of St. Bartholomew.

Also, to provide for all needs of the society which fall within the time of their proctorship.

Moreover, those of the feast of St. Bartholomew are required to provide wood unless it has been provided by others and for the making of verjuice unless their predecessors have attended to it, and especially to do what should be done in vintages of *salinato, rapeto* and other wines as far as the money will go.

Those, moreover, of Christmas are required to make provision for Lent of peas, beans, spices and other things as the time requires.

Also, the same are required to make in the accustomed way a collection for common expenses, namely, wood for the hall, the service of domestics, sheets, towels and other things of the sort, having summoned four or five discreet fellows a little after Christmas, in order that the collection may be fully attended to before Brandons[3] at least. Moreover, the fellows residing for the year personally in the house or the absent who have those answering for them in the house shall alone contribute to the collection. If, however, others who were absent through the year wish for some reason to contribute to the collection and if they have property in the house, they

---

[3]Term sometimes used in France for Invocavit, the sixth Sunday before Easter.

may contribute in this way, that the amount be beyond the sum to be placed in the collection, so that always without debts the money assigned to the society in the accounts of the proctors remain an integral whole, but in annual income and cold cash, lest by lack of cash money and reason of debts the utility of the society be retarded. Those not paying the collection shall be held at the stated term to the customary fine which we estimate at twelve pence for delinquency of one day, and one penny for each subsequent day of default.

In what we have said about fines for those not paying the rolls and collections and all other dues, in which particular fellows are bound to the society, we intend to bind both absent and present by the same law, so that they may be careful before they leave to inquire what obligations they have and to pay them, or at least leave other fellows in their place to answer for them and give satisfaction as carefully as they would for themselves.

These are the duties of the janitor. First he is required to reply courteously to every comer, and, if such a person asks for some fellow of the house, he is required to seek him and call him, unless the caller be some scholar for whom some fellow of the house was specially told him that he may have free access to his room.

When, moreover, the janitor goes to find some fellow in his room or elsewhere, he shall close the door after him. If the caller is a man of note, he shall allow him to wait in the court. If not, he shall remain between the two gates.

Also, the janitor is required to keep clean the entire court within and without and all the street so far as our house extends, and the walks and steps and all the rooms of the fellows and also the common passage to the private rooms, to provide water for the lavatory and keep the lavatory clean inside and out.

Also, he shall serve no one eating or drinking in a private room, unless after curfew when the gate is locked with a key, which key he is to carry with him.

Also, under no circumstances shall he go to town for anyone. But if for some urgent need of his own he has to go to town, he is required to have someone of the house to guard the gate, which if he does not do and the gate is found unguarded, he shall forfeit sixpence from his salary as penalty.

Also, he shall under no circumstances linger in the kitchen nor shall he do anything there.

Also, after curfew he must close the great gate and at the sign of St. James always open it and always keep the keys with him. If anyone of the house has to leave before the hour, he must rise and close the gate after him. If, moreover, any persons are accustomed to enter after the aforesaid hour or anyone to go out before, he is required by his oath to report this to the prior. Similarly, if he sees any faults in the domestics, or any of the goods of the house carried outside by anyone, he is required to reveal this. Also, if he sees any outsider carrying anything out of the house under his garment, he shall not permit him to leave, unless someone from the house accompanies him to the gate.

Also, at lunch he shall have the portion of a fellow without wine; at dinner however he shall have bread and soup as much as is deemed enough for him once, and a half trayful of the fragments remaining after the fellows are served and the domestics have their share. Also each day he shall have a pint of wine.

Moreover, he ought always to eat these at the gate while the fellows are at table. Moreover, he should reserve nothing in his room but return the fragments for the common benefit of clerics. If he shall have transgressed these provisions, let the prior himself correct him. If, by the testimony of the fellows or the majority of them he is found incorrigible, the prior may freely expel him. . . .

London Assize of Nuisance

Medieval cities were small, crowded, and filthy. The largest cities of Europe perhaps had a hundred thousand people; London in the early fourteenth century may have counted fifty thousand. Because of ramshackle houses and the preponderant use of wood as a building material, fire was a constant worry. So was pollution, from businesspeople such as tanners and butchers and from individuals at home as well. The proximity of homes to one another led to frequent quarrels. A neighbor's garbage and waste were of immediate concern. Water was a problem—clean water had to be found and maintained, and there was no adequate sewer system for disposing of waste material.

The following records from a London municipal court, the Court of Assize, show what day-to-day issues bothered Londoners. (Of course, the parties settled many grievances informally by themselves.) What types of matters drove people to file complaints against their fellow citizens? To what extent were Londoners concerned with cleanliness? With privacy? Can you say something about physical space, about the layout of homes, from these documents?

What types of judgments did the court hand down? Do you find those decisions fair? Did the court's rulings follow a consistent pattern? Did women fare as well as men before the court? What comparisons can you make between the living conditions and concerns of these London residents and those of medieval peasants?

Fri. 10 Feb. 1301, Elias Russel, mayor, Geoffrey de Nortone, Walter de Finchingfeld, William le Marezerer, Thomas Romeyn, John de Dunstaple, Solomon le Coteler, John de Canterbury (Cantuaria), Simon de Paris, Hugh Pourte, Nicholas Pycot, aldermen.

William de Béthune . . . complains that the cess-pit of the privy . . . of William de Gartone adjoins so closely his stone wall that the sewage penetrates his cellar. . . . The def.[1] says that he and his ancestors have been seised[2] of the privy in question time out of mind, and prays that the assize do nothing in prejudice of his free tenement. The pl.[3] says that long seisin[4] contrary to the statute ought not to prejudice his case. After adjournment the assize comes upon the land on Fri. 3 Mar. 1301, and it is adjudged that within 40 days the def. remove his cess-pit 2½ ft. of masonry . . . from the pl.'s wall. . . .

Fri. 23 Feb. 1302, John le Blund, mayor, Elias Russel, Geoffrey de Nortone, Thomas Romeyn, William de Leyre, Walter de Finchingfeld, John de Armenters, John de Dunstaple, Solomon le Coteler, Nicholas Pycot, Richer de Refham.

John Duly, kt.,[5] pl., appears against John le Riche and Rose his wife, defs., complaining that the stone wall which he holds in common with them in the par.[6] of St. Nicholas Shambles is ruinous because the cess-pit of their privy adjoins it too closely. The sheriff testifies that the defs. were summoned but they make default. It is adjudged that they rebuild the wall within 40 days etc. and be in mercy.[7] . . .

Fri. 27 July 1302, John le Blunt, mayor, Geoffrey de Nortone, William de Béthune, Thomas Romeyn, Solomon le Coteler, Nicholas Pycot, Simon de Paris, William de Leyre.

The essoin[8] of Agnes wife of Simon son of . . . Robert le Pesshoner, pl., by Robert de Leycestre, is quashed because Simon was essoined at the last court. The same Simon and Agnes complain that John le Bonde and Joan his wife have built the stone cess-pit of a privy too close to their tenement. The def. denies the charge and a day is given to the parties to hear judgment at Guildhall[9] on Tues. 31 July. Afterwards, on Fri. 3 Aug. 1302, the assize comes upon the land by John le Blunt, mayor, William de Béthune, Walter de Finchingfeld, Geoffrey de Nortone, Richard de Gloucestre, Solomon le Coteler, Simon de Paris and Nicholas Pycot, etc.; and because it is found that the cess-pit is at a sufficient distance from the pls.' tenement it is

---

[1]Defendant.

[2]That is, owned by possession.

[3]Plaintiff.

[4]Ownership by possession.

[5]Knight.

[6]Parish.

[7]They must await the pardon of the sheriff upon completing the wall.

[8]Excuse for not appearing in a law court at the prescribed time.

[9]Hall in London where the Court of Common Council met and administered the city.

adjudged that the defs. complete their building operations. Pls. in mercy for a false plaint. . . .

> *Fri. 7 Sep. 1302. John le Blunt, mayor, Elias Russel, Geoffrey de Nortone, William de Leyre, Thomas Romeyn, John de Canterbury, John Darmenters, John de Dunstaple, Solomon le Coteler, and Nicholas Pycot.*

. . . Solomon le Coteler complains that Michael de Tullesan has broken down the fence . . . of his house in the same par., so that his tenants have a view into his courtyard . . . and can see his private business; and that the water from the def.'s house floods the courtyard and submerges his trees and plants. . . . The def. comes and agrees to do all that he ought to do. He is given a day at the quindene[10] but afterwards the parties agree out of court. . . .

> *Fri. 2 Aug. 1303. John le Blund, mayor, William de Leyre, Walter de Finchingfeld, William de Béthune, Solomon le Cotiller, John de Dunstaple, Adam de Foleham, Nicholas Pycot, and Hugh Pourte, sheriff, and Simon de Paris, sheriff, John de Armenters.*

. . . William de Leyre complains that Master John de Egemere, rector of All Hallows the Less upon the Cellar, and his parishioners have a stone wall at the west end of the church on the verge of ruin, to the great peril of the pl. and other inhabitants and passers-by. The sheriff testifies that the rector was summoned but he makes default; the parishioners come but show no reason why the verdict of the assize should be delayed. Judgment that the defs. rebuild the wall *within 40 days etc.* . . .

> *Fri. 29 May 1304. John le Blond, mayor, William de Combematin, sheriff, John de Wangrave, William de Béthune, Walter de Finchingfeld, Richer de Refham, Richard de Gloucestre, John de Dunstaple, Nicholas de Farndone, Thomas Romeyn, Ralph de Honilane, Nicholas Pycot.*

Osbert de Braye and Isabel his wife complain that the water draining from the house of Adam de Hallingbury through his gutter . . . falls upon the tiles . . . of the side . . . of their house in the par. of St. Michael de Wodestrete and that whereas they own the stone wall 16 ft. high, for which reason he ought to convey away the water falling from their house under their eaves, he has constructed a gutter and nailed it to the beams . . . above their wall aforesaid. The def. says that the pls. are not entitled to an assize, because he and his predecessors have been seised of the gutter and fall of water . . . for many years, and the plaint ought to have been raised within a year and a day. Afterwards the parties agree to the arbitration of four aldermen, the pls. choosing John de Wangrave and William de Leyre, and the def. Walter de Finchingfeld and Richer de Refham. On Fri. 26 June 1304 the parties come, but the arbitrators say that they have not yet met.

[10]The fifteenth day after a Church festival.

The assize is further adjourned until Fri. 10 July, when the pls., because they cannot deny that the def. has been seised for many years of the gutter and fall of water, are advised to seek a remedy on that count by another process of law. Since, however, the stone wall 16 ft. high belonging wholly to the pls. is opposite the def.'s kitchen where the gutter is to be newly built it is adjudged that *within 40 days etc.* the def. make it so as to receive the water from the pls.' house and convey it into his own, beneath the pls.' eaves and so onto his own land. . . .

Fri. 19 June 1304, John le Blound, mayor, John de Burreforth, sheriff, John de Wangrave, William de Leyre, William de Béthune, Walter de Finchingfeld, Thomas Romeyn, Richer de Refham, Simon de Paris, Solomon le Cotiller.

. . . Luke, parson of St. Benet Fink, and his parishioners complain that Roger de Euere has overthrown the fence . . . of the churchyard, so that pigs and other animals and even men enter it by night and day, and carry off the plants growing there . . . , and commit other enormities in contempt of God and to the great damage of the church. The def. admits his obligation to rebuild the fence, and asks to be given until Michaelmas to do it. The pls. agree, on the understanding that, in the event of his failure, they are to be given 3 ft. of his land on which to erect a wall. To this he freely consents. . . .

Fri. 12 Mar. 1305, John le Blound, mayor, John de Wangrave, William de Leyre, John de Dunstaple, Richer de Refham, Hugh Pourte, Thomas Romeyn, Solomon le Cotiller, John de Lincoln and Roger de Paris, sheriffs, William de Combemartin, Adam de Rokesle.

Robert le Barber complains that William le Mareschal has constructed a gutter . . . from which the water falls at his door . . . , and has built a jetty . . . above . . . his beams . . . opposite his door and windows . . . which obstructs his view, and that his chimney . . . is too near the pl.'s party-wall . . . , causing danger of fire to his house in the par. of All Hallows de Grascherch. The def. comes but says nothing to delay the verdict of the assize. Judgment that *within 40 days etc.* he remake the gutter in dispute so that the water falls within his own tenement; that he remove all that part of the jetty which obscures the pl.'s view; and that he rebuild his chimney so that neither the pl. nor any other neighbours are in danger from fire. . . .

Fri. 4 Nov. 1306. John le Blund, mayor, John de Wengrave, William de Coumbemartin, Hugh Pourte, Adam de Rokesle, John de Dunstaple, Solomon le Cotiller, Richard de Gloucestre, Richer de Refham.

. . . Isabel relict of Estmar de Wynton' complains that Peter de Hatfeld and Juliana his wife have built the gutter . . . carrying off the water from their houses in the par. of St. Lawrence de Candelwykstrete leading into hers, which is unable to contain or convey away so great a quantity of water, so that it rots her timber . . . and floods her house. Peter after essoin makes default. Juliana comes and says that her father, Fulk de St. Edmunds, gave her the tenement, built as at present, and that she and her father before her were seised of the said fall of water . . . ; but because long seisin cannot prejudice the pl.'s case or give to the possessor the right and fee . . . , it is adjudged that *within 40 days etc.* the defs. receive the water from their houses and convey it on to their own land without damage to the pl. and her free tenement. . . .

Fri. 4 Dec. 1310.

John le Luter complains that the cess-pit of Robert de Chiggewelle's privy adjoins too closely his earthen wall in the par. of St. John Zachary, so that his house is inundated and his wall rotted by the sewage. The def. says that the cess-pit is common to both parties, since their respective tene-ments were formerly a single whole; and the wall simply marks the bound-ary between their pourparties.[11] Judgment after view that they clean the cess-pit at their common charges; and, at their discretion, either combine to build a stone wall in place of the earthen one, or each build a stone wall on his own pourparty. The cleansing of the cess-pit to be carried out within 40 days. Otherwise the sheriff is to act at the expense of the defaulting party. . . .

Fri. 20 Sep. 1314.

Margery de Somery complains that she has a tenement in the par. of St. Michael de Wodestrete, with right of free entry and exit as well by night as by day through a great entrance . . . adjoining the tenement of William le Chaundeler and Christine his wife; but they have so filled it with stalls . . . ,[12] timber and other impedimenta that she cannot go freely in and out to transact her business; and that she and the defs. had a well . . . in the entrance, common to both their tenements, from which to draw water, but the defs. have obstructed it; and, further, that the rainwater from their house falls upon her land and floods it. The defs come and say that they hold their tenement for life only, and that the reversion belongs to Robert Burdeyn, goldsmith, without whom they cannot answer. The sheriff is or-dered to summon him for the quindene[13] [4 Oct.]. On that day the pl. ap-pears but the sheriff testifies that Robert has not yet been summoned. He is ordered to summon him for the octave[14] [11 Oct.] when the mayor and aldermen and the parties duly come. The pl. proffers a deed in which Phi-lip the Palmer of Wodestrete granted to Maud de Bentele, his sister, and to

---

[11]A pourparty is a share of an estate held by joint owners that is assigned to one of them after they have divided the estate.

[12]Probably boxes or stands placed in the street for the sale of wares. . . . (Original editor's note.)

[13]That is, in fifteen days.

[14]In eight days.

all Christians acquiring it by inheritance, gift, sale or bequest, the great hall with its appurtenances which she now holds, with free entry and exit through the gate . . . with horses and other beasts of burden . . . and carts, by day and by night, and with the right to draw water from the well . . . by the hall door. . . . Robert can say nothing in rebuttal of her claim and it is therefore adjudged that *within 40 days etc.* the well be repaired at the common charges of Robert and the pl., and that he allow her free entry and exit by the gate and entrance aforesaid and further, since the cess-pit of the defs. adjoins too closely the pl.'s wall, Robert is ordered to remove it to a distance of 2½ ft. if it is walled in stone or 3½ ft. if in earth. . . .

Fri. 5 Nov. 1322.

Christine Tylly and Henry de Denecombe, pls., appear against Nicholas de Perndon, def., complaining that whereas an open drain . . . used to carry off to la More the water from their adjoining houses, and those of other neighbours, the def. has so obstructed it that when it rains the pls.' garden and the plants growing therein are flooded to a depth of 1½ ft. The def., summoned by Robert de Dunmowe and Roger de Wyndesore, makes default, and no one appears for him. Judgment after view that *within 40 days etc.* he remove the obstruction so that the water can be carried off to la More as formerly. . . .

Fri. 6 Dec. 1325. Hamo de Chigewell, mayor, John Cotun and Gilbert de Mordon, sheriffs, Robert de Swaleclive, John Hauteyn, Roger le Palmere and others, aldermen.

. . . John de Hemenhale complains that the earthen wall between his land and that of John de Havering in the par., of St. Ethelburga within Bisshopesgate, which stands wholly on his land, is ruinous and broken down, so that men and dogs, pigs and other animals can come in and out freely; and he asks that the wall be rebuilt in accordance with the assize. The def. comes and the parties agree together, the pl. undertaking to build the wall at his own expense, and the def. to provide the land. The work is to be done within 40 days when the weather is suitable. At present it cannot be done because of wintry conditions. . . .

Fri. 20 Aug. 1333. Continuation.

John de Brycheford and Alice his wife are summoned to answer William de Causton and Denise his wife who complain that, whereas a dispute occurred between Walter le Waleys, citizen, and Thomas de Brauncestre, citizen, in 1276–7, when Gregory de Rokesle was mayor, and Robert de Arraz and Ralph le Feure, sheriffs, concerning their adjoining tenements, and was settled by the mayor and other good men summoned for the purpose, the parties agreeing that Thomas and his heirs and assigns should have and hold in perpetuity a new building . . . , with the use of a courtyard . . . and well, and with the right of free entry and exit towards Westchepe and the church of St. Matthew de Fridaistrete, as appears in an indenture made between them; and the pls. hold the tenement which then belonged to Walter, and John de Brycheford and Alice his wife that of Thomas, the same John and Alice have obstructed the courtyard by building there and have placed a cistern in an inconvenient position, reducing the space available to the pls. The defs. come and say that the courtyard is not common to the parties, because in the time of Henry III the tenement which the defs. now hold belonged to Henry fitz Stephen, with half the adjoining courtyard or plot of land, and he granted the same to Hugh de Rokyngham, goldsmith, who granted it to Thomas de Brauncestre, who, in his will, provided for it to be sold by his executors . . . , who sold it to John de Dallyngg, mercer, from whom the defs. bought it. On Fri. 22 Oct. the assize comes by J. de Preston, mayor, Nicholas de Farndon, J. de Granthan, Gregory de Norton, Reginald de Conduit, Benedict de Fulsham, H. de Cumbemartyn, J. de Causton, J. Priour and Henry de Sechford, aldermen, and John Hamond and William Hanisard, sheriffs, and the parties likewise; but because of various difficulties the proceedings were adjourned to the next Husting of Common Pleas to be terminated there. On Mon. 6 June 1334, the parties come and ask for the record and judgment. The customary discussion . . . having been held between the mayor and aldermen the record is read, and the allegations of the parties considered together with the indenture between Walter le Waleys and Thomas de Brauncestre previously produced by the pls., and it appears to the court that the courtyard and well are common to the parties, and that no partition was made at the time of, or subsequent to, the drawing up of the indenture. Afterwards the mayor and aldermen go to the site and find that the defs., as alleged, had moved the cistern from the place where it used to stand and built a fence . . . in a new position without the consent of the pls. Judgment by view of the carpenters and masons sworn to the assize, that *within 40 days etc.* they replace the cistern in its former position, and rebuild the fence as it was before. . . .

Fri. 14 May 1333. John de Preston, mayor, John de Pulteneye, John de Grantham, Nicholas de Farndon, Richard de Betoyne, Henry Darcy, Gregory de Norton, John Priour, Robert le Bret, Robert de Ely, Benedict de Fulsham, Anketin de Gisors and William de Causton, aldermen.

. . . William de Thorneye complains that when he hired workmen to build the cess-pit of a privy in his house in the par. of St. Mary de Aldermaricherche, Andrew Aubrey and Joan his wife had the work prohibited. The defs. say that the cess-pit is not build in accordance with the custom of the City, since the fence . . . is not 2½ ft. from their wall. After repeated adjournments, the mayor and aldermen come on Fri. 25 June, and having viewed the cess-pit, find that it is not to the nuisance of the pl., but sufficient and tolerable according to the custom of the City. Judgment that the pl. continue his building in stone without further impediment. . . .

Fri. 25 June 1333. Mayor, Nicholas de Farndon, John de Grantham, Richard de Betoigne, John de Pulteneye, Gregory de Norton, Benedict de Fulsham, Anketin de Gysors, William de Causton, John de Causton, Henry de Gysors and Robert le Bret, aldermen, John Husebonde and Nicholas Pyk, sheriffs.

Andrew de Aubrey and Joan his wife complain that whereas they possess an easement in the use of a cess-pit common to their tenement and those of Thomas Heyron and Joan relict of John de Armenters, and the same was enclosed by a party-wall . . . and roofed with joists and boards . . . , so that the seats . . . of the privies of the pls. and the others could not be seen, Joan de Armenters and William de Thorneye have removed the party-wall . . . and roof so that the extremities of those sitting upon the seats can be seen, a thing which is abominable and altogether intolerable. Judgment, after the site has been viewed, that the defs. roof and enclose the cess-pit as it was before, under the penalty prescribed by the law and custom of the City in such cases.

As regards the aperture which the same Andrew and Joan his wife made in their room over the cellar of John de Armenters, now held by William de Thorneye, through which his private business . . . can be seen by those in the room above, and concerning which Joan de Armenters and the above-named William have made complaint, it is adjudged by the mayor and aldermen that it be blocked up.

Sentences against Heretics

Heresies beset the Church following the reforms of the eleventh century. Increasing centralization of power in the Church and the solidification of special status for the celibate clergy left some laypeople disenchanted with the clergy and the type of religious experience that was available to them. In the course of the twelfth and thirteenth centuries, especially in southern France, heresies thus arose that captured the imagination and dedication of some of the laity. The two most famous were the Waldensian and the Catharist heresies. The Waldensians, named for their founder, Peter Waldo, embraced a life of poverty and preaching. They rejected the Church's clergy because they were corrupt and had refused to allow Waldensians to preach. The Cathars, also called Albigensians after the French city of Albi, were dualists; they believed in a good god of light, purity, and spirit who was locked in an eternal battle against the prince of darkness, maker of the material world. Material possessions and all aspects of the body were thus evil entrapments for the soul. The Albigensians themselves consisted of two sorts of practitioners. The "perfect ones" held to high moral standards, especially regarding the rejection of meat and sex (or anything produced by sexual union). The "believers" married and had more relaxed lives, though they tried, at the moment of death, to reject all material aid, even so much as a glass of water, and so willed their deaths.

The Inquisition was the Church's mechanism to seek out, investigate, and punish heretics—in theory, if not to save the heretics' souls, then to protect the rest of the faithful from contamination by heretical ideas. That branch of the Inquisition based in Toulouse was very active in seeking out signs of heresy. Even as late as the first decades of the fourteenth century (when the following documents were drawn up), the Toulouse Inquisition was pursuing heretics in the villages around the city. The records of the Inquisition tell us less of what the heretics thought of themselves than of what the inquisitors thought of them. From these sources, can you tell what the heretics believed? What they practiced? What did these people do wrong in the eyes of the clergy who interrogated and prosecuted them? What sorts of punishments did the inquisitors mete out? Why, in other words, were the inquisitors so eager to pursue these heretics? Finally, what sorts of people were the heretics? What did they do? How much wealth and education did they have?

GUILIELMUS

"Guilielmus de Bayssanis, son of Peter de Bayssanis, of Bornum, in the diocese of Montauban (as legally appears by his judicial confession, made 21st of Sept. 1321) eighteen years, or thereabouts, before the time of his confession, on a certain night, while his father, and Petrona his mother, and John his brother, were sitting near the fire, his father asked him, 'If he wished to see the good men?' And he asked 'What sort of men they were?' And his mother gave him a box on the ear. And then his said father, and he, and his brother, went up to a certain loft of his house, and found there two men; of whom afterwards his father told him, that one was called Peter Auterius, and the other Amelius. And they sat with them. And the said Peter Auterius said, 'You are welcome—do not be afraid, for we will do you no harm'; and said some words, which he stated that he did not remember. And after the matters aforesaid, he, and his father, and his brother, came down from the loft, and left them there. The said Guilielmus de Bayssanis was at that time, as he says, of the age of eight or nine years. Also, the third night after the matters aforesaid, while he Guilielmus, and other persons whom he names, were sitting in the aforesaid house near the fire, the aforesaid two, Peter Auterius and Amelius, came down from the loft, and sat with them. And one of them said, 'Maynada, we are good men, and are of those whom people call heretics, but we are not heretics'; and he began to read in a certain book some words which he said that he did not remember. Also, on the following night, he, and his father, went up to the said loft, and found there the aforesaid two, Peter Auterius and Amelius; and while they were there, two other men, whom he names, came up; and then his father told him to go to bed; and he went, and left them there. Also, on the following night, or another night after, while he and his father, and his mother, and his brother, were sitting in his house, near the fire, the aforesaid two, Peter Auterius and Amelius, the heretics, came from out of doors, and Guilielmus Mercaderius of Bornum with them; and then, when they were in the house, the said Guilielmus Mercaderius bowed his knees, two or three times, before the said heretics, saying some words which he did not understand, and afterwards went away. The heretics remained there; and then his aforesaid father, and mother, and John his brother, one after the other, adored the said heretics, by bowing their knees three times upon the ground, and putting their hands upon a bench, with their heads uncovered, saying certain words which he did not understand. And after them he Guilielmus adored the aforesaid heretics in the aforesaid heretical manner. Being asked concerning his belief of the heretics, he answered that he was then of the age of eight or nine years; and did not know what to believe about them; and had not faith in their sect, and was led to do what he did by his father, and mother. Being interrogated why he so long deferred coming to confess the matters aforesaid, he answered that when his father was cited by the Inquisitor to come to the Sermon, at which he was imprisoned, he said to him, 'Son, I do not know whether I shall see you again; but take care that, as long as I and your mother live, you do not tell any body what you have seen, and known, of the proceedings of the heretics.' And this he said was the cause why he had deferred so long to come and confess the matters aforesaid." . . .

PETRONA

"Petrona, wife of Petrus Sicardus of Villemur, (as appears to us by her confession, legally and judicially made) frequently saw the heretics, in her own house, and elsewhere, and adored them with joined hands, and bended knees, bowing herself profoundly three times, saying, 'Benedicite.' Also, she was present at the heretication[1] of William, the son of Gerald Ysarnus of Villemur, and saw, and heard, and at the end adored, James Auterius the heretic, who hereticated the said William. Also, she twice ate of the consecrated bread of the heretics. Being asked if she believed the heretics to be good men, she answered, that she did not. The heretics whom she saw are these; James Auterius, Amelins de Perlis, Guilielmus Auterius, and Peter Auterius,"[2] . . .

PETRUS

"Petrus Sicardus otherwise called De la Boyssa, living in Villemur, a native of Bornum, (as appears to us, by his confession legally and judicially made, after he had made another confession of the crime of heresy, three years

[1] Process of pronouncing someone a heretic.

[2] A marginal note, by the Inquisitor, states that, "because she had many little children, and because her husband, whom she feared, made her do it, she was let off without imprisonment." This was at the second Sermon, the 25th of May, 1309, at which time her husband, under whose influence she is supposed to have acted, was imprisoned. . . . (Original editor's note.)

before that time) on the Vigil of St. Michael last past, a certain man whom he did not then know because it was night, asked him if he would take him into his house for the night, and he answered that he would not; and, the next morning, a certain youth, who lived with Sancius Mercaderius, asked him if he had seen Amelius the heretic that night? And he answered, 'Not that he knew of; but a certain man had come, and asked him to take him in'; and the other replied, that he was Amelius the heretic, and was in Villemur, but he did not tell him in what place he was. And he asked and required of him to pay to him, the money which he owed to Vitalis, the brother of that Amelius, who was dead. And he answered, that he had it not ready; but when he had it he would willingly pay it to the said Amelius. Also, after the aforesaid, Arnaldus Sicardus, the brother of the said Peter, many times told him that he did wrong, in not paying that money to the said Amelius the heretic. And once the said Arnaldus told him, that the said Amelius the heretic, remained in the country on that account, and it caused him to labour . . . and afterwards, he told the said Arnaldus that he should receive fifty *albus's*[3] of Tours, from a certain man whom he named to him, and that he would deliver them to the said heretic, which he had before delivered to that man. And the following day the said Arnaldus told him, that Peter Auterius, and Amelius, the heretics, charged him, that what remained of the money, he held at the peril of his soul, because he did not hold it with their consent. And that he should go to them, and should pay them the said money. And he, Arnald, said that he would bring them at night to a place that he might speak to them; and he answered that he did not want to see them. Also, about three years before last Whitsuntide, he visited Petrona his mother, in that illness of which she afterwards died; and then Stephana, the sister of the said Petrona, told him that a certain man whom she named to him might have one of these heretics, who would receive the said sick person into their Order, or would direct how they might have one, and that they were in the house of Raymond Durand. And then he saw him talking with his said mother. And, afterwards, on another day, the said sick person was very weak, and then the said Stephana told Bernard Sicardus, her brother, to go quickly for the said heretics, and he went. And when the said sick person became more weak, the said Stephana told him, Peter Sicardus, to go to the wife of that man of whom she had said that he would direct them to get one of the heretics; and that he should go quickly for this. And he doubts whether he went, or not, to the said Petrona; but, if he went, he found her in the road; and told her the aforesaid words, and thereupon the said Petrona went away. And he believes that she, and the said Bernard, went to the house of Raymond Durand, for one of the heretics to come and receive the said sick

[3]A minor coin of Germany and the Low Countries in the thirteenth and fourteenth centuries.

person. And after a little while, Peter Auterius, the heretic, came to the house where the sick person lay; and he, Peter Sicardus, was there present, and saluted the said heretic. And then the said sick person had already lost her speech. And he [Peter Auterius] asked if she had previously made the agreement, or covenant; and he, [Peter Sicardus] and the said Stephana, answered, that they did not know. And then the heretic said he would not receive her, but yet she would be saved in another tunic, and in another body. . . . And, afterwards, the heretic drank there, and went away. And he, Peter Sicardus, went to Arnald Mercator, and told him to accompany the said heretic. He did not apprehend the said heretic, nor cause him to be apprehended, nor tell anybody that might have apprehended him."

PONCIUS

"In the name of our Lord Jesus Christ the Crucified. Amen. Some time since Poncius Arnaldus de Puiolibus, of the parish of St. Faith, near Taravellum, in the Diocese of Thoulouse (coming, uncalled for, before us, Brother Bernard Guido, of the Dominican Order, Inquisitor of heretical pravity in the kingdom of France, deputed by the Apostolic See, and being judicially placed before us, and sworn to speak the truth) spontaneously, and of his own free will, confessed and said, that about twenty years before, while he was ill in a sickness from which he afterwards recovered, Peter Arnald, his son, brought to him, Poncius, then sick, two heretics whom the said Peter called good men, telling him that those heretics would deliver his soul to God . . . and that the same Peter invited him, Poncius, to eat of the consecrated bread of the heretics, which he then shewed him. Moreover, that so far as in him lay, he induced him when thus sick, to the love, and belief, of the heretics; and that the above mentioned Poncius believed, that the aforesaid Peter had in like manner induced Bruna, the daughter of him, Poncius, and sister of the aforesaid Peter, to the belief of the heretics.

"We, therefore, Brother Bernard, Inquisitor aforesaid, justly presuming that Poncius the Father had not deposed what was false, or with a design to slander his son Peter, caused the said Peter Arnald, son of the said Poncius, to be called before us; and he, being judicially before us, and sworn to speak the truth, we required him to tell the whole truth, and nothing but the truth, concerning the matters aforesaid. He constantly denying the aforesaid matters, and persisting long and steadily in his denial, from this, and from certain probable conjectures, justly suspecting that the above-mentioned Poncius, maliciously, and calumniously, deposing falsehoods against his own son Peter, was endeavouring to involve him in a crime so nefarious, we caused the said Poncius to be cited and brought to our presence. Poncius the Father, and Peter his son, aforesaid, we caused to be confronted; and since, after having been sworn to speak the truth, the said Poncius constantly persisted in his affirmative, and the said Peter in his negative, we had the said Poncius detained until we should become, as it was our duty to be, more fully informed respecting the matters aforesaid. And, finding that the said Poncius, at the time mentioned in his deposition, was not lying ill of any sickness, but was in good health; and that at that time and place the heretics were not active . . . we caused the above-mentioned Poncius to be brought out of prison; and when he was judicially placed before us, and sworn, we again admonished, and canonically required, him to tell us, whether there was any truth in those things which he had deposed against his aforesaid son Peter; and then this Poncius, being conscious of his malice, and coming to his right mind, and being judicially placed before us, spontaneously and freely acknowledged, that all, and every thing, which he had confessed, and deposed, against his aforesaid son Peter, was false, and containing no truth, either in whole, or in part; and that he had deposed such things being moved with hatred against the said Peter his son, as these matters are more fully contained in the processes thereupon had. All which things we caused to be intelligibly recited in the vulgar tongue to the aforesaid Poncius, in the presence of the venerable men Dominus Petrus de Lacu, Official of Thoulouse, and Dominus Barranus de Perhissacho, Vicars of the Reverend Father in Christ and Lord, the Lord G. by the grace of God Bishop of Thoulouse, and of us, and of Brother Geoffry de Ablusiis, our Co-inquisitor; and Poncius (by virtue of the oath which he had then and previously taken) spontaneously, freely, and without force, acknowledged and affirmed, that all and singular the matters aforesaid, were true; humbly praying that a salutary penance might be enjoined him on account of the matter aforesaid.

"We, therefore, Inquisitors and Vicars, above mentioned, having considered the premises, and other circumstances by which the decision of our mind, and of every person giving judgment, could be rightly informed—being convinced that the aforesaid Poncius Arnaldus, as far as in him lay, would have deceived our Court, destroyed that truth which is the only object to be sought after in matters of faith, and corrupted the sincerity of the office of the Inquisition which we hold, to the prejudice of the Catholic faith, and the scandal of an innocent son, whom he maliciously and falsely endeavoured to involve in so detestable a crime, by knowingly bearing false witness, when judicially placed before us, contrary to his own oath, as has now been recited and read to him intelligibly in the vulgar tongue—that the punishment of this Poncius may afford an example to others, and deter them from the like proceedings—this day and place being peremptorily assigned to the said Poncius for the hearing our definitive sentence—sitting as a tribunal, the Holy Gospels being placed before us, that our judgment may go forth from the face of God, and that our eyes may see equity—having taken counsel with persons both regular, and secular, learned in either law[4]—by virtue of the authority which we exercise, do by

---

[4]That is, the Roman civil law or the canon law—both taught in universities in the Middle Ages.

these presents sentence, and condemn, the said Poncius Arnaldus, false witness or accuser, to perpetual imprisonment, therein to do salutary penance, with the bread of affliction, and the water of affliction, leaving him out of pity only his life. And moreover, that the aforesaid false witness shall publicly stand with his hands bound, raised up on a ladder in an elevated place before the door of this Cathedral Church of St. Stephen to-day, and to-morrow from early in the morning until nine o'clock, with his head bare, in his tunic without a girdle, with two red tongues, a palm and a half long, and three fingers broad, on his breast, and two hanging between his shoulders; so that he may be seen, and recognised, by the by-standers; and that in the same manner he shall be placed, and stand, before the doors of the Church of St. Saturninus on the following Sunday; and the Sunday after before the door of the Gilded Church—canonically admonishing the same Poncius, and enjoining and commanding him by the oath which he has taken, that he shall constantly wear the said tongues on every upper garment; and shall not go about, either in or out of doors or of prison, without having them prominent and apparent; and shall repair them if they are torn, and renew them if, and so often as, they shall be worn out; and that immediately on his coming, or being taken, down from the ladder, he shall betake himself without delay to the prison near the Castle of Narbonne, and put himself in there, to remain for ever. . . . And if he shall contemn or neglect to fulfil these our injunctions, and commands, by not wearing the said tongues, or by not going into the said prison, or by rashly quitting it without the leave of us or our successors in this office, or by acting at any time contrary to his oath, we do, by the authority which we exercise, excommunicate him by these presents, for this, and all future times, and occasions . . . , as a person perjured, impenitent, and liable for his former crimes—canonically admonishing all and singular, that no person of whatsoever condition, or state, he may be, shall knowingly afford counsel, help, or favour, to the said Poncius, if he neglects the matters aforesaid, or to assist him to avoid them; and let them know, that if they shall do otherwise, we do by these presents excommunicate them. These things however we have enjoined upon the aforesaid Poncius, retaining to ourselves, and our successors in this office, full power of adding, diminishing, changing, aggravating, or alleviating, this penance, or punishment, or otherwise sentencing, as often as to us, and our successors in this office, by the advice of good men, it shall be deemed expedient.

"This sentence, and that which immediately precedes it, was given in the Church of St. Stephen at Thoulouse, on Saturday, the 22nd of April, in the year 1312, in the presence of," & c. . . .

GALHARDUS

"Galhardus Faber, weaver, Son of the late Arnald Faber of Soricinium [Soreze, in the diocese of Lavaur] as legally appears to us by his confession judicially made 25th Sept. 1310, frequently heard the heretics commended confidentially, and secretly, by certain persons whom he names in his confession; and agreed with them that he would see one of them. And, afterwards, on a certain day, they brought to his house, a certain heretic who was called Peter Auterius, who dined in his house, with certain other persons who accompanied him . . . ; and there he saw the aforesaid heretic adored by some of those who then accompanied . . . the said heretic; and there the said heretic drew him, Gallhardus, apart, and told him, that no one could be saved unless he was received by them at the time of his death, and made the agreement . . . with them. And he asked him if he would enter into the agreement with them? and he answered him 'yes.' Also he heard, and knew, that the said heretic then went to receive a certain sick person, whom he did not hear named, nor the place. Also he believed the heretics to be good men, and true; and that a man might be saved in their faith, and sect; and was in that belief for half a year. The things aforesaid he committed six years before he made a judicial confession of them; nor did he confess until he was apprehended and detained in prison." . . .

GUILIELMUS

"Guilielmus de Bosco, Son of the late Guilielmus de Bosco, of Bornum, in the diocese of Montauban (as by his confession judicially made the 22nd of August, in the year of our Lord 1321, legally appears) on one occasion was led by his mother, Johanna, at night, after supper, to the house of Petrus de Bayssanis, where they found the said Peter, and his wife, and sons whom he names, sitting by the fire—and there were there with them two strangers . . . whom he did not know, and whose names he did not hear. And one of them asked of him who he was? And Ricarda, his grandmother, answered that he was the son of the aforesaid Johanna her daughter. And there came Sancius Mercaderius, who talked with one of the two strange men apart, and afterwards they called the other, and those three went away together, and he did not know where they went to, or why they went away. And afterwards, when he and his mother had returned home, he asked his mother what sort of men they were? who answered that they were of the good men; but he did not understand her to say this of heretics, and knew nothing else about them. The things aforesaid he saw and heard sixteen, or eighteen years before he came to reveal them. Being asked why he had so long delayed to reveal, and confess, the things aforesaid, when his mother had been imprisoned on account of heresy, and P. his brother sentenced to wear crosses, he answered that 'It was his simplicity, and he wished he had come before to reveal the the things aforesaid.' ". . .

ARNALDUS

"Arnaldus Sicredus, son of the late Petrus Sicredus, of Salieth, near Seguervilla (as legally appears to us by his own confession judicially made on the 5th of February, in the year of our Lord 1311) heard and knew from Guilielmus Sicredus, his brother, that Petrus Sicredus, their father, had been hereticated in the sickness of which he died, by a certain heretic, which heretic was still in the house of their father. And the said Guilielmus asked if he would see the heretic, and speak with him, and he consented. And, afterwards, on two occasions by night, the said Arnaldus came to the said house, where he saw the said heretic, who was called Petrus Sancius, and heard the words of the preaching of the said heretic which he was reading in a certain book, with other persons whom he names in his confession. Also, afterwards, at the request of Raymundus de Morovilla, he granted and agreed that the said heretic should return to the same house; and he, Arnaldus, with Guilielmus and Petrus, his brothers prepared a certain secret place in which the said heretic might remain concealed; and made a hole in the wall, by which the heretic might go in and out secretly. And afterwards the said heretic was brought to the said house by Raymundus de Morovilla, in which house the said Arnaldus saw the aforesaid heretic on a certain night, and heard his words and preaching, with other persons whom he names. And the same night, having heard that the said Raymundus de Morovilla was taken by the Inquisitor of Thoulouse, the said heretic went away by night, fearing lest he should be taken. And on the following day, the messengers of the Inquisition came to apprehend the said heretic; and the said Arnaldus, though frequently asked, and though he was offered grace on the part of the Inquisitor, if he would give up the heretic, or direct how he might be taken, would not disclose any of the matters aforesaid. Being interrogated as to his belief of the heretics, he denied any. The things aforesaid he committed three months before he judicially confessed them; nor did he confess till he was detained in prison, and at the first he denied the truth.". . .

The Annals of Ghent

Located in present-day Belgium and northern France, Flanders in the High Middle Ages was the most urbanized area of Europe, surpassing Tuscany in population density. In the early fourteenth century, Ghent had a population of approximately eighty thousand, Bruges sixty to sixty-five thousand, and Ypres thirty thousand. By comparison, London's population was perhaps fifty thousand. Flanders was strategically placed and famous for the manufacture of woolen cloth. English, French, German, Italian, and Castilian merchants came there to trade.

Notwithstanding its title, The Annals of Ghent *actually concerns the entire county of Flanders. The anonymous chronicler, a man of Ghent (most certainly a Franciscan), who wrote these annals discusses in the excerpt here the visit of the king of France to Flanders in 1301, as well as the social conflict that was endemic in Flemish towns.*

Most of Flanders was a fief held by the French king, so his visit had great political significance and was an occasion for much pomp and festivity. What does the greeting that the Flemish gave to King Philip IV, who reigned from 1285 to 1314, indicate about the wealth of the towns and his relationship to the different urban social groups? Did the Flemings appreciate the king's lordship over Flanders? What grievances did the Flemings have? In what ways and over what issues did the common people (the commonalty) and the ruling oligarchy (the patricians) clash? Based on the social and political quarrels recounted here, can you say anything about the nature of violence in early-fourteenth-century Flanders? How does the violence here compare to the urban unrest in northern France that Guibert of Nogent describes in a previous selection? What does the temporary conclusion to the conflict say about notions of justice and punishment? Where do you think the sympathies of the chronicler lay?

In the year of our Lord 1301, about the end of May, King Philip[1] came into Flanders with the queen of Navarre, his wife, as new prince and direct lord: With him came John, count of Hainault, who had injured his paternal uncle in many ways and helped to expel him from his lands. Now the king arrived in great pomp and majesty, to hold tourneys and inspect the land and the finest towns of Flanders; but that tourney was later the cause and occasion of a result most grievous and serious for him and his followers. He came first to Douai, next to Lille, afterwards to Ghent. The men of Ghent went forth in procession to meet him and pay their respects, all clad in new garments, the patricians in two fashions, because they disagreed among themselves, the commonalty after their own fashion. They held divers joustings, and the *échevins*[2] sent him lavish and magnificent presents. Indeed, on the presents sent to the king and queen, and on the tournaments held in their honour, the *échevins* and patricians of Ghent spent fully as much as 27,000 pounds. Now when the king entered Ghent, the commonalty hastening to meet him, cried out loudly and begged earnestly to be freed from a certain heavy tax which there was at Ghent and Bruges upon articles for sale, especially beer and mead. The men of Ghent call it "the evil money," those of Bruges "the assize." And the king, in cheerful mood and freshly arrived, acceded to the requests of those who clamoured thus. This greatly displeased the patricians of the town, who were used to making profit from the said exaction, as at Bruges also. From Ghent the king went on to Ardenburg, then to Damme, afterwards to Bruges. The men of Bruges came to meet him with extravagant adornments of their garments, and with divers joustings, and sent him presents of great value. Now the *échevins* and patricians of Bruges had forbidden the commonalty, on pain of death, to clamour to the king for the abolition of the assize, or make supplication to him, as had been done at Ghent. The commonalty, offended by this, stood on the king's arrival as though they were dumb, at

[1]Philip IV, king of France, 1285–1314.
[2]Aldermen, town councillors.

which, it is said, the king was much surprised. When the king had gone on to Wynendaele, a very beautiful residence of the former count, the *échevins* and patricians of Bruges, being desirous that the presents made to the king and the ornaments of the garments which they had prepared to wear when meeting him should be paid for out of the assize, and that the tunics and raiment of the commonalty should be paid for out of the commonalty's own resources, still further excited the commonalty to anger. Great disturbance and dissension therefore arose in the town. Its originator is said to have been a certain weaver called Peter, surnamed Coninck, and some of his adherents. So the bailiff, on the advice of the patricians and *échevins* of Bruges, seized him, together with about twenty-five leaders of the commonalty, and shut him up in the king's prison, formerly the count's that is called the Steen. When the commonalty heard of this, stirred and provoked, they gathered together, forced those in charge of the prison to open it, and brought out all their friends unharmed, both Peter and his followers. So their agitation calmed down for a while, though they were still suspicious of the ill-will of the patricians.

From Wynendaele the king went on to Ypres, and from Ypres he returned to his own land. About the end of June, on the vigil of the apostles Peter and Paul, when the men of Ghent were carrying [the statue of] St. Livin to Hautem, they fell out with countryfolk and others who had collected there for a festival and dedication, and were wounded and ill-treated by them; for they had been unprepared for such a quarrel. When the commonalty of Ghent heard what had happened, coming out in armed force and with battle standards, they burnt the country town of Hautem, killed or wounded many there, and did serious damage to the monastery of St. Bavon.[3]

After the departure of the king and queen from Flanders, the aforesaid James of St. Pol, still left by the king as ruler and governor of Flanders, much resented, proud and spirited as he was, the contumacy of the city of Bruges in having broken the king's prison, that it is to say, having caused it to be opened by force. So he assembled a force of about five hundred mounted men and stationed it near Bruges, and by the advice of Sir John of Ghistelles, who had always borne that city ill-will, and of the patricians of Bruges, tried by various subtleties and deceptions to take vengeance for the action of the commonalty and grind it under foot. After consultation, therefore, on the ringing of a certain bell, arranged by them for this purpose, all the patricians armed themselves (the commonalty suspecting no evil), intending with the help of the aforesaid James, who was ready outside the town with his army, and whom they meant to admit by one of the gates as soon as the fighting had begun, swiftly to destroy and weaken the

---

[3]Seventh-century missionary from Ireland to Flanders and Brabant; patron saint of Ghent.

power of the commonalty. When the commonalty discovered this, hastening to arms, they most manfully resisted the patricians, who began to advance against them at the signal aforesaid. They forced the patricians to flee to a safe place called the Bourg, near [the church of] St. Donatian. Finally, they attacked that place also and obtained it by assault, slew some of the patricians, wounded many, and took the rest prisoner. When the commonalty began to get the upper hand, John of Ghistelles fled from the town, and James of St. Pol did not dare to enter it. This fight took place about the middle of July, on a Thursday. James, highly indignant about the said fight, calling to advise and help him his brother the count of St. Pol and a great army of Flemish nobles and patricians of other Flemish towns, retired to the neighborhood of Bruges. By the efforts of certain mediators, peace was made between the said count and his brother on the one hand, and the town of Bruges on the other, on the following terms. Those of the commonalty who admitted themselves responsible for the aforesaid disturbance and fighting were to leave the town of Bruges and the land of Flanders within a fixed period, as though banished, never to return. Peter Coninck and his followers did this. The rest of the townsfolk were to submit to the decision and judgment of the count and his brother in all points. The count and his brother entered the town, but did not dare to wreak savage vengeance. First, prudently as it seemed to them, they caused certain stone towers and gates to be destroyed, the wooden towers and all fortifications to be thrown into the ditch, the ditch itself to be filled up in places, and the rampart encircling the town to be at various points thoroughly dug up and destroyed. They said and decreed that through the aforesaid fight the town had forfeited all the liberties and noble customs and privileges granted to it by kings of France or counts of Flanders. This decree and judgment was resented both by the patricians and the humbler folk. In the following winter, therefore, a suit concerning it was begun in the king's court between the count and his brother and the town.

About the end of summer, the count aforesaid returned to France, but his brother was left, as before, as governor of Flanders. That year and the year before, at the French king's cost, he caused two very strong castles and fortresses to be erected, one in Lille and the other in Courtrai. He also began one at Bruges, which he did not finish.

The following winter, John, count of Namur and Guy his brother, the count's sons, with William of Jülich, provost of Maestricht, son of their sister, their hearts touched by the cruel and unjust imprisonment of their father and brothers, began like men of spirit to conspire and hold secret counsel with some of their Flemish friends, and to send private messengers and letters to some of the commonalties of Flanders who were unsettled and disturbed, [desirous of] recovering the rich land of their ancestors. So about mid-winter Peter Coninck, with some of his followers, returned by their advice to Bruges, and obtained such a hold over the weavers, fullers, and some others of the commonalty (for he was genial, and won them with smooth and sweet words) that the king's bailiff and the *échevins* and patricians of Bruges dared not touch him or his associates. About the end of winter, when spring was beginning, the envoys of the town of Bruges, unable to bring to a conclusion their suit in the king's court against the count of St. Pol and his brother, or recover their liberties and privileges, returned to Flanders wrathful and indignant. And Peter Coninck gained such a hold upon the commonalty of Bruges that he publicly forbade those who were destroying the rampart of Bruges and filling up the ditch, by order of James of St. Pol, to continue to obey his command, and threatened them from the rampart. When this became known, the king's bailiff and his judge and the *échevins* of Bruges, and many of the patricians, fearing for their lives, fled from the town, and Peter and his friends remained as it were lords of it.

While matters stood thus at Bruges, about the middle of March there arose in the town of Ghent a serious disturbance, most acceptable and consoling to the men of Bruges. The *échevins* and patricians, wishing that the debts contracted for the presents made to the king should be paid out of the exaction already mentioned, on Quadragesima Sunday[4] caused public proclamation to be made on behalf of James of St. Pol, in the presence of the bailiff, that the said exaction, as to which the king had indulged the commonalty, and annulled it, so to speak, should run and persist in its pristine vigour. When the commonalty heard this, they began to rage fiercely and complain and grumble shrilly, particularly because proclamation had been made that anyone who opposed the edict of the patricians would be banished from the town and country or be beheaded. Assembling in consultation about dusk, the men of the commonalty came to an agreement that next day they would do no work at their crafts, but would remain idle and discuss among themselves how they could get rid of the aforesaid exaction. When the king's bailiff and the *échevins* and the patricians heard of this, they took counsel together, and at dawn, just about sunrise, some eight hundred of them took up arms, and marching in bands of thirty or forty or fifty through the lanes and squares, designed to capture or massacre those of the commonalty who were unwilling to work. When the commonalty saw the patricians in arms, and heard the haughty words of some of them, they remained quiet for the time being, and many of them went to work. But about terce on the second day, the morrow of Quadragesima Sunday, some of the commonalty secretly armed themselves, took their banners and battle standards, and went forth openly. By beating upon [metal] bowls (as they dared not approach the town bell) they roused all the commonalty, who left their work *en masse* and took up arms, and meeting the patricians in conflict began a fight. Getting the upper hand,

---

[4] 11 March 1302. Quadragesima Sunday, the first Sunday in Lent, marked the fortieth day after Pentecost. Quadragesima is short for the Latin words for fortieth day.

they forced the bailiff, the *échevins* and many others, to the number of about six hundred, to flee to the castle, once the count's, near [the church of] St. Pharaildis. The rest returned each to his own house. The commonalty, therefore, possessed with rage and massing together, attacked the said castle with crossbowmen on every side, and before noon took it, on the surrender of the patricians. Of the latter they slew two *échevins* and eleven others, and sorely wounded about a hundred. They compelled the rest, with the bailiff, to swear fidelity to them; otherwise they would have killed them all. James of St. Pol, arrogant and proud, was excessively indignant at this exploit, and gave a sharp answer to certain mediators, who would gladly have brought about peace between him and the commonalty of Ghent. He sent back to the commonalty by them threatening, haughty and outrageous messages.

The Black Death

JEAN DE VENETTE

Arguably the greatest catastrophe in European history, the plagues known as the Black Death killed perhaps twenty-five million Europeans in a decade, one-quarter to one-third of the population. It also remained endemic in Europe and recurred frequently over the subsequent three centuries.

The chronicler Jean de Venette discusses the arrival of the plague in France in 1348 and its effects. After recounting an omen, he records a rather clinical description of those who contracted plague. How did various people react to the disease? How do Venette's strong Christian beliefs underscore his reporting of the Black Death?

What explanations did contemporaries give to the outbreak of plague? Why were Jews blamed? Does Venette condone the massacres of Jews? Does he see this virulent anti-Semitism as Christian? Does he express sympathy toward the Jews? What does Venette think caused the plague? After the plague had stopped, what, according to Venette, were its effects on society?

Venette relates the work of the Flagellants, bands of men who whipped themselves in order to convince God to remove the plague. Why does Venette not approve of their activities? After all, they were in the Christian tradition of extreme asceticism, and people did admire their courage and religious zealotry.

How do the persecutive attitudes of Venette and his contemporaries toward Jews compare with those of the earlier Romans toward Christians?

In A.D. 1348, the people of France and of almost the whole world were struck by a blow other than war. For in addition to the famine . . . and to the wars . . ., pestilence and its attendant tribulations appeared again in various parts of the world. In the month of August, 1348, after Vespers[1] where the sun was beginning to set, a big and very bright star appeared above Paris, toward the west. It did not seem, as stars usually do, to be very high above our hemisphere but rather very near. As the sun set and night came on, this star did not seem to me or to many other friars who were watching it to move from one place. At length, when night had come, this big star, to the amazement of all of us who were watching, broke into many different rays and, as it shed these rays over Paris toward the east, totally disappeared and was completely annihilated. Whether it was a comet or not, whether it was composed of airy exhalations and was finally resolved into vapor, I leave to the decision of astronomers. It is, however, possible that it was a presage of the amazing pestilence to come, which, in fact, followed very shortly in Paris and throughout France and elsewhere, as I shall tell. All this year and the next, the mortality of men and women, of the young even more than of the old, in Paris and in the kingdom of France, and also, it is said, in other parts of the world, was so great that it was almost impossible to bury the dead. People lay ill little more than two or three days and died suddenly, as it were in full health. He who was well one day was dead the next and being carried to his grave. Swellings appeared suddenly in the armpit or in the groin—in many cases both—and they were infallible signs of death. This sickness or pestilence was called an epidemic by the doctors. Nothing like the great numbers who died in the years 1348 and 1349 has been heard of or seen or read of in times past. This plague and disease came from *ymaginatione* or association and contagion, for if a well man visited the sick he only rarely evaded the risk of death. Wherefore in many towns timid priests withdrew, leaving the exercise of their ministry to such of the religious as were more daring. In many places not two out of twenty remained alive. So high was the mortality at the Hôtel-Dieu[2] in Paris that for a long time, more than five hundred dead were carried daily with great devotion in carts to the cemetery of the Holy Innocents in Paris for burial. A very great number of the saintly sisters of the Hôtel-Dieu who, not fearing to die, nursed the sick in all sweetness and humility, with no thought of honor, a number too often renewed by death, rest in peace with Christ, as we may piously believe.

This plague, it is said, began among the unbelievers, came to Italy, and then crossing the Alps reached Avignon, where it attacked several cardinals and took from them their whole household. Then it spread, unforeseen, to France, through Gascony and Spain, little by little, from town to town, from village to village, from house to house, and finally from person to person. It even crossed over to Germany, though it was not so bad there as with us. During the epidemic, God of His accustomed goodness

---

[1]Evening worship service.

[2]The main hospital in Paris.

deigned to grant this grace, that however suddenly men died, almost all awaited death joyfully. Nor was there anyone who died without confessing his sins and receiving the holy viaticum.[3] To the even greater benefit of the dying, Pope Clement VI through their confessors mercifully gave and granted absolution from penalty to the dying in many cities and fortified towns. Men died the more willingly for this and left many inheritances and temporal goods to churches and monastic orders, for in many cases they had seen their close heirs and children die before them.

Some said that this pestilence was caused by infection of the air and waters, since there was at this time no famine nor lack of food supplies, but on the contrary great abundance. As a result of this theory of infected water and air as the source of the plague the Jews were suddenly and violently charged with infecting wells and water and corrupting the air. The whole world rose up against them cruelly on this account. In Germany and other parts of the world where Jews lived, they were massacred and slaughtered by Christians, and many thousands were burned everywhere, indiscriminately. The unshaken, if fatuous, constancy of the men and their wives was remarkable. For mothers hurled their children first into the fire that they might not be baptized and then leaped in after them to burn with their husbands and children. It is said that many bad Christians were found who in a like manner put poison into wells. But in truth, such poisonings, granted that they actually were perpetrated, could not have caused so great a plague nor have infected so many people. There were other causes; for example, the will of God and the corrupt humors and evil inherent in air and earth. Perhaps the poisonings, if they actually took place in some localities, reenforced these causes. The plague lasted in France for the greater part of the years 1348 and 1349 and then ceased. Many country villages and many houses in good towns remained empty and deserted. Many houses, including some splendid dwellings, very soon fell into ruins. Even in Paris several houses were thus ruined, though fewer here than elsewhere.

After the cessation of the epidemic, pestilence, or plague, the men and women who survived married each other. There was no sterility among the women, but on the contrary fertility beyond the ordinary. Pregnant women were seen on every side. Many twins were born and even three children at once. But the most surprising fact is that children born after the plague, when they became of an age for teeth, had only twenty or twenty-two teeth, though before that time men commonly had thirty-two in their upper and lower jaws together. What this diminution in the number of teeth signified I wonder greatly, unless it be a new era resulting from the destruction of one human generation by the plague and its replacement by another. But woe is me! the world was not changed for the better but for

---

[3]Communion administered to a dying person.

the worse by this renewal of population. For men were more avaricious and grasping then before, even though they had far greater possessions. They were more covetous and disturbed each other more frequently with suits, brawls, disputes, and pleas. Nor by the mortality resulting from this terrible plague inflicted by God was peace between kings and lords established. On the contrary, the enemies of the king of France and of the Church were stronger and wickeder than before and stirred up wars on sea and on land. Greater evils than before pullulated everywhere in the world. And this fact was very remarkable. Although there was an abundance of all goods, yet everything was twice as dear, whether it were utensils, victuals, or merchandise, hired helpers or peasants and serfs, except for some hereditary domains which remained abundantly stocked with everything. Charity began to cool, and iniquity with ignorance and sin to abound, for few could be found in the good towns and castles who knew how or were willing to instruct children in the rudiments of grammar. . . .

In the year 1349, while the plague was still active and spreading from town to town, men in Germany, Flanders, Hainaut, and Lorraine uprose and began a new sect on their own authority. Stripped to the waist, they gathered in large groups and bands and marched in procession through the crossroads and squares of cities and good towns. There they formed circles and beat upon their backs with weighted scourges, rejoicing as they did so in loud voices and singing hymns suitable to their rite and newly composed for it. Thus for thirty-three days they marched through many towns doing their penance and affording a great spectacle to the wondering people. They flogged their shoulders and arms with scourges tipped with iron points so zealously as to draw blood. But they did not come to Paris nor to any part of France, for they were forbidden to do so by the king of France, who did not want them. He acted on the advice of the masters of theology of the University of Paris, who said that this new sect had been formed contrary to the will of God, to the rites of Holy Mother Church, and to the salvation of all their souls. That indeed this was and is true appeared shortly. For Pope Clement VI was fully informed concerning this fatuous new rite by the masters of Paris through emissaries reverently sent to him and, on the grounds that it had been damnably formed, contrary to law, he forbade the Flagellants under threat of anathema to practise in the future the public penance which they had so presumptuously undertaken. His prohibition was just, for the Flagellants, supported by certain fatuous priests and monks, were enunciating doctrines and opinions which were beyond measure evil, erroneous, and fallacious. For example, they said that their blood thus drawn by the scourge and poured out was mingled with the blood of Christ. Their many errors showed how little they knew of the Catholic faith. Wherefore, as they had begun fatuously of themselves and not of God, so in a short time they were reduced to nothing. On being warned, they desisted and humbly received absolution and penance at the hands of their prelates as the pope's representatives. Many honorable women and devout matrons, it must be added, had done this penance with scourges, marching and singing through towns and churches like the men, but after a little like the others they desisted.

The Testament of Michele di Vanni Castellani (c. 1370)

The Castellani were a wealthy and prominent Florentine clan, actively involved in the feverish political life of their city in the fourteenth century. For men of such families, politics, business, and family were inextricably intertwined. Michele di Vanni was the head of one branch of the Castellani, the best-known and most powerful bearer of that name in the turbulent 1360s, 1370s, and 1380s. He possessed considerable wealth from his cloth-manufacturing ventures and from activities in international trade and finance. This document is his record of his testament (his will), not a copy but a paraphrase that indicates better than a legal document what he was really thinking. Men like Castellani made wills well in advance of their deaths and might have several drawn up in the course of their lives as their financial situation changed and as children were born or died. This document, therefore, may bear little resemblance to what happened to his patrimony following his death sometime in the 1380s or 1390s. It does, however, indicate what his wishes were at one point in his life as he experienced concerns and worries shared by many other heads of families in Italian and other cities.

How did he treat his sons? His daughters? What other relatives were left anything? What was left to them? Under what conditions? What religious themes and overtones run through this testament? What does this text tell us about kinship and property in the fourteenth century, an era of plagues and wars?

This is the record of what I have bequeathed to Vanni and Niccolò, my sons, because it is my desire that they do the same to Alberto and Giovanni and Matteo [his younger sons]. I gave to each son, Vanni and Niccolò, the sum of 2,000 florins,[1] as it is recorded in the account book of my shop, in which these sums are credited to their accounts and debited to mine. And furthermore, when they took wives, I paid all of the costs of their wardrobes, their rooms, and the festivities. Moreover, if I die before I have given 2,000 florins to Alberto, Giovanni, and Matteo, I bequeath to each of them that sum from my estate. . . . Then, if God should grant them such life that they would marry, then let each receive the same expenses for their marriage as Vanni and Niccolò. . . . I further bequeath the sum of 1,000 florins to my daughter Antonia for the dowry, as I have already done for [her sisters] Caterina and Margherita. . . .

---

[1]Gold coin established by Florence in 1252.

If I were to die at the time of this writing, God has shown me such grace and has made me guardian of so much of his substance that I leave my sons with great wealth. Therefore, it is my will that my heirs be required, in the event that any of my daughters be widowed, to establish them in my house, to allow them to live there as though it were their own, and to give them the wherewithal to live decently. And if it should happen that any one of my daughters becomes a widow, and my sons do not treat them with the proper respect (in the judgement of Messer[2] Lotto or Niccolò), then it is my will that my heirs pay her the sum of 50 florins annually during her lifetime. . . . And in the event that any one of my daughters is widowed and cannot recover her dowry, then my heirs are hereby ordered to provide her with another dowry of 1,000 florins, if she wishes to remarry. If, however, she recovers her dowry, then they are not required to give her anything, except as good brothers or good sisters might wish to do.

If God should call me to Himself, I also order my heirs to give each of my daughters a farm worth 500 florins, or a house of the same value. And furthermore I desire that the income from the farm or house go to them, with the stipulation that after their death, the property should revert to my male heirs. . . .

I also desire that my male heirs maintain in their house the children of Guido Federighi and of Gostanza, my sister, and to give them the wherewithal for their subsistence until they reach the age of fifteen. . . . If God should claim me within a year, I order my heirs to arrange for the marriage of my niece Andreuola, daughter of Guido, and to provide her with a dowry of 500 florins. If they grant her more, they will be contributing to her welfare, for she has no one else in the world—neither father nor relative—but ourselves.

Furthermore, it is my will that my sisters, Filippa and Cicilia, may return to live with my heirs if they have need, and they shall not be denied sustenance. I shall bequeath nothing else to them because I do not believe that they require anything. But my heirs shall give annually to Cicilia 50 bushels of grain and 200 pounds of pork and two cords of wood, without which she will not be able to live on the income from her dowry. I also desire that she and the other [Filippa] should perform deeds for my soul and pray to God for me.

I see that Messer Lotto [Castellani] is a young knight and is not as wealthy as his station requires. I therefore order my sons and heirs to grant him 200 florins annually during his lifetime if he wishes to accept it. However, I know that he will not take this money except for the benefit of my sons, and if he has need of it. Stefano [Castellani, brother of Messer Lotto] is prospering and he does not need to spend above his income, and therefore I shall not treat him in the same manner as Messer Lotto. But when his

---

[2]Term of address accorded those of noble rank.

daughter Ghita reaches the age of matrimony, I order my heirs to give her and her sister Catalana 200 florins each for their dowry. If only one marries, then her dowry shall be 300 florins.

If, in the opinion of Messer Lotto and my sons and heirs, Antonio di Lotto Castellani lives and works well, then he shall be given the farm in Avignon . . . and also the houses which I have bought from Pagolo di Ser Francesco. From my estate I also bequeath him 150 florins to purchase household furnishings or for whatever purpose he desires. However, if Messer Lotto judges him unworthy of this benefit, then my heirs are not bound to give him anything. I make this bequest out of pity, because he has nothing of his own. It is my will that the house of Stafole, in which is located the hospital where Master Simone stays, shall be the haven of Christ's poor. The income from the farm at Poggio a Mensola shall be used to sustain those who live there. I place the burden for maintaining this house upon the consciences and the souls of my heirs, and I charge them with keeping it, as I have done, or better, in the service of God.

When our Lord Jesus Christ calls me to Himself, I pray Him that out of His pity and mercy He pardon my sins and receive me into His holy kingdom. I desire that my body be buried in the church of the Friars of St. Francis in Florence, if I die in the city or the *contado*.[3] If I die elsewhere, then I wish to be buried in the Franciscan church of the locality. If there is none, then whoever arranges my burial can bury me wherever he wishes. Since I do not have a tomb in the Franciscan church, and since I wish my son to be buried with me, I order my heirs to build a chapel costing 1,000 florins in the church where I am buried, and there they should bury my body and that of my son Rinieri. This should be done with the counsel of my confessor, Fra Marco de' Ricci and of Fra Francesco of the Friars [of S. Croce in Florence].

If there be any person who petitions my heirs for repayment of my legitimate debts, he should be paid. I have not contracted any debts in this world save those which I have recorded in my own books, or in the yellow book which belonged to Vanni [his dead partner] in the shop. . . . And there it is written that I owe Giovanni di Ser Pierozzo 600 florins. . . .

I bequeath 100 florins to the bishop as compensation for money which I may have gained illegally, and this should be used in benefit of the souls of those from whom I received the money. But I do not believe that I obtained any [illicit income].

As my equal heirs, I name my sons Vanni, Niccolò, Alberto, Giovanni, and Matteo with the charges that I have recorded in this document or which I have yet to record. I pray God to grant them the grace to act for the benefit of my soul and theirs.

I bequeath 100 lire to the church of the order of St. Francis in Florence.

[3] The "county" or countryside around Florence subject to its control.

To the Dominican, the Augustinian, and Carmelite Friars,[4] I bequeath 25 lire each. To every [other] order of Friars of our city, I leave 10 lire; to every house of monks or nuns, 5 lire; to every hospital in Florence, 2 lire, except that I wish to give 25 lire to S. Maria Nuova. I bequeath 5 lire to each priest in the *pieve* [ecclesiastical district] of Cascia, so that they may pray for my soul, as they would pray for their friend. I bequeath 50 lire to Ser Michele of Ruota, so that he will say a mass for my soul with the priests of the *pieve*. I give 60 lire to Fra Federigo of Bibbiena to spend on behalf of the convent of Vernia. I bequeath 25 florins to Master Battista of Poppi to refurbish the chapel which I built.

How to Succeed in Business

AN ANONYMOUS MERCHANT

Italian bankers and merchants dominated the European commercial scene in the late Middle Ages. Their remarkable inventiveness led to many forms of commercial contracts, the first types of insurance, and new banking procedures and accounting techniques. The following selection reveals something of the temperament and energies of one such merchant who lived in the middle of the fourteenth century. From this text, we can gain some insight into why and how these merchants were so technically innovative.

One key feature in this brief treatise of advice is the problem of trust, or lack of it. Can the merchant trust anyone? Why, or why not? With what sorts of persons is he supposed to deal? How is he supposed to treat them? What are the sources of danger that threaten the merchant's enterprise?

As a final consideration, it may be useful to compare the life and outlook of this merchant with that of peasants, as seen in earlier selections.

Whoever wishes to be a merchant must be endowed with three qualities: good sense, experience, and money.

GOOD SENSE

In order to know how to behave and act in every circumstance, that is, to know how to recognize and choose whatever must be done, and avoid whatever must be left alone. This means that one should not over extend oneself, nor undertake more than his purse allows him, and not to have

---

[4]The friars ("brothers") were members of mendicant orders established in the Middle Ages.

patience with those whom one cannot trust, for these people are lords [*signiori*], or men with similar inclinations, poor and of ill repute.

One must take good account of the types of people one deals with, or to whom one entrusts one's goods, for no man is trustworthy with money.

It is convenient to be shrewd in words and actions which one undertakes, for many tricks are used to distract the merchant from his goal, everyone trying to improve himself at his expense. And everyone feels that all of the merchant's transactions are successful, and that in his hands bird droppings turn into gold, and that he earns from each transaction as much as he wishes.

It is not advisable to have everyone's friendship, particularly of those who are of low station and do not enjoy a good reputation, that is sharpsters and slanderers and people who, in general, take pleasure by defaming others.

One must learn to protect oneself from jealousy, which is always disloyal, and a very bad enemy; thus, one should always act secretly, without advertising one's affairs, nor boasting of one's gains or riches, for then, whatever your gains, they would not be profitable to you, but would bring you great damage. For, some men, observing you speak in such fashion, would try to appropriate some of your goods, and a great loss would result to you only because of their jealousy and not because they had some good reason.

And keep in mind that this jealousy is found in the heart of everyone. I do not believe that there is any sin which is so great and ubiquitous as is this.

One should not be ambitious or aspire to fame only in order to show off, but only because he leads a judicious life. A good name is always derived when one leads a moderate life, for it is a precious and praiseworthy thing. This kind of life often aids and defends a man in circumstances in which ordinarily he would not be appreciated. Man does not have a clearer or dearer friend than his good name. For, whoever enjoys a good reputation cannot help but be good, just, and upright. All the things on this earth under the sky are here for whoever enjoys this condition of life.

Always guard yourself from bad habits, for in the end they always damage you.

If ever visitors come to your house who are not well-disposed toward you, you should not invariably throw them out or snub them. It is rather advisable to deal with them nicely and to feign good intentions toward them. For there are many who can harm a merchant, particularly when he is a foreigner. This last word means nothing more than a man who enjoys no favours at all.

Sometimes your actions should depend on the status of the men with whom you deal. For you may have to deal with someone who is more powerful than you are, or with a man of bad reputation, or with someone who always procrastinates, and in these cases it is better that they be in a position to ask favours of you, than you depending on them. The essence is that you recognize your own and your comrade's status. You should act accordingly.

It is not always a bad thing to pay more for something than it is worth, particularly to messengers, to one's employer, to a broker, or to such men in general. For, if ever they take offense they can cause a good deal of damage, particularly brokers and middlemen who are in a position to do much harm, and who should always be kept on good terms.

It is always good to have friends from every condition of life, but not useless men. Whoever can have good, wise, and wealthy friends would have the very best kind; if that is not possible, let them be good and wise.

One can never be too careful, particularly when collecting money, for the condition of the merchant is such that it is always subjected to infinite dangers. And one cannot collect money on short notice as some people seem to believe.

You should not postpone tending to your correspondence. Paper is cheap, and often it brings in good profit.

Expenses should always be curtailed, for they always bring damage, and money never returns to one's purse. Thus, if you save a little bit at a time, you will have a respectable sum at the end of the year. Let us say that you save 10 lire;[1] in 10 years, if they are accumulated, they constitute a great sum; so great, in fact, that he who does not calculate it carefully would never believe it.

Careless and immoderate expenditures for clothes result in bad and dishonest earnings.

There is nothing that inflames one's ego more than a desire to lead an ostentatious life. There are some people who, before reducing their standard of living, would be willing to give their soul to the devil. There are many dangers inherent in leading a luxurious life which requires large expenditures.

Moreover, if ever you have an excess of money, it should always be saved. For, whoever spends moderately and with foresight is called wise and discreet. Whereas he who spends lavishly is called a bad provider and scatterbrained. The reason is that all temporal possessions are subjected to many dangers, and incessant expenses are like a continuous fever which kills men.

If you live in a foreign land keep in mind that your aid, defense, honour, profit and support come from your money; if you lose it one could say that you lived as if you were damned.

There are only a few reasons for which a citizen of a state would seek the friendship of a foreigner: either to improve his position by associating

---

[1] Italian currency is still designated by this term derived from Latin *libra*, meaning "pound" (hence the abbreviation *lb.* for pound).

with the foreigner, or to have some of his money, or because he knows him to have a fine and subtle mind, or even because the foreigner is a good conversationalist or an imaginative historian, or is endowed with some such qualities. If you do not possess any of these qualities and, while living in a strange land a citizen seeks your friendship, beware, for he is probably trying to trick you.

If, while a foreigner, you have to sign an agreement with the citizen of a state do your utmost to behave as a mature and intelligent man. Keep in mind that your generosity toward him, rather than justice or reason, will dispose him favorably toward you. Remember that authority which says: "Gifts blind the eye of the wise, and alter the words of the just." [Deuteronomy, XVI, 19]

Even if I were to prolong this statement I would not be able to include anything on the question of accidents, which are infinite in number. Everything could not be specified here. Nevertheless, one must not have a frail mind, but one must have discretion which is the best of judges and most sensible. Discretion instructs you that you must not judge a document by its contents, but by its intentions. You must not say: Such and such authority, or that precedent instruct this course. But ask yourself: What was the intention of whoever wrote the document? Only then will you be able to understand and act according to the exigencies of a situation. And this is the most beautiful discretion.

EXPERIENCE

So that you may judge the quality of the merchandise, if it is good, average, or poor, and how long it may last without spoiling. It is also important to know the season in which each must be sold, and when it is the best time of the year to send it by boat or by an overland route. Moreover, one should know how to repair these goods if they are damaged on the way, for they can be damaged easily. Similarly, there are many remedies which may be used to conserve or repair them so that they may be better in appearance. In this question of adorning merchandise, there are any number of ways which may be used, and one must be an expert in such things so that he may not be tricked.

It is a very grave error to base one's commercial activities on mere opinion, and not on reason. That is why one must have experience, or at least be accompanied by an experienced person in mercantile affairs.

One must know how to keep books and records; to write and answer letters, which is not a small thing, particularly that of knowing how to dictate letters. For, of all the great friends that we have, language is one of the best, particularly to the man who knows how to use it well.

It is a most useful thing to know how to keep records properly; and this is among the principal lessons a merchant can learn.

MONEY

It is needed so that one may act with his own resources and not with those of others. For, whoever depends on the money of someone else has to pay a high price for it, even if he can borrow it at low interest rates, for it is always certain that the money has to be repaid, while profits are never certain.

Paying interest in order to be a merchant means nothing more than tiring oneself for someone else's benefit, and in the end with damage to oneself.

The Goodman of Paris

Medieval food might appear strange to us. The culinary differences between various regions were not as pronounced as those between the elite and the common people. The elite ate more meat than the commonalty, and their banquets overwhelmed by the prodigiously gaudy variety and amount of dishes served. Fish and rare birds (such as heron and swan) were aristocratic delicacies; stoutness was a sign of wealth and therefore beauty. Feasting alternated with fasting. For the common rural folk, soup, some vegetables, black bread, and dairy products sufficed; malnutrition accompanied vitamin deficiency.

The medieval cookbooks that survive concern the diet of well-placed social groups. An elderly Parisian, perhaps a magistrate, wrote The Goodman of Paris *sometime between 1392 and 1394 for his recent bride, a fifteen-year-old girl. What husbandly advice does he offer her? What is his ideal of the good wife? How does his religion influence the marital wisdom he bestows on his spouse? Does he think cleanliness is important in a marriage? What does this cookbook indicate about the medieval home? Why is there so much advice to the wife in this cookbook? What does this selection tell us about the situation of medieval women, especially of married women?*

Finally, the Goodman includes recipes for his wife. What are some common features of these recipes? What do these recipes indicate about medieval tastes and customs? From the ingredients, what can you infer about the writer's social position? Do any of the dishes described here appeal to you? Why, or why not?

Dear Sister,

You being the age of fifteen years and in the week that you and I were wed, did pray me to be indulgent to your youth and to your small and ignorant service, until you had seen and learned more; to this end you promised me to give all heed and to set all care and diligence to keep my peace and my love, as you spoke full wisely, and as I well believe, with other wisdom than your own, beseeching me humbly in our bed, as I remember, for the love of God not to correct you harshly before strangers nor before our own folk, but rather each night, or from day to day, in our chamber, to remind you of the unseemly or foolish things done in the day or days past, and chastise you, if it pleased me, and then you would strive to amend yourself according to my teaching and correction, and to serve my will in all things, as you said. And your words were pleasing to me, and won my praise and thanks, and I have often remembered them since. And know, dear sister, that all that I know you have done since we were wed until now and all that you shall do hereafter with good intent, was and is to my liking, pleaseth me, and has well pleased me, and will please me. For your youth excuses your unwisdom and will still excuse you in all things as long as all you do is with good intent and not displeasing to me. And know that I am pleased rather than displeased that you tend rose-trees, and care for violets, and make chaplets, and dance, and sing: nor would I have you cease to do so among our friends and equals, and it is but good and seemly so to pass the time of your youth, so long as you neither seek nor try to go to the feasts and dances of lords of too high rank, for that does not become you, nor does it sort with your estate, nor mine. And as for the greater service that you say you would willingly do for me, if you were able and I taught it you, know dear sister, that I am well content that you should do me such service as your good neighbours of like estate do for their husbands, and as your kinswomen do unto their husbands. Take counsel privily of them, and then follow it either more or less as you please. For I am not so overweening in my attitude to you and your good intent that I am not satisfied with what you do for me therein, nor with all other services, provided there be no disorder or scorn or disdain, and that you are careful. For although I know well that you are of gentler birth than I, nathless that would not protect you, for by God, the women of your lineage be good enough to correct you harshly themselves, if I did not, and they learnt of your error from me or from another source; but in you I have no fear, I have confidence in your good intent. Yet although, as I have said, to me belongs only the lesser service, I would that you know how to give good will and honour and service in great measure and abundance more than is fit for me, either to serve another husband, if you have one, after me, or to teach greater wisdom to your daughters, friends, or others, if you list and have such need. For the more you know the greater honour will be yours and the greater praise will therefore be unto your parents and to me and to others about you, by whom you have been nurtured. And for your honour and love, and not for my service (for to me belongs but the common service, or less,) since I had pity and loving compassion on you who for long have had neither father nor mother, nor any of your kinswomen near you to whom you might turn for counsel in your private needs, save me alone, for whom you were brought from your kin and the country of your birth, I have often wondered how I might find a simple general introduction to teach you the which, without the aforesaid difficulties, you might of yourself introduce into your work and care. And lastly, me-seems that if your love is as it has appeared in your good words, it can be accomplished in this way, namely in a general instruction that I will write for you and present to you, in three sections containing nineteen principal articles. . . .

The first section of the three is necessary to gain the love of God and the salvation of your soul, and also to win the love of your husband and to give you in this world that peace which should be in marriage. And because these two things, namely the salvation of your soul and the comfort of your husband, be the two things most chiefly necessary, therefore are they here placed first. And this first section contains nine articles. . . .

The fifth article of the first section telleth that you ought to be very loving and privy towards your husband above all other living creatures, moderately loving and privy towards your good and near kinsfolk in the flesh and your husband's kinsfolk, and very distant with all other men and most of all with overweening and idle young men, who spend more than their means, and be dancers, albeit they have neither land nor lineage; and also with courtiers or too great lords, and with all those men and women that be renowned of gay and amorous and loose life. . . .

For to show what I have said, that you ought to be very privy and loving with your husband, I set here a rustic ensample, that even the birds and the shy wild beasts, nay the savage beasts, have the sense and practice of this, for the female birds do ever follow and keep close to their mates and to none other and follow them and fly after them, and not after others. If the male birds stop, so also do the females and settle near to their mates; when the males fly away they fly after them, side by side. And likewise wild birds, be they ravens, crows, jackdaws, nay, birds of prey such as hawks, falcons, tercels and goshawks and the like, that be nurtured by persons strange to them in the beginning, after that they have taken food from those strangers, they love them more than others. So likewise is it with domestic and field animals, as with wild beasts. Of domestic animals you shall see how that a greyhound or mastiff or little dog, whether it be on the road, or at table, or in bed, ever keepeth him close to the person from whom he taketh his food and leaveth all the others and is distant and shy with them; and if the dog is afar off, he always has his heart and his eye upon his master; even if his master whip him and throw stones at him, the dog followeth, wagging his tail and lying down before his master to appease him, and through rivers, through woods, through thieves and through battles followeth him.

Another ensample may be taken from the dog Macaire, that saw his master slain within a wood, and when he was dead left him not, but lay down in the wood near to the dead man, and by day went to find food afar off and brought it back in his mouth and there returned without eating it, but lay down and drank and ate beside the corpse of his master, all dead within the wood. Afterwards this dog several times fought and attacked the man that had slain his master, and whenever he found him did assail and attack him; and in the end he overbore the man in the fields on the island of Notre Dame at Paris, and even to this day there be traces there of the lists that were made for the dog and for the field [of battle]. . . .

Now have you see divers strange ensamples, which be true and visible to the eye, by the which ensamples you see that the birds of the sky and the shy wild beasts and even the ravening beasts have the sense perfectly to love and be privy with their owners and those that be kind to them, and to be strange with others; wherefore for a better and stronger reason women, to whom God has given natural sense and who are reasonable, ought to have a perfect and solemn love for their husbands; and so I pray you to be very loving and privy with your husband who shall be.

The sixth article of the first section saith that you shall be humble and obedient towards him that shall be your husband, the which article containeth in itself four particulars.

The first particular saith that you shall be obedient: to wit to him and to his commandments whatsoe'er they be, whether they be made in earnest or in jest, or whether they be orders to do strange things, or whether they be made concerning matters of small import or of great; for all things should be of great import to you, since he that shall be your husband hath bidden you to do them. The second part or particular is to understand that if you have some business to perform concerning which you have not spoken to him that shall be your husband, nor hath he bethought him concerning it, wherefore hath he nothing ordered nor forbidden, if the business be urgent and it behoves to perform it before he that shall be your husband knoweth it, and if you be moved to do after one fashion and you feel that he that shall be your husband would be pleased to do after another fashion, do you act according to the pleasure of your husband that shall be, rather than according to your own, for his pleasure should come before yours.

The third particular is to understand that if he that shall be your husband shall forbid you to do anything, whether he forbid you in jest or in earnest or whether it be concerning small matters or great, you must watch that you do not in any manner that which he has forbidden.

The fourth particular is that you be not arrogant and that you answer not back your husband that shall be, nor his words, nor contradict what he saith, above all before other people.

Taking the first of the four particulars, which biddeth you to be humble and obedient to your husband, the Scripture bids it. . . . That is to say, it is the command of God that wives be subject to their husbands as their lords, for the husband is the head of the wife, even as our Lord Jesus Christ is the head of the Church. Thus it followeth that even as the Church is subject and obedient to the commandments, great and small, of Jesus Christ, as to her head, even so wives ought to be subject to their husbands as to their head and obey them and all their commandments great and small. . . .

The seventh article of the first section showeth how you should be careful and thoughtful of your husband's person. Wherefore, fair sister, if you have another husband after me, know that you should think much of his person, for after that a woman has lost her first husband and marriage, she commonly findeth it hard to find a second to her liking, according to her estate, and she remaineth long while all lonely and disconsolate and the more so still if she lose the second. Wherefore love your husband's person carefully, and I pray you keep him in clean linen, for that is your business, and because the trouble and care of outside affairs lieth with men, so must husbands take heed, and go and come, and journey hither and thither, in rain and wind, in snow and hail, now drenched, now dry, now sweating, now shivering, ill-fed, ill-lodged, ill-warmed and ill-bedded. And naught harmeth him, because he is upheld by the hope that he hath of the care which his wife will take of him on his return, and of the ease, the joys and the pleasures which she will do him, or cause to be done to him in her presence; to be unshod before a good fire, to have his feet washed and fresh shoes and hose, to be given good food and drink, to be well served and well looked after, well bedded in white sheets and nightcaps, well covered with good furs, and assuaged with other joys and desports, privities, loves and secrets whereof I am silent. And the next day fresh shirts and garments.

Certes, fair sister, such services make a man love and desire to return to his home and to see his goodwife, and to be distant with others. Wherefore I counsel you to make such cheer to your husband at all his comings and stayings, and to persevere therein; and also be peaceable with him, and remember the rustic proverb, which saith that there be three things which drive the goodman from home, to wit a leaking roof, a smoky chimney and a scolding woman. And therefore, fair sister, I beseech you that, to keep yourself in the love and good favour of your husband, you be unto him gentle, and amiable, and debonnair. Do unto him what the good simple women of our country say hath been done to their sons, when these have set their love elsewhere and their mothers cannot wean them therefrom. Sure it is that when fathers and mothers be dead and stepfathers and stepmothers that have stepsons rail at them and scold them and repulse them and take no thought for their sleeping, nor for their food and drink, their hose and their shirts, nor for their other needs or affairs, and these same children find elsewhere a good refuge and counsel from some other woman, that receiveth them unto herself and taketh thought to warm them by some poor gruel with her, to give them a bed and keep them clean and mend their hosen, breeches, shirts and other clothes, then do these same children follow her and desire to be with her and to sleep and be warmed between her breasts, and they be altogether estranged from their mothers and fathers, that before took no heed of them, and now be fain to get them back and have them again; but it may not be, for these children hold more dear the company of strangers that think and care for them, than of their kinsfolk that care no whit for them. Then they lament and cry and say that these same women have bewitched their children and that the lads be spell bound and cannot leave them and are never at ease save when they are with them. But, whatever they may say, it is no witchcraft, but it is for the sake of the love, the care, the intimacies, joys and pleasures that these women show unto them in all things and, on my soul, there is none other enchantment. For whoever giveth all its pleasure to a bear, a wolf, or a lion, that same bear, wolf, or lion will follow after him, and so the other beasts might say, could they but speak, that those thus tamed must be bewitched. And, on my soul, I trow that there is none other witchcraft than well doing, and no man can be better bewitched than by giving him what pleaseth him.

Wherefore, dear sister, I beseech you thus to bewitch and bewitch again your husband that shall be, and beware of roofless house and of smoky fire, and scold him not, but be unto him gentle and amiable and peaceable. Have a care that in winter he have a good fire and smokeless and let him rest well and be well covered between your breasts, and thus bewitch him. And in summer take heed that there be no fleas in your chamber, nor in your bed, the which you may do in six ways, as I have heard tell. For I have heard from several that if the room be strewn with alder leaves, the fleas will be caught thereon. Item I have heard tell that if you have at night one or two trenches [of bread] slimed with glue or turpentine and set about the room, with a lighted candle in the midst of each trencher, they will come and be stuck thereto. The other way that I have tried and 'tis true: take a rough cloth and spread it about your room and over your bed, and all the fleas that shall hop thereon will be caught, so that you may carry them away with the cloth wheresoe'er you will. Item, sheepskins. Item, I have seen blanchets [of white wool] set on the straw and on the bed, and when the black fleas hopped thereon, they were the sooner found upon the white, and killed. But the best way is to guard oneself against those that be within the coverlets and the furs, and the stuff of the dresses wherewith one is covered. For know that I have tried this, and when the coverlets, furs or dresses, wherein there be fleas, be folded and shut tightly up, as in a chest tightly corded with straps, or in a bag well tied up and pressed, or otherwise put and pressed so that the aforesaid fleas be without light and air and kept imprisoned, then will they perish forthwith and die. Item I have sometimes seen in divers chambers, that when one had gone to bed they were full of mosquitoes, which at the smoke of the breath came to sit on the faces of those that slept, and stung them so hard, that they were fain to get up and light a fire of hay, in order to make a smoke so that they had to fly away or die, and this may be done by day if they be suspected, and likewise he that hath a mosquito net may protect himself therewith.

And if you have a chamber or a passage where there is great resort of flies, take little sprigs of fern and tie them to threads like to tassels, and hang them up and all the flies will settle on them at eventide; then take down the tassels and throw them out. Item, shut up your chamber closely in the evening, but let there be a little opening in the wall towards the east, and as soon as the dawn breaketh, all the flies will go forth through this opening, and then let it be stopped up. Item, take a bowl of milk and hare's gall and mix them one with another and then set two or three bowls thereof in places where the flies gather and all that taste thereof will die. Item, otherwise, have a linen rag tied at the bottom of a pot with an opening in the neck, and set that pot in the place where the flies gather and smear it within with honey, or apples, or pears; when it is full of flies, set a trencher over the mouth and then shake it. Item, otherwise, take raw red onions and bray them and pour the juice into a bowl and set it where the flies gather and all that taste thereof will die. Item, have whisks wherewith to slay them by hand. Item, have little twigs covered with glue on a basin of water. Item, have your windows shut full tight with oiled or other cloth, or with parchment or something else, so tightly that no fly may enter, and let the flies that be within be slain with the whisk or otherwise as above, and no others will come in. Item, have a string hanging soaked in honey, and the flies will come and settle thereon and at eventide let them be taken in a bag. Finally meseemeth that flies will not stop in a room wherein there be no standing tables, forms, dressers or other things whereon they can settle and rest, for if they have naught but straight walls whereon to settle and cling, they will not settle, nor will they in a shady or damp place. Wherefore meseemeth that if the room be well watered and well closed and shut up, and if nought be left lying on the floor, no fly will settle there.

And thus shall you preserve and keep your husband from all discomforts and give him all the comforts whereof you can bethink you, and serve him and have him served in your house, and you shall look to him for outside things, for if he be good he will take even more pains and labour therein than you wish, and by doing what I have said, you will cause him ever to miss you and have his heart with you and your loving service and he will shun all other houses, all other women, all other services and households. All will be as naught to him save you, who think for him as is aforesaid, and who ought so to do, by the ensample that you see of horsemen riding abroad, for you see that as soon as they be come home to their house from a journey, they cause their horses to be given fresh litter up to their bellies; these horses be unharnessed and made comfortable, they be given honey and picked hay and sifted oats, and they be better looked after in their own stables on their return than anywhere else. And if the horses be thus made comfortable, so much the more ought the persons, to wit the lords, to be so at their own expense on their return. Hounds returning from the woods and from the chase be littered before their master and he maketh their fresh litter himself before the fire; their feet be greased at the fire with soft grease, they be given sops and be well eased, for pity of their labour; and likewise, if women do thus unto their husbands, as men do unto their horses, dogs, asses, mules, and other beasts, certes all other houses, where they have been served, will seem to them but dark prisons and strange places, compared with their own, which will be then a paradise of rest unto them. And so on the road husbands will think of their wives, and no trouble will be a burden to them for the hope and love they will have of their wives, whom they will be fain to see again with as great longing as poor hermits and penitents are fain to see the face of Jesus Christ; and these husbands, that be thus looked after, will never be fain to abide elsewhere nor in other company, but they will withhold, withdraw and abstain therefrom; all the rest will seem unto them but a bed of stones compared with their home; but let it be unceasing, and with a good heart and without pretence.

But there be certain old hags, which be sly and play the wise woman and feign great love by way of showing their heart's great service, and naught else; and wot you, fair sister, that the husbands be fools if they perceive it not; and when they perceive it, if the husband and wife be silent and pretend one with another, it is an ill beginning and will lead to a worse end. And some women there be, that in the beginning serve their husbands full well, and they trow well that their husbands be then so amorous of them and so debonnair that, trow they, those husbands will scarce dare to be wroth with them, if they do less, so they slacken and little by little they try to show less respect and service and obedience, but—what is more—they take upon themselves authority, command and lordship, at first in a small thing, then in a larger, and a little more every day. Thus they essay and advance and rise, as they think, and they trow that their husbands, the which because they be debonnair or peradventure because they set a trap, say nought thereof, see it not because they suffer it thus. And certes, it is an ill thought and deed, for when the husbands see that they cease their service, and mount unto domination, and that they do it too much and that by suffering ill good may come, then those women be all at once, by their husband's rightful will, cast down even as Lucifer was. . . .

CINNAMON BREWET. . . . Break up your poultry or other meat and stew it in water, putting wine therewith, and [then] fry it; then take raw dried almonds in their shells unpeeled and great plenty of cinnamon and bray them very well and moisten them with your broth or with beef broth and boil them with your meat; then bray ginger, cloves and grain [of Paradise] etc., and let it be thick and red. . . .

SORINGUE OF EELS. . . . Skin and then cut up your eels; then have onions cooked in slices and parsley leaves and set it all to fry in oil; then bray ginger, cinnamon, clove, grain [of Paradise] and saffron, and moisten with verjuice and take them out of the mortar. Then have toasted bread brayed and moistened with purée and run it through the strainer, then put in the purée and set all to boil together and flavour with wine, verjuice and vinegar; and it must be clear. . . .

STUFFED PIGLING. . . . Let the pig be killed by cutting his throat and scalded in boiling water and then skinned; then take the lean meat and throw away the feet and entrails of the pig and set him to boil in water; and take twenty eggs and boil them hard and chestnuts cooked in water and peeled. Then take the yolks of the eggs, the chestnuts, some fine old cheese and the meat of a cooked leg of pork and chop them up, then bray them with plenty of saffron and ginger powder mixed with the meat; and if your meat becometh too hard, soften it with yolks of eggs. And open not your pig by the belly but across the shoulders and with the smallest opening you may; then put him on the spit and afterwards put your stuffing into him and sew him up with a big needle; and let him be eaten either with yellow pepper sauce or with cameline in summer. . . .

SWAN. Pluck him like a chicken or a duck and scald or do again [in hot water]; put him on a spit skewered in four places and roast him whole with beak and feet and pluck not his head; eat with yellow pepper sauce.

IV

EARLY MODERN EUROPE (FIFTEENTH TO SEVENTEENTH CENTURIES)

Beginning in the fourteenth century, even as the plagues began to haunt Europe, as wars waged, and as the popes became mired in the Great Schism, an intellectual and artistic revival of the classical culture of Greece and Rome began in Italy that has come to be known (largely through the influence of the nineteenth-century Swiss historian Jakob Burckhardt) as the Renaissance ("rebirth"). Many, following Burckhardt, saw the Renaissance as a break from the Middle Ages and thus the beginning of the modern age. Of course, what we mean by "modern" is open to varying interpretations.

To Burckhardt and his followers, the Renaissance was distinguished by the flourishing of an intellectual and literary humanism that gave rebirth to serious study of the linguistic style and moral outlook of the Latin and Greek classics. This humanism, in turn, was marked by two trends, secularism and individualism. Secularism espoused that human life on earth is an appropriate subject of sophisticated examination and contemplation. Individualism advocated that moral and intellectual self-improvement should be the goal of this contemplation of human life. This new outlook was first formulated in Italy, where city-states such as Florence provided economic support and an urbane audience for humanists' teaching and writing.

When we look beyond intellectual, literary, and artistic activities, however, it is harder to find any momentous changes. Scholars who disagree with Burckhardt claim the Renaissance represents no sharp break with the past but, rather, rests upon a continuation of social and economic structures of the Middle Ages. Humanism, in fact, affected very few people beyond an educated elite and the wealthy who patronized them. The lives of most people remained untouched. On the other hand, insofar as members of the Florentine elite were influenced by humanist writings (and we know they read them, at least in excerpts), we cannot say that humanism had no social impact. At least for the elites, as they arranged their marriages and drew up their wills, they did so with greater self-consciousness about the meanings of family life and its relation to social and political existence. Indeed, the sort of learning the humanists advanced crystallized into a new social ideal of the gentleman. That ideal, with its corresponding gender image of the gentlewoman, was also clearly for the noble and educated. Its individualism was socially limited to those with the resources to realize and exploit it.

In the course of the fifteenth and sixteenth centuries, Renaissance humanism and related artistic styles spread from Italy to northern Europe. There it came to influence powerfully literary styles and vigorous discussions of religious life, taking on the form often called Christian humanism. *A more revolutionary stance was taken by Martin Luther (1483–1546), a German monk and professor of theology who followed out the implications of his insights on the saving nature of faith in Jesus Christ (as opposed to performing sacramental and charitable works). Justification by faith alone was Luther's insight into Christian salvation and lay at the heart of the Protestant reformers' break with the Catholic church. The theological and institutional implications of this insight were enormous. Marriage was now regarded as an appropriate state for all, including clergy, and marriage was not a sacrament. Monasteries and convents were to be closed, canon law's jurisdictions taken over by secular courts, and much Church property turned over to lay control.*

The religious ideas of Luther and other reformers fell on fertile ground as, for a variety of reasons (by no means all of them religious), many people were willing to listen to alternatives to traditional Roman Catholicism. In Germany, discontent with social and economic conditions had been manifest for some time, especially among the knights, peasants, and urban artisans, who had seen their economic standing deteriorate. Their grievances proved a fertile ground for Luther's challenge to ecclesiastical authority and imperial government. What made his message different from earlier figures, many of whom had taught religious views similar to his, was that Luther's Ninety-five Theses protesting the sale of indulgences provoked a movement that forever sundered doctrinal and ecclesiastical unity in Europe. The Reformation, as this movement came to be called, split the peoples of Europe into two broad but in some cases overlapping political, intellectual, and spiritual camps—Protestant and Roman Catholic—each of which was intent on extirpating the other. Religion was a dominant or contributing factor in conflicts ranging from the civil wars in France in the late sixteenth century and in England in the seventeenth to the Dutch rebellion against Spanish rule and the Thirty Years' War that racked Germany from 1618 to 1648.

Both Protestants and Catholics had powerful interests in seeing that their people were educated in the proper doctrine. Alternative and subversive ideas were to be eliminated and "superstition" eradicated. It was in this climate that trials and executions for witchcraft went on throughout Europe. With the witch-hunts, we are also confronted with the deadly effects of the breakdown of expected social order (as the accuser and the accused usually knew each other) played out on gender stereotypes that saw women as weak and irrational creatures open to the devil's influence (over 80 percent of those executed were women). These trials should be seen against the larger backdrop of concerns about heresy and radical religious ideas, religious wars, intolerance, and the migration of people, even to North America, to seek a space in which to live by their beliefs and impose them on others.

The early modern period of European history also saw the growth of government. The modern state, in its secular rather than religious character, with its bureaucrats and soldiers, has been hailed erroneously as an achievement of the Renaissance. Humanism revived knowledge of Roman and Greek governments and political events, as well as knowledge of classical political theories. New technologies in warfare, like the cannons and other weapons made possible by gunpowder, as well as new infantry tactics and techniques of fortification, put greater power in the hands of those rulers who could afford the new weapons and larger armies. Colonial discoveries and expansion furnished the basis of a global economy; and those regions that were best able to take advantage of the essentially exploitative colonial trade were able to finance more extensive government administrative machinery. Even religious strife tended to strengthen the hand of government, as Protestants and Catholics alike looked to rulers to foster and spread their faith. Governments developed more sources of revenue to finance their armies; they spread their influence over more areas of life through law and administration. When governments found ways to control or confine the marginal and deviant, they were able to stop witchcraft prosecutions and more violent means of addressing the problem of social order. In the end, perhaps more so than ever before, it was still a world of privilege. These privileges would come under attack forcefully in the eighteenth century.

Florence: Catasto of 1427

In 1427, the city of Florence revised its fiscal structure. The city relied on forced loans from its citizens, and these loans were supposed to be proportional to each citizen's wealth. In a desire to make the distribution of fiscal responsibility more equitable, the city fathers enacted an enormous bureaucratic undertaking—a census (catasto) of all households in the city of Florence and the regions of Tuscany under Florentine control. The result, for the historian, is an important source of information on households. This selection presents five examples, varying from the rather wealthy Conte di Giovanni Compagni (with taxable assets of more than 11,837 florins) to modest craftsmen. The monetary sums are given as florins (the gold currency devised by Florence in 1252 that was a standard for commercial transactions in most of Italy and Europe), which were subdivided into soldi and denari (twelve denari to a soldo, twenty soldi to a florin—on the model of the Carolingian silver currency of the eighth century that also served as a model until the 1970s for the later British pound sterling).

Florentines were supposed to list all properties they owned and other assets, including sums owed to them by others. They could deduct what they owed to others and two hundred florins for each member of their household. What forms of wealth did these Florentines have? What forms of wealth did the rich have that the poor did not? From the information on debts and credits, what can you tell about the business and financial dealings of Florentines? What do the lists of personal exemptions (literally, "mouths") tell us about Florentine family relations? How old, for example, were the husbands in relation to their wives? How many children did each family have? In what order are names given in the list, and what might that tell us about family relations?

THE DECLARATION OF CONTE DI GIOVANNI COMPAGNI

Assets of Conte di Giovanni Compagni . . .

A house with furnishings which I inhabit, located in the parish of S. Trinita on the street of the Lungarno
[not taxable]   0

A house in the parish of S. Trinita on the street of the Lungarno . . . which is rented to Niccolò and Tommaso Soderini for 24 florins per year, [capitalized] at 7 percent   342–17–2

A house on the Lungarno in that parish . . . rented to Giovanni di Simone Vespucci for 24 florins per year, [capitalized] at 7 percent
342–17–2

A house located in that street . . . rented to Michele di Piero Dino for 12 florins per year. . . .   171–8–9

Two shops . . . with courtyards and basements for selling wine, located in the parish of S. Agostino in the Via de' Terni . . . rented to Daddo di Zanobi, wineseller, for 20 florins per year. . .   285–14–6

One-half of two-thirds of some shops in the palace of the Aretti of Pisa. . . . My share [of the rent] is 28 florins per year, more or less. . . .   400–0–0

A farm in the parish of S. Maria a Quarto . . .   238–11–6

A farm in the parish of S. Giorgio in the *contado* of Prato, with laborer's cottage, including several plots of vineyard and pieces of woodland adjacent to the farm. . . . Bartolomeo di Filippo cultivates this farm; he has borrowed 38 ½ florins [from me] and he keeps a pair of oxen at his risk.
. . . [The farm is valued at]   353–15–2

A small farm in the Valdimarina in the parish of S. Margherita a Torre with a villa and a laborer's cottage and olive trees and woods [valued at]
                                  139–13–0

A piece of woodland [valued at]   35–14–0

He [Conte] has invested in a shop of the Lana [woolen cloth manufacturers] guild in the company of Michele di Benedetto di Ser Michele, the sum of   2000–0–0

In another account with Michele in that shop, he is to receive   911–0–0

And in another account, he is to receive   66–0–0

Money which is owed to him by:

Francesco and Niccolò Tornabuoni	1130–0–0
Bartolomeo Peruzzi and company	335–5–0
Lorenzo di Messer Palla Strozzi and company	465–0–0
Michele Dini	75–0–0
Lorenzo di Messer Palla [Strozzi] and company	500–0–0
Michele di Benedetto di Ser Michele	325–0–0
Giovanni and Rinaldo Peruzzi and company	17–2–0

[Compagni estimated his holdings in *Monte*[1] shares (communal bonds) and accrued interest at   4390–3–0

He also estimated that he would collect only 500 florins of some 1,079 florins owed to him by delinquent debtors.]   500–0–0

Obligations

Money owed to:

Creditors of Gino	39–0–0
Giovanni and Rinaldo di Rinieri Peruzzi	33–0–0
Lorenzo di Messer Palla [Strozzi] and company	118–18–6
Lorenzo di Messer Palla and company	45–11–0
Baldo, my servant	12–0–0
Marco di Bernardo and company, druggists	15–0–0
Monna Guida of the Mugello, my servant	10–0–0
[other obligations]	128–11–6

---

[1]Funded public debt (literally *monte* means "mountain" or "heap") in which people held shares resulting from voluntary investment or, more likely, forced loans. Shares were transacted at a discount.

Personal exemptions:

Conte, aged 61	200–0–0
Monna Nanna, his wife	200–0–0
Ilarione, his son, aged 15	200–0–0
Giovanni, his son, aged 11	200–0–0
[Total estimated value of Conte's taxable assets]	13,039–6–3
[Total debts and exemptions]	1,202–1–0
[Net assets subject to taxation]	11,837–5–3

THE DECLARATION OF
FRANCESCO DI MESSER GIOVANNI MILANESE

One-fourth of a cloth factory . . . Bartolomeo Corbinelli operated this shop and paid a rent of 42 florins, but he didn't want to pay that much and he left on March 6, 1425. Since then, the shop has been closed . . .
150–0–0

One-half of a cottage, which I inhabit, with . . . orchard in the parish of S. Michele a Castello. 0

An adjoining vineyard in the same parish. The vineyard is cultivated by Fede di Domenico . . . 64–0–0

One house with vineyard in the same parish. . . . I receive a rent of 9 florins 128–11–0

One peasant's cottage in the same parish with vineyard . . . 163–8–0

In Tunis, I commissioned Piero di Ser Naddo to arrange for the shipment of 204 bales of wool to Pisa on the ship owned by Giovanni Uzzino. But this wool was never loaded and it remained at the port. It was a total loss, and was valued at 600 florins or more. I have not yet been able to investigate the cause of this loss. . . . Since my return from Tunis, I have been unable to pursue this matter on account of the litigation in which I have been involved. . . . 0

Also, this Piero di Ser Naddo received 150 florins from Bernardo di Caccione which he was obligated to give me in Tunis but did not. I believe that Bernardo paid him that money without any letter or instruction from me. I have not yet legally demanded the return of that money but have only made an oral request. . . . I don't know how this will end. When this business is settled, I will inform the authorities. 0

Also, Marco di Messer Forese Salviati and company owe me 100 florins or thereabouts, the price of leather which I sent him from Tunis. . . . This debt is not yet settled, but I fear that I will not be repaid, and I don't expect to win a lawsuit against them since they are very influential. 0

[Milanese estimated that his holdings of *Monte* shares amounted to 65 florins.] 65–0–0

Obligations

[Milanese estimated his commercial and personal debts at 115 florins.]

Personal exemptions: 115–0–0

Francesco, aged 56	200–0–0
Monna Ginevra, his wife, aged 50	200–0–0
Antonio, his son, aged 24	200–0–0
Bernardo, his son, aged 24	200–0–0
Michele, his son, aged 21	200–0–0
Gabriello, his son, aged 7	200–0–0
[Total estimated value of Giovanni's taxable assets]	572–7–0
[Total debts and exemptions]	1315–0–0

THE DECLARATION OF LORENZO GHIBERTI, SCULPTOR

. . . A house located in the parish of S. Ambrogio in Florence in the Via Borgo Allegri . . . with household furnishings for the use of myself and my family . . .   0

A piece of land in the parish of S. Donato in Franzano . . .   100–0–0

In my shop are two pieces of bronze sculpture which I have made for a baptismal font in Siena. . . . I estimate that they are worth 400 florins or thereabouts, of which sum I have received 290 florins; so the balance is 110 florins.   110–0–0

Also in my shop is a bronze casket which I made for Cosimo de' Medici,[2] I value it at approximately 200 florins, of which I have received 135 florins. The balance owed to me is 65 florins.   65–0–0

I have investments in the *Monte* of 714 florins.   714–0–0

I am still owed 10 florins by the Friars[3] of S. Maria Novella for the tomb of the General [of the Dominican Order, Lionardo Dati].

Obligations

Personal exemptions:

Lorenzo di Bartolo, aged 46	200–0–0
Marsilia, my wife, aged 26	200–0–0
Tommaso, my son, aged 10 or thereabouts	200–0–0
Vettorio, my son, aged 7 or thereabouts	200–0–0

[2]Patriarch of the Medici family who became de facto ruler of Florence later in 1434. He died in 1464.

[3]Derived from the Latin *frater* ("brother"). Term used for those in the mendicant orders—Dominicans and Franciscans.

I owe money to the following persons:

Antonio di Piero del Vaglente and company, goldsmiths	33–0–0
Nicola di Vieri de' Medici	10–0–0
Domenico di Tano, cutler	9–0–0
Niccolò Carducci and company, retail cloth merchants	7–0–0
Papi d'Andrea, cabinet-maker	16–0–0
Mariano da Gambassi, mason	7–0–0
Papero di Meo of Settignano	
Simone di Nanni of Fiesole	
Cipriano di Bartolo of Pistoia (my apprentices in the shop)	48–0–0
Antonio, called El Maestro, tailor	15–0–0
Domenico di Lippi, cutler	2–0–0
Alessandro Allesandri and company	4–0–0
Duccio Adimari and company, retail cloth merchants	8–0–0
Antonio di Giovanni, stationer	3–0–0
Isau d'Agnolo and company, bankers	50–0–0
Commissioners in charge of maintenance and rebuilding of the church of S. Croce	6–0–0
Lorenzo di Bruciane, kiln operator	3–0–0
Meo of S. Apollinare	45–0–0
Pippo, stocking maker	8–0–0
[Total of Lorenzo's taxable assets]	999–0–0
[Total obligations and exemptions]	1074–0–0

THE DECLARATION OF AGNOLO DI JACOPO, WEAVER

He and his mother own a house, in which they live, in the Via Chiara . . .

      0

A loom which we operate, valued at	40–0–0
Giano di Masotto owes me	3–5–0
Antonio di Fastello, parish of S. Stefano, owes me	25–0–0
Michele di Piero Serragli owes me	21–0–0
Niccolò di Andrea del Benino owes me	15–8– 0

Obligations

Personal exemptions:

Agnolo di Jacopo, aged 30	200–0–0
Mea, his wife, aged 28	200–0–0
Taddea, his mother, aged 72	200–0–0
I owe Giano di Manetto	3–5–0
[Agnolo's taxable assets]	104–13–0
[His obligations and exemptions]	603–5–0

THE DECLARATION OF BIAGIO DI NICCOLÒ, WOOL CARDER

He owns one-third of a house in the parish of _____; his father bought it for 30 florins. . . . He lives in it.   0

One-half of a cottage located in the Via delle Romite. He receives 3¼ florins of rent annually   46–0–0

Next to the cottage is a small piece of garden . . .   0-8-8

Obligations

He owes Braccio di Giovanni, cloth manufacturer

                                                                        20–0–0

Personal exemptions:

Biagio di Niccolò   200–0–0
Monna Fiora, his wife   200–0–0
Gemma, his daughter, aged 9   200–0–0
Chola, his daughter, aged 5   200–0–0

He pays rent on the two-thirds of his house which he does not own . . .
                                                                        14-5-0

[Biagio's taxable assets]   65–18–8
[His obligations and exemptions]   834–5–10

On the Family

LEON BATTISTA ALBERTI

The Florentine humanist Leon Battista Alberti (1404–1472) was the illegitimate son of Lorenzo Alberti. The Alberti were one of the most prominent and wealthy Florentine clans in the late fourteenth century. However, the Alberti became caught up in political schemes in the 1390s and were exiled from Florence by the other patrician families of the ruling elite. Their exile ended only in 1428, and Battista himself did not set foot in Florence until 1434. By that time, he had forsaken legal studies in Bologna for the works of humanists and entered holy orders. He ended his career in Rome with a position in the papal chancery.

In 1432, Alberti began writing, in Italian, his dialogues On the Family. *These conversations among various of his Alberti relatives are set against the background of the impending death of his father, which had occurred eleven years earlier. It was aimed stylistically at a wide audience among literate Florentines, yet it also sparkled with the erudition in the classics that Alberti had acquired in his humanistic studies.*

Entire passages and lines of argument were lifted from classical sources, including Xe-
nophon. A humanist's writing cannot be held to our standards of originality, for origi-
nality was not a virtue to the humanist. It is thus a work that shows us where, and
how imperfectly, the Renaissance met social realities. Alberti himself was a beneficed
cleric who never married or had children, and he lived in Florence among the Alberti
only for relatively brief periods; yet he offered in his work an idealized picture of family
life and relationships.

The speaker at the beginning of this selection is Alberti's father, Lorenzo, who re-
counts the words of his own father on the duties and responsibilities of fathers. How
are they supposed to treat their sons? For what are they training their sons? Later in
the dialogue, younger Alberti (Lionardo and Adovardo) exchange ideas on the joys and
troubles of fatherhood. Why is the father so crucial to the operation of the family? In
consequence, having agreed that it is a good idea for Alberti men to become fathers, Li-
onardo and the older Giannozzo then go on to discuss marriage. What are the attri-
butes to be sought in the ideal wife? What is her role in relation to her husband and his
household?

Finally, compare this selection to others you have read on the family. How do Al-
berti's views and concerns differ from those of Xenophon or Aristotle? How well does
Alberti's advice square with other evidence you have from his society—the catasto rec-
ords, the Castellani testament?

BOOK ONE

Here, however, I am reminded of our father, Benedetto Alberti, a man of
wisdom and authority, and of a fame that was not vulgar. He was diligent
in all things, but especially in pursuing and carefully tending the fortune
and honor of our family. When he was encouraging other members of the
Alberti family of that time to be, as they certainly were, careful and industrious in all they did, he used to speak in the following words:

"The duty of a father is not only, as they say, to stock the cupboard and
the cradle. He ought, far more, to watch over and guard the family from all
sides, to check over and consider the whole company, to examine all the
practices of every member, inside and outside the house, and to correct
and improve every bad habit. He ought preferably to use reasonable rather
than indignant words, authority rather than power. He should appear to
give wise counsel where this would help more than commands, and
should be severe, rigorous, and harsh only where the situation really calls
for it. He ought in every thought always to put first the good, the peace,
and the tranquility of his entire family. This should be a kind of goal toward which he, using his intelligence and experience, guides the whole
family with virtue and honor. He knows how to steer according to the
wind's favor, the waves of popular opinion, and the grace given him by his
fellow citizens, toward the harbor of honor, prestige, and authority. He
also knows how to remain afloat there, how to strike and furl the sails, and
how, in storms and in such misfortunes as have unjustly afflicted our
house these last twenty-two years, to restrain the spirits of the young men.

He must neither let them yield to the blows of fortune nor leave them to lie in defeat. He must never allow them to try something irresponsible and wild, either for revenge or to satisfy some youthful and frivolous optimism.

"When fortune is tranquil and goodnatured, but still more when the times are stormy, the good father never departs from the pilot of reason and the careful conduct of life. He remains alert, foresees from a good distance every mist of envy, every storm cloud of hate, every lightning stroke of enmity threatening on the faces of his fellow citizens. Encountering any contrary wind, any shoal and danger which may confront the family, he acts the part of the experienced expert sailor. He recalls with what winds others have sailed, how they rigged their ships and how they sighted and avoided every danger. He never forgets that in our country no one ever spread all his sails, even though they might not be the greatest of all, without having to take them down again, not whole any longer but ripped and torn. Also he knows that there is more harm done by one badly navigated voyage than good by the successful accomplishment of a thousand. . . .

"Let fathers realize that excellent sons rejoice and support their parents at every age. In the father's watchfulness lies the son's character. Laziness and sloth corrupt and disgrace the family; anxious and responsible fathers restore it to honor. Greedy, lascivious, wicked, and proud men load the family with ill fame, misfortunes, and troubles. The good ones, however gentle, moderate, and humane they may be, ought to realize that if they are not also very concerned, diligent, foresightful, and active in correcting and restraining the young, when any part of the family falls, they too will be ruined. The more greatness and wealth and rank was theirs in the family, the greater will be their downfall. The top stones in the wall shatter most when they fall.

"Therefore let the elders be ever alert and busy for the well-being and honor of the whole family, counseling, correcting, and keeping a firm hold, as it were, on the bridle of the whole family. For it is nothing if not an honorable, pious, and blessed labor to rein in with words and courtesy the appetites of the young, to wake up the lazy spirits, to enflame the wills that are cold, at the same time doing honor to oneself and glorifying one's country and one's house. Nor does it seem to me less than a very noble and pleasant work for fathers of families to contain and to restrain with seriousness and moderation the excessive license of youth. Anyone who wants to deserve well of the young will most appropriately maintain in himself the jewel of old age, which consists, I believe, in nothing else than authority and reverence. . . .

"They must not do like certain old men used to do who were perhaps given to avarice. These, when they meant to make their children thrifty, made them unhappy and servile. They appreciated money more than honor, and so they taught them ugly and low occupations. I do not praise that sort of liberality which would be harmful unless rewarded by fame or friendship, but I do condemn extremely every form of stinginess. I have also always found every sort of excessive pomp displeasing.

"The old, then, should be common fathers to all the young. Indeed they are mind and soul to the whole body of the family. And just as having dirty naked feet brings dishonor on the face and on the whole man and is a disgrace, so the old, any of the elders, should realize that neglecting the least member of the house brings justified blame on them. They are to blame if they have allowed any part of the family to fall into misery or dishonor. Let them keep in mind that the first duty of the elders is to work for everyone of the house, like those good ancient Lacedaemonians who considered themselves fathers and tutors of every young person. Each of them corrected all the errors of any young citizen that might be, and his closer, more immediate kinsmen were glad and fully accepted the improvement produced by others. It brought honor to fathers that they showed gratitude and thanks to whoever had made their youth more reasonable and more responsible in carrying out any undertaking. Because of this good and most useful system of moral discipline, their land was glorious and honored with immortal and well-earned fame. There was no enmity among them. Anger and hostility were immediately rooted up and overthrown. There was but a single will among the citizens, and that directed to making the country virtuous and disciplined. Such were the goals for which everyone labored, exerting energy, mind, and will. The old offered their counsel, their memories, and their good example, while the young gave their obedience and imitation."

These things and many others that Messer Benedetto used to mention are indeed the duties of fathers of families. If the young should really receive care not only from their fathers but also by the merit of others, surely no one can question the justice of my efforts, like other fathers, to apply every argument, consideration, and art to assure my own very dear sons of being well recommended and as cherished as possible by their own kinsmen and by everyone's good faith and piety.

I conclude, my children, that the duty of the young is to love and obey the old, to respect age, and to have toward all their elders the same attitude as toward their father, showing them all the required submissiveness and reverence. In the accumulation of years is long experience of things, and the knowledge of many sorts of conduct, of many ways, and of many human souls. The old have seen, heard, and thought through innumerable practical solutions and excellent and noble answers to every condition of fortune. . . .

Indeed who could doubt that in great age there is a vast memory of the past, long experience of things, intelligence practiced in predicting and in assessing the causes, purposes, and results of things? There is the knowledge of how to relate present affairs to those of yesterday so as to foretell what may become of them tomorrow. The old, therefore, give by their foresight sure and highly relevant counsel. By their counsel they provide the best solutions to maintain the family in a tranquil and honorable state. With faith and diligence may they always protect it from any sudden ruin, and with strength and virility of soul guide and restore it if it has already been in part shaken or bent by fortune's blows. The intelligence, wisdom, and knowledge of the old together with their diligence constitute the very means to maintain the family in a flourishing and happy state of fortune and to ornament it with splendor and praise. What do the old deserve, then, who have the power to do this for their people, to keep them fortunate, to strengthen their resistance to misfortune, to support them in a life not deprived of adornment and pleasure? Do they not deserve great respect?

The young should respect the old, but more especially their own fathers. To these both for their age and for other reasons the young owe all too much. From your father you have your being and many principles to guide you in acquiring excellence of soul. Your father, with his sweat and zeal and hard work, made you the man you are. He gave you your years, your fortune, your condition. If you owe something to him who helps you in necessity and trouble, certainly to him who as far as he was able never allowed you to suffer the least need, to him you owe much indeed. If you ought to share every thought, every possession, every gift of fortune with your friend, and to suffer discomfort, fatigue, and strain for one who loves you, still more should you do for your father to whom you are dearer than anyone and to whom you owe almost more than to yourself. If your friends ought to enjoy a good portion of your possessions and goods and wealth, far more ought your father, from whom you have received, if not your goods, still life itself, and not only life but nurture for so long a time, and if not nurture, still being and name. Therefore ought young people to refer every wish, thought, and plan of their own to their fathers and elders and to take counsel with them about everything, especially with those to whom they know they are dearer than to the others. They should listen eagerly to them as to very wise and experienced men, and gladly submit to the guidance of men of judgment and age. Nor let the young be slow to help any of their elders in their old age and infirmity. Let them hope for the same humanity and sense of duty in their juniors that they have shown to their elders. Let them be quick and eager, then, to give them, in the staleness of old age, comfort, contentment, and repose. Nor let them imagine that any contentment or joy of the old surpasses that of seeing the young turn out well and worthy of love. Surely nothing can be a greater comfort to the old than to see those on whom they have long lavished their hope and expectation, those for whom they have been ambitious, rise through their conduct and character to attain general esteem, love, and honor. Very happy will be the old age which witnesses all the young people directed toward or engaged upon a peaceful and honorable life. A life which is well conducted will always be peaceful; a life guided by virtue will always be honorable. Nothing is such a source of anxiety in human life as vice.

Your duty, then, young men, is to try to satisfy your fathers and all your elders by your character in general, and particularly by doing things which bring praise and fame to you and, to your kinsmen, happiness, pleasure, and delight. So, my sons, follow virtue, flee from vice, respect your elders, act so as to be well liked, to live in freedom, to be happy, honored, and loved. The first step toward being honored is to make yourself liked and loved; the first step toward acquiring good will and love is to make one's goodness and honorableness apparent; the first step toward acquiring that grace of virtue is to feel a horror of vice and to flee from the vice-ridden. One should keep oneself ever worthy of the praise and love of good men. . . .

Lionardo: I do not see, Adovardo, how a diligent father can have sons who are stubborn and proud, unless you mean that he does not begin to be diligent until his son has been totally corrupted. If the father is really alert and provides against vices as they appear, if he is conscientious about uprooting them when he sees they have been started, if he is foresightful and careful not to wait lest a vice become so great and so thick that its infamy shadows and obscures the whole house, surely I think he will not have to fear any stubbornness or lack of obedience in his sons. It may even be that by his negligence and inaction some wickedness has grown and put out some of its branches. The father will never, by my advice, cut these off in such a way that they may in some manner strike his fortune or reputation. He will not separate his son from himself or send him out of the house as some uncontrolled and irate fathers do. Thus do young men already bursting with wickedness and filled with indulgence fall to doing vile things under pressure of necessity, committing dangerous deeds, and living in a way that disgraces themselves and their family. The father of the family will be careful and conscientious from the beginning about correcting every error in the appetites of any of his children. He will make an immediate effort to put out the sparks of any wicked greed. Then he need not later take on the heavy task of extinguishing with labor, grief, and tears a greater fire. . . .

A father must always act like a father, not odious but dignified, not overly familiar, but kind. Every father and elder should remember always that power sustained by force has always, inevitably, proved less stable than authority maintained by love. No fear can last very long: love lasts much longer. Fear diminishes in time: love grows always from day to day. Who would be so mad, then, as to think he must at all times appear severe and harsh? Severity without kindness produces more hate than obedience. Kindness, the more easy and free of any harshness it is, the more it wins love and acceptance. Nor do I call it diligence if a man, more like a tyrant than like a father, inquires too exactly into everything. This kind of severity and harshness usually makes young minds resentful and ill disposed to their elders rather than submissive. A noble mind by nature resents being treated like a slave instead of like a son. . . .

If the father finds nonetheless that as a result of past negligence he has a grown son who is bad, let him rather incline not to wish to call him son than to watch his own boy being dishonest and wicked. Our excellent laws, the custom of our country, the judgment of all good men, permit a useful remedy in such a case. If your son does not want you for a father, you need not have him for a son. If he does not obey you as a father is obeyed, you may be considerably harsher with him than with an obedient son. You should prefer the punishment of a bad man to the disgrace of your house. Be less sorry to have one of your children in prison or in chains than to have an enemy free in your house or a public disgrace outside. A man who causes you sorrow and grief is a real enough enemy.

But certainly, Adovardo, if a man is diligent and cares in time for his children, as you do for yours, he will never encounter at any age anything but reverence and honor from his own offspring. He will always find in them contentment and joy. The character of the sons lies in the power of the elders and the father. Nor should anyone imagine that obedience and submissiveness toward their elders will diminish in children, unless laziness and sloth are on the increase in their elders.

Adovardo: If all fathers could listen to these admonitions of yours, Lionardo, what sons they might raise to their satisfaction! How much joy and wisdom they might gain! Fortune cannot take all from us, I do see, not all, I admit. She cannot give us certain things either—character, virtue, letters, or any skill. All these depend on our diligence, our interest. What of those things, however, which are said to be subject to fortune: riches, power, and similar conveniences in life? They are almost necessities for the attainment of virtue and fame. Fortune has been ungenerous with us in these things. Fortune is unjust toward diligent fathers, as we have often seen. Most of the time she harms good men rather than less esteemed ones. Lionardo, what would be your grief if you were a father and not able to achieve the honorable goals you set yourself and toward which you had expected to strive? What if fortune did not permit you to do what you would and could do with her help, namely to guide your young sons toward the fame and honor you had expected for them and had already taught them to desire?

Lionardo: Are you asking me whether I would be ashamed to be poor, or whether I would be afraid that virtue might despise us and flee our poverty?

Adovardo: What, would poverty not cause you grief? Would it not weigh on your heart to be interrupted in every honorable course? Lionardo, what would you think then?

Lionardo: What do you think? I would be concerned to live as happily as I could. It would not grieve me much to suffer with a just mind, without annoyance, that which, as you say, often afflicts the good. Nor is being poor so ugly a thing, Adovardo, that I would be ashamed of it. Do you imagine that I think poverty would be so bad, so perfidious and unkind as to leave me no occasion for excellence, that it would give no reward of any kind to the efforts of a man who was hard-working and modest? Yet if you will look about you carefully, you will see more virtuous poor men than rich ones. Human life can content itself with little. Virtue is very well contented with itself. And the man who lives contentedly is rich enough.

Adovardo: Now, Lionardo, don't be such a Stoic[1] about everything I mention. You can say what you will, I would never admit that poverty is not a very mischievous and miserable thing for everyone, and particularly for a father. I willingly agree with your opinion that diligent fathers receive true delight from their sons, but I shall like this still better if I see you supporting your view of all these things not only with most subtle arguments but also with the wisdom of experience. A way should be found, Lionardo, to provide you and the others with a mate and sons. You should take a wife, add to our Alberti family, and diligently raise many offspring. You should use your excellent education so that our house might multiply, as Lorenzo was saying before, in the number of its famous and immortal men. I don't doubt that, by following all the learned ideas which you have just been teaching me, our house may become more glorious from day to day and richer in fine young men.

Lionardo: In this discussion of ours my mind was fixed on nothing less than on teaching you how to be a father. Who is so mad as to take on himself the burden of making you more learned in anything, you who, in every particular field, are more knowledgeable than anyone. In this one, besides, you are taught by experience as well as by the ancient writers. What fool would try to be your teacher concerning the excellent thing which we call a liberal education, or try to contradict you in a discussion of it? But all the cunning was yours, for you spoke to me against having children, and led me to throw away and give up all my old excuses for not taking a wife. I am left with no excuse to avoid this nuisance. I am willing, Adovardo, since you have thus convinced me, that you should have the freedom and discretion to choose me a wife wherever you think wise. Do realize, however, that you owe me a labor in return for what I have done? If I have lifted from your mind the troubles you said beset a father, you likewise should arrange for me to be free of anxiety and continual strife. These, if I follow your advice and get married, I am afraid will not be easy to escape. . . .

---

[1]One who adheres to Stoicism, a moral philosophy prominent among the ancient Greeks and Romans, which taught that humans should be free from passion, impassive or indifferent to pleasure or pain.

BOOK TWO

Lionardo: In our discussion we may establish four general precepts as sound and firm foundation for all the other points to be developed or added. I shall name them. In the family the number of men must not diminish but augment; possessions must not grow less, but more; all forms of disgrace are to be shunned—a good name and fine reputation is precious and worth pursuing; hatreds, enmities, rancor must be carefully avoided, while good will, numerous acquaintances, and friendships are something to look for, augment, and cultivate. . . .

Families increase in population no differently than do countries, regions, and the whole world. As anyone who uses his imagination will quickly realize, the number of mortal men has grown from a small number to the present almost infinite multitude through the procreation and rearing of children. And, for the procreation of children, no one can deny that man requires woman. Since a child comes into the world as a tender and delicate creature, he needs someone to whose care and devotion he comes as a cherished trust. This person must nourish him with diligence and love and must defend him from harm. Too much cold or too much sun, rain, and the wild blowing of a storm are harmful to children. Woman, therefore, did first find a roof under which to nourish and protect herself and her offspring. There she remained, busy in the shadow, nourishing and caring for her children. And since woman was busy guarding and taking care of the heir, she was not in a position to go out and find what she and her children required for the maintenance of their life. Man, however, was by nature more energetic and industrious, and he went out to find things and bring what seemed to him necessary. Sometimes the man remained away from home and did not return as soon as his family expected. Because of this, when he came back laden, the woman learned to save things up in order to make sure that if in the future her husband stayed away for a time, neither she nor her children would suffer. In this way it seems clear to me that nature and human reason taught mankind the necessity of having a spouse, both to increase and continue generations and to nourish and preserve those already born. It also became clear that careful gathering and diligent preserving were essential to the maintenance of human life in the married state.

Nature showed, further, that this relationship could not be permitted with more than one wife at a time, since man was by no means able to provide and bring home more than was needed for himself and one wife and children. Had he wished to find food and to gather goods for more wives and families, one or another of them would certainly sometimes have lacked some of the necessities. And the woman who found herself lacking what are or ought to be the necessities of life, would she not have had sufficient reason even to abandon her offspring in order to preserve her own life? Perhaps under pressure of such need she would even have had the right to seek out another companion. Marriage, therefore, was instituted by nature, our most excellent and divine teacher of all things, with the provision that there should be one constant life's companion for a man, and one only. With her he should dwell under one roof, her he should not forget or leave all alone, but to her return, bearing things with him and ordering matters so that his family might have all that was necessary and sufficient. The wife was to preserve in the house the things he brought to her. To satisfy nature, then, a man need only choose a woman with whom he can dwell in tranquility under one roof all his life.

Young people, however, very often do not cherish the good of the family enough to do this. Marriage, perhaps, seems to them to take away their present liberty and freedom. It may be, as the comic poets like to tell us, that they are held back and dissuaded by some mistress. Sometimes, too, young men find it hard enough to manage one life, and fear as an excessive and undesirable burden the task of supporting a wife and children besides. They may doubt their capacity to maintain in honorable estate a family which grows in needs from day to day. Viewing the conjugal bed as a troublesome responsibility, they then avoid the legitimate and honorable path to the increase of a family.

If a family is not to fall for these reasons into what we have described as the most unfortunate condition of decline, but is to grow, instead, in fame and in the prosperous multitude of its youth, we must persuade our young men to take wives. We must use every argument for this purpose, offer incentive, promise reward, employ all our wit, persistence, and cunning. A most appropriate reason for taking a wife may be found in what we were saying before, about the evil of sensual indulgence, for the condemnation of such things may lead young men to desire honorable satisfactions. As other incentives, we may also speak to them of the delights of this primary and natural companionship of marriage. Children act as pledges and securities of marital love and kindness. At the same time they offer a focus for all a man's hopes and desires. Sad, indeed, is the man who has labored to get wealth and power and lands, and then has no true heir and perpetuator of his memory. No one can be more suited than a man's true and legitimate sons to gain advantages by virtue of his character, position, and authority, and to enjoy the fruits and rewards of his labor. If a man leaves such heirs, furthermore, he need not consider himself wholly dead and gone. His children keep his own position and his true image in the family. Dido,[2] the Phoenician, when Aeneas left her, his mistress, cried out with tears, among her great sorrows no desire above this one: "Ah, had I but a small Aeneas now, to play beside me." As you were first poisoned, wretched and abandoned woman, by that man whose fatal and consuming love you

[2]In Virgil's epic poem *The Aeneid*, Dido, the queen of Carthage, falls in love with the Trojan hero Aeneas and kills herself when he leaves for Italy.

did embrace, so another little Aeneas might by his similar face and gestures have offered you some consolation in your grief and anguish.

It will serve our purpose, also, to remind the young of the dignity conferred on the father in the ancient world. Fathers of families wore precious jewels and were given other tokens of dignity forbidden to any who had not added by his progeny to the population of the republic. It may also help to recall to young men how often profligates and hopeless prodigals have been restored to a better life by the presence of a wife in the house. Add to this what a great help sons can be as hands to get work done—how they give zealous and loyal aid and support when fortune is hard and men unkind—and how your sons more than anyone spring to your defense and are ready to avenge the injury and harm inflicted upon you by evil and outrageous men. Likewise, our children are our comfort and are apt at every age to make us happy and give us great joys and satisfactions. These things it is good to tell them. It also helps to point out how much children come to mean in old age, when we live under the pressure of various needs. As Messer Niccolaio Alberti in his wisdom and experience used to say, children are the natural and reliable crutch of the old. These and similar arguments, which it would take too long to detail here, will help to teach young men not to spurn an honorable mate. . . .

Let it be the responsibility of the whole house to see that once they have the desire they have also the ability honorably to establish a family. Let the entire family contribute, as if to purchase its own growth, and let them all join by gathering something from each member to put up a sufficient sum for a fund which will support those who shall be born. In this way an expense which would have been disastrously heavy for one alone shall be shared among many and become merely a light obligatory payment. . . .

Perhaps it will help to put our young people under some compulsion like this: fathers could say in their wills, "If you do not marry when you reach the appropriate age, you are no heir of mine." As to what is the appropriate time of life to take a wife, to relate all the ancient opinions on this matter would take a long time. Hesiod[3] would have a man marry at thirty; Lycurgus[4] wanted fatherhood to begin at thirty-seven; to our modern minds it seems to be practical for a man to marry at twenty-five. Everyone at least agrees that to give this kind of responsibility to the willful and ardent youth under twenty-five is dangerous. A man of that age spends his fire and force better in establishing and strengthening his own position than in procreating. The youthful seed, moreover, seems faulty and frail and less full of vigor than that which is ripened. Let men wait for solid maturity.

---

[3]Eighth-century B.C. Greek poet.
[4]Spartan lawgiver.

When, by the urging and counsel of their elders and of the whole family, young men have arrived at the point of marriage, their mothers and other female relatives and friends, who have known the virgins of the neighborhood from earliest childhood and know the way their upbringing has formed them, should select all the well-born and well-brought-up girls and present that list to the new groom-to-be. He can then choose the one who suits him best. The elders of the house and all of the family shall reject no daughter-in-law unless she is tainted with the breath of scandal or bad reputation. Aside from that, let the man who will have to satisfy her satisfy himself. He should act as do wise heads of families before they acquire some property—they like to look it over several times before they actually sign a contract. It is good in the case of any purchase and contract to inform oneself fully and to take counsel. One should consult a good number of persons and be very careful in order to avoid belated regrets. The man who has decided to marry must be still more cautious. I recommend that he examine and anticipate in every way, and consider for many days, what sort of person it is he is to live with for all his years as husband and companion. Let him be minded to marry for two purposes: first to perpetuate himself in his children, and second to have a steady and constant companion all his life. A woman is needed, therefore, who is likely to bear children and who is desirable as a perpetual mate.

They say that in choosing a wife one looks for beauty, parentage, and riches. The beauty of a man accustomed to arms, it seems to me, lies in his having a presence betokening pride, limbs full of strength, and the gestures of one who is skilled and adept in all forms of exercise. The beauty of an old man, I think, lies in his prudence, his amiability, and the reasoned judgment which permeates all his words and his counsel. Whatever else may be thought beautiful in an old man, certainly it differs sharply from what constitutes beauty in a young cavalier. I think that beauty in a woman, likewise, must be judged not only by the charm and refinement of her face, but still more by the grace of her person and her aptitude for bearing and giving birth to many fine children.

Among the most essential criteria of beauty in a woman is an honorable manner. Even a wild, prodigal, greasy, drunken woman may be beautiful of feature, but no one would call her a beautiful wife. A woman worthy of praise must show first of all in her conduct, modesty, and purity. Marius,[5] the illustrious Roman, said in that first speech of his to the Roman people: "Of women we require purity, of men labor." And I certainly agree. There is nothing more disgusting than a coarse and dirty woman. Who is stupid enough not to see clearly that a woman who does not care for neatness and cleanliness in her appearance, not only in her dress and body but in all her behavior and language, is by no means well mannered?

---

[5]Roman general during the turbulent first century B.C.

How can it be anything but obvious that a bad mannered woman is also rarely virtuous? We shall consider elsewhere the harm that comes to a family from women who lack virtue, for I myself do not know which is the worse fate for a family, total celibacy or a single dishonored woman. In a bride, therefore, a man must first seek beauty of mind, that is, good conduct and virtue.

In her body he must seek not only loveliness, grace, and charm but must also choose a woman who is well made for bearing children, with the kind of constitution that promises to make them strong and big. There's an old proverb, "When you pick your wife, you choose your children." All her virtues will in fact shine brighter still in beautiful children. It is a well-known saying among poets: "Beautiful character dwells in a beautiful body." The natural philosophers require that a woman be neither thin nor very fat. Those laden with fat are subject to coldness and constipation and slow to conceive. They say that a woman should have a joyful nature, fresh and lively in her blood and her whole being. They have no objections to a dark girl. They do reject girls with a frowning black visage, however. They have no liking for either the undersized or the overlarge and lean. They find that a woman is most suited to bear children if she is fairly big and has limbs of ample length. They always have a preference for youth, based on a number of arguments which I need not expound here, but particularly on the point that a young girl has a more adaptable mind. Young girls are pure by virtue of their age and have not developed any spitefulness. They are by nature modest and free of vice. They quickly learn to accept affectionately and unresistingly the habits and wishes of their husbands. . . .

Now we have spoken of beauty. Let us next consider parentage, and what are the qualities to look for there. I think the first problem in choosing a family is to investigate closely the customs and habits of one's new relatives. Many marriages have ruined the family, as one may hear and read every day, because they involved union with a litigious, quarrelsome, arrogant, and malevolent set of men. For brevity's sake I cite no examples here. I think that no one is so great a fool that he would not rather remain unmarried than burden himself with terrible relatives. Sometimes the links of family have proved a trouble and disaster to the man, who has had to support both his own family and that of the girl he married. Not infrequently it happens that the new family, because they feel unable to manage their own affairs or because they really are so unfortunate, all settle down in the house of their new kinsman. As the new husband you cannot keep them without harm to yourself, nor can you send them away without incurring censure.

To sum up this whole subject in a few words, for I want above all to be brief on this point, let a man get himself new kinsmen of better than plebeian blood, of a fortune more than diminutive, of a decent occupation, and of modest and respectable habits. Let them not be too far above himself, lest their greatness overshadow his own honor and position. Too high a family may disturb his own and his family's peace and tranquility, and also, if one of them falls, you cannot help to support him without collapsing or wearing yourself out as you stagger under a weight too great for your arms and your strength. I also do not want the new relatives to rank too low, for while the first error puts you in a position of servitude, the second causes expense. Let them be equals, then, and, to repeat, modest and respectable people.

The matter of dowry is next, which I would like to see middling in size, certain, and prompt rather than large, vague, or promised for an indefinite future. I know not why everyone, as if corrupted by a common vice, takes advantage of delay to grow lazy in paying debts. Sometimes, in cases of marriage, people are further tempted because they hope to evade payment altogether. As your wife spends her first year in your house, it seems impossible not to reinforce the new bonds of kinship by frequent visiting and parties. But it will be thought rude if, in the middle of a gathering of kinsmen, you put yourself forward to insist and complain. If, as new husbands usually do, you don't want to lose their still precarious favor, you may ask your in-laws in restrained and casual words. Then you are forced to accept any little excuse they may offer. If you make a more forthright demand for what is your own, they will explain to you their many obligations, will complain of fortune, blame the conditions of the time, complain of other men, and say that they hope to be able to ask much of you in greater difficulties. As long as they can, in fact, they will promise you bounteous repayment at an ever-receding date. They will beg you, and overwhelm you, nor will it seem possible for you to spurn the prayers of people you have accepted as your own family. Finally, you will be put in a position where you must either suffer the loss in silence or enter upon expensive litigation and create enmity.

What is more, it will seem that you can never put an end to the pressure from your wife on this point. She will weep many tears, and the pleadings and insistent prayers of a new love that has just begun are apt to have a certain force. However hard and twisted your temperament you can hardly impose silence on someone who pleads with an outsider, thus softly and tearfully, for the sake of her own father and brothers. Then imagine how impossible for you to turn a deaf ear on your own wife doing so in your own house, in your own room. You are bound, in the end, to suffer either financial loss or loss of affection. This is why the dowry should be precisely set, promptly paid, and not too high. . . .

Battista: I would not interrupt your rapid exposition, if you had not yourself given me leave to do it. But it would help to stop a moment and let me turn my head to fix in my memory what you have traversed to this point, if I can remember it rightly. You have said, I gather, that one should select a virtuous woman of good parentage, one well dowered and suited to bear a fair number of sons. All these things are very difficult. Lionardo, do you think one could easily find them all combined in one woman, let alone in as many as a large family like ours requires? In various marriages I have noted that if a girl is well born she often comes without dowry. There is even a common saying, "If you desire gold, take her ugly or old." It is my impression that we regulate our lives rather like the ancient Thracians, among whom ugly virgins purchased their husbands at high prices, while, for the beautiful girls, sums to be paid were established by official assessors. Do you see what I mean, Lionardo?

Lionardo: I do see, and I am glad you listened so patiently to what we have been saying so far. I am glad, too, that you did not let me run on like this. For, yes, it is as you say: all marriages cannot be as I wish. Nor can all wives be like that Cornelia, the daughter of Metellus Scipio, who was married to Publius Crassus,[6] a woman who was beautiful, well educated, skilled in music, geometry, and philosophy, and, most praiseworthy of all in a woman of such abilities and virtue, not at all haughty or aloof or demanding. But let us take the advice of the slave girl, Birria, in Terence:[7] "If you can't do what you want, want what you can do." One marries the girl who seems to have less faults than the others. One does not give up beauty for parentage or parentage in order to get a dowry. Cato,[8] who excelled as the father of a family, used to praise the girl who showed an old fashioned refinement of manners above the one who was loaded with money. Personally, I can well believe that both may be rather forward and self-willed, but that the one born and brought up not in the luxurious shade of wealth but under the bright influence of good character and habits will probably be a little more sensitive about bringing shame on herself and far more obedient. One takes a wife, in fact, mainly to have children by her. One then considers, further, that good kinsmen are a more reliable advantage than good fortune. They are worth more, in the judgment of good men, than wealth. Wealth is a fleeting and perishable thing, while kinsmen, if you think of them as such and treat them accordingly, remain kinsmen forever. . . .

BOOK THREE

Lionardo: . . . The system and diligence of the master makes even the heaviest and most difficult tasks easy and manageable. For some reason, however, I don't know why, it still does seem that public affairs get in the way of private ones, while private needs often conflict with our attention to public affairs. I am led to doubt, therefore, that all our devotion, given to all things at once, will prove sufficient.

Giannozzo: Don't take that view when there is a quick and excellent remedy at hand.

---

[6]A member, with Pompey and Julius Caesar, of the First Triumvirate of Rome (59 B.C.).
[7]Roman poet and playwright.
[8]Cato the Censor (second century B.C.), paragon of conservative Roman civic values.

Lionardo: What remedy?

Giannozzo: Let the father of the family follow my example. Since I find it no easy matter to deal with the needs of the household when I must often be engaged outside with other men in arranging matters of wider consequence, I have found it wise to set aside a certain amount for outside use, for investments and purchases. The rest, which takes care of all the smaller household affairs, I leave to my wife's care. I have done it this way, for, to tell the truth, it would hardly win us respect if our wife busied herself among the men in the marketplace, out in the public eye. It also seems somewhat demeaning to me to remain shut up in the house among women when I have manly things to do among men, fellow citizens and worthy and distinguished foreigners.

I don't know whether you will approve of my solution. I know some people are always checking on their own household and rummaging around in every nook and cranny lest something remain hidden from them. Nothing is so obscure that they do not look into it and poke their fingers in. They say that it is no shame or harm to a man to attend carefully to his own affairs and to lay down the law and custom in his own house. They point out that Niccolo Alberti, who was a very diligent person, said diligence and universal vigilance was the mother of wealth. I too admire and like this saying, for diligence always helps; but I cannot convince myself that men who are engaged in other concerns really ought to be or to seem so very interested in every little household trifle. I don't know, perhaps I am wrong about this. What do you say, Lionardo, what do you think?

Lionardo: I agree, for you are, indeed, precisely of the opinion of the ancients. They used to say that men are by nature of a more elevated mind than women. They are more suited to struggle with arms and with cunning against the misfortunes which afflict country, religion, and one's own children. The character of men is stronger than that of women and can bear the attacks of enemies better, can stand strain longer, is more constant under stress. Therefore men have the freedom to travel with honor in foreign lands, acquiring and gathering the goods of fortune. Women, on the other hand, are almost all timid by nature, soft, slow, and therefore more useful when they sit still and watch over our things. It is as though nature thus provided for our well-being, arranging for men to bring things home and for women to guard them. The woman, as she remains locked up at home, should watch over things by staying at her post, diligent care and watchfulness. The man should guard the woman, the house, and his family and country, but not by sitting still. He should exercise his spirit and his hands in brave enterprise, even at the cost of sweat and blood. No doubt of it, therefore, Giannozzo, those idle creatures who stay all day among the little females or who keep their minds occupied with little feminine trifles certainly lack a masculine and glorious spirit. They are contemptible in their apparent inclination to play the part of women rather than that of men. A man demonstrates his love of high achievements by the pride he takes in his own. But if he does not shun trifling occupations, clearly he does not mind being regarded as effeminate. It seems to me, then, that you are entirely right to leave the care of minor matters to your wife and to take upon yourself, as I have always seen you do, all manly and honorable concerns.

Giannozzo: Yes, you see that's my long-standing conviction. I believe that a man who is the father of a family not only should do all that is proper to a man, but that he must abstain from such activities as properly pertain to women. The details of housekeeping he should commit entirely into their hands. I always do.

Lionardo: You, however, can congratulate yourself on having a wife who probably surpasses other women. I don't know how many women one could find as vigorous and as wise in their rule of the household as your wife.

Giannozzo: My wife certainly did turn into a perfect mother for my household. Partly this was the result of her particular nature and temperament, but mainly it was due to my instruction.

Lionardo: Then you taught her?

Giannozzo: Many things.

Lionardo: And how did you do it?

Giannozzo: Well, I'll tell you. After my wife had been settled in my house a few days, and after her first pangs of longing for her mother and family had begun to fade, I took her by the hand and showed her around the whole house. I explained that the loft was the place for grain and that the stores of wine and wood were kept in the cellar. I showed her where things needed for the table were kept, and so on, through the whole house. At the end were no household goods of which my wife had not learned both the place and the purpose. Then we returned to my room, and, having locked the door, I showed her my treasure, silver, tapestry, garments, jewels, and where each thing had its place.

Lionardo: All those valuables, then, were assigned some place in your room, I suppose because they were safer there, better secluded and more securely locked up.

Giannozzo: Yes, but primarily so that I could look them over whenever I liked without witness. You may be sure, children, that it is imprudent to live so openly that the whole household knows everything. It is less difficult to guard a thing from a few persons than from all. If something is known only to a few, it is easier to keep safe. If it does get lost, it is easier to get it back from a few than from many. For this and for many other reasons, I have always thought it a good precaution to keep every precious thing I had well hidden if possible, and locked up out of the reach of most hands and eyes. These treasures, I always felt, should be kept where they are safe from fire and other disaster, and where I can frequently, whether for my pleasure or to check them over, shut myself up alone or with whomever I choose while giving no cause for undue curiosity to those outside. No place seemed more suited for this purpose than the room where I slept. There, as I was saying, I wanted none of my precious things to be hidden from my wife. I opened to her all my household treasures, unfolded them, and showed them to her.

Only my books and records and those of my ancestors did I determine to keep well sealed both then and thereafter. These my wife not only could not read, she could not even lay hands on them. I kept my records at all times not in the sleeves of my dress, but locked up and arranged in order in my study, almost like sacred and religious objects. I never gave my wife permission to enter that place, with me or alone. I also ordered her, if she ever came across any writing of mine, to give it over to my keeping at once. To take away any taste she might have for looking at my notes or prying into my private affairs, I often used to express my disapproval of bold and forward females who try too hard to know about things outside the house and about the concerns of their husband and of men in general. . . .

I always tried to make sure, first that she could not, and second that she did not wish, to know more of my secrets than I cared to impart. One should never, in fact, tell a secret, even a trivial one, to one's wife or any woman. I am greatly displeased with those husbands who take counsel with their wives and don't know how to confine any kind of secret to their own breast. They are madmen if they think true prudence or good counsel lies in the female brain, and still more clearly mad if they suppose that a wife will be more constant in silence concerning her husband's business than he himself has proved. Stupid husbands to blab to their wives and forget that women themselves can do anything sooner than keep quiet! For this very reason I have always tried carefully not to let any secret of mine be known to a woman. I did not doubt that my wife was most loving, and more discreet and modest in her ways than any, but I still considered it safer to have her unable, and not merely unwilling, to harm me. . . .

When my wife had seen and understood the place of everything in the house, I said to her, "My dear wife, those things are to be as useful and precious to you as to me. The loss of them would injure and grieve you, therefore should you guard them no less zealously than I do. You have seen our treasures now, and thanks be to God they are such that we ought to be contented with them. If we know how to preserve them, these things will serve you and me and our children. It is to you, therefore, my dear wife, to keep no less careful watch over them than I."

Lionardo: And what did your wife say to that?

Giannozzo: She replied by saying that her father and mother had taught her to obey them and had ordered her always to obey me, and so she was prepared to do anything I told her to. "My dear wife," said I, "a girl who knows how to obey her father and mother soon learns to please her husband. But do you know how we shall try to be? We shall imitate those who stand guard on the walls of the city; if one of them, by chance, falls asleep, he does not take it amiss for his companion to wake him up that he may do his duty for his country. Likewise, my dear wife, if you ever see any fault in me, I shall be very grateful to you for letting me know. In that way I shall know that our honor and our welfare and the good of our children are dear to your heart. Likewise be not displeased if I awaken you where there is need. Where I am lacking, you shall make it good, and so together we shall try to surpass each other in love and in zeal.

This property, this family, and the children to be born to us will belong to us both, to you as much as to me, to me as much as to you. It behooves us, therefore, not to think now much each of us has brought into our marriage, but how we can best maintain all that belongs to both of us. I shall try to obtain outside what you need inside the house; you must see that none of it is wasted.

Lionardo: How did she seem to take all this? Was she pleased?

Giannozzo: Very much so. She said she would be happy to do conscientiously whatever she knew how to do and had the skill to do, hoping it might please me. To this I said, "Dear wife, listen to me. I shall be most pleased if you do just three things: first, my wife, see that you never want another man to share this bed but me. You understand." She blushed and cast down her eyes. Still I repeated that she should never receive anyone into that room but myself. That was the first point. The second, I said, was that she should take care of the household, preside over it with modesty, serenity, tranquility, and peace. That was the second point. The third thing, I said, was that she should see that nothing went wrong in the house.

Lionardo: Did you show her how to do what you commanded, or did she already have an expert knowledge of these things?

Giannozzo: Do not imagine, my dear Lionardo, that a young girl can ever be very well versed in these matters. Nor is such cleverness and cunning required from a young girl as it is from the mother of a family. Her modesty and virtue, on the other hand, must be greater. And these very qualities my wife had in abundance. In these virtues she surpassed all other women. I could not describe to you how reverently she replied to me. She said her mother had taught her only how to spin and sew, and how to be virtuous and obedient. Now she would gladly learn from me how to rule the family and whatever I might wish to teach her. . . .

When I had given the house over to my wife's keeping, I brought her back to our own locked room, as I was saying. Then she and I knelt down and prayed to God to give us the power to make good use of those possessions which he, in his mercy and kindness, had allowed us to enjoy. We also prayed with most devoted mind that he might grant us the grace to live together in peace and harmony for many happy years, and with many male children, and that he might grant to me riches, friendship, and honor, and to her, integrity, purity, and the character of a perfect mistress of the household. Then, when we had stood up, I said to her:

"My dear wife, to have prayed God for these things is not enough. Let us also be very diligent and conscientious and do our best to obtain what we have prayed for. I, my dear wife, shall seek with all my powers to gain what we have asked of God. You, too, must set your whole will, all your mind, and all your modesty to work to make yourself a person whom God has heard and to whom he has granted what you prayed for. You should realize that in this regard nothing is so important for yourself, so acceptable to God, so pleasing to me, and precious in the sight of your children as your chastity. The woman's character is the jewel of her family; the mother's purity has always been a part of the dowry she passes on to her daughters; her purity has always far outweighed her beauty. A beautiful face is praised, but unchaste eyes make it ugly through men's scorn, and too often flushed with shame or pale with sorrow and melancholy. A handsome person is pleasing to see, but a shameless gesture or an act of incontinence in an instant renders her appearance vile. Unchastity angers God, and you know that God punishes nothing so severely in women as he does this lack. All their lives he makes them notorious and miserable. The shameless woman is hated by her whose love is true and good. She soon discovers that, in fact, her dishonored condition pleases only her enemies. Only one who wishes us to suffer and be troubled can rejoice when he sees you fall from honor.

"Shun every sort of dishonor, my dear wife. Use every means to appear to all people as a highly respectable woman. To seem less would be to offend God, me, our children, and yourself. To seem so, indeed, brings praise and love and favor from all. Then you can hope that God will give some aid to your prayers and vows.

"To be praised for your chastity, you must shun every deed that lacks true nobility, eschew any sort of improper speech, avoid giving any sign that your spirit lacks perfect balance and chastity. You will disdain, first of all, those vanities which some females imagine will please men. All made up and plastered and painted and dressed in lascivious and improper clothing, they suppose they are more attractive to men than when adorned with pure simplicity and true virtue. Vain and foolish women are these who imagine that when they appear in make-up and look far from virtuous they will be praised by those who see them. They do not realize that they are provoking disapproval and harming themselves. Nor do they realize, in their petty vanity, that their immodest appearance excites numerous lustful men. Such men all besiege and attack such a girl, some with suddenness, some with persistence, some with trickery, until at last the unfortunate wretch falls into real disgrace. From such a fall she cannot rise again without the stain of great and lasting infamy upon her." . . .

Lionardo: Did she seem to agree and to realize you were telling the truth?

Giannozzo: What sort of silly girl would fail to realize this was the truth? Besides, to make sure she did believe me, I asked her about a neighbor of mine, a woman who had few teeth left in her mouth, and those appeared tarnished with rust. Her eyes were sunken and always inflammed, the rest of her face whithered and ashen. All her flesh looked decomposed and disgusting. Her silvery hair was the only thing about her that one might regard without displeasure. So I asked my wife whether she wished she were blond and looked like her?

"Heavens, no," said she.

"And why not? Does she seem so old to you? How old do you think she is?"

To that she replied most modestly that she was no judge of these matters, but to her the woman seemed about the age of her mother's wetnurse. Then I assured her of the truth, namely that that neighbor of mine was born less than two years before me and had certainly not yet attained her thirty-second year. Thanks to make-up, however, she had been left in this diseased condition and seemed old before her time.

When I saw she was really amazed at this, I reminded her of all the Alberti girls, of my cousins and others in the family. "You see, my dear wife," I said, "how fresh and lively our girls all are, for the simple reason that they never anoint themselves with anything but river water. And so shall you do, my wife," said I. "You'll not poison yourself or whiten your face to make yourself seem more beautiful for me. You are white and bright enough complexioned for me as you are. Rather, like the Alberti girls, you will just wash and keep clean with water alone. My dear wife, there is no one but me for you to think of pleasing in this matter. Me, however, you cannot please by deception. Remember that. You cannot deceive me, anyway, because I see you at all hours and know very well how you look without make-up. As for outsiders, if you love me, think how could any of them matter more to you than your own husband. Remember, my dear wife, that a girl who tries harder to please outsiders than the one she should be pleasing shows that she loves her husband less than she does strangers."

The *Très Riches Heures* of the Duc de Berry

Little is known of the three Limbourg brothers (Pol, Hennequin, and Hermann), who in the early fifteenth century painted thirty-nine miniatures for Jean, duke of Berry (1340–1416) that illustrated the manuscript book, The Très Riches Heures (Very Rich Hours). A book of hours was a book of prayers to be said privately. (The canonical hours were the stipulated times of daily prayer.) It is extraordinary that the Limbourgs' calendar, one of the most celebrated works of art in Western civilization, appears in a library manuscript (in Chantilly, in northern France) rather than being displayed to the public in a museum.

The six months reproduced here (February, March, May, July, September, and November) give us vivid glimpses of late medieval French life, even if we take into account that the Limbourgs (and a later artist, Jean Colombe, who painted the illuminations for November and for parts of March and September) idealized much of what they painted. Of course, in using these illustrations, the historian must decide the extent to which they depict reality as opposed to the way the aristocracy wished to see the world.

The illustration of the month of February portrays the height of winter. What does this picture tell us about peasant work, costume, and living conditions? How did the people keep warm? In March, we see a landscape with fields in the foreground and a castle (the château of Lusignan) in the background. How did the peasants work their fields? May describes the duke and his court in a pageant, where the wearing of green was traditional. How did these noble men and women dress? Note that musicians and dogs accompanied this merry frolic through the woods. In the distance looms the exquisitely detailed royal palace in Paris. What can you learn about Paris from this depiction of the Parisian skyline?

The Limbourgs show peasants reaping and shearing in the month of July. How do their costumes differ from those peasants wore in the February illustration? In comparing the castle of Saumur in the September painting with the castles in the March and July pictures, can you say something about fifteenth-century castle architecture? Do the castles appear to have been built with comfort, beauty, or defense in mind? September also shows the peasants harvesting grapes and is another good rendition of peasant costume. The final illustration, of November, portrays the traditional acorn harvest. Peasants and pigs scour the forest for acorns. Taken together, what do these six illustrations indicate about peasant diet and life? How do these illustrations confirm or revise the impression of peasant life you derived from the earlier selections on peasants?

February

March

May

July

September

November

Articles of the Peasants of Stühlingen and Lupfen

The territorial county of Stühlingen was situated in southwestern Germany in a region of petty domains, small towns, and monastic territories. Unrest and rebellion began to occur among the rural population there in the spring of 1524. In June of that year the peasants of Stühlingen, irate over demands that they leave harvest work in order to collect snail shells on which the ladies of the manor could wind their thread, rose against their territorial and ground lord, Count Sigmund von Lupfen. The Count, who had been left in desperate financial straits by his spendthrift father and was bent on extracting as much revenue as possible from his subjects, turned a deaf ear to his peasants' demands. When attempts at mediation failed, the peasants organized military units, chose a captain, and sought help from the nearby city of Waldshut and from Duke Ulrich of Württemberg, who had recently been exiled from his lands by the Habsburgs and was looking for a cause to help him restore his fortunes. These events, and their consequences, led to the great peasant war of 1525.

In the end, the demands of the Stühlingen peasants were arbitrated and transferred to the Imperial Chamber Court (an extraterritorial, national appeals tribunal) for action. The list of articles below, translated with a few minor omissions, was drawn up for the justices of this high court. A detailed statement of grievances and demands, it is an excellent summary of the conditions of peasant life in western Germany at the end of the Middle Ages. Appealing on nearly every point to the "ancient traditions and customs" that were thought to have guarded village autonomy against attempts at state-building by centralizing territorial princes, peasant spokesmen pleaded for a reversal of the Count's steady encroachment on their independence and for a mitigation of the innumerable petty chicaneries, exactions, and regulations that stunted and frustrated rural existence at almost every turn. The articles are notable also for the absence of any references to the Church and the religious question. Issues in Stühlingen were practical and mundane. (Original editor's introduction.)

What specific customs do the peasants feel that their lord, Count Sigmund von Lupfen, has violated? What recommendations do the peasants make?

What can you say about the court system on manors from this document? That is, how did it operate and what roles did the peasants play in it?

What were the customs affecting inheritance and marriage? Do the obligations, such as services, that the peasants owed the count appear to be onerous? Do the peasants' demands regarding their relationship with Count von Lupfen appear to be reasonable?

1. The counts of Stühlingen and Lupfen should not imprison any resident involved in a civil action.

In the old days it was the custom and usage in the above-mentioned county to imprison no one against whom a civil action was pending, as long as the man held some property in the county and was willing to furnish surety for the matter or sum being asked of him. In recent times, however, our lords have ignored our village courts, where, according to our laws and customs, they should bring action. If they think that a man owes them something or if they suspect that someone has committed an offense, they order the bailiff to take the accused to prison and let him lie there until he has made his peace with them according to their bidding. . . .

2. No one should be tried for felony in a court other than the one with jurisdiction over his place of residence or the place where the offense was committed.

Although we have our own courts for criminal, including capital, matters and although it has been the custom up to now to try no offender in a superior court or away from the court in whose jurisdiction he committed his offense and was apprehended, our lords have introduced an innovation by transferring cases from our village courts to their superior court. This practice does us much harm, for a man who enjoys the counts' favor will not be punished in their court according to the gravity of his offense. Furthermore, it is up to us to escort the prisoner to this distant court, which is a venture requiring much trouble, pain, cost, and risk. . . .

3. Our lords confiscate both the stolen and the personal property of a condemned thief.

When a man is hanged for theft, our lords take not only the stolen goods, or as much of them as can be recovered, but his other property as well, which is a practice against all law and custom. For, according to custom, damage may not be added to damage; to act contrary to this custom is most unjust to the poor widow and orphans, who are obliged to repay the debt out of their own pockets. We request that the counts be made to realize that in the case of a condemned and executed thief the stolen property should be returned to the man from whom it was stolen and that the wife and children of the condemned man should not be done out of the remaining property, no matter how it was acquired. . . .

5. If a man snatches a stolen article from the thief, he is obliged to surrender it to the counts.

If it should happen that a man from whom something has been stolen succeeds in forcing the thief to surrender the loot, either in part or in its entirety, he is forced to hand it, that is to say, his own property recovered by him, to the counts. And if he should conceal from the counts the recovery of his property and they become aware of it, they punish him. . . .

6. What happens when a marriage partner dies and the deceased is claimed by the lord as a bondsman.

Marriage is an institution sanctioned by divine and Christian laws and is, moreover, free, so that in case of death nothing should be taken away from either of the partners. But when a man or a woman of the county takes for wife or husband a person not from the county and not bonded to the count, and the man dies and is claimed by the count as his bondsman, the count's officials come and take the best head of cattle. If the woman dies, they take her best frocks, even her wedding garments, and sometimes also a bed. In some places they also take clothes when the husband has died. It is our request that in future such exactions cease and we be no longer compelled to surrender cattle, clothes, beds, or anything else in case of death.

7. What happens when a man takes for a wife a woman not in bondage to the count.

If a man should take a woman from another village who is not the property of the count, and the woman dies, the count takes the third part of the entire property without any compensation, regardless of debts remaining to be paid off and orphaned children to be raised. Sometimes he takes our cattle even though half of it may still be unpaid for. . . .

8. Marriage with a person from another county is forbidden without the count's approval.

We are further oppressed by the unchristian practice of refusing a man or woman permission to wed a person not subject to the lord. Even when this permission is granted, it is given only after a long delay. And if one of us should enter into such a marriage without permission, he is punished for it by the lord or his bailiffs. . . .

9. If our jurors give judgments displeasing to our lords' bailiffs, they hale the jurors before the territorial court, which means that our jurors cannot judge freely.

Although our jurors have sworn an oath binding them to judge freely, fairly, and according to their true understanding of the matter brought before them, neither favoring nor disadvantaging anyone, it often happens that when a bailiff takes a matter pertaining to the count's business before one of our village courts and is displeased with the judgment given by our honorable jurors, he summons the jurors before the territorial court, claiming that they did not judge correctly in the matter and demanding that they be punished. From this practice it follows that jurors cannot be free and secure in their deliberations and that parties against whom the bailiff appears as plaintiff must always be prepared for an unjust verdict. . . .

10. We are all, young and old, summoned to court when a capital case is tried.

When a man is tried for a capital crime in the counts' court, the bailiffs round up all villagers above fourteen years of age and tell them to assist at the trial and to remain there on pain of punishment until it is ended. From this we have no benefit whatever; on the contrary, it does us much harm, for we must abandon our work and leave our houses unguarded. . . . It is our plea that the counts should cause to be summoned only one from each village to be present at court along with the judges. . . .

11. Sub-bailiffs should be appointed with the approval of the community or elected by the majority of its members.

Although it used to be the custom of the county to appoint a sub-bailiff with the knowledge and approval of the community or else to have him chosen by a majority of its members, our lords have in recent times undertaken to appoint sub-bailiffs without our knowledge and will, selecting them according to their own pleasure and taking only such men as are pleasing to them. A sub-bailiff appointed in this way is bound to wish to please the lords and their bailiffs, for if he fails to do so, he loses his office. Moreover, many men are now appointed sub-bailiffs who are not suitable for this post. . . .

12. We are forced to have our legal documents notarized by the territorial scribe . . . even though territorial courts have no authority over our written business.

Our lords oblige us to have our papers, such as purchasing agreements, contracts, bills of sale, and other documents, drawn up by the territorial scribe, although the old laws give us leave to have them done and sealed at our own village courts at nominal cost. It is therefore our request that in future all documents pertaining to our affairs be written and sealed by the authority of our own courts. . . .

13. We are forced to provide carting service and other help to foreign lords and noblemen.

Although we are always willing to give aid in body and goods to our own lords, we feel sorely oppressed by our lords' demand that we journey to meet visiting foreign rulers and nobles, from which obligation we suffer heavy costs and risks. According to our old laws and customs we do not owe such service to foreigners, and it is our plea and request that our lords henceforth refrain from demanding it of us. . . .

14. We are prevented, in violation of the old customs, from gathering wood in the county's forest.

In the old days we were always free to go to the forests to fill our need of lumber and firewood. But in recent times our lords have abolished this ancient custom, and we are now no longer permitted to gather wood in the forest as of old, which is much to our harm and injury. . . .

15. Our lords and their bailiffs and retainers do their hawking and hunting on our fields without showing consideration for the condition of our crops.

We till our fields and meadows with great effort, cost, and work so as to be able to fulfill our obligations to our lords and to nourish our wives and children. In return for this our lords and their bailiffs ought to guard us and our property and protect us from harm. Instead, they ride and tramp over our meadows and fields in pursuit of the pleasure of hunting, hawking, and the chase. They do this without giving a thought to the harm and grief that come to us as we see our crops so brutally destroyed. It is our plea that our lords be made to realize that they should refrain from this destructive sport, but if they persist and we continue to suffer the ruin of our crops, they should be held accountable for the damage.

16. In violation of the old customs our lords have appropriated the brooks running through our property and given the fishing right to other persons.

Many of us have lands and meadows watered by brooks and rivers, and these we have always, according to tradition, had the right to employ for irrigating our fields and driving our mills, for it is generally accepted that water is free and common to all. But in recent years our lords have taken this right away from us and leased the waters to fishermen, who have inflicted grave damage on our properties by tearing down dams and weirs, thus making it impossible for us to use our mills and water our meadows. . . .

18. The widow and heirs of a murdered man are obliged to pay the costs of the murder trial even though the guilty party may have escaped and the widow has taken no legal action.

In our county, when a man is slain and the killer escapes and the friends and heirs of the victim do not press charges, the counts arrogate to themselves the right to initiate the trial, the costs for which must be borne by the victim's widow and children. Inasmuch as it is not right that a widow who does not press charges should bear court costs, we ask that our lords not insist in such cases that the widow or children or next of kin meet the expenses of the trial.

19. Our lords claim to be the legal heirs of all children born out of wedlock, to the exclusion of next of kin.

When an illegitimate child dies, our lords lay claim to the deceased's belongings and goods, excluding the next of kin, though this may be a brother or a sister. We wish it recognized that brother, sister, father, mother, or next of kin should inherit in such cases ahead of our lords. . . .

20. The penalty for assault used to be three or five shillings, but now this offense is treated as a felony.

The old customs hold that when a man strikes another on the face and is convicted of it, he forfeits a fine not to exceed five shillings and is tried before his own sub-bailiff or bailiff. But nowadays our lords have begun to treat the offense as a felony and transferred jurisdiction over it from our sub-bailiffs to their own officials. We ask that the old custom be restored and the offense in question be treated as nothing more than a misdemeanor and not as a felony. . . .

22. We are forced to grind our grain in distant and inconveniently located mills.

Although the county of Lupfen and Stühlingen has many mills conveniently situated to meet our needs, we are compelled to take our grain to a mill in the counts' domain at a great distance from our villages. It is our plea that we be left free to grind our grain wherever it is convenient for us. . . .

23. We do not know the origins of the interest and rents we are said to owe the counts.

Although we have for many years made annual payments of interest, dues, and rents to our lords, we confess that we do not know the origins of these payments, nor do we know for what reason we are obliged to make them, nor what obligations our lords owe us in return for them. We ask that the counts be required to inform us of the origins and causes of these interests, dues, and rents by showing us credible documents stating why we must pay them and what duties they owe us in return. . . .

24. We are aggrieved and oppressed by a great number of required services.

Over and above what we have stated so far, our lords and their bailiffs burden us with insufferable servile tasks, in the performance of which we are forced to neglect our plowing and other work so that we do not know how to nourish our wives and children. We ask to be relieved of services such as the following:

We are obliged to harvest oats, bind hemp, till and sow, plow, cut grain and cart it to the threshing floor, thresh, take the grain to the manor house, mow the grass, do the haying, and take the hay to the barn; we must also repair yokes and reins, lay traps, and take captured game to the manor or from the manor to other places wherever it pleases our lord to command us to take it.

We must transport wine at our own expense from wherever his grace the count buys it . . . to Stühlingen. We must supply the manor not only with firewood but also with building lumber. We must clean the fields and cart an spread manure. When it is time for us to sow, the counts ask us to dig roots, gather mushrooms, cut juniper berries, and break barberries so that our gracious lords may enjoy their blackthorn sloe stew. Our wives and servant girls must pluck hemp and prepare it for the distaff.

We must transport grain from Schleitheim to Schaffhausen, cart oats to Stühlingen and Schaffhausen, and take grain and oats from Bondorf to Stühlingen and Schaffhausen. We have to mow and cut for the bailiff and weed the manor gardens—and this we must do three times a year. We must mind the bailiff's cattle, and, even though we are supposed to be relieved of plowing duties (in return for which freedom we give tributes in grain, hay, seed corn, and money), we are often forced to till and plow the lord's fields.

We are obliged to keep the counts' hunting dogs, which not only means an expense for us in feeding them but causes great loss of chickens and other fowl killed by the dogs. . . .

Furthermore, we have always in the past been allowed to cut sticks and hazelnut staffs for basket making, such baskets being a good source of added income for a poor man. But our lords have now forbidden this. We ask that the counts return to the old custom and let us cut sticks without inference or punishment.

26. The village of Witzen in the county of Lupfen is forbidden to keep geese and ducks.

In some villages in the county of Lupfen, among them Witzen, the villagers are forbidden to keep geese and ducks though they make good eating and are a source of income for the poor. . . .

27. When a man is burned at the stake we must furnish the wood for the pyre.

Whenever a criminal is to be burned at the stake, a number of villagers are required to furnish the wood regardless of the fact that this deprives the poor of their property.

31. The counts collect the toll, but we are the ones who build roads, paths, and bridges.

Although it is customary to levy tolls only for the purpose of building and maintaining roads and bridges, the counts of Stühlingen take the tolls for their own treasury while we are forced to expend money, pain, and labor for building roads and bridges and keeping them in good repair. . . .

32. If a man finds an article he must surrender it to the counts. If a man inadvertently comes upon something useful or valuable he must notify the counts, and if he fails to do so, he is harshly punished for his omission.

34. A man's first trial should be before his own judge.

Although we have our own [village] courts and jurisdictions and although our rights as well as the laws of the empire demand that each man should in the first instance be tried before his own judge, we are frequently summoned before the counts' territorial courts, a practice which imposes grave burdens on us through loss of time and travel expenses. . . .

Concerning the "bailiff's dues."

Although we have been faithful in giving our lords all that we owe them according to the old customs and traditions, they have recently introduced an innovation by imposing an excise upon our properties, the payment of which we are forced to render annually. This excise is called "the bailiff's dues," and we are much aggrieved by it. . . .

36. Our lords treat non-criminal offenses as though they were criminal offenses and cite them before the criminal court.

Although the common written law explicitly identifies offenses that are to be regarded as criminal and other offenses that are not criminal and should not come before a criminal judge, our lords are inclined to bring criminal actions against persons accused only of civil offenses. . . .

38. A man may not pour wine unless he does so throughout the year.

If a man has a barrel or two of wine and retails it for a period of two or three weeks but not for a whole year, he must pay a fine of three pounds of silver. It should be recognized that a poor man cannot afford to buy enough wine to retail it for an entire year; hence, we ask that each of us be allowed to buy and sell wine according to his ability and desire and to cease selling it whenever he wishes without fear of punishment.

39. One who leaves the county, or inherits property in the county, must pay heavy taxes.

If a man wishes to move from the county or if a man inherits something in the county and wants to remove it, he is forced to pay a heavy and unjust exit tax on everything he takes abroad. Moreover, this tax is inequitably assessed according to whether our lords are well or ill disposed toward a man. . . .

40. Concerning the forester.

Although, according to the common law, animals and wild game are free and available to everyone, we have been sorely oppressed by the imposition of a forester. If a man wishes to hunt or trap birds, foxes, rabbits, or small game, or to cut himself a stick or a piece of bark, he is now forced to pay the forester. If the forester favors him he sets a low price, if, on the other hand, he does not like a man, he charges a large sum.

41. Wild game ought to be altogether free.

We perform long and hard labor on our fields in order to raise crops (of which we are obliged to give a portion to our lords) and to make a living for ourselves and our wives and children. But much of our work is brought to nothing by the profusion in our land of wild game, which is ruinous to our crops. Though God and the common law decree that wild game, having been created to supply the common needs of mankind, may be trapped and hunted by everyone, our lords have proclaimed injunctions and heavy penalties against the snaring, trapping, hunting and catching of game. If a man violates these prohibitions and is caught, they gouge out his eyes or torture him in other ways according to the counts' or their bailiffs' pleasure. It is our plea that, by the authority of divine and common law, we be henceforth permitted to hunt, shoot, and trap all game found on our fields and properties and use it to fill our requirements. . . .

42. Concerning the game fences placed on our fields.

They have come to our fields (for which we must pay steep taxes and on which we perform hard labor) and put up game fences, though some of them are never used for anything. When, wishing to plow or rake, we undertake to remove the fence or a section of it, they punish us and, moreover, they refuse to allow us to shut the fence again, so that animals may enter freely and damage our crops. . . .

44. Concerning the bathhouse built by the community and then taken over by the counts.

Not long ago the community of Stühlingen built, at its own cost and with its own labor, a public bathhouse. . . . Recently, however, the counts illegally confiscated and expropriated this bathhouse, without offering any compensation to us, and gave it to a bathing master, who now boasts charter and seal to prove his ownership. Inasmuch as no one should be deprived of his property without legal action nor should be forced illegally to surrender what belongs to him, we ask that the bathhouse be restored to the community and the bathing master be given his leave. . . .

50. Contrary to the old customs we are forbidden to buy and sell salt.

The ancient laws and customs of Stühlingen entitle every burgher to buy and sell whatever he wants to. Not long ago, however, the counts issued a decree and command preventing everyone but the territorial scribe from selling and retailing salt. We ask it to be recognized that this should be abolished, the ancient traditions and customs be left undisturbed, and we be permitted to buy and sell salt as we please.

52. We are forbidden to sell geese and ducks except to the manor house.

We may not buy or sell ducks and geese without the knowledge and approval of the count. We are forced to take our ducks and geese to the manor and offer them for sale there and take for them whatever the bailiffs are willing to give us.

59. Concerning bondage and serfdom.

Although by rights every man is born free and neither we nor our ancestors have been guilty of anything that should have made serfs of us, our lords claim that we are and ought to be their bondsmen and that we are obliged to do whatever they command us to do as though we were born slaves—and it may well happen in time that we will be sold like slaves. It is our strong plea and request that the counts be made to recognize that they ought to release us from serfdom and should never press another man into bondage. Apart from this plea, we pledge ourselves to act as loyal subjects, and we promise faithfully to perform all the duties we owe to our lords according to custom and tradition.

PETITION

We reserve to ourselves the right to augment, reduce, or otherwise alter the above list of grievances and complaints. We ask that each and every article on our list be carefully considered with a view to examining our right and just demands. And if one or the other of our wishes, as stated in the above articles, is found not to be in accordance with a strict interpretation of the law and is therefore judged unjustified (which, however, we hope will not be the case) we ask your graces to consider not only the law in its strict sense but, in judging our claims, also to ponder the dictates of divine and natural law, of fairness, reason, and common sense so that we might be released from the above-mentioned insufferable grievances and be permitted to live our lives as honest, Godfearing men in our land and among our wives, children, belongings, and property. . . .

On Marriage Matters

MARTIN LUTHER

The Protestant Reformation affected German society in many ways, including marriage. Catholics had extolled celibacy for both men and women and viewed marriage as an institution for those who had neither the strength nor the calling for a celibate life. For centuries, convents had existed for women and monasteries for men who for a variety of reasons would not marry and/or who desired sincerely a religious life free from social pressures. Martin Luther (1483–1546) and other Protestant reformers abolished these religious houses where they could and advocated marriage for those cloistered men and women (Luther himself married an ex-nun). Marriage came to be accepted

and expected for all Protestants. Although Luther broke with the Roman church for re-
ligious reasons, he felt compelled, as reformed religion spread, to examine the conse-
quences of his theology for a host of institutions. In this selection, he advises ministers
on marriage.

One theme in his advice is authority: the authority of parents, of husband, of law,
and of scripture. How does this concept of authority color his views on engagement?
Why is he opposed to secret betrothals? If parental authority is so important to Luther,
why does he object to forced engagements? Did he believe people should marry in order
to be happy?

What are Luther's views concerning divorce? Under what conditions might a di-
vorce be granted? In what ways does he criticize the attitudes of the Roman church to-
ward marriage and divorce? How did his views of marriage differ from those seen in
medieval canon law?

From reading Luther's feelings on marriage, do you think women would have pre-
ferred his views or those of the Roman church? With which view would men have been
more comfortable? To what extent does this selection stress the subordination of
women? How does Luther help us understand the workings of European patriarchy?

To the worthy gentlemen, Messrs. N. and N.,[1] pastors and preachers at N.,
my dear brothers in Christ.

Grace and peace in Christ, our Lord and Savior. You are not the only
ones, my dear sirs, who are having a great deal of trouble with marriage
matters; others are having the same experience. I myself am greatly plagued by them; I put up a stiff resistance, calling and crying out that these
things should be left to the temporal authorities, and as Christ says, "Leave
the dead to bury their own dead" [Matt. 8:22]. God grant that they may do
this, rightly or wrongly, for we are supposed to be servants of Christ, that
is, we are to deal with the gospel and conscience, which gives us more than
enough to do against the devil, the world, and the flesh.

No one can deny that marriage is an external, worldly matter, like
clothing and food, house and property, subject to temporal authority, as
the many imperial laws enacted to the subject prove. Neither do I find any
example in the New Testament where Christ or the apostles concerned
themselves with such matters, except where they touched upon consciences, as did St. Paul in I Corinthians 7 [:1-24], and especially where
unbelievers or non-Christians are concerned, for it is easy to deal with
these and all matters among Christians or believers. But with non-Christians, with which the world is filled, you cannot move forward or back-
ward without the sharp edge of the temporal sword. And what use would
it be if we Christians set up a lot of laws and decisions, as long as the world
is not subject to us and we have no authority over it?

Therefore I simply do not wish to become involved in such matters at
all and beg everyone not to bother me with them. If you do not have sover-

[1]Luther means any minister. (Original editor's note.)

eigns, then you have officials.[2] If they do not render just decisions, what concern is it of mine? They are responsible, they have undertaken the office. I am horrified too by the example of the pope, who was the first to get mixed up in this business and has seized such worldly matters as his own to the point where he has become nothing but a worldly lord over emperors and kings. So here too I am afraid that the dog may learn to eat leather by nibbling at his own rags and we too may be misled with good intentions, until finally we fall away from the gospel into purely worldly matters. As soon as we begin to act as judges in marriage matters, the teeth of the millwheel will have snatched us by the sleeve and will carry us away to the point where we must decide the penalty. Once we have to decide the penalty, then we must also render judgment about the body and goods, and by this time we are down under the wheel and drowned in the water of worldly affairs.

Now the whole world knows (praise God) what effort and zeal I have already expended and how hard I am still toiling to see that the two authorities or realms, the temporal and the spiritual, are kept distinct and separate from each other and that each is specifically instructed and restricted to its own task. The papacy has so jumbled these two together and confused them with each other that neither one has kept to its power or force or rights and no one can disentangle them again. This is what I dread, and with God's help I want to avoid it and stay within the charge of my own office, and as I said above, "Leave the dead to bury their own dead; you go and proclaim the kingdom of God," Matthew 9. Now this is to be my answer to you, may you do likewise.

But since you persist so strongly in asking instruction of me, not only for yourselves and your office, but also for your rulers who desire advice from you in these matters, and ask me what I for my part would do if I were asked for advice—especially since your rulers complain that it is burdensome to their consciences to render decisions according to the spiritual or papal laws, which in such cases are unreliable and often run counter to all propriety, reason, and justice, and since the imperial laws too are ineffective in these matters—I will not withhold my opinion from you. Yet I give it with this condition (which I hereby wish to have stated clearly to you and to everyone), that I want to do this not as a judge, official, or regent, but by way of advice, such as I would in good conscience give as a special service to my good friends. So, if anyone wishes to follow this advice of mine, let him do so on his own responsibility; if he does not know how to carry it out, let him not seek shelter or refuge with me, or complain to me about it. I do not wish to place myself under the restraint of any authority or court, and since I am under none now, I do not wish to be under any in the future. Let whoever is supposed to rule or wants to rule

---

[2]Luther means a judge of the bishop's court, the chief legal officer in a diocese. (Original editor's note.)

be the ruler; I want to instruct and console consciences, and advise them as much as I can. Whoever wishes to or can comply, let him do so; whoever will not or cannot, let him refrain. This has been my position up to now, and I intend to adhere to it in the future.

Well then, let us in God's name get down to the business at hand and summarize these opinions and this advice of mine in several articles and points, so that they may be understood and retained that much the better.

The First Article

Secret engagements should not be the basis of any marriage whatsoever.

The Second Article

A secret engagement should yield to a public one.

The Third Article

Of two public engagements, the second should yield to the first and be punished.

The Fourth Article

If anyone touches another woman after a public engagement, so to marry her in order thereby to break the first engagement, this action is to be regarded as adultery.

The Fifth Article

Forced engagements should not be valid.

We will let these articles be sufficient for the first part of this little book. Now let us state our reasons for these articles. The reasons for the first article are:

First, the divine law, that because marriage is a public estate which is to be entered into and recognized publicly before the church, it is fitting that it should also be established and begun publicly with witnesses who can testify to it, for God says, "Every word should be confirmed by the evidence of two or three witnesses" [Matt. 18:16]. But where two people become engaged secretly, no one can be sure whether it is true or not, because husband and wife (and likewise bride and bridegroom) are one flesh and one voice, on whose testimony and witness nothing is to be based, nor can such an uncertain marriage be confirmed thereby.

To prevent anyone from wrangling with words here, I define a secret engagement as one which takes place without the knowledge and consent of those who are in authority and have the right and power to establish a marriage, such as, father, mother, and whoever may act in their stead. Even if a thousand witnesses were present at a secret betrothal and it nonetheless took place without the knowledge and consent of the parents, the whole thousand should be reckoned as acting in the darkness and not in the light, as only one voice, and as assisting treacherously in this beginning without the presence of orderly public authority.

Second, we also have here the temporal imperial law which clearly forbids such secret betrothals. Now in our external conduct we are bound to obey the temporal law. We should not cause the imperial laws to yield and subjugate themselves to papal laws because these same papal laws often run counter to public ordinances, reason, and good sense.

Third, this is also confirmed by the ancient canons and by the best points of the canon law, all of which forbid such secret engagements, indeed, even today the pope forbids the making of such engagements. But on the other hand, once they have taken place he wants them to be kept, to be valid and binding, so he makes them merely a sin of disobedience, thus rewarding them with the joy and satisfaction of those who disobey, so that they achieve their purpose with the sin of disobedience, which is contrary to all that is right and proper.

Fourth, add to this the example of the old law and all the fathers, among whom it was both law and custom that the parents gave their children in marriage by parental authority, as is clearly stated in Exodus 21 [:9], and as the examples of Isaac, Jacob, Joseph, Samson, etc., show.

Fifth, it was also in the natural law among the heathen, and also with the Greeks, who were the wisest people on earth. We read these words in the works of the Greek poet Euripides, "It is my father's business to arrange for my marriage. It is not fitting that I have anything to do with it." St. Ambrose[3] finds this passage very pleasing, . . . and he admonishes all women not to betroth themselves or to choose husbands according to the example of Rebecca, but to leave this care and right to their parents. . . .

Seventh, we should be influenced by the great dangers and mischief that have so often resulted from such secret betrothals and still do. Here I want to show what impelled me, even before I had considered these causes, to advise and act against secret engagements. It often happened that a married couple came to me (not counting those who came to others all over the world), one or both of whom had previously become secretly engaged to others, and now there was misery and distress. Then we confessors or theologians were supposed to counsel these captive consciences. But how could we do this? There was the law and custom of the officials which decreed that the first secret betrothal was a true marriage in God's sight, and that the second one was an open act of adultery. So they went ahead and tore up the second marriage and ordered them to keep the first secret betrothal, even if they had ten children together in the second mar-

---

[3]Bishop of Milan, c. 340–397.

riage and had joined their inheritance and property into one.[4] They had to separate, whether God granted that the first betrothed was present and claimed the woman, or whether he was elsewhere, even though he had married elsewhere and no longer wished to have her. Further, if this engagement was so secret that it could not be attested by a single witness, and the second one was openly confirmed in the church, then they were forced to comply with both: first, they must consider the secret betrothal as the true marriage in their consciences before God, and on the other hand the woman was forced on pain of excommunication and by obedience to share the table and bed of the second man as her true husband, because this marriage was publicly attested, while the former secret engagement no one dared to acknowledge except she herself, and that in her conscience before God. What should a poor conscience do in a case like this? How could the situation be more confused than by such contradictory laws and decisions? If she were to run from the second husband to the first she would be regarded as an adulteress, put under the ban, and deprived of the sacraments and of all her Christian rights. But if she remained with the second man she would again be looked upon as an adulteress before God. So she could not stay in any one place and yet she had to stay there.

Now what kind of real advice do they give to such a conscience? This is what they give: they say she should keep the first engagement, and if she is forced by the ban to stay with the second man, she should suffer this ban as one that did her no harm in the sight of God. If she could not come to the first man in person and was compelled to share the bed of the second one and render to him the conjugal duty, to which he is entitled, she should bear with this, too, and perform her duty with her body, but with her heart she should cling to the first betrothal, and she should demand no conjugal duty from the second husband, for she has no power over his body, but should desire and demand it from the first man. This is called consoling and instructing consciences. These are the fruits of secret engagements and such were the conditions at the time.

My dear fellow, what strange kind of wife is this? She is the second man's wife, but this same second man is not her husband. The first man is not her husband, but she is his wife nevertheless, for as a wife she has the right and power to demand conjugal duty from him, but he does not have to grant it to her, for she does not have to go to him. On the other hand, the second man is her husband, but she is not his wife, for she has neither the right nor the power as a wife to demand conjugal duty from him. I will not mention the danger of forcing a woman into a man's bed to perfrom the conjugal duty and yet not allowing her to demand it of him. Indeed, it

---

[4]Pope Innocent III had commanded that if a man had become engaged to a woman with whom he had already been intimate, and then married another, he should return to the first woman even if there were children by the second woman. (Original editor's note.)

is easy to cut into someone else's hide; it is easy to impose laws upon others which do not affect us. . . .

Forced engagements should not be valid.

The whole world is unanimous in this article, for God has created man and woman so that they are to come together with pleasure, willingly and gladly with all their hearts. And bridal love or the will to marry is a natural thing, implanted and inspired by God. This is the reason bridal love is so highly praised in the Scriptures and is often cited as an example of Christ and his church. Therefore parents sin against God and nature when they force their children into marriage or to take a spouse for whom they have no desire. We read in Genesis, Chapter 24 [:58], that when Rebecca's relatives betrothed her, they demanded and inquired of her whether she would have Isaac, and they thought it right to have the girl's prior consent. The Holy Spirit did not cause such an example to be written down in vain; he wished by this to confirm the natural law, which he created in such a way that marriage partners are to be joined together without force or compulsion, but willingly and with pleasure.

Our daily experience teaches and shows us what kind of mischief has resulted from forced marriage. Indeed, so much grace is required for marriage to be successful against the devil, the flesh, and the world even when it is begun amiably with God's blessing and commandment, obediently and with pleasure, that one would not dare to begin it contrary to God's law and with animosity and ill will, thus painting the devil over the door when he comes by himself. And it is a strange thing for someone to want to have a bride when he knows that she does not want or care to have him, and for parents to be so foolish as to force their children into external animosity and aversion. Dumb animals would not do it, and even if God and nature had not already commanded that marriage should be without compulsion, a fatherly or motherly heart should still not allow children to enter into anything other than that which takes place agreeably and with pleasure. But Mammon and the belly are mighty gods, and this is why pastors should diligently urge this point and frighten the people away from such compulsion.

It may well be that until now neither children nor parents have known that it is a sin against God and nature to force anyone into marriage, and so the parents have had no scruples about compulsion and did not regard it as a sin, but found satisfaction in it as if they had done a good deed and it were completely within their power to do this with their children. No, my dear fellow, no one should allow you to have this power, but should deny it to you and take it from you by God's word and commandment, so that you may know that you have no such power over your child. This power of compulsion is not a paternal power, but an unpaternal, tyrannical, criminal power, not much better than if a thief or robber took away your property or kept it from you by force. And the authorities should not permit any father to do this. Instead the authorities should punish him and force him to stay within the limits of his paternal power and not allow him to go further than a father ought to. It would be a horrible sin if someone wantonly murdered his child or made him blind or lame, but how much better do you think you are doing when you force your child into a marriage for which he has no wish or desire, even though it might be that your child would rather be dead? Take care that you do not become a murderer of your own child by striving against the nature and essence of marriage, which is ordered by God, and fall into a grievous, damnable, mortal sin.

Yes, the crude masses have been quick to learn this from the gospel: that paternal power is to be feared and that children are not to become secretly engaged. In this matter they can accept the gospel and go ahead and misuse it; it has to serve as a cloak for their shame, and they want to make of paternal might a criminal might, and they do this as freely and unscrupulously as if they had earned indulgence by it. Yes, my dear fellow, if you want to accept the gospel when it gives you power over your child and demands filial obedience to you, then you should also accept it when it commands you to treat your child in a paternal way and forbids you to use your power shamefully and criminally in this matter, since the salvation of your child is in danger, for you cannot give your child the desire and love for his spouse that he should have according to the commandment of God, who desires that husband and wife shall love one another. If you now can make a big thing out of the sin of filial disobedience on the basis of the gospel, then one can also make a big thing out of your unpaternal crime on the same basis, and if filial disobedience is a sin, then your unpaternal criminal power is two sins. So that you may know that you are to be regarded as tyrants who keep or force their children away from the Christian faith, according to which they are not obliged to be obedient, but are free and are to be disobedient, Christ says, "He who loves father and mother more than me is not worthy of me" [Matt. 10:37]. How a pastor may further emphasize and elaborate upon this!

What if a child has already been forced into marriage? Shall this be and remain a marriage? Answer: Yes, it is a marriage and shall remain one, for although she was forced into it, she still consented to this coercion by her action, accepted it, and followed it, so that her husband has publicly acquired conjugal rights over her, which no one can now take from him. When she feels that she is being coerced, she should do something about it in time, resist, and not accept it, call upon some good friends, and if that were of no avail she should appeal to the authorities or complain to the pastor or give public, verbal testimony that she did not want to do it, and thus cry out openly against the compulsion. For these four means, namely, calling upon good friends, appealing to the authorities, complaining to the pastor, and protesting openly, should be powerful enough to prevent a forced marriage. Indeed, the authorities with the law or the pastor with good counsel can probably do it alone.

If the girl remains silent during her public betrothal, however, and leaves these means untried, then she is to keep the promise she has made and afterward keep silent and not complain or pretend that she was forced. One is not to believe her if she does complain. "Yes," you say, "Who knew that one could resist force by these means?" Answer: Learn it now, anyone who can or will. Why haven't your preachers or judges taught you this? And why did you not seek advice from your pastor? People no longer want to have preachers or pastors; they do not heed them or need them and they act as if they could do all things and well live without them. Well then, people will have to suffer the consequences of this and take it as their reward and spare us the complaint and howling. That is the way you wanted it, it serves you right! Why does God provide you with parents, pastors, and authorities if you do not need them?

However, if a case could be found where a child was closely guarded and could not gain access to these means and was betrothed without her co-operation through intermediaries who married her off by force, and she could afterward furnish witnesses that she had not given her consent, I would pronounce her free, even after the consummation. . . .

But because the world is filled with cunning and deceit and a child may easily make excuses and pretend that she is not doing this out of caprice or foolish love, but cannot or is not able to love this one or that one, well then, we must let the fathers use their common sense and understanding and decide how to deal with such children. But the preachers likewise are to be diligent in informing the young people and must hold their conscience to filial obedience by pointing out the position in which they find themselves and that they are unjustly excusing themselves, that they are twice sinning against paternal authority, both with disobedience and deception. This will do them no good later on, and it is to be feared that they will receive as punishment an unhappy marriage or a short life. They should be careful not to trifle in these matters, for it is certain that they will not deceive the father but themselves, for God will surely discover their lying and deception. If the fact that I preferred something else and did not want to give it up were any kind of sufficient reason, then there would be no obedience left, either in heaven or on earth. Abraham, too, loved his son Isaac, yet he had to give him up and surrender him [Gen. 22:2]. Let this be enough for the time being on the five articles.

Necessity demands that we also say something about divorce and other subjects, such as degrees of kinship and the like. We have heard above that death is the only reason for dissolving a marriage. And because God has commanded in the law of Moses that adulterers should be stoned [Deut. 22:22-24], it is certain that adultery also dissolves a marriage, because by it the adulterer is sentenced and condemned to death, and also because Christ, in Matthew 19 [:19], when he forbids married people to divorce each other, excepts adultery and says, "Whoever divorces his wife, except for unchastity, and marries another, commits adultery." This verse is also confirmed by Joseph in Matthew 2 [1:19], when he wanted to leave Mary because he considered her an adulteress, and yet he is praised by the evangelist as a pious man. Now he certainly would not be a pious man if he wanted to leave Mary unless he had the power and right to do so.

Accordingly, I cannot and may not deny that where one spouse commits adultery and it can be publicly proven, the other partner is free and can obtain a divorce and marry another man. However, it is a great deal better to reconcile them and keep them together if it is possible. But if the innocent partner does not wish to do this, then let him in God's name exercise his right. And above all, this separation is not to take place on one's own authority, but it is to be declared through the advice and judgment of the pastor or authorities, unless like Joseph one wanted to go away secretly and leave the country. Otherwise, if he wishes to stay, he is to obtain a public divorce.

But in order that such divorces may be as few in number as possible, one should not permit the one partner to remarry immediately, but he should wait at least a year or six months. Otherwise it would have the evil appearance that he was happy and pleased that his spouse had committed adultery and was joyfully seizing the opportunity to get rid of this one and quickly take another and so practice his wantonness under the cloak of the law. For such villainy indicates that he is leaving the adulteress not out of disgust for adultery, but out of envy and hate toward his spouse and out of desire and passion for another, and so is eagerly seeking another woman.

Second, the pastors should diligently see to it that the guilty partner (if the authorities do not punish him) shall humble himself before the innocent one and beg forgiveness. When this has been done, they are confidently to entreat the innocent partner with the Scriptures, where God commands us to forgive, and on this basis press hard upon his conscience and point out what a grave sin it is not to forgive his spouse (if the latter remains unpunished and has not been expelled by the authorities) and takes her back in the hope that she will mend her ways. For it can very easily happen to all of us that we fall, and who is without sin? [John 8:7]. And how would we have our neighbor act toward us if we had fallen? So we too are to act toward others and be strong, continuing to practice Christian love and the duty we have to forgive another if he mends his ways, and thus aid in restraining the law of divorce as much as we can. If that does not help, well, then let the law take its course.

In addition, there is another case, namely, when one spouse runs away from the other, etc. May this one in turn marry still another? Here my answer is this: Where it happens that one spouse knowingly and deliberately leaves the other, such as merchants or those required to go to war, or for any other reason of necessity, and both of them agree to this—here the other partner shall wait and not marry again until there is certain and trustworthy evidence that the spouse is dead, even if the pope in his decretals decrees and permits more than I do. Inasmuch as the wife consents to this journey of her husband and enters into this risk, she is to adhere to it, especially if it takes place for the sake of goods, as may happen with merchants. If for the sake of goods she can consent to her husband's making dangerous trips, let her have the same danger if it comes; why does she not keep him at home with less goods and be content in her poverty?

But if he is such a villain, and I have found many in my time, who takes a wife and stays with her for a while, spends a lot of money and lives well, then runs away without her knowledge and consent, secretly and treacherously, leaves her pregnant or with children, sends her nothing, writes her nothing, offers her nothing, pursues his villainy, and then returns in one, two, three, four, five, or six years and relies on her having to take him back when he comes, and on the city and house being open to him,[5] then it would be high time and necessary for the authorities to issue a stern decree and take severe measures. And if a villain were to undertake such an action or trick, he should be forbidden to enter the country, and if he were ever caught, he should be given his deserts as befits a villain. Such a villain shows his contempt for matrimony and the laws of the city. He does not consider his wife as his wedded wife, nor his children as his lawful children, for he withholds from them the duty, food, service, provision, etc., that he owes them, against their knowledge and consent. And he is acting contrary to the nature and character of marriage, which is and imposes a way of life, an estate in which a man and a woman are joined together and stay together and live and reside together until death, as the temporal laws also state: *Individuam consuetudinem vitae*, etc.,[6] and they are not to be apart or live apart without mutual consent or unavoidable necessity.

And in addition he withholds his person and services from the authorities and the community as a faithless, disobedient person, contrary to his oath, and uses the city, his wife, house, and property like a robber and a thief when he comes running back, and no one would or should have any use for him. There is no villain whom I would rather have hanged or beheaded than this scoundrel. . . .

For whenever such a case or error or doubt comes up, where the conscience could not be aided unless the law or statute were repealed, and yet this same law cannot be publicly repealed because it is universal, one should, before God and secretly in one's conscience, respect the conscience

---

[5]I.e., without fear of prosecution or exile. (Original editor's note.)

[6][M]aintaining an undivided relationship for life. . . . (Original editor's note.)

more than the law. And if conscience or law has to yield and give way, then it is the law which is to yield and give way, so that the conscience may be clear and free. The law is a temporal thing which must ultimately perish, but the conscience is an eternal thing which never dies. It would not be right to kill or ensnare an eternal thing for a transient thing to remain and be free. Rather, the opposite should be true; a transitory thing should perish rather than an eternal one be destroyed. It is better to strangle a sparrow so that a human being may survive than to strangle a human being so that a sparrow may survive. The law exists for the sake of the conscience, not the conscience for the sake of the law. If one cannot help both at the same time, then help the conscience and oppose the law.

I am saying this because I have often heard confessors complain that marriage matters, of such a nature that they were impossible to decide, have come before them and they said, "We must commend these matters to the unfathomable goodness of God." I have also seen how much the doctors, especially Gerson,[7] had to deal with *perplexis conscientiis*, confused consciences. All this comes from commingling spiritual and temporal law and regarding the external transitory laws as equal to the internal, eternal laws. One is not well learned in the law, however, if one confuses consciences by them; laws are supposed to instil fear and punish, prevent and forbid, not to confuse and ensnare. But where they do confuse they are certainly no longer laws, or else they are not rightly understood. Therefore, if you find that a confusion of conscience is about to arise over the law, then tear through the law confidently like a millstone through a spiderweb, and act as if this law had never been born. And if you cannot tear it up outwardly before the world, then let it go and tear it up in your conscience. It is better to leave the body and one's property confused in the law than the conscience and the soul.

And one should especially observe this rule or method *in preteritis*,[8] that is, when a thing has happened, and say, "What has happened, has happened; gone is gone; who can gather it together again as it was before, when it has been spilled?" See to it that it does not happen again, and forgive and forget what has happened to spare consciences. An intelligent physician does well when he spares the medicine as long as a man is healthy, but if a man is sick and he wants at first to leave him unattended to save medicine, he is a fool. So here, too, whoever wishes to restore the law which has been transgressed to its entirety, so that he would rather let consciences choke on it before he would omit one bit of the law—he is the biggest fool on earth; that was the practice of the monks and clergy under

[7]John Gerson (1363–1429) was a prominent medieval theologian and conciliarist. As a moral theologian he held to the doctrine that the sinfulness or goodness of an act depended solely on the will of God. (Original editor's note.)

[8]With regard to past things.

the papacy. To learn or know laws is no great art, but to use the laws correctly and keep them within their goals and province requires that one use restraint, and that is an art.

I should probably also have treated the canon law or the pope's decretals in this work, but the canon law is thrown together in so disorderly a fashion, often contradictory, and gathered together out of circular letters of the pope which have been issued at many times and for many reasons, that it would be too great an effort for me and would lead to a great disputation which I could not cover in many pages, as has happened to the jurists and still happens daily, when they are to abridge it and compare it. It is true that there are many good decisions and verdicts in it, but some are just so-so. . . .Therefore my advice is this: Let the temporal laws apply here, but in conscience our canon shall be this: Because public betrothals take precedence over secret and private ones, so also prior lying together takes precedence over future betrothals, other things being equal.

Galateo: A Book of Manners

GIOVANNI DELLA CASA

Giovanni della Casa (1503–1556) was a member of an old and eminent patrician family of Florence. While in Bologna to study law in 1525, he became attracted to the lectures and writings of humanists; later he moved to Rome to pursue a life of study and dissipated elegance. He took holy orders after a few years and quickly began a successful ecclesiastical career, thanks to family connections. He became archbishop of Benevento in 1544. However, he then lost his patrons in Rome and retired to Venetian territory, where he wrote the Galateo *between 1552 and 1555.*

Della Casa's life coincided with the tumultuous events of the Italian Wars, which began in 1494, and the Reformation, begun by Martin Luther in 1517. Having experienced the devastation of Italy, the humiliation of popes, princes, and republics, della Casa offered in Galateo *a remedy—a sense of order, manners, rules, and structure.*

Galateo *draws on a tradition of courtesy books, the most famous of which was Baldassare Castiglione's* Courtier. *Basic assumptions of this genre of writings were that humans, but especially males, can improve themselves, and that external manners express the quality of the person within. Books like* Galateo *were written for those with humanistic educations who would occupy visible and public posts. What kind of manners does della Casa want such people to cultivate? What does he mean by "grace"? What is the lesson to be drawn from the incident of Bishop Giberti and Count Ricciardo? What are the key ingredients to getting along with others? What sorts of people would have been able to follow through on the ideals and models in this book?*

So that you may learn this lesson more easily, you must know that it will be to your advantage to temper and adapt your manners not according to your own choices but according to the pleasure of those with whom you are dealing and act accordingly. This you must do with moderation, for when someone delights too much in favouring someone else's wishes in conversation or in behaviour he appears to be more of a buffoon or a jester, or perhaps a flatterer, rather than a well-mannered gentleman. And, on the contrary, someone who does not give a thought to another's pleasure or displeasure is boorish, unmannered, and unattractive.

Therefore, our manners are considered pleasant when we take into consideration other people's pleasures and not our own. And if we try to distinguish between the things which generally please the majority of men and those which displease them we can easily discover what manners are to be shunned and what manners are to be selected for living in society.

Let us say, then, that every act which is disgusting to the senses, unappealing to human desire, and also every act that brings to mind unpleasant matters or whatever the intellect finds disgusting, is unpleasant and ought to be avoided.

Dirty, foul, repulsive or disgusting things are not to be done in the presence of others, nor should they even be mentioned. And not only is it unpleasant to do them or recall them, but it is also very bothersome to others even to bring them to mind with any kind of behaviour.

Therefore, it is an indecent habit practised by some people who, in full view of others, place their hands on whatever part of their body it pleases them. Similarly, it is not proper for a well-mannered gentleman to prepare to relieve his physical needs in the presence of others. Or, having taken care of his needs, to rearrange his clothing in their presence. And, in my opinion, when returning from nature's summons, he should not even wash his hands in front of decent company, because the reason for his washing implies something disgusting to their imaginations.

For the same reason it is not proper habit when, as sometimes happens, one sees something disgusting on the road to turn to one's companions and point it out to them. Even less so should one offer something unpleasant to smell, as some insist on doing, placing it even under a companion's nose saying: "Now Sir, please smell how this stinks," when instead he should be saying: "Don't smell this because it stinks."

And just as these and similar actions disturb those senses which they affect, so grinding one's teeth, or whistling, or shrieking, or rubbing together rough stones, or scraping metal is unpleasant to the ear, and a man ought to abstain as much as possible from doing such things. Not only this, but he must avoid singing, especially solo, if his voice is out of tune and unharmonious. But few refrain from doing this; in fact it seems that whoever has the least natural talent for singing is the one who sings most often.

There are also some who cough or sneeze so loudly that they deafen everybody. And some who are so indiscreet in such actions that they spray those near them in the face.

You will also find the type who, when he yawns, howls and brays like an ass; or someone who opens his mouth wide as he begins to speak or carries on with his argument, producing thus a voice, or rather a noise, that a mute makes when he attempts to speak. And these vulgar manners are to be avoided because they are bothersome to the ear and to the eye.

Indeed, a well-mannered man ought to abstain from yawning too much because, besides the above-mentioned reasons, it seems that yawning is caused by boredom and regret, because whoever yawns would much rather be somewhere else and dislikes the company he is with, their conversation, and their activities. Certainly, even though a man is inclined to yawn at any time, it will not occur to him to do it if he is involved in some pleasure or thought; but when he is inactive and indolent he easily remembers to yawn. And so when someone else yawns in the presence of idle and carefree persons, everybody else will immediately start to yawn, as you may have seen many times, as if that person had reminded them of something which they would already have done themselves, had they thought of it first. And many times have I heard learned men say that in Latin the word for yawning is the same as that for lazy and careless. It is therefore advisable to avoid this habit which, as I have said, is unpleasant to the ear, the eyes, and the appetite, because by indulging in it we show that we are not pleased with our companions, and we also give a bad impression of ourselves, that is to say, that we have a drowsy and sleepy spirit which makes us little liked by those with whom we are dealing.

And when you have blown your nose you should not open your handkerchief and look inside, as if pearls or rubies might have descended from your brain. This is a disgusting habit which is not apt to make anyone love you, but rather, if someone loved you already, he is likely to stop there and then. The spirit in the Labyrinth, whoever he may have been, proves this: in order to cool the ardour of Messer Giovanni Boccaccio[1] for a lady he did not know very well, he tells Boccaccio how she squats over ashes and coughs and spits up huge globs.

It is also an unsuitable habit to put one's nose over someone else's glass of wine or food to smell it. By the same token I would not want someone to smell even his own drink or food for fear that some things that men find disgusting may drop from his nose, even if it should not happen. And I would advise you not to offer your glass of wine to someone else after someone very close to you. And even less should you offer a pear or some other fruit into which you have bitten. Do not consider the above

---

[1]Italian novelist and poet (1313–1375), author of the *Decameron*.

things to be of little importance, for even light blows can kill, if they are many.

I want you to know that in Verona there was once a wise bishop, very learned in Scripture, named Messer Giovanni Matteo Giberti.[2] Aside from his other praiseworthy habits, he was also courteous and generous with the noble gentlemen who came and went about him, honouring them in his house with a magnificence which was not overdone, but moderate, as was fitting to a cleric. And it happened that a nobleman by the name of Count Ricciardo was passing by at that time and stayed several days with the bishop and his household, which was composed, for the most part, of well-mannered and learned men. Because he seemed to them a very polite gentleman adorned with pleasant manners, they praised and esteemed him highly, except for one small fault in his deportment. The bishop, who was a discerning man, noticed it and, having sought the advice of some of his closer friends, decided that the count ought to be made aware of it without, however, causing him any distress. Since the count was to depart the following morning and had already taken his leave, the bishop called a discreet gentleman of his household and told him to ride out and accompany the count part of the way and then, when he thought the time was right, to tell him politely what they had decided upon together. This gentleman was a man of advanced age, very learned as well as extremely pleasant, a good conversationalist and handsome, all beyond belief, who in his time had much frequented the courts of great lords. He was, and perhaps still is, called Messer Galateo[3] and it was at his bidding and on his advice that I first started to dictate this treatise. Riding with the count, he soon engaged him in pleasant conversation, moving from one topic to the next, until he thought it was time to return to Verona. Asking for permission to take his leave of the count, with a cheerful countenance, he said delicately: "My lord, my lord bishop extends your lordship his infinite thanks for the honour you have bestowed upon him by entering and dwelling in his humble house. Furthermore, as recompense for all the courtesy you have shown towards him he has commanded me to present you with a gift on his behalf. And he begs you dearly to receive it with a happy heart. This is the gift. You are the most graceful and well-mannered gentleman the bishop thinks he has ever met. For this reason, having carefully observed your manners and having examined them in detail, he has found none which was not extremely pleasant and commendable except for an unseemly motion you make with your lips and mouth at the dinner table,

---

[2]Giberti (1495–1543), made bishop of Verona in 1524, was involved in theological publishing and was an active supporter of church reform.

[3]Galeazzo Florimonte (1478–1567), bishop of Sessa, who wrote an unfinished book of manners that served as della Casa's model.

when your chewing makes a strange sound which is very unpleasant to hear. The bishop sends you this message, begging you to try to refrain from doing it, and to accept as a precious gift his loving reprimand and remark, for he is certain no-one else in the world would give you such a gift." The count, who had never before been aware of his fault, blushed slightly on being chastised for it; but, being a worthy man, he quickly re-covered himself and said: "Please tell the bishop that men would be far richer than they are if all the gifts they gave each other were like this. And thank him profusely for all the courtesy and generosity he has shown to-wards me, assuring him that from now on I will diligently and carefully avoid this fault. Now go, and God be with you."

Now what do we think the bishop and his noble friends would have said to those we sometimes see who, totally oblivious like pigs with their snouts in the swill, never raise their faces nor their eyes, let alone their hands, from the food in front of them? or to those who eat or rather gulp down their food with both their cheeks puffed out as if they were blowing a trumpet or blowing on a fire? or to those who soil their hands nearly up to the elbows, and dirty their napkins worse than their toilet towels? Often they are not ashamed to use these same napkins to wipe away the sweat which, be-cause of their hurry and their over-eating, drips and drops from their fore-heads, their faces and from around their necks. They even use them to blow their noses whenever they feel like it. Truly, men like these are not worthy of being received, not just in the very elegant house of that noble bishop, but should even be banished from any place where there are well-mannered men. A well-mannered man must therefore take heed not to smear his fingers so much that his napkin is left soiled, for it is a disgusting thing to see. And even wiping one's fingers in the bread one is about to eat does not seem to be a polite habit. . . .

One should not speak ill either of other men or of their affairs, even though it is clear that, because of the envy we generally have for other peoples' wealth and honour, ears will gladly stoop to hear it. But in the end every-one flees the charging bull and men avoid the friendship of slanderers because they think that what they said to us about others they also say to others about us.

Some people who contradict every word and always question and ar-gue show that they do not know the nature of men very well, because everyone likes victory and hates defeat both in speech and in action, and also because to contradict others eagerly is a sign of enmity, not friendship. For this reason whoever likes to be a friendly and charming conversational-ist must not have a ready, "That's not what happened," or a, "On the contrary, it was as I say," nor set up wagers. Instead, he must make an effort to be conciliatory to others in those matters that are of little account. Victory in such cases turns to our detriment for in winning a point in a frivolous question we will often lose a dear friend and become annoying to people, so much so that they dare not deal with us so as not to be constantly arguing. And they nickname us Mister Win-it-all, or Sir Contradiction, or Sir Know-it-all, and sometimes the Subtle Doctor.[4]

Although it may sometimes happen that someone becomes involved in a dispute at the invitation of those present, this should be done gently and without that thirst for the sweetness of victory that will make the other man choke. Instead, it is proper to let everyone have his say and, whether the opponent is right or wrong, to abide by the opinion of the majority or of the more importunate and leave the field of battle to them, so that others and not you will be the ones to do battle, work hard, and sweat. These are unseemly occupations not suited to well-behaved men, and so one acquires their hatred and dislike. . . .

To offer your advice without having been asked is nothing else but a way of saying that you are wiser than the man to whom you are giving advice, and even a way of reprimanding him for his limited knowledge and his ignorance. For this reason, it should not be done with everyone you know, but only with the closest friends and with people whom you have the right to rule and guide, or in fact only when someone—even if a stranger to us—is in great and imminent danger. In daily matters, however, one must abstain both from giving advice and from remedying other people's faults. Many fall into these errors, and most often it is the least intelligent, because slow-witted men have little on their minds and so do not spend much time in reaching a decision, like those who do not have many alternatives available to them. Whatever the case, whoever goes about offering and disseminating his advice shows that he is of the opinion that he has more wisdom than he needs and that others lack it. And there are some who think so highly and with conviction of this wisdom of theirs that not to follow their advice is like wanting to come to blows with them, and they say, "That is fine: a poor man's advice is never taken," and, "So-and-so wants to do as he wants," and, "So-and-so does not listen to me." As if demanding that someone else follow your advice does not show greater arrogance than wanting to follow one's own opinion!

A sin similar to this is committed by those who take it upon themselves to correct other men's failings and reprimand them, and want to pass final judgement upon everything and lay down the law to everyone. "Such a thing should not be done." Or, "What a word you have said!" Or, "Stop doing and saying such things." "The wine you drink is not healthy for you. You should drink red wine, instead." Or, "You should use some of this potion, and some of those pills." And they never cease reprimanding or correcting. Not to mention that at times they busy themselves in weeding

---

[4]Famous theologians received names from their students. The Subtle Doctor was John Duns Scotus (1266?–1308) of Oxford.

someone else's garden while their own is full of weeds and nettles. But it is too much bother to listen to them. Just as there are few or no men who could stand to live with their doctor or with their confessor, or even less with a criminal court judge, similarly there are few men to be found who will risk becoming familiar with this type of person because everyone loves freedom and by appearing to be our teachers they deprive us of it. For this reason it is not a pleasant habit to be eager to correct and teach others. This must be left to teachers and fathers. Even from these will sons and students eagerly distance themselves, as you well know.

One should never mock anyone however great an enemy he may be, because it seems that one shows greater contempt in mocking someone than in doing him wrong. This is so because a man wrongs another man out of anger or out of some covetous desire, and no one is upset by something that he esteems worthless or desires something which he despises completely. So one has some esteem for the man one injures, but none at all or very little indeed for the man one mocks. Mocking consists of taking pleasure, for no personal benefit to ourselves, in the shame we bring on others. Therefore, it is good manners to abstain from mocking anyone. They behave badly who reprove others of some defect either with words, as Messer Forese da Rabatta did when he laughed at Master Giotto's appearance,[5] or with actions, as many do, mimicking those who stutter, or limp, or are hunchbacked. It is also bad manners to laugh at people who are deformed, misshapen, thin or short; or to laugh loudly and make a fuss about a silly thing someone has said; or to take pleasure in making others blush. Such spiteful behaviour is properly detested.

Like these people are the jokers, those who enjoy playing tricks on someone and leading him along not because they want to jest with him or deride him, but simply for the fun of it. You must know that there is no difference between joking and mocking except in purpose and intention; for joking is done for amusement, and mocking is done to hurt. In common speech and writing the two words are often confused, but the difference is that whoever mocks is pleased with the shame he inflicts on another, while he who jokes is not pleased, but rather is amused by the other man's error, and would probably be pained and feel sorry if the other man were made to feel shame. . . .

You must know that there is wit that bites and wit that does not bite. Let Lauretta's wise advice suffice for the former, and that is that wit must bite like a sheep, and not like a dog, for if it bit like a dog it would not be wit but insult.[6] In nearly every city the law is such that whoever insults someone else should be severely punished, and perhaps one should also have or-

---

[5] Reference to one of the hundred stories in Boccaccio's *Decameron*.
[6] Another reference to the *Decameron*.

dained no light penalty for anyone who used overly biting witticisms towards someone else. Well-mannered men should consider that the law against slander applies to wit as well, and so mock someone else only rarely and gently at that.

Besides all this, you must realize that unless a witty remark, whether biting or not, is pleasant and subtle, those who hear it will not delight in it. Rather, they will be bored by it or, if they laugh, they will laugh at the "wit" and not at the witticism. Witty remarks are nothing else but deceptions, and deceptions, being subtle and crafty, must be carried out only by astute men with a quick wit, and, above all, unexpectedly. Therefore, they are not suitable to stolid persons with thick heads, nor to anyone with a good, solid head on his shoulders. . . .

. . . Where a pleasant witticism has been said, there immediately is gaiety, laughter, and a kind of astonishment, but where your pleasantries are not rewarded with the laughter of those around you, you will desist from telling witticisms for the fault will be with you and not with your listeners. People are tickled by quick or charming or subtle answers of propositions and even if they try they cannot hold back their laughter and laugh despite themselves. Your listeners are like a lawful and just jury against whose judgment you must not appeal by choosing to make a further trial of yourself based solely on the grounds of your own opinion.

One should not, for the sake of making someone else laugh, say obscene words, or indulge in such ignoble or unsuitable act as distorting one's face and disguising oneself, for no one should debase himself in order to please others. This is the habit not of a gentleman, but of jesters and clowns. . . . Nor should one pretend to be crazy or foolish, but if he can he should say, at the proper time, something nice and interesting which no one else has thought of, or else keep quiet. For these are matters of the mind, and if they are pleasant and lively they are an indication and a testimonial of the nimble mind and the good habits of the speaker, and this is particularly liked by other men and endears us to them. But if they are without grace and charm, they have the contrary effect and then it seems that an ass is joking, or that someone very fat with an enormous derrière is dancing and hopping about in his shirt-sleeves. . . .

Both in extended speaking and in other manners of speech, words must be so clear that everyone in the group can understand them with ease, and also beautiful in sound and meaning. And so if you must choose one of these two words, you will rather say "stomach" than "belly," and where your language will bear it you will rather say "tummy" than "belly" or "body" and thus you will be understood, not misunderstood, as we Florentines say, and you will not bring anything unpleasant to your listener's mind. Wanting to avoid such implications in this very word, I believe Petrarch,[7] our most excellent poet, sought to discover another one even if it

[7]Italian poet (1304–1374).

meant using periphrasis. And so he said: "Remember that our sins made God take on, to save us, human flesh in your virginal cloister."

Because Dante,[8] also a most excellent poet, thought very little about such precepts, I find that little good can be said of him for this reason. I would certainly not advise you to make him your teacher in this art of being elegant, since he himself was not. In fact, in some chronicle I find this written about him: "Because of his knowledge, Dante was presumptuous, scornful, and disdainful, and lacking in grace, as philosophers are, he did not know very well to converse with laymen." But to return to our discussion, I say that words ought to be clear; this will be the case if you know how to choose those that are native to your region, and not so ancient that they have become rancid and corrupt and, like worn-out clothes have been cast aside and rejected. . . . Furthermore, the words you use should not have double meanings, but must be simple; for if these ambiguous words are combined one creates that kind of speech which is called enigmatic or, as is said more clearly in the vernacular, a jargon. . . .

Your words should also be, as far as possible, appropriate to what you want to demonstrate, and as little applicable to other matters as possible. In this manner it will seem that you are bringing forth the things themselves and that they are being described not with words but with your finger. Therefore it is preferable to say that a man is recognized by his features rather than by his figure or by his image. Dante described the event better when he said "that the weight makes their balances creak thus," than if he had said either shrieked, screeched, or made a noise. It is more precise to say "the shivers of a fever" than the "cold of a fever"; and "fat meat makes one feel nauseous" rather than "we have had our fill of fatty meat"; and "hang out" the laundry rather than "spread it out"; and "stumps" rather than "severed arms"; and at the edge of a ditch, "the frogs lie . . . with only the muzzle out" rather than their "mouths." These are all words that have only one meaning. And similarly we should say the "hem" of a cloth rather than the "extremity."

I know very well that if, as my ill luck would have it, a foreigner came across this little treatise of mine he would mock me and say that I was teaching you how to speak in jargon, that is a code, since these words are for the most part particular to our region and no other nation uses them and if it were to use them they would not be understood. . . .

Therefore, no one can speak effectively with someone who does not understand the language in which he is speaking. If a German does not understand Latin, we must not ruin our own speech when communicating with him, nor engage in mimicry like Master Brufaldo,[9] as do some people who are so foolish as to force themselves to speak in the language of the

---

[8]Italian poet (1265–1321), author of *The Divine Comedy.*
[9]No one is certain to whom della Casa is here referring.

person with whom they are speaking, whatever it may be, and say everything backwards. It often happens that a Spaniard will speak Italian with an Italian, and the Italian, to show off and to be pleasant, will speak to him in Spanish, and yet it is easier to realize that they are both speaking in a foreign language than to keep from laughing at the silly things that come out of their mouths.

We shall speak then in a foreign language when that is necessary in order to make some need of ours understood; but generally let us continue to use our own language, even if inferior, rather than another one, though it may be superior to ours. For a Lombard will speak more properly in his own language, though it is the ugliest dialect of all, than he would in Tuscan or any other because he will never have easily at hand, try as he might, the correct and specific words which we Tuscans have. And if anyone, in order to show consideration for the people with whom he is speaking, seeks to avoid using the local words which I mentioned and in place of them uses generally accepted, standard words, his conversation will thus become much less pleasant.

Every gentleman must also avoid saying indecent words. Decency in words is dependent on their sound, or on their pronunciation, or on their meaning. Some words signify a decent thing, yet one can hear something indecent in pronouncing them, such as "rinculare,"[10] which is nevertheless used daily by everybody. But if anyone, man or woman, were to use some word to mean "to draw forth" coined in the same manner as that word for "to draw back," then the indecency of the word would become apparent. Because of usage, however, our taste for this word perceives its wine rather than its mildew. . . .

In fact, one should not only refrain from indecent and obscene words, but also from base words, especially where one speaks of high and noble matters. For this reason, perhaps, Beatrice[11] deserved some blame when she said: "God's high decrees would be broken if Lethe were passed and such a draught were tasted without some scot of penitence." In my opinion, the base word appropriate to an inn did not fit in such a noble discussion. Nor should one say "the lamp of the world" in place of "the sun" because for some persons such a word implies the stink of oil and of the kitchen. Nor would any prudent man say that Saint Dominic[12] was the "lover" of theology, nor would he say that the glorious saints had uttered such base words as: "and then let them scratch where it itches," which are sullied with the filth of the common people, as anyone can readily ascertain.

Therefore, when you speak at length you must consider those things

---

[10] A word capable of an off-color pronunciation, as could happen in English, for example, with a word like *asset*.

[11] A woman loved by Dante who leads him to heaven in the *Paradiso* part of *The Divine Comedy*.

[12] Founder of the Order of Friars Preachers, known as the Dominicans (ca. 1170–1221).

mentioned above and some others which you may easily learn from your teachers and from the art that they call Rhetoric. In other manners of speech you must accustom yourself to using words that are polite, simple and sweet, so that there is no bitter flavour to your language. You will sooner say, "I did not explain myself well," rather than, "You do not understand me;" and, "Let us just consider if we are interpreting things correctly," rather than, "You are wrong," or, "That is not true," or, "You do not know." It is a polite and pleasant habit to excuse a man's fault even when you know him to be in the wrong. In fact, one should share a friend's own error and first claim a portion of it oneself, and then reprove him for it and correct him. You should say, "We have taken the wrong road" and "Yesterday we did not remember to do this," even though it was your friend alone who was forgetful, and not you. What Restagnone said to his companions was not right: "You, if your words do not lie . . ."[13] because it is not proper to question other people's good faith. In fact, if someone promised you something and did not deliver, it is not correct for you to say, "You did not keep your word," unless you are forced to say it by some necessity, for the safeguarding of your honour, for example. If someone has deceived you, you should sooner say: "You did not remember to do this"; and if he did not remember you should sooner say, "You could not do it," or, "It slipped your mind," rather than "You forgot," or, "You did not care to keep your promise to me," because such words have the sting and poison of protest and spite in them. Because of this, those people who make it a habit to use such words often are considered to be mean and rough fellows, and one avoids their company as much as one avoids becoming tangled up in thorns and thistles. . . .

It is therefore not true that against nature there is neither rein nor master. On the contrary, there are two of them: one is good manners, the other reason. But, as I have said to you shortly before, without good manners which are a child and a product of time, reason cannot make an uncouth man into a courteous one.

Consequently, one should begin to listen to reason early on, not only because a man thus has a longer period of time in which to become accustomed to follow her teachings and become her servant and be one of her train, but also because youth in its purity takes on colours more easily; and also those things to which one first grows accustomed always tend to be more pleasing. For this reason it is told that Diodato[14] a great master in reciting comedies, always wanted his own play to be staged first, in spite of the fact that those who were to come before him were not highly thought of, because he did not want his voice to find the ears of his spectators

---

[13] Another *Decameron* reference.

[14] A Greek actor of the fourth century B.C.

accustomed to other voices, even though they would have been worse than his.

Since, for the reasons I have told you, I cannot suit my deeds to my words as did Master Chiarissimo who knew how both to do and to teach, let it suffice for me to have said at least in part what one should do; for I am unfit to put any part of it into practice. But just as in seeing darkness one learns what light is, and in hearing silence one learns what sound is, so also you will be able to perceive, in looking at my poor and uncouth manners, what the light of pleasant and praiseworthy manners may be. Returning to the discussion of these manners, which will shortly come to an end, let us say that pleasant manners are those which delight or at least do not irritate any of the senses, the desires or the imagination of those with whom we are dealing. It is about these things that we have talked till now. . . .

Therefore, a man must not be content with doing what is good, but he must also seek to do it gracefully. Grace is nothing else but something akin to a light which shines from the appropriateness of things that are suitably ordered and arranged one with the other, and in relation to the whole. Without this measure, even that which is good will not be beautiful, and beauty will not be pleasing. Just as with food which, although it is wholesome and nutritious, will not please the guests if it has no taste or a bad taste, so it will sometimes be with a man's manners. Even if there is nothing harmful in them, they will appear silly or distasteful unless he flavours them with that certain sweetness which is called, as I believe, grace or charm.

For this reason alone, every vice must be in itself offensive to other people, for vices are such ugly and improper things that their unsuitability displeases and disturbs every sober and well-balanced spirit.

Therefore, it is most advisable for those who aspire to be well liked in dealing with other people to flee vices, especially the fouler ones such as lust, avarice, cruelty, and the like. Some of these vices are despicable, such as gluttony or drunkenness; some are filthy, such as being a lecher; some are evil, such as murder. Similarly, other vices are despised by people, some more than others, each for its own nature and quality. But, as I have shown you before, all vices in general, because they are disordered things, render a man unpleasant in the company of others. However, since I undertook to show you men's errors and not their sins, my present care must be to deal not with the nature of vice and virtue, but only with the proper and improper manners we use toward each other. One of these improper manners was the one used by Count Ricciardo, of whom I told you above. It was so different from and discordant with his other beautiful and fitting manners that the worthy bishop immediately noticed it, as a good and well-trained singer notices wrong notes.

It is therefore suitable for well-mannered persons to be mindful of this balance of which I have spoken in their walking, standing, sitting, movements, bearing, and in their dress, in their words, in their silence, in their repose, and in their actions. Thus, a man must not embellish himself like a woman, for his adornments will then contradict his person, as I see some men do, who put curls in their hair and beards with a curling iron, and who apply so much make-up to their faces, necks, and hands that it would be unsuitable for any young wench, even for a harlot who is more anxious to hawk her wares and sell them for a price.

One should not smell either foul or sweet, so that a gentleman does not smell like a beggar or a man like a common woman or a harlot. Still, I do not say that at your age certain simple fragrances made from distilled waters are not suitable.

For the reasons I have mentioned above, your clothes should be according to the custom of those like you in age and condition. We do not have the power to change customs as we see fit, for it is time that creates them and likewise it is time that destroys them. Everyone, however, may adapt the current fashion to his own need. For example, if your legs are very long and the fashion calls for short clothes, you could make your garments a little less short. If someone has very thin legs, or unduly fat ones, or perhaps crooked ones, he should not wear hose of bright or attractive colours so as not to invite others to gaze at his defect.

Your garments should not be extremely fancy or extremely ornate, so that no one can say that you are wearing Ganymede's hose,[15] or that you have donned Cupid's doublet. But whatever clothes you are wearing should fit your body well and suit you, so that it does not look as if you are wearing someone else's clothing. And above all they must befit your condition, so that a priest does not look like a soldier,[16] or the soldier like a jester. . . .

We must therefore take care that our garments fit not only the body but also the status of the person who wears them. And, furthermore, they should be suitable to the place where we live. For as in other lands there are other weights and measures and yet one sells, buys, and trades in every country, so in different places there are different customs and yet in every land a man can behave and dress himself properly.

The feathers that Neapolitans and Spaniards wear on their hats, and their elaborate trimmings and embroideries, do not suit the apparel of serious men or the clothes of city-dwellers. Armour and chain-mail are even less suitable. So, what is perhaps suitable in Verona in Venice may not do, for these men, so feathered, decorated, and armed are out of place in that venerable city of peace and orderliness. In fact, they appear like nettles and burrs among good and sweet garden greens, and for this reason are ill

---

[15]According to ancient Greek legend, Ganymede was a Trojan boy carried off to Olympus by Zeus.

[16]Possible reference to Pope Julius II, in office from 1503–1513, who often personally led troops into battle.

received in noble gatherings, because they are so out of keeping with them.

A noble man must not run in the street, nor hurry too much, for this is suitable for a groom and not for a gentleman. Besides, a man will tire himself out, sweat and pant for breath, all of which are unbecoming to men of quality. Nor, on the other hand, should one proceed as slowly or demurely as a woman or a bride does. Also, it is unsuitable to wiggle too much when walking. One should not let his arms dangle, nor swing them around, nor throw them about so that it looks like he is sowing seed in a field. Nor should one stare a man in the face as though there was something to marvel at. . . .

Spanish Society in the Reign of Philip II

GIANFRANCESCO MOROSINI

In this 1581 report, the Venetian ambassador to Spain, Gianfrancesco Morosini, describes the people and society of Spain. Venice was the birthplace of the institution of the resident ambassador, and Venetian ambassadors are famous for their long and detailed reports to their governments describing the countries in which they were stationed. These reports dealt not only with political developments but with all facets of life. Thus, these ambassadorial writings are of great value to the historian.

How does Morosini depict the appearance and habits of the Spaniards? Does Morosoni believe in "national" character, personalities and attributes that are typical of people in a particular country? For what does he find fault with the Spanish, and for what does he admire them? Why does he feel that the people do not like their king and his ministers? Why do the common people not rebel? How does Morosini explain the prevalence of poverty in Spain? What does he think of the Church? Of the nobility? What is the relationship between the Crown and the aristocracy?

How were the different parts of Spain governed? What does Morosini consider to be the greatest problems that Spanish society faced? Morosini wrote his report when Spain was the leading power in Europe, during the period that some historians have termed the "Golden Age" of Spain. Does Morosini at least recognize Spanish greatness, or does he emphasize obstacles to Spanish greatness? Overall, is his portrayal of Spanish society flattering? In what ways might Morosini have been biased?

Most of the men in this country are small in stature and dark in complexion, haughty if they belong to the upper classes or prudently humble if they are common people, and unsuited for any kind of work. As farmers they are the most lackadaisical in the world, and as artisans they are so lazy and slow that work that would be done anywhere else in one month in

Spain requires four. They are such stupid craftsmen that in all their provinces you can hardly find a building or anything else of interest except for antiquities done in Roman times or works built by the Moorish kings. Most of the Spanish live in houses so ineptly built of inferior materials that it is remarkable if one lasts as long as the man who built it. The cities are badly run and dirty; they throw all their refuse into the public streets instead of having the conveniences in their houses which are used in Italy and other parts of the world. They give no thought to food supplies; as a result the common people often have to fight each other to get bread, not so much because there is a shortage of grain as because there is no official whose job it is to make sure that there is bread. . . .

On the other hand, in bearing arms and making war they have worked miracles. They put up well with discomforts, and very comradely with each other, and are particularly clever at battlefield strategems (they make a specialty of this). In battle they are bold, eager, and united, as they have shown not only in their own country, where they won fame for the prowess they showed in driving out the Moors, but also outside of Spain. I have in mind the conquest of the Indies and the new world, their attacks on France, Germany, and Italy, and their warfare on land and sea with the Turks, in none of which they have ever suffered any real damage to their homeland. More recently there were the events in Flanders when a mere three thousand Spaniards, garrisoned in the citadel of Antwerp, had the courage to assault and sack the city. Antwerp had a large population and more than fourteen thousand friendly soldiers with fairly experienced officers, but all of these were not enough to prevent the sack. The Antwerp soldiers considered themselves lucky to escape, after killing only a dozen of the Spanish.[1] The Spaniards reached the point where they were a threat to all countries, and even to their own king,[2] who dreaded their return to Spain because he thought that when they had been paid off these capable soldiers might stir his whole kingdom into rebellion.

Spain might be quick to rebel if there were a leader courageous enough to direct a revolt. All of the people are discontented with their king and his current ministers. The nobles are dissatisfied because they are virtually ignored, and everyone else because they pay such unbearably heavy taxes; no other people in the world carry such a tax burden as the Castilians. True, the Aragonese and Castilians have ended their quarrels and there have been no more of those rebellions of the cities against the kings which happened in the reign of the emperor Charles V,[3] and earlier during the

---

[1]The sack of Antwerp, or "Spanish Fury" (1557), cost the lives of about seven thousand persons. The Spanish dead probably numbered nearer two hundred than the twelve of which Morosini speaks. (Original editor's note.)

[2]Philip II, king of Spain, 1556–1598.

[3]King of Spain, 1516–1556, and Holy Roman Emperor, 1519–1556.

reign of King Ferdinand.[4] But when the king dies—or if he should get into serious problems—these and even more unpleasant humors might recur in the body politic. There would be a special danger if the rebels used religion as a battle standard, since religious faith lends itself very well to subverting and destroying monarchies. Spain would be particularly susceptible because there are so many there who are Moors at heart, many others who secretly remain Jews, and even some heretics. They are all very cautious because they fear the Inquisition, a high tribunal so powerful and harsh that everyone is terrified of it. Without the Inquisition Spain would be more lost than Germany and England, even though the Spanish look at first glance like the most devout Catholics in the world.

Most Spaniards are either very rich or very poor, and there would seem to be a cause-and-effect relationship between the wealth of some and the poverty of the rest. It is as if four men had to divide this [Senate] chamber among them. If one man took three-quarters there would be very little to divide among the other three. The Spanish clergy is very rich; the church in Toledo alone has revenues of 400,000 ducats a year, and all the other fifty-seven bishoprics are also very wealthy. The incomes of the churches have been estimated at four million in gold per year. Then there are twenty-two dukes, forty-seven counts, and thirty-six marquises in those lands, and their incomes total nearly three million in gold a year. The richest of all is said to be the duke of Medina Sidonia,[5] the governor-elect of Milan, whose income exceeds 150,000 ducats a year.

One group among these nobles are called the "grandees" of the kingdom. The only things that set them apart are that they remain covered in the presence of the king, whereas everyone else must remove his hat, and when His Majesty is in church they sit on a bench, called the grandees' bench, while everyone else stands. These grandees are all addressed as "*Vuestra Señoria*"[6] even though they are dukes. (The sole exception is the duke of Alva, whom many call "Your Excellency.") All the nobles *except* the grandees—including the counts and marquises—are addressed as "*Vuestra Merced.*"[7] But then the rest of the men and women right down to the peasants and the scoundrels who beg in the streets and churches are called "*Señor*" and "*Señora.*"[8]

The grandees then are those to whom previous kings or the present one conceded the right of remaining covered in their presence. Many of the other nobles constantly implore the king to grant them this honor, which

---

[4] Also of Spain, 1474–1504.

[5] Alonso Pérez de Guzmán (1550–1615), commander of the Spanish Armada in 1588.

[6] "Your Lordship."

[7] "Your Honor."

[8] What strikes the ambassador as paradoxical is that the highest social group (the grandees) and the lowest are both addressed in approximately the same way. (Original editor's note.)

the mere fact of being dukes, counts, or marquises, and very rich, does not entitle them to have. The honor is conferred on them only if the king so desires, and he grants it to those he likes best. He does not confer it only on Spaniards; recently he indicated that he plans to give this honor to Sir Giovanni Andrea Doria,[9] who had never received it. Doria plans to go to court to be given the dignity. The king makes as little use as possible of the grandees; on the contrary, he does all he can to keep them from becoming important. If one of them manages his affairs well or has a stroke of luck and becomes very rich, the king finds a way to make him spend his money and thus weaken him. As a result, even though they have large incomes, as I said, none of them has money to spend. Quite the opposite; they are deep in debt.

Because the king does not use them in his service, very few of the grandees know anything about running a government, nor do they know anything else. They consider it beneath them to leave their estates unless to take major government positions; on the other hand, they are not suited for life on their own estates. They do not read; they do not discuss anything of value; they simply live in ignorance. The only noteworthy thing about them is a certain loftiness and dignity which in Italy we call "Spanish composure" and which makes all foreigners hate them. They let it be understood that not only is there no other people which bears comparison with them, but that everyone should be grateful to be ruled by them. And they do not forget to use this haughtiness even among themselves. Before addressing a person as *"Señor," "Vuestra Merced,"* "you" (plural), "you" (singular), or *"el,"* they give the matter a great deal of thought, because they believe that any distinction they confer on someone else reduces their own importance.

Because they remain on their own lands they have seen and they know nothing about the world. Their lack of schooling makes them ignorant and their lack of contacts with others makes them arrogant. This arrogance is very common among the young people, especially those who are surrounded by great wealth. Revered and deferred to by their own domestic servants, they soon come to believe that everyone should behave that way toward them, and that no one is so important as they. The result is that they look down on others—indeed, they often despise them—and only late or never do they realize their error, when they have been damaged and shamed.

The Spanish grandees consider attending to business matters just as ridiculous as book reading; both pursuits are detestable, or at least completely at odds with the life of a knight. And yet they do not take much pleasure in horsemanship. Instead they pass the time idly, even de-

---

[9]Genoese naval commander in Spanish service, grand-nephew of the more famous admiral of the same name. (Original editor's note.)

pravedly. The reasons for this are that they have been poorly brought up and they believe that exercise in Spain is "unhealthy," and also that the king lives in great seclusion and has no interest in watching tournaments.

The grandees and other nobles are subject to the laws of the kingdom just as much as the poorest, wretchedest commoner. Not even the richest and proudest of them would dare to refuse to go to prison if a constable (called an *alguacil*), armed only with a billy club, came to arrest him. While I was in Spain the duke of Alva[10] provided an example of this obedience. The duke is closely related to many of the grandees and nobles of Castile, is respected, dignified, and more than eighty years old. He has served the emperor Charles V and the present king more than fifty years continually and received honors that those rulers never conferred on anyone else. And yet a single *alguacil* with a warrant from the king took him to prison. If he had refused to go, and turned not toward Uceda, where he was imprisoned, but toward his own easily defended district of Alva, he would have frightened the king and agitated the country so much that those who know the kingdom well think the king would have had to leave him alone.

Spain is divided into two major sections. One is Castile, which in 1034 was changed from a county into a kingdom, with the kingdoms of Leòn, Galicia, Granada, Toledo, Murcia, Andalusia, and Seville added to it. The Indies and the king's lands in Africa are also linked to Castile. The other section is Aragon, with Valencia and Catalonia (to which Majorca and those other islands are attached) and the kingdoms of Naples, Sicily, and Sardinia. The kingdom of Navarre is not grouped with these, nor is Portugal,[11] because the former is not completely under Castile and the system of government for Portugal had not yet been decided when I left. The king was planning to join it to Castile, but I will discuss it separately.

The people of Aragon claim to be independent, as in effect they are, since they govern themselves almost as if Aragon were a republic. The king is the head of the state, but he does not inherit the position, they elect him to it. He appoints no official there except a viceroy, who has no part in governing the land or administering justice. These tasks are the responsibilities of officials elected in that kingdom. The viceroy has charge only of the armed forces, and the safety and defense of the region. His Majesty collects no revenues from this region unless he goes there to conduct a meeting of the Cortes,[12] in which case they grant him 600,000 ducats. They keep the rest of the taxes and duties and spend them for the benefit of their own land. They guard their liberties very jealously and bitterly contest each point so that the king and his ministers cannot enlarge their control

---

[10]Ferdinand Alvarez de Toledo, duke of Alva (or Alba) (1508–1582), general.

[11]Portugal was added to Philip II's lands in 1580 and remained under Spanish rule until 1640. (Original editor's note.)

[12]Representative assembly.

over them. As a result they frequently and unnecessarily hinder measures which are not their business.

The kingdom of Castile, however, is governed very differently, because there the king has supreme authority. It is he who chooses all the judges, officials, ministers, and councillors, assigns the bishoprics (as he does throughout all of Spain), grants all the benefices and sinecures of the kingdom, and draws up whatever laws he chooses. He abolishes old laws and imposes new ones entirely as he sees fit, although with the apparent consent of the Cortes of Castile, who assemble whenever he gives so much as a hint and then do just about what he wants. He has total control over the revenues, completely controls the courts (that is, pardons, executions, and fines), and generally does whatever he pleases. The one exception is the imposing of new taxes and customs duties, which he cannot change without the consent of the Cortes, which represent all of Castile. But this requirement serves more as a salve to his conscience and a way of facilitating the collection of the money than anything else. Even in tax matters he has such power and is so revered and respected that if he wants something, not one of the deputies in the Cortes would dare to oppose him openly. What makes them all the more docile is their knowledge that when the Cortes are over, the king invariably rewards with presents those who openly supported him. He does this to help his projects along; it keeps everyone from speaking out against him and he always has his way.

The nobles and other aristocrats are all tax exempt; they pay the king no head or property tax at all. Their only obligation is to serve in his army at their own expense, and even then only when it is a question of defending Spain from attack. They are very firm and determined about guarding their tax immunity, just as the Aragonese defend all of their liberties. Once when the government tried to impose a very light tax on them they raised such an uproar that the matter was dropped.

The nobles and grandees of Castile have so little legal authority in their own jurisdictions that most of them have courts only of the first instance; and few of their courts may hear appeals. All appeals eventually go to the chancelleries and the royal council. Their own vassals can have them summoned to these higher courts on the slightest of grounds, and they are often treated worse there than the lowliest subjects. This happens both because such is the king's wish and because the judges usually come from the lower classes. The reason for this is that judges have to be university graduates; since the nobles consider it beneath them to study anything, the power of the courts goes by default into the hands of plebeians. Professional learning is the only route by which men from the lower classes can rise to important posts. This explains why not only the law courts but almost all of the bishoprics are also in the hands of commoners, who are enemies of nobility. This in turn is another of the grudges the upper classes have against the present regime. At one time most of the bishoprics were given as a matter of course to younger sons of the grandees, as a way of compensating them for not being the heirs. Despite all I have said, however, the king still has ample means to gratify the nobles, since he has many knighthoods in the military orders to distribute, all of which may be conferred only on nobles. Some of these have incomes of up to twelve thousand ducats.

The king rules the people of Castile with an iron hand, as experience has proved is necessary. They are an obstreperous people by nature, and if he treated them otherwise they would be violent and ungovernable. If someone resists the authorities even slightly, by word rather than deed, they punish him as harshly as another government would only for very serious and important crimes. The law officers behave so outrageously that no other country would tolerate them. Frequently they will arrest prominent people without reason, showing no respect for them, and put them in prison. If these people then complain to higher officials about the damage and injustice done to them, these officials are so determined to support the authority of their subordinates that they merely release the injured parties. And even then they have to pay the expenses of their arrest and imprisonment! Because of this there is no shame attached to going to jail in Spain, so at least one does not have insults added to his injuries. . . .

Life in Paris during the French Civil Wars

PIERRE DE L'ESTOILE

From 1562 to 1598, France experienced eight terribly destructive civil and religious wars. Spanish meddling in French affairs and later war against Spain added to an already appalling situation. Catholic fought Protestant (the Huguenots), Catholic often combated Catholic, and the French of both religions took up arms against their lawful government. It was the worst of times.

Pierre de L'Estoile (1546–1611), a Parisian magistrate, is famous because of his Journal, *an excellent historical source for Parisian life during the reigns of Henry III, 1574–1589, and Henry IV, 1589–1610. It is important to recognize L'Estoile's bias— he was an ardent royalist, a supporter of the French kings. L'Estoile was a* politique, *a Frenchman who placed the interests of the state above those of any religion. Therefore he opposed the Holy League, the extreme Catholic organization bent on rolling back Protestantism no matter what.*

The following selection describes certain events that occurred in Paris in 1583. How did the civil strife affect life in Paris? How did L'Estoile view the recent uprising in Antwerp? What does L'Estoile think of the Parisian clergy? How does he explain the popular opinion of King Henry III? Religious processions constituted an integral part of Parisian life. What does the March procession and ceremonies of the Confraternity of Penitents and the September processions tell us about French religion? How does the November anecdote concerning Cardinal du Perron illustrate French attitudes toward religion?

In April, the government imprisoned an author of a book. Why? How does this episode speak to the sixteenth-century attitude toward censorship? In August and November, L'Estoile recounts yet more arrests. What crimes had been committed? Or rather, why was the behavior described considered to be criminal?

What similarities and differences do you perceive between the urban violence in Paris and that depicted in the earlier excerpt from The Annals of Ghent?

JANUARY

Flood Waters Cause the Cost of Living to Rise.

In this month of January the Seine river overflowed, due to the great and continuous rains. It rose almost as high as last November, and as a result wheat rose to 11 francs, feed grain to 8, and hay to 15.

Kings in the Matter of Money are Inexorable. A Blow to the Bonds of the City.

At this time the King[1] levied a tax of 1,500,000 crowns on the cities of the kingdom . . . of which the quota of Paris is 200,000, which the King, without any consultation or deliberation, commanded the Prévost[2] and Échevins[3] to collect from the bourgeois of the city. . . . An assembly was held at the Hôtel de Ville[4]. . . where it was resolved . . . that his town of Paris could not furnish such a sum. The King was much irritated at this response and forthwith commanded de Vigny, treasurer of the city, to take it out of the income of the municipal bonds, which was about to be paid out.

The King's Dream, Remarkable for What Has Happened Since.

January 21 . . . the King returned to the Louvre, and had the lions, bears, bulls, and other animals he has kept for purposes of amusement killed. This was due to a dream he had had in which these animals were eating him up. This dream seemed to presage what we have seen since, when the furious beasts of the League threw themselves on this poor prince, tore, and ate him, with his people.

The Uprising in Antwerp.

January 28 there came to Paris news of the terrible rioting and fighting in Antwerp between the French and the inhabitants, on the 17th of this

---

[1]Henry III, king of France, 1574–1589.
[2]Provost of the merchants, the head of the city government.
[3]Town councilors.
[4]City Hall.

month. This was on the occasion of the French, under M. le Duc d'Alençon,[5] trying to make themselves masters of the city and loot it, as the Spaniards did six or seven years ago. . . . Fifteen or sixteen hundred were killed, including three or four hundred French gentlemen, all of the flower of the nobility, a terrible loss. Other Frenchmen, found unarmed, were arrested and put out of the town. . . . The Duke . . . retired to his camp . . . where he was without provisions. . . . He was much criticized for such a rash and ill-advised enterprise which really cannot be called by any other name than treason, although if it had been successful it would be called something else! Indeed, by this day the name of Frenchman lost greatly in the eyes of foreigners, and Monsieur, the King's brother, much of his reputation. . . .

FEBRUARY

Of the King Frequenting the Streets, and of the Reproaches of Rose.

On the day of Mardi Gras the King and his *mignons*[6] went about the streets masked, going from house to house and committing a thousand insolences, up to six in the morning of Ash Wednesday. On that day most of the preachers of Paris openly blamed him for this in their sermons. This annoyed the King very much, especially the reproaches of Rose, doctor of theology, whom he sent for.[7] Rose tried to avoid going, saying that he feared maltreatment . . . but he finally appeared and received a light reprimand from the King . . . with the order not to do it again. . . . The King not only pardoned him but, several days later, sent him 400 crowns "to buy sugar and honey, to help pass Lent, and to sweeten your bitter words."

MARCH

The King at the Palais for His Edicts. The League.[8]

Monday, March 1, the King, accompanied by his two *mignons* and a few other gentlemen, went to the Palais[9] to have published in his presence a number of financial edicts which the Court[10] had refused to register, on the grounds that they tended to the manifest oppression of the people. . . .

---

[5]François Hercules (1555–1584), duke of Alençon and the king's brother.

[6]Favorites.

[7]William Rose, Bishop of Senlis, one of the founders of the Paris League. He was among the most violent of the League preachers during the rebellion. (Original editor's note.)

[8]The Catholic League, an organization led by the Guise family. The league opposed King Henry III and any compromise with French Protestants.

[9]Palace of Justice.

[10]The Parlement of Paris, a sovereign judicial court whose jurisdiction covered approximately one-half of France.

[They were registered] although the money is used only for the profit of the Italians and the *mignons,* and even more does it give advantage to those of Guise, who stir the people up more against the King on this account. The League is beginning now to develop their *mystique* of [Henry III's] inequity.

The Confrairie des Pénitents,[11] Their Processions and Ceremonies.

In the present year 1583 the King instituted a new brotherhood which is called the Penitents, of which he and his two *mignons* are members. . . . The first ceremonies were held on the 25th of March, Feast of the Annunciation, with a solemn procession at four in the afternoon from the monastery of the Augustinians to the great church of Notre Dame. They marched two by two . . . dressed in white cloth from Holland . . . the King among them, without any guard, indistinguishable from the others. The Cardinal of Guise carried the cross, the Duke of Mayenne, his brother, was Master of Ceremonies . . . the King's singers marched in the procession, dressed like the others, singing the litany melodiously.

When they arrived at Notre Dame they all sang the *Salve Regina*[12] accompanied by beautiful music. The hard and continuous rain which fell all day long did not in the least hinder these ceremonies. This occasioned a gentleman of equality to write the following quatrain about the King's wet robe, which, being found very timely and apropos, is being repeated everywhere:

> After having pillaged France
> And put the people to sack,
> Isn't it a fine penitence
> To wear a dripping wet sack?

The Boldness of Poncet's Preaching, for Which He Was Imprisoned.

Sunday, the 27th of the said month of March, the King had the monk Poncet arrested. He had preached a Lenten sermon at Notre Dame the day before, in which he attacked this new brotherhood, calling it a brotherhood of hypocrites and atheists.

On the same day the King had over a hundred pages and lackeys at the Louvre beaten because they had mocked the procession of the Penitents by putting white handkerchiefs over their heads, with holes cut for their eyes, and had imitated the ceremonies in an obscene and disrespectful manner. . . .

---

[11]Confraternity of Penitents, a religious association that organized public spiritual activities. Such associations were common in late-sixteenth-century France.

[12]"Hail, Holy Queen," a Catholic hymn.

APRIL

Author of the Book: Stemmata Lotharingiae.

At this time M. François de Rosières, Archdeacon of Toul, subject of the Duke of Lorraine, was imprisoned in the Bastille at the King's command for having said many things against the truth of history and against the honor of the King and his predecessors in his book entitled *Stemmatum Lotharingiae ac Barri Ducum, Tomi Septem.*[13]

. . . Arrived at the Bastille, he threw himself on both knees and begged for mercy. . . . And although such a crime can really only be wiped out by loss of his life (as M. de Cheverny, Garde des Sceaux, told him in no uncertain terms), His Majesty, at the request of his mother . . . pardoned him. . . .

It is the most inept and impertinent book possible, and the worst advocate of the House of Lorraine[14] and the League that has appeared. It would have been worth their money to have it repressed rather than published. . . .

The Marshal of Montmorency Defies the King.

In this month the King grew angry at the Marshal of Montmorency, Governor, or to speak plainly King, of Languedoc, because he wouldn't give up his office to the Marshal of Joyeuse, father of his *mignon* and brother-in-law . . . but Montmorency defied the King, and made himself so strong, with the support of the local nobility, that he could not be dislodged even by force without provoking civil war. . . .

JULY

Dunkirk Besieged and Taken by the Spaniards.

In the month of July, Dunkirk, which had been held by Monsieur,[15] was besieged by the Duke of Parma[16] and taken. The opinion is that this was done by secret agreement between Monsieur and the King of Spain, who paid him well for it.

---

[13]*Geneological Tree of the Dukes of Lorraine and Berry, in Seven Volumes.*

[14]The Guise family, the leaders of the ultra-Catholic faction in France.

[15]The duke of Alençon, the king's brother.

[16]Alessandro Farnese (1546–1592), duke of Parma and governor of the Spanish Netherlands.

AUGUST

Affront to the Queen of Navarre[17] Which Has Cost France Dear.
Joking Remark of the King of Navarre.[18]

Monday, the 8th day of the present month of August, the Queen of Navarre left Paris after having spent eighteen months—with great pleasure—at her brother's court, to rejoin the King of Navarre, her husband, in Gascony. This was at her brother's command. In fact the King had said that it would be better for her to be with her husband than at the court, where she served no useful purpose. . . . The King sent a company of sixty archers after her . . . and arrested two of her ladies, whom he accused of moral misdemeanors, as well as her secretary, her doctors, and others of her suite, ten in all. They were taken to Montargis, where the King himself interrogated them on the behavior of the said Queen, including a child she was supposed to have had while at the court. . . . He didn't learn anything of consequence and finally sent them back to the Queen with permission for her to continue on her way.

[Henry III] wrote to the King of Navarre about these matters . . . but when the latter resolved not to take her back . . . he wrote again and urged him to reconsider because he had discovered that the charges were all false and greatly damaging to the honor of the Queen. But the King of Navarre said he would follow the information of the first letters . . . and would not take her back. The King was much irritated by this time and sent M. de Bellièvre[19] with letters signed by his own hand to command the King of Navarre . . . to obey him. In one of these letters the King said, "That he knew that kings were liable to be deceived by false reports, and that even the most virtuous princesses were not always exempt from calumny, and he would remind him that false accusations had even been made against the late Queen, his [Navarre's] mother."

When he saw this letter the King of Navarre took to laughing, and said to Bellièvre, "The King does me too much honor in these letters. In the first he called me a cuckold, and by this one, son of a prostitute."

Hièronimites.[20]

In this month the King . . . had built in the Bois de Boulogne[21] a chapel for a new religious group which he calls Hièronimites . . . he loses himself each day in new devotions with them, living the life of a monk more than that of a king.

---

[17]Margaret of Valois (1553–1615), sister of King Henry III.

[18]Henry of Bourbon, the future King Henry IV of France, 1589–1610.

[19]Pomponne de Bellièvre (1529–1607), royal councillor.

[20]Hermits of Saint Jerome, the biblical scholar (ca. 342–420) whose Latin name is Hieronymus.

[21]Forest west of Paris.

SEPTEMBER

Processions in Paris on All Sides.

September 10, eight or nine hundred people came in a procession to Paris, dressed in white with veils over their heads, bare feet, and carrying in their hands either a large burning candle or a wooden cross. They marched two by two, as pilgrims do. They were inhabitants of the villages of St. Jean des Deux Gemeaux and D'Ussy, in Brie. They were escorted by two gentlemen of the village, on horseback, with their ladies following in a coach. The people of Paris gathered in great crowds to see them offering their prayers and gifts in Notre Dame, and were moved by pity and admiration for their long and devout voyage in bare feet. . . .

[Later in the autumn there came five other such companies] in supplication that it would please God and Our Saviour . . . to soften His wrath and turn away the plague, which is severe and widespread in the whole kingdom.

NOVEMBER

Ladies of Paris Imprisoned for Their Luxurious Clothes and Baubles.

Sunday, November 13, fifty or sixty bourgeois ladies were taken prisoner for having broken the edict about the reform of dress by their lavish attire and jewels . . . this was excessive as the edict really only required a fine to be paid . . . in the following days the *commissaires*[22] of Paris collected quite a lot of money from other offenders, depending on the degree of the offense and the financial standing of the victim.

Death of Cardinal Biragues.

Thursday, November 23, M. René de Biragues, Cardinal and Chancellor, died at the age of seventy-six . . . in Paris. He was laid out dressed as a bishop, with his red hat at his feet, and his Penitent's costume beside him. He remained thus for eight days, and great crowds of Parisians went to see him.

This Cardinal was Italian in nationality and in religion [*sic*], well versed in affairs of state but very little in those of justice . . . for the rest he was liberal, voluptuous, a man of the times, absolute slave of the King's whims, having often said that he was not Chancellor of France but Chancellor of the King of France. . . . He died poor for a man who had always served kings . . . and did better for his friends and servants than for himself. He said, a little before he died, that he would die Cardinal without title, priest without benefice, and Chancellor without seal.

---

[22]Agents of the city government.

The King, Offended by an Affront to the Honor of God (A Rare Thing in Princes),
    Dismissed Du Perron, and in This Acts as a Very Christian King.

Friday, the 25th of this month, M. du Perron,[23] great talker and philosopher, made a fine discourse on the proof of the existence of God . . . with
clear and cogent reasons . . . which the King enjoyed and praised. . . . But
Du Perron . . . carried away by conceit . . . said to the King, "Sire, I proved
today by good and sufficient reasons that there is a God. Tomorrow, if it
please your Majesty to hear me again, I'll prove by equally good reasons
there is no God." The King flew into a rage at this, dismissed Du Perron
and forbade him his presence. This just anger was very cheering to all good
men, and it was regarded as the best and most Christian thing he had ever
done in his whole life. . . .

DECEMBER

Burial of Biragues.

Tuesday, December 6, M. René de Biragues, Cardinal and Chancellor of
France, was magnificently buried. . . . The princes of the houses of Bourbon[24] and Guise wore mourning, followed by all the chambers of the Parlement, the officials of the city, and the body of the University of Paris. . . .

December 13 a great and important impetuous windstorm blew up
over Paris, which lasted about two hours. About three days later the following "prediction" appeared and was circulated in the city. It is attributed
to the Huguenots.[25] Whether it is put into their mouths to make them more
and more odious to the King, or whether they are really responsible . . . is
not certain. But from whatever quarter it comes, it is just as stupid and
ridiculous as malicious and seditious.

The Miseries of War

JACQUES CALLOT

Jacques Callot (1592–1635) was an etcher and engraver who captured in his many
works slices of seventeenth-century life. Born in Nancy, capital of the duchy of Lor-
raine, Callot first etched scenes of aristocratic culture. He then went to Florence, a cen-

---

[23]Jacques Davy, Cardinal du Perron, 1556–1618, convert from Calvinism, made Bishop
of Evreux by Henry IV in 1591. He was influential in obtaining papal absolution and recognition for the King in 1595. . . . (Original editor's note.)

[24]Rivals to the Guise and future royal dynasty with the accession in 1589 to the throne
of Henry of Bourbon, king of Navarre, as King Henry IV.

[25]French Protestants.

ter of the engraver's art, where he learned new techniques, especially a hard varnish that allowed him to produce a wide range of lights and darks not previously achieved. He also broadened his choice of subjects to include satire, the theater and actors, religion, and the lives of ordinary people. Callot returned to Nancy in 1621. The following year a German army pillaged and devastated Lorraine, which was drawn into the terrible Thirty Years' War (1618–1648). As a result, in 1633 Callot published one of his masterpieces, The Miseries of War, doubtless the best representation of the effects of war on the seventeenth-century population.

The selections reproduced here concern the recruitment of troops, the plundering of a farmhouse, the plundering and burning of a village, an attack on a coach, the hanging of thieves, the judicial method of punishment known as the wheel, men dying by a roadside, and the peasants' revenge on soldiers. In good seventeenth-century style, a poem at the bottom of each engraving explains the subject matter while offering a moral lesson.

How do these pictures help us gain an idea of various aspects of life, such as dress, architecture, soldiers' behavior and lives, methods of execution, travel, and ideas of justice? Do these etchings provide other glimpses into seventeenth-century life? What were the moral lessons that Callot attempted to impart?

It has been argued that The Miseries of War condemns the horrors of war while glorifying the lives of soldiers. Do you agree with this assessment?

Recruitment of Troops.

The poem reads: "That metal which Pluto encloses within his veins, which at the same time causes peace and war, draws the soldier, without fear of danger, from the place of his birth to foreign lands, where, having embarked to follow the military, he must arm himself with virtue to combat vice."

Plundering a Large Farmhouse.

The poem reads: "Here are the fine exploits of these inhuman hearts. They ravage everywhere. Nothing escapes their hands. One invents tortures to gain gold, another instigates his accomplices to perform a thousand misdeeds, and all with one accord spitefully commit theft, kidnapping, murder and rape."

Ceux que Mars entretient de ses actes meschans
Accommodent ainsi les pauures gens des champs

Ils les font prisonniers ils bruslent leurs villages,
Et fur-le bestail mesme exercent des rauages,

Sans que la peur des Loix nonplus que le deuoir,
Ny les pleurs et les cris les puissent esmouuoir. 7

Plundering and Burning a Village.

The poem reads: "Those whom Mars nourishes with his evil deeds, treat in this manner the poor country people. They take them prisoner, burn their villages and even wreak havoc on their livestock. Neither fear of the law, nor sense of duty, nor tears and cries can move them."

Ifrael ex cum Priuil. Reg.

A l'escart des forests, et des lieux solitaires . Ces infames Voleurs viuent en Maslins
Bien loing de l'exercice et des soings militaires , Et leur bras tout sanglantre se plaist quaux larcins

Tant ils sont possedez, d'vne cruelle enuie
D'oster aux Voyageurs et les biens et la vie .

8

Attack on a Coach.

The poem reads: "In the seclusion of forests and deserted places, quite far from military drill and discipline, these ignoble thieves lead the life of assassins, and their bloody arm deals only in robbery, so possessed are they with the cruel desire to take travelers' property and life."

The Hanging.

The poem reads: "Finally these ignoble and abandoned thieves, hanging from this tree like ominous fruit, show that crime (horrible and black spawn) is itself the instrument of shame and vengeance, and that it is the fate of vice-ridden men to experience the justice of Heaven sooner or later."

Israel ex. Cum Priuil. Reg.
L'œil tousiours surueillant de la diuine Astrée
Bannit entierement le dueil d'vne-contrée,
Lors que tenant l'espée, et la Balance en main
Elle iuge et punit le voleur inhumain,
Qui guette les passans, les meurtrit, et s'en ioüe,
Puis luy mesme deuient le ioüet d'vne roüe.
14

The Wheel.

The poem reads: "The ever-watchful eye of divine Astraea [Justice] completely banishes mourning from a region when, holding the sword and scales in her hands, she judges and punishes the inhuman thief who awaits passersby in ambush, wounds them and toys with them, then becomes himself the plaything of a wheel."

Dying Men by the Roadside.

The poem reads: "How lamentable is the lot of the poor soldier! When the war is over, his misfortune starts again. Then he is compelled to go begging, and his poverty arouses the laughter of the peasant, who curses him when he asks for alms and considers it an insult to see before him the object of the sufferings he endures."

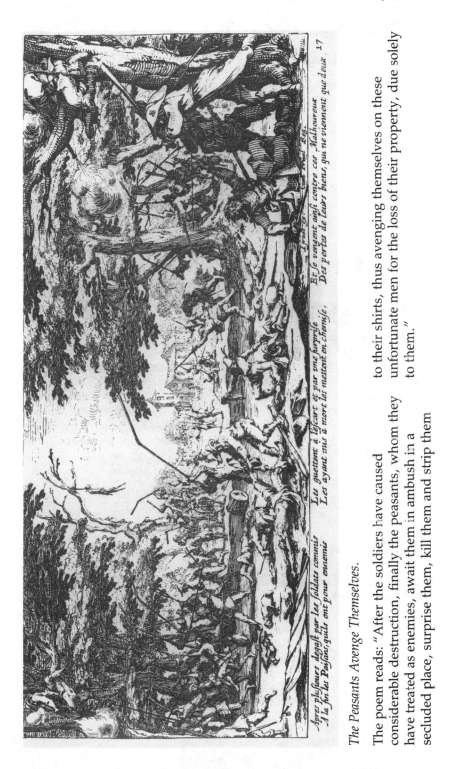

*Apres plusieurs degasts par les soldats commis
A la fin les Paysans, quils ont pour ennemis,*

*Les guettent à l'escart et par une surprise
Les ayant mis à mort les mettent en chemise,*

*Et se vengent ainsi contre ces Malhoureux
Des pertes de leurs biens, qui ne viennent que d'eux.* 17

The Peasants Avenge Themselves.

The poem reads: "After the soldiers have caused considerable destruction, finally the peasants, whom they have treated as enemies, await them in ambush in a secluded place, surprise them, kill them and strip them to their shirts, thus avenging themselves on these unfortunate men for the loss of their property, due solely to them."

The Witches of Huntingdon, Their Examinations and Confessions

Historians refer to the mass persecution of alleged witches during the sixteenth and seventeenth centuries as the great European witch-hunt (or craze or mania). From Russia to the British Isles, sixty to one hundred thousand people were executed for supposedly practicing the diabolical art of witchcraft. Courts accused innumerable others, who were usually tortured, punished in different ways, or even acquitted. This selection is a pamphlet relating a trial that occurred in England in 1646.

Witchcraft was endemic in English society; there were probably as many witches as priests. English witches were either beneficent—helping fellow villagers by foretelling the future, trying to locate buried treasure, mixing love potions—or malevolent—using curses and magic to cause illness, injury, or death. Nevertheless, unlike continental demonologists, who stressed the witch's complicity with Satan and his demons, English judges normally looked only for the carrying out of evil deeds. The great exception occurred in 1645–1646, when Matthew Hopkins, the so-called Witch-Finder General, conducted a witch-hunt that was similar to those on the Continent and that resulted in the execution of over one hundred witches. Hopkins was able to convince the populace of the reality of the demonic threat and could act because of the breakdown of central authority and hence control during the Puritan Revolution.

According to the testimony of the accusers and the accused, what type of crimes did witches commit? Why did the witches agree to consort with demonic spirits? Why did witches try to harm their neighbors? That is, what sort of situation could lead a person to harm another villager by occult means? How does all of this testimony help us to understand village society, relationships, and conflicts? How are accusations of witchcraft to be proved? Why do you think most accused witches were women? How are these demonic spirits different from those in the life of Saint Germanus?

The Examination of Elizabeth Weed *of great* Catworth *in the county of* Huntington, *widow, taken upon the last day of* March, 1646, *before* Robert Bernard, *and* Nicholas Pedley, *Esquire; two of His Majesty's Justices of the Peace for this county.*

She says that about twenty-one years since she being saying her prayers in the evening about bedtime, there did appear unto her three spirits, one in the likeness of a young man or boy, and the other two of two puppies, the one white and the other black, and that which was in the shape of a young man did speak unto her, asking her if she would renounce God and Christ; she answered, she would. And the devil then offered her that he would do what mischief she should require him; and said she must covenant with him that he must have her soul at the end of twenty-one years, which she granted. And says that he came to her about a week after, about ten o'clock in the night, with a paper, and asked her whether she were willing to seal the covenant. She said she was. Then he told her it must be done with her blood, and so pricked her under her left arm and made her bleed in the place; a great lump of flesh did rise, and has increased ever since, and she scribbled therewith. And being demanded what light was there, she answered, none but the light of the spirit, and presently he came to bed to her, and had the carnal knowledge of her, and so did divers times after, and says, the other two spirits did then and at other times come into her bed also, and sucked upon other parts of her body where she had teats. Being demanded the name of the lesser spirits, she says the name of the white one was *Lilly*, and the black one *Priscill*; and that the office of *Lilly* was to hurt man, woman, or child; and the office of *Priscill* was to hurt cattle when she desired. And the office of the man-like spirit was to lie with her carnally, when and as often as she desired, and that he did lie with her in that manner very often; and that the spirit *Lilly*, according to the covenant, did kill the child of *Mr. Henry Bedells* of *Catworth*, aforesaid, as she this examinate desired him to do; and that she wished him to do the same when she was angry; but does not well remember for what: and says that about two or three days before that, she sent the same *Lilly* to the said *Henry Bedells* commanding him to kill him, who returned and said he had no power: and confesses she sent her said spirit another time to do some hurt to *Edward Musgraves* of *Catworth*, aforesaid, who likewise returned answer, he had no power: And that she sent her spirit *Priscill* to kill two horses of the said *Edward Musgraves*, and one of *John Musgraves*, and to kill one cow of *William Musgraves*, and one cow of *Thomas Thorps* of the same town, which was done accordingly. And being demanded when the twenty-one years would be out, she answered about *Low-Sunday* next, to the best of her remembrance, and being further demanded what was the reason, she did duly resort to church to sermons, and also to the minister's house to repetition, which *Mr. Poole* the minister being present did affirm; she says she was well pleased with his preaching and had a desire to be rid of that unhappy burden which was upon her. And further she says not.

The Examination of John Winnick *of Molseworth in the said county, labourer, taken upon the 11th day of* April, 1646, *before* Robert Bernard *Esquire, one of His Majesty's Justices of the Peace for this county.*

He says that about twenty-nine years since, the twenty-ninth year ending about midsummer last past, he being a bachelor, lived at Thorpston with one *Buteman*, who then kept the inn at the *George*, and with-all kept husbandry: this examinate being a servant to him in his husbandry, did then lose a purse with seven shillings in it, for which he suspected one in the family. He says that on a Friday being in the barn, making hay-bottles for his horses about noon, swearing, cursing, raging, and wishing to himself that some wise body (or wizard) would help him to his purse and money again: there appeared unto him a spirit, black and shaggy, and having paws like a bear, but in bulk not fully so big as a coney. The spirit asked him what he ailed to be so sorrowful, this examinate answered that he had lost a purse and money, and knew not how to come by it again. The spirit replied, if you will forsake God and Christ, and fall down and worship me for your God, I will help you to your purse and money again. This examinate said he would, and thereupon fell down upon his knees and held up his hands. Then the spirit said, tomorrow about this time of day, you shall find your purse upon the floor where you are now making bottles. I will send it to you, and will also come myself. Whereupon this examinate told the spirit he would meet him there, and receive it, and worship him. Whereupon at the time prefixed, this examinate went unto the place, and found his purse upon the floor and took it up, and looking afterwards into it, he found there all the money that was formerly lost; but before he had looked into it, the same spirit appears unto him and said, there is your purse and your money in it; and then this examinate fell down upon his knees and said, my Lord and God I thank you. The said spirit at that time brought with him two other spirits, for shape, bigness and color, the one like a white cat, the other like a grey coney: and while this examinate was upon his knees, the bear spirit spoke to him, saying, you must worship these two spirits as you worship me, and take them for your gods also: then this examinate directed his body towards them, and called them his lords and gods. Then the bear spirit told him that when he died he must have his soul, whereunto this examinate yielded. He told him then also that they must suck his body, to which this examinate also yielded, but they did not suck at that time. The bear spirit promised him that he should never want victuals. The cat spirit that it would hurt cattle when he would desire it. And the coney-like spirit that it would hurt men when he desired. The bear spirit told him that it must have some of his blood wherewith to seal the covenant, whereunto this examinate yielded and then the bear spirit leapt upon his shoulder, and pricked him on the head, and from thence took blood: and after thus doing, the said three spirits vanished away. The next day about noon, the said spirits came to him while he was in the field, and told him they were come to suck his body, to which he yielded, and they sucked his body at the places where the marks are found, and from that time to this, they have come constantly to him once every twenty-four hours, sometimes by day, and most commonly by night. And being demanded what mischief he caused any of the said spirits to do, he answered never any, only he sent his bear spirit to provoke the maid-servant of *Mr. Say* of *Molmesworth* to steal victuals for him out of her master's house, which she did, and this examinate received the same.

The Examination of Frances Moore, *taken before Nicholas Pedley Esquire; one of His Majesty's Justices of Peace for this county, the ninth day of* April, 1646.

This examinate says that about eight years since she received a little black puppy from one *Margaret Simson* of great *Catworth*, which dog the said *Margaret* had in her bed with her, and took it thence when she gave it to the examinate: The examinate further says, that the said *Margaret* told her, that she must keep that dog all her lifetime; and if she cursed any cattle and set the same dog upon them, they should presently die, and the said *Margaret* told her that she had named it already. His name was *Pretty*.

And the said examinate further says, that about the same time one goodwife *Weed* gave her a white cat, telling her, that if she would deny God, and affirm the same by her blood, then whomsoever she cursed and sent that cat unto, they should die shortly after. Whereupon this said examinate says that she did deny God, and in affirmation thereof she pricked her finger with a thorn, whence issued blood, which the cat presently licked; and the said goodwife *Weed* named the cat *Tissy*. And the said examinate further says, that one *William Foster*, about sixteen years since, would have hanged two of her children for offering to take a piece of bread; and for that cause about six years since she cursed the said *William Foster*; whereupon the white cat went to him, and he immediately fell sick, and lying in great pain for the space of seven or eight days, and then died. But being demanded what the cat did to him, or what she bid it do, she says she remembers not. And she further says that about five years since, she keeping cows in the field, a cow of *Edward Hulls* went into the grain, she cursed her, and set *Pretty* on her, and she swelled and died shortly after; and after that a cow of one *Peter Browne* went into the corn, and she likewise cursed her, and set *Pretty* on her, and she died within two or three days after. And she further says that she killed the said dog and cat about a year since; and yet after that the like dog and cat haunted her familiarly: and when she was apprehended, they crept under her clothes, and tortured her so that she could not speak to confess freely, and more she said not.

The Information of Peter Slater *of Little* Catworth *in the said county, shepherd, taken upon oath, before* Robert Bernard, *Esquire; one of His Majesty's Justices of Peace for this county, upon the 7th day of April,* 1646.

This informant says, that his wife dying about twenty-one years since in child-bed, and one *Frances Moore* being suspected for a witch, and in custody. He went to her upon Friday last, and asked her, if she did his wife any harm? She answered she did, by cursing her. And he says, his wife did of a sudden change and die, after she had lain in a week; and that a little before this informant's wife was brought to bed, the said *Frances Moore* falling out with her, said she hoped she should never be untwined, as this informant has since called to mind.

The Information of William Searle *of Little* Catworth, *yeoman,*[1] *taken upon oath the said day and year.*

This informant says, he was present when *Frances Moore* did confess herself to be a witch, and that she had done much harm; and among other things, that she sent her spirit *Pretty* to this informant's capons, who did kill them; and he says that she coming to bake a loaf at his house about three or four years since, being denied, the capons did fall a fluttering, and

[1]A farmer who cultivated his own land.

would never eat after. Also says, that about the said time, she having a hog in his yard, some of his servants set a dog on the same; for which she said she would be revenged; and the next day one of his hogs died.

The Information of Thomas Becke *of Bythorn* in Com. Hunt. *yeoman, against* Anne Desborough, *taken upon oath before* Nicholas Pedley *Esquire, one of His Majesty's Justices of Peace for the said county, the 9th day of* April, 1646.

This informant says, that *Anne Desborough*, widow of Bythorn aforesaid, being apprehended upon suspicion of being a witch, on the eighth day of this present April, he in the presence of Master Coyst and others, heard the said *Anne Desborough* (in answer to questions asked her) freely confess, that about thirty years since, there appeared unto her a thing somewhat bigger than a mouse, of a brown color, when she lived at Titsmarsh in the county of Northamptom, she being in bed and asleep, which nipped her on the breast and awakened her, then it told her that it must have part of her soul: she prayed then to God, and it left her at that time, and the said informant heard the said *Anne* further say, that about five or six days after, the same mouse appeared again to her with another much like the former, it being a little less than the former, and had a white belly. Then the mouse that came first said, we must abide with you and suck your blood. She said that they should. About three days after both the mice came to her again, and told her that she must forsake God and Christ: and when she died, they must have her soul, to all which she yielded: this informant says further, that he heard the said *Anne* confess that she named one of the mice *Tib*, which promised her to hurt men, and she named the other *Fone*, which promised her to hurt cattle when she wished it: and after the third time they kept not away from her above twenty-four hours together, but did frequent her, and familiarly such on her body, until she was apprehended.

April the 8th day, Anno 1646

Anne Desborough of Bythorn in the county of Huntingdon, confesses, that about thirty years since, the first week of Clean Lent, there appeared unto her a thing somewhat bigger than a mouse, of a brown color, and the likeness of a mouse. This was while she lived at Tichmarsh in the county of Northampton: she being there in bed, and in a dream, the said likeness then gave her a nip, and thereby awakened her out of her dream, and then told her (when she was awakened) that it must have part of her soul; whereupon she was in a great fear, and gave him no answer, but prayed to God, and thereupon it vanished away from her. About five days after, the same mouse appeared to her again, bringing with it another mouse, about the bigness of an ordinary mouse, or very little bigger, brown like the former, save only that this latter had some white about the belly, whereas the former was all brown. Then the mouse that first appeared, said, we must suck of your body. She yielded to them, and said, they should. Upon her yielding they went to her, and sucked of her body, where the marks are found. The bigger mouse she called *Tib*, and the lesser *Fone*. *Tib* told her that she must forsake God and Christ, and take them for her gods: telling her that when she died, they must have her soul, to all which she yielded. *Tib* promised her to hurt cattle if she should desire. Within two days after they appeared again: and ever after till she was discovered, they appeared once every twenty-four hours.

The Examination of Jane Wallis *of* Keiston *in the county of Huntingdon spinster taken the 16th day of* April, 1646 *before Sir* Robert Osborn *Knight, one of His Majesty's Justices of the Peace for the county of* Huntington.

This examinate says, as she was making of her bed in her chamber, there appeared in the shape of a man in black clothes and blackish clothes about six weeks past, and bid her good-morrow, and she asked what his name was, and he said his name was *Blackeman*, and asked her if she were poor, and she said aye; then he told her he would send one *Grissell* and *Greedigut* to her, that shall do anything for her. She looking upon him, saw he had ugly feet, and then she was very fearful of him for that he would seem sometimes to be tall, and sometimes less, and suddenly vanished away.

And being demanded whether he lay with her, she said he would have lain with her, but she would not suffer him: and after *Blackeman* was departed from her, within three or four days, *Grissell* and *Greedigut* came to her, in the shapes of dogs with great bristles of hogs' hair upon their backs, and said to her they were come from *Blackeman* to do what she would command them, and did ask her if she did want anything, and they would fetch her anything: and she said she lacked nothing: then they prayed her to give them some victuals, and she said she was poor and had none to give them, and so they departed. Yet she confessed that *Blackeman*, *Grissell*, and *Greedigut* divers times came to her afterwards, and brought her two or three shillings at a time, and more says not.

April 14, 1646.

Ioane Wallis confessed to me and John Guyle that she had three spirits, she called them *Blackeman*, *Grissell*, and *Greedigut*, and that *Blackeman* gave her the other two, and told her they should do anything for her that she should desire. She said *Blackeman* came first to her, about a twelve-month since, like a man something ancient, in blackish clothes, but he had ugly feet uncovered. Sometimes she said it was longer since he first came to her, and ever since he appeared in the like shape, but *Grissell*, and *Greedigut* did come in several shapes, yet most commonly like hounds with bristles on their backs. I asked her what use she put them to, and if any of them had the use of her body besides sucking; she said he would have had once, but she denied him: then presently of herself she said, if I would not tell, she would confess but she hoped I would love her never the worse, and then she said that *Blackeman* had the use of her body once, twice, and sometimes thrice in a week, but the other two only sucked her where her marks are found; she said *Blackeman* never sucked her; she would not confess that she ever sent them to do any harm, but said the filthy rough *Blackeman* would send them; but what hurt they did she confessed not to us. I asked her to what purpose she let *Grissell* and *Greedigut* suck her if she made no use of them? She said, they would sometimes bring her money, two or three shillings at a time, and that was all they did for her; and once they told her they robbed a man, and pulled him from his horse, and brought her some money.

The Examination of John Clarke Junior, of Keiston, in the county of Hunt. labourer, taken before me John Castell, Esquire, one of His Majesty's Justices of the Peace for the said county, the 2nd day of May, 1646.

Who says, that true it is that he did overtake one man and three women upon the Sabbath day last was seven-night, between *Stanwick* and *Raunce*, being about three miles from *Keiston*, whither this examinate was going. But this examinate denies that he ever told or said that he had any marks cut off, or that he had any place of meeting with any witches, or that he had any consultation, or made any compact with the devil, or ever knew what belonged to any such matter. And further says not.

The Information of John Browne of Raunce in the county of Northamptom, tailor, taken upon oath the second day of May, 1646, before me John Castell, Esquire, one of His Majesty's Justices of the Peace for the county of Hunt.

Who says, that upon the Sabbath day last was seven-night, he (this informant), coming from *Higham-Ferris* to *Raunce* in the county of *Northamptom* aforesaid, where he quarters, and sitting down by *Stanwick Town* end, saw one coming from *Artlebroward*; who when he came near to this informant, this informant said, I have stayed for you a long time; but he answered, I saw you not all the way I came. Then this informant said to him, from whence came you? who answered, that he came from his uncle's at *Artlebroward*. Then this informant asked him who was his uncle? And he said one *Clarke*: this informant asked him, if he were not *Clarke* son of Keiston, he answered, he was. And then this informant asked him, what haste was he in? who said he was in haste; for his father and mother were accused for witches, and that himself had been searched; and this informant answered and so have I. Then *Clarke* asked this informant, whether anything were found about him, or not? He (this informant) answered, that they said there were marks: *Clarke* said again, had you no more wit but to have your marks found? I cut off mine three days before I was searched. And then after some further communication past concerning who searched them, *Clarke* said to this informant, I do not believe you are a witch, for I never saw you at our meetings: who answered, that perhaps their meetings were at several places, and so fell out and parted.

The Trial of Diogo Henriques before the Portuguese Inquisition

The Spanish Inquisition has become synonymous with religious prejudice and repression. That is in many ways an unfair view, a myth propounded during the later Enlightenment, when thinkers rejected much of conventional religion in the name of rationality, as they understood it. The inquisitors saw themselves as rooting out both superstitious beliefs and dangerous heretics, who could undermine the ecclesiastical and political order to the detriment of the souls of all. In Spain, the perceived danger lay not with Protestants, for Protestantism had no real chance to take hold there, but with Jews, or with those Christians called conversos—*people descended from Jews who had forsaken Judaism at the end of the fifteenth century rather than be expelled from the kingdom. (Spain had driven out 150,000 Jews in 1492.) The same concern animated the Inquisition in Portugal after Philip II, the king of Spain from 1556 to 1598, took over Portugal in 1580.*

Diogo Henriques was a humble Portuguese of Jewish stock who traveled to the Portuguese colony of Brazil, where he encountered Jews who practiced their faith. Henriques took advantage of being outside the kingdom itself to learn and practice Judaism, but he was ultimately denounced before the Inquisition in 1646 to answer charges that he was not truly Christian. The selection that follows contains his "voluntary" confession, which the inquisitors in fact elicited from him after a lengthy process of investigation and interrogation. Just what did he confess? What types of information did he give about himself? Why did the inquisitors ask for that information? To what punishment did they subject him? In the end, how harsh was his treatment? Finally, how does this inquisitional process compare to that used on fourteenth-century heretics, which you saw in an earlier selection ("Sentences against Heretics")? Is the later process more thorough and comprehensive? Is it harsher?

GENEALOGY AND SENTENCE

Names Other Persons and Declares His Genealogy

On the 19th day of December, 1646, in Lisbon, in the first Audience Hall of the Offices of the Holy Inquisition, his Worship Inquisitor Melchior Dias Pretto, holding the morning Audience, summoned to appear before him Diogo Henriques, with whom this Process deals, he having asked for an audience, who, being present, said that he had asked for an audience, in order to name other persons with whom he remembers he had communication, when in error. And that he might in all things speak the truth, and preserve secrecy, he was told to take oath on the Holy Gospels on which he placed his hand, and having taken oath accordingly under seal thereof: He said that having reached the country of Brazil, five years ago or thereabouts, he became acquainted in Pernambuco with Manoel Nunes, does not know his native city, but who lived for some time in Madrid, and deponent has heard that he fled from thence to France fearing the justice of the Holy Office, and then proceeded to Pernambuco, where he followed the

profession of surgeon; he was married to Catherina da Costa, who, deponent has heard, was burnt in effigy, in Madrid. And the said Manoel
Nunes appeared to be about forty-five years of age and spoke Portuguese,
and confessant saw him attending the Sinagogues and publicly professing
belief in the Law of Moses, as he did also when his profession brought him
to confessant's house, and he was accustomed to seeing him in the sinagogue where they assembled, and on various occasions they declared to
one another their belief in the aforesaid Law, in which Law Catherina da
Costa, wife of the aforesaid, also lived publicly.

Further declares that at the same time he was acquainted with
Abraham Israel, whose name as a Catholic he does not know, native of
Portalegre, cousin of Luis Mendes, of whom confessant has spoken, and
confessant has heard the said Abraham Israel say that he left this kingdom
and went to Holland, for fear of the justice of the Holy Office; and in Pernambuco, where confessant knew him, the said Abraham Israel publicly
professed his belief in the Law of Moses, and attended the sinagogue in
confessant's company in the manner customary to Jews; and the said
Abraham Israel would be about forty at the time, tall, and stout, and followed the calling of barber, besides having certain commercial dealings;
and he said that he was married to a niece of his, who was also a Jewess by
belief, and lived in Amsterdam.

Further says that at the same time he was acquainted in Pernambuco
with David Zuzarte, whose name as a Catholic he does not know, native of
Thomar, married in Amsterdam, but does not know to whom; and at that
time he appeared to be about forty years of age, short and black bearded;
and he also publicly professed the Law of Moses, continuing in the belief
and observances thereof, attending the sinagogues in company with confessant. And all the said persons were in Arrecife at the time confessant
was brought to the Fortress of the River of San Francisco, and further saith
not, and has nothing to declare as to good or ill will. And since he had
nothing further to say the usual questions as to his genealogy were put to
him.

Asked his name, age, race, native town and place of residence: Says,
he is named Diogo Henriques, is of the race of New Christians,[1] native of
Medina de Rio Secco in Castile; is twenty-six years of age or thereabouts;
that his father was named Pedro Henriques, and his mother Anna Vas; he
does not know, and does not remember having been told, the names of his
paternal or maternal grandparents, nor where they were born; and that on
his father's side he had four uncles, though he has never heard any but
Antonio Henriques spoken of, who, as deponent has already said, left this
kingdom for Italy.

And that the said Anonio Henriques was married to Fillipa de Mes-

[1]Recent converts from Judaism.

quita, sister to confessant's mother, who had one daughter only, also named Fillipa de Mesquita, married to Francisco Alvares, of whom he has spoken, and he does not know whether they have any children. And he does not know the names of his other uncles, nor whether they were married, since he has never known children of theirs, nor has he any information concerning them, but has heard his father say that he had four brothers; and he now remembers that his said father had a sister named Isabel Henriques, who lives in the town of Padua, widow, and deponent does not know when she married; and she has two sons, one a Doctor of Medicine, and the other also follows a learned profession, but does not know which; both sons unmarried; he does not know their names.

And that on his Mother's side he has one uncle only, Francisco Vas by name, of whom deponent has spoken, and who was married to Beatriz Rodrigues, deceased, by whom he had two daughters, who have remained unmarried, the oldest is named Fillipa de Mesquita, he cannot remember the name of the other.

And this deponent has three brothers, namely, Antonio, João and Fernando, all unmarried and younger than deponent; and two sisters, namely, Violante Henriques, married to Isaac Baru, of whom deponent has spoken, and they have no children, and Catherina Henriques married to Jacob Vas, whom deponent spoke in his confession, and they, also, have no children.

And that this deponent is unmarried, and, as he has said, he was baptized in the Church of Santa Maria Maior of Medina de Rio Secco, but he does not know by whom, nor who were his godparents, and that he is not confirmed. And that notwithstanding his being baptized, he did not at any time go to Church, as Catholic Christians do, nor perform any action or work as such, because from his earliest years he was instructed in the ceremonies and beliefs of the Law of Moses, having no knowledge whatever of the mysteries of our holy faith: and in this blindness he ever persisted, for the reason that he did not know the prayers of the church, nor was he at any time instructed therein, but on the contrary his said parents warned him that the Law of Moses forbade any knowledge of the Law of the Gospel. And he only knows how to read, write and count as much as is needed for his business and commerce. And that he has nothing further to say concerning the faith other than what he has already declared before this Tribunal, and does not know of any relation of his being brought before the Inquisition, or who was arrested or penanced by the Holy Inquisition.

Asked whether he, the prisoner, has understood the reason why he was summoned before the Inquisition and detained, says, that he was brought here as a Jew, and that he was detained because the fact of his having been baptized was known. He was informed that the Holy Office has sufficient reason to detain him, without which it is not customary to take proceedings against any person whatever; and that since God, Our Lord, through this detention has granted him the special privilege of realising his errors, and has given him understanding to bring him to repentance of them, which is necessary for the salvation of his soul, since the Law of Moses was ended by the promulgation of the Law of Grace, he is exhorted, therefore, after rendering thanks to that same Lord for so great a privilege, to persist most firmly in his resolution, being certain that only in the belief of our holy Faith lies salvation, and that for his benefit it is necessary he should declare before this tribunal all that he further remembers concerning his faults or the questions which have been put to him; and in particular whether before or after following the Law of Moses, he had received instruction or had knowledge of the matters and mysteries of our holy Faith, as all the aforesaid is necessary for the better discharge of his conscience, and the despatch of his cause: And as he said that he would render thanks to God our Lord for the favour granted him, and that he had never at any time received instruction in the mysteries of our holy Faith, in which he earnestly begged to be instructed, and that should he remember anything further touching his errors he would come to declare it before this tribunal, the session was read to him, the which having heard he declared it to be well and truthfully written, and signed with his Worship, whereupon he was formally admonished and sent to his cell.

Belchior Dias Pretto.
Diogo Henriques.

Written by Gaspar Clemente.

Diogo Henriques

The Inquisitors in ordinary and Deputies of the Holy Inquisition are agreed:

That taking into consideration these autos, errors and confessions of Diogo Henriques, new Christian, unmarried, son of Pedro Henriques, native of Medina de Rio Secco, Kingdom of Castile, resident in Pernambuco, State of Brazil, the prisoner here present:

By which is shown that being a baptized Christian, and as such obliged to hold and believe all that the Holy Mother Church of Rome holds, believes and teaches, he acted to the contrary and since the last General Pardon, finding himself outside of this said kingdom and circumcised, he took the name of Abraham Bueno, and being persuaded and instructed in the false doctrine by certain persons of his race, he adopted the Law of Moses, and publicly professed it, even holding it to be good and true, hoping to be saved therein, and not in the Faith of Christ, Our Lord, in whom he did not believe, nor hold Him to be true God, the Messiah promised in the Law, but still waited for Him, as do the Jews: and believed only in the God of Abraham, Isaac and Jacob, Creator of heaven and earth, who gave the Law to the people of Israel, and to Him he commended himself by Jewish prayers; and in observance of the said Law he kept the Sabbath beginning on Friday afternoon, doing no work on that day, wearing his best clothes and clean linen; celebrating the Jewish holy days, and in particular the feast of Peça[2] in memory of the exodus of the people of Israel from Egypt, eating unleavened bread at that time, doing no work for eight days, keeping them as days of festival; observing also the festival they call Jacoth[3] in commemoration of God's mercy to the said people in bringing them to the Promised Land: And another festival known as Salvuoth[4] (*sic*) in commemoration of the aforesaid Law, which lasts for two days; and keeping also, in observance of the said Law, the feast of Kippur, vulgarly known as the Pardons, which falls in September, remaining on that day without food or drink until the rising of the star; also that of Thebeth[5] observed in the same way; and that of Purim[6] in memory of Queen Esther, remaining without food or drink for twenty-four hours; Observing also another fast, which they name the three weeks in memory of the people of Israel, and another in memory of the destruction of Temple.[7] . . .

Publicly attending the Synagogues, observing therein all further rites of the aforesaid Law: speaking of these things publicly more especially with other observers of the Law, to whom he declared himself to be a Jew. Behaving in Catholic countries only exteriorly as a Catholic, in dissimulation and conformity whilst among them, attending the churches, and performing acts and outward observances of a Catholic Christian; knowing and understanding that the aforesaid Law of Moses was contrary to that which the Holy Mother Church of Rome holds, believes and teaches; persevering in his belief of the aforesaid errors, until he made his confession before the tribunal of the Holy Office.

All of which being considered, as well as what further appears from the autos, they declare:

That the offender Diogo Henriques was a heretic and apostate from our holy Catholic faith, and that he has incurred the sentence of major excommunication and confiscation of all his goods to the Royal Fisc and Treasury, and all other penalties as by law established in similar cases: But seeing that following better counsel he confessed his faults to the tribunal of the Holy Office with signs of repentance, asking pardon and mercy; and taking into account what further appears in the Acts, they receive the offender Diogo Henriques into the fold, and into union with holy Mother Church,

---

[2]Passover.

[3]Sukkot.

[4]Shavvot.

[5]Asarah B'Tebet, in remembrance of the beginning of the Babylonian siege of Jerusalem in 586 B.C.

[6]Festival commemorating the deliverance of the Jews from massacre by the Persians in 473 B.C.

[7]Tisha B'av, in remembrance of the destruction of the First Temple in 586 B.C. and of the Second Temple in A.D. 70.

as he asks: And in penalty, and in penance for his faults they commanded that he shall appear in the Auto da Fe[8] in customary manner; and hear his sentence, and shall formally abjure his heretical errors; and they assign to him a prison, and he shall wear a penitential habit perpetually; and in prison he shall receive instruction in matters of our holy Faith necessary to the salvation of his soul. And he shall perform all other spiritual pains and penalties that may be imposed on him. And they command that he be absolved from the major excommunication, which he has incurred, according to ecclesiastical custom.

(Signed) Luis Martins da Rocha

The above sentence was read to the offender Diogo Henriques in the public Auto da Fe celebrated on the Terreiro do Paço of this city of Lisbon, on Sunday, 15th day of December, of 1647.

Written by Gaspar Clemente.

Formal Abjuration

I, Diogo Henriques, in presence of your Worships, take oath upon the Holy Gospels, on which I place my hand, that of my own free will, I do anathematize, and reject every kind of heresy that has been or may be put forward against our holy Catholic Faith and the Apostolic See, especially those into which I fell, and which have been here read to me in my sentence, which I hold to be here repeated and set forth, and I swear ever to hold and to keep the holy Catholic Faith, as it is held and taught by the holy Mother Church of Rome, and that I will ever be most obedient to our most holy Father, Pope Innocent X, at present presiding over the Church of God, and to his Successors, and I confess that all who rebel against that holy Catholic Faith are worthy of condemnation; and I do swear never to join with them, but to pursue them and to make known any heresies I know anyone to hold, to the Inquisitors, or the Prelates of holy Mother Church; and I do swear and make promise to fulfil as far as in me lies the penance which is, or may be, imposed on me; and should I fall again into these errors, or into any other heresy whatsoever, I desire, and it is my pleasure that I shall be held to be relapsed, and punished in conformity with the law, and if at any time anything should be proved against me in contrary to my confession sworn before your Worships, I desire that this absolution be of no avail, but I submit myself to the severity and correction of the Sacred Canons, and I request the Notaries of the Holy Office to issue an Instrument accordingly, and those here present to be witnesses thereof, and to sign with me:

[8]Elaborate public sentencing of convicted heretics that included sermons and processions of penitents. Executions occurred after the auto-da-fé.

Joao Mendes de Vasconcellos, and Francisco Dias Castro signed as witnesses.

Written by Gaspar Clemente.
Diogo Henriques.

Deed of Secrecy

On the 10th day of the month of December, of 1647, in Lisbon, in the Casa do Despacho of the Offices of the Holy Inquisition, their Worships the Inquisitors holding their morning audience, summoned to appear before them, from the Penitential Cell, Diogo Henriques, with whom these Acts deal, to whom being present oath was administered on the Holy Gospels on which he placed his hand, under seal of which he was charged to keep secrecy as to all that he might see or hear in these prisons, and might occur with reference to his process, and neither by word or writing or any other method whatsoever to disclose the same, under pain of severe punishment, all of which he promised under seal of the aforesaid oath, whereupon this document was issued by order of their Worships aforesaid, the which he signed.

Written by Gaspar Clemente.
Diogo Henriques.

Deed of Penance

On the 11th day of the month of January, 1648, in Lisbon, in the Casa do Despacho of the Offices of the Inquisition, their Worships the Inquisitors holding their afternoon audience, summoned to appear before them Diogo Henriques, prisoner with whom these Acts are concerned, who being present, was informed that in penalty and for penance for his offences he must perform the following spiritual acts: Namely, he shall go to confession on the four principal festivals of the year, Christmas, Easter, Pentecost and the Assumption of our Lady, but shall not receive Communion without licence from this Tribunal; he shall recite every Saturday the Rosary of Our Lady the Virgin Mary, and on one Friday in the month he shall fast in honour of the Passion of Christ, all this during the coming year, at the end of which he shall send a certificate to this Tribunal in witness of having done so, to be annexed to his Process: and this city is assigned to him as prison, from which he may not absent himself without licence from this Holy Office; and on Sundays and Holy Days he shall attend the principal Mass in the Church of São Lourenço, wearing his penitential habit, until it is removed by order of the most Illustrious Lord Bishop, Inquisitor General; all of which he promised to perform, whereupon this Deed was drawn up by order of the Worshipful Inquisitors, and signed by Domingos Esteves, notary of the Holy Office, who wrote it, and by the prisoner Diogo Henriques.

Most Illustrious Lord,

Diogo Henriques, a poor youth, a wanderer in this Kingdom, who appeared in the last Auto, as a Judaizer, and who was ordered to attend the principal Mass in the Church of São Lourenço, wearing a penitential habit, the which he has done up to the present, suffering much distress both from sickness and want of necessities, which distress he cannot remedy during the period in which he must wear the said penitential habit. For which reason he addressed two petitions to your Lordship's tribunal, neither of which was granted, and since he is still suffering from the aforesaid distress, with none to succour him, he begs your Lordship and the most Reverend Senate, by the death and passion of our Lord Jesus Christ, to take compassion on his distress and poverty, and to give order that his penitential be removed, which will be a great charity. R. M.

Let the Inquisitions be informed of the decision:
Lisbon, 28th February, 1648 (a rubric).

The Bishop, Dom Francisco de Castro, Inquisitor General of the Kingdom and Dominions of Portugal, and member of his Majesty's Council of State, etc. We make known that the above petition of Diogo Henriques reconciled in the last Auto-da-Fe, and the information given by the Inquisitors being taken into consideration:

We think fit to dispense the aforesaid for the period remaining for the performance of his penance. And we command that the penitential habit be removed, and we commute the said penance to any spiritual penances which their Worships the Inquisitors think necessary for the salvation of his soul, which he shall perform, as well as all else contained in his abjuration: this shall be annexed to his process, with the deed of Admonition made to him, and the declaration of the penances imposed on him. Given in Lisbon over our Seal only this 4th day of March, 1648.

Written by Diogo Velho.
Dom Francisco de Castro, Bishop.

Your Lordship thinks fit to dispense Diogo Henriques, reconciled, for the period remaining for the performance of his penance.

* * *

On the 4th day of March, 1648, in Lisbon in the Casa do Despacho of the offices of the Holy Inquisition, their Worships the Inquisitors, holding their morning audience, summoned to appear before them Diogo Henriques, who was reconciled in the last Auto, who, being present was informed that his illustrious Lordship has shown him mercy, and taking into consideration the time during which he has performed his penance, and the information given by this Tribunal, has thought fit to dispense him for the period remaining for the fulfilment of his penance, and has given order for his penitential habit to be removed, which was done, and his sentence commuted to such spiritual penances as were imposed on him in the first instance, which he must perform for another year, and must further comply with all else contained in his abjuration, the which he promised to do;

whereupon their Worships the Inquisitors gave order for this deed to be issued, the which he signed. Diogo Henriques.

Domingo Esteves, who wrote this deed.

Edict Establishing the General Hospital for the Confining of the Poor Beggars of Paris

In 1656, the "Great Lockup" occurred in Paris, whereby the government incarcerated the poor, about one thousand people, perhaps 1 percent of the city's population. Prostitutes and beggars were the two major groups of indigent. The impetus behind this drastic action was the Company of the Holy Sacrament, an aristocratic and bourgeois organization that desired to reform French society according to the company's religious and social beliefs. The company itself was a product of the French Catholic Reformation. An upsurge in religious fervor, which dated back to the second half of the sixteenth century, found expression in the reform and establishment of religious houses and orders, in the conversion of French Protestants, in missionary work, in an attack on what was seen to be the licentious and sinful habits of peasants and lower-placed social groups, and in an increase in charity.

The mid-seventeenth century was a time of economic depression, open rebellion against the government (the revolts of the Fronde), extraordinarily high taxation, and probably an increase in the numbers of poor. Thus, the Crown and the Church worked to extend charity. The Company of the Holy Sacrament had influence here, as the Great Lockup demonstrated. The company saw the poor as being lazy, responsible for their own pitiable state. It interpreted poverty and unemployment as a result of sin, not of the prevailing socioeconomic conditions. The company wanted the poor confined, not only to make society a better place for devout people, but also because the devout had an obligation to reform the souls of the poor. The development of absolutism and the rise in religious zealotry of a puritanical nature combined with social and economic distress to produce the program against vagabondage that led to the massive confinement described in this selection.

How does the introduction to the edict justify the incarceration of beggars and other poor people in the General Hospital? The penalties stipulated for begging were harsh, yet the edict still permitted certain groups to beg. Which groups? Why? What means did the edict give to the directors of the hospital to enforce its strictures against begging? How was the General Hospital to obtain funds to carry on its charitable work? Do you think the lockup and creation of the General Hospital were successful in reforming the poor and in relieving poverty?

Issued at Paris in the month of April 1656. Verified in the Parlement[1] the first of September following, and in all the other Sovereign Companies.

[1]The Parlement of Paris, a sovereign judicial court whose jurisdiction covered approximately one-half of France.

Louis,[2] by the grace of God, King of France and of Navarre, to all present and to come, hail. The kings our predecessors during the last century issued several ordinances for the maintenance of order, and strove by their zeal as much as by their authority to prevent begging and idleness, the sources of all disorders. And although our Sovereign Companies have supported by their efforts the execution of these ordinances, they nevertheless became with the passage of time fruitless and ineffectual, either through the lack of the funds necessary to support such a great plan, or through the lack of a well-established board of directors suitable to the nature of the work. So that recently and during the reign of the late King[3] our very honored lord and father of blessed memory, the evil having grown even greater as a result of public licentiousness and the dissoluteness of morals, it was recognized that the chief fault in the execution of this program to maintain order lay in the fact that beggars were free to wander everywhere, and that the relief obtained did not prevent secret mendicity and did not make them cease their idleness. On this basis was planned and carried out the praiseworthy plan to confine them in the House of Pity and its dependencies. And *letters patentes*[4] were granted to this end in the year one thousand six hundred and twelve, registered in our Court of the Parlement of Paris, according to which the poor were confined; and the adminstration was entrusted to good and renowned bourgeois who, successively, one after the other, contributed their industry and their good conduct to make this plan succeed. And nonetheless no matter what efforts they made, it was effective for only five or six years, and then very imperfectly, as much from a failure to employ the poor in public works and manufactures as because the directors were not supported by the powers and authority necessary for the great size of the undertaking, and because as a result of the disorders and the misfortunes of the wars, the number of poor increased beyond common and ordinary credence, and the illness became more powerful than the remedy. So that the libertinage of beggars went to excess, by their unfortunate abandoning of themselves to all sorts of crimes, which bring down God's curse upon states when they remain unpunished. Experience having shown the persons involved in these charitable undertakings that several of [the beggars] of one or the other sex are living together without being married, many of their children are unbaptised, and they are almost all living in ignorance of religion, in scorn of the sacraments, and in the continual practice of all sorts of vices. That is why, since we are indebted to Divine Grace for so many favors and for a visible protection which it has made apparent in our actions at our accession, and

---

[2]Louis XIV, king of France, 1643–1715.

[3]Louis XIII, king of France, 1610–1643.

[4]Letters patent, royal acts that usually granted a privilege, concession, pardon, or establishment.

in the happy course of our reign, by the success of our arms and the happiness of our victories, we believe we are more obliged to show [Divine Grace] our gratitude by a royal and Christian attention to the things involving its honor and its service, by considering these poor beggars as living members of Jesus Christ, and not as useless members of the state, and by acting in carrying out such a great work not in the name of the maintenance of public order, but with the sole aim of charity.

Firstly,

For these reasons . . . we desire and order that poor beggars both healthy and invalid, of both sexes, be confined in a hospital to be employed there at works, manufactures, and other tasks according to their capacities. . . .

V

We desire that the localities serving to confine the poor be called the General Hospital for the Poor; that the inscription be placed with our coat of arms over the portal of the House of Pity and its dependencies.

VI

We intend to be the preserver and protector of the said General Hospital and of its dependencies, since it is a royal foundation. . . .

IX

We very strictly prohibit and forbid all persons of all sexes, and places, and ages, whatever their social standing or birth, and in whatever state they may be, healthy or invalid, sick or convalescent, curable or incurable, to beg in the city and faubourgs[5] of Paris, or in the churches, or at their doors, or at the doors of houses, or in the streets, or anywhere else publicly or secretly, by day or by night, no exception being made for solemn feast days, pardons, or jubilees, or assemblies, fairs, or markets, or for any other reason or pretext whatsoever, under penalty of being whipped for the first offense; and for the second offense the galleys for men or boys, and banishment for women and girls.

X

If anyone begs in houses, we permit and specifically command owners and tenants and their domestic servants and others to keep the said beggars until the directors or the officials named below can be notified to impose upon them the above penalties, as the case demands.

---

[5]Suburbs.

XI

We do not intend the above prohibitions to include the alms collections for the Hôtel Dieu [hospital] and its dependencies; those for the Grand Bureau of the Poor [maintained for the non-begging poor] and its dependencies, the blind of the Hospital of the Quinze-vingts, the children of the Hospital of the Trinity, of the Holy Spirit, and of the Red Children,[6] begging monks, the Sisters of the Ave Maria, and others entitled to poor boxes or alms collections, all of whom we exempt, such privileges being generally forbidden to all others; and on condition that the blind, the children, and others entitled to seek alms remain at the doors of the churches, or near their boxes; and that they are forbidden to solicit elsewhere in the churches, under penalty of being stripped of their rights.

XII

We give and confer upon the directors . . . all power and authority for the direction, administration, legal authority, jurisdiction, policing, correction, and chastisement of all the poor beggars in our city and faubourgs of Paris, both within and without the said General Hospital. . . .

XIII

To this end the directors shall have posts, iron collars, prisons, and dungeons in the said General Hospital and its dependencies. . . .

XIV

The directors shall have a hospital bailiff, sergeants of the poor, [and] guards at the gates and entrances, with halberds and other suitable weapons, and all other necessary officials, both to carry out their ordinances, and to capture the beggars and escort to the hospital or its dependencies those who are to be admitted, to send away, eject, or arrest those who are to be excluded from it, and to accompany passersby. . . .

XV

We enjoin the bailiff, and the other officials who shall be appointed by the directors, to make a careful search each day with the sergeants of the said hospital, to remove all sorts of beggars from the streets, . . . under penalty of being sent away and punished; [and they shall carry out this search] without taking anything from the poor, or others, or granting them favors

---

[6]The children in the Hôpital des Enfants Rouges wore red uniforms. (Original editor's note.)

or tolerating them, or mistreating them, the whole under penalty of corporal punishment. . . .

XVII

We prohibit and forbid all persons, whatever their social standing and position, to put alms into the hands of beggars in the streets and above-mentioned locations, no matter how moved by compassion, urgent necessity, or other pretexts whatsoever, under penalty of a fine of four livres parisis,[7] which shall be given to the hospital. . . .

XVIII

We likewise forbid owners and tenants of houses and all other persons to lodge, shelter, or keep with them . . . the poor who are or would be beggars, under penalty of hundred livres' fine for the first offense, of three hundred livres for the second, and higher, in case of repetition, the whole to be given to the poor of the General Hospital; to which end the owners, tenants, and others can be compelled by seizure of their belongings and imprisonment of their persons. . . .

XX

We forbid the soldiers of our guards, even the bourgeois of our said city and faubourgs, and all other persons, whatever their social position, to molest, insult, or mistreat the bailiff, officials, or any of those employed in capturing or escorting, expelling, ejecting, or accompanying the poor . . . under penalty of being imprisoned at once and criminal proceedings being lodged against them. . . .

XXI

We order the commissioners of the quarters . . . and others not to allow anyone to reside in their quarter without first verifying at the police office that he has the possessions, industriousness, or vocation sufficient to nourish himself and to support his family: with the exception of the humble poor who are being helped by parishes or elsewhere, and the married poor now begging, who will receive alms from the General Hospital according to the certificate which they will bring back from [the hospital] . . . ; and that every month [the commissioners] will bring in the list to the office of the said hospital, under penalty of a fine of forty-eight livres parisis for each person not appearing on the list. . . .

---

[7]A local monetary unit.

XXXV

Inasmuch as the care of the poor concerns all sorts of persons, and since by our ordinances, police regulations, and old edicts, each one is obliged to contribute to the feeding of the poor, according to his means, we desire and order that . . . all secular and regular religious communities [with the exception of those serving the poor], of both sexes, in our city and faubourgs, *prévôté*,[8] and viscounty of Paris, and all lay groups, the vestrymen[9] of the churches, the guild chapels and confraternities, and others of that nature, even the trade guilds and all other persons shall contribute to the establishing and maintenance of the said work, each in proportion to his wealth. They are invited to do this, and if they fail to do so willingly, they will be assessed in accordance with the former edicts, by our Court of the Parlement. . . .

XXXVI

We permit the directors [to use] all alms collections, poor boxes, collection plates, and large and small boxes in all the churches, crossroads, and public places of our said city, faubourgs, and *prévôté* and viscounty of Paris; and that the said boxes may be placed in the merchants' warehouses, offices, and shops, in inns and coach halts, in public markets, covered markets, and fairs, at bridges, city gates, and passageways, and in all localities where one might be urged to give alms, even on such occasions as baptisms, marriages, funerals, burials, and memorial services, and others of that sort. . . .

XXXVIII

[We grant the said hospital] a quarter of the fines or sentences stipulating that the guilty party give alms, ordered for misdemeanors, malversations, and usurpations of the Waters and Forests of France, both in the past and in the future, for which the directors, as litigants, can carry out the prosecutions in our Council or elsewhere.

XXXIX

A quarter of the police fines, and of all merchandise or other things declared acquired and confiscated.

XL

And also a third of all the [fees paid for] letters of [guild] mastership, which have been and shall be by us in the future and by the kings our successors

---

[8]Royal jurisdiction in Paris.
[9]Those who administer the financial affairs of the parish.

issued and registered in our Parlement, either owing to the marriage or birth of [royal] children of France, an accession to the throne, or other special cause, intending by this to include those previously issued by us, and not yet registered.

XLI

All officials who are received into our Sovereign Companies established in our city of Paris, others besides those of the said companies, and also those who will be received into subordinate seats and jurisdictions, both ordinary and extraordinary, similarly established outside our said city, will upon their reception be obliged to contribute some modest sum to the said General Hospital, and they shall be obliged to bring back the receipt before the edict or judgment of their reception shall be delivered to them. This sum or tax shall be determined by our said Sovereign Companies, each one individually, and a list of them [shall be] drawn up, taking into account the rank of the said officers.

XLII

We also desire all journeymen in trades, when they receive their certificates of apprenticeship, and masters, when they complete their masterpiece or test, or are elected as guild officials, also be obliged to give some modest sum to the said General Hospital, and likewise to bring back the receipt before the said certificates of apprenticeship or letters of mastership shall be delivered to them. . . .

LV

In order to favor and patronize further the establishment and subsistence of the said General Hospital, we desire each trade guild of our said city and faubourgs of Paris to be obliged to provide, when they are asked, two journeymen, and the mistress seamstresses two girls, to teach their trade to the children of the said General Hospital, as they shall see fit; and in doing this the said two journeymen and girls will acquire a mastership in their guilds and trades, after having served for the period of six years in the said General Hospital, and certificates shall be delivered and signed by the directors, to the number of at least six, with the right to keep a shop, as do other masters and mistresses, and with no distinctions between them. . . .

LVII

We also want the apothecaries' and surgeons' guilds to each give two members of their said group, capable of serving free in the said hospital, and of helping the poor there and its officials and domestic servants; and after a similar six-year period, the said apothecary and surgeon members shall likewise earn their mastership, with certificates from the directors in like number, and shall have the same rights and privileges as all other masters.

LVIII

And those who have served as schoolmasters and mistresses for ten years in the General Hospital, with the approval of the directors, can be masters and mistresses in the city and faubourgs, with no examination, letters, and permits beyond the directors' certificate confirming their service. . . .

LXIV

We also forbid all inhabitants, assessors, and collectors for the parishes, and all others, to tax or to assess, or to cause to be taxed or assessed, upon the lists of the *tailles*,[10] *taillons*,[11] subsistences, utensils, or other ordinary or extraordinary duties, either for us or for individuals, levied or to be levied, of any nature whatsoever, the tax farmers, sub-tax farmers, receivers, or clerks of the said General Hospital, or its farms, houses, and their dependencies; but in the event that they are eligible to pay, they will be taxed for a modest amount by the *élus*[12] according to the regulations and considering their possessions, without including in them the possessions and the income of all or part of the said General Hospital, which we intend to be entirely exempt, under penalty of the said assessors, collectors, and others, and even the chief inhabitants of the parishes being held answerable for it jointly, in their own and private names, and being compelled by seizures, distraint, and sale of their possessions, of furniture, and buildings, and imprisonment of their persons, to repay the money which had been paid, and all expenses, damages, and interest. Even in the cases of surtaxes on surtaxes which were routinely issued; for which reason we permit the directors to intervene or to take the affair in hand, and to settle it directly in our *Cour des aides*,[13] without the need to make any previous appeals. . . .

Issued in Paris, in the month of April in the year of grace one thousand six hundred and fifty-six, and the thirteenth of our reign.

LOUIS

[10]Direct tax levied by the king on individuals and on land.
[11]Supplement to the *taille*.
[12]Government officers who assessed the *taille*.
[13]Court dealing with disputes over taxes.

Acknowledgments (continued from p. iv)

Loeb Classical Library from *Demosthenes: Volume VI. Private Orations (L–LVIII), In Neaeram (LIX)*, translated by A. T. Murray, Cambridge, Mass.: Harvard University Press, 1939.

"Hellenistic Family Documents." Reprinted by permission of the publishers and the Loeb Classical Library from *Papyri: Volume I. Non-Literary Papyri: Private Documents*, translated by A. S. Hunt and C. C. Edgar, Cambridge, Mass.: Harvard University Press, 1932.

"The Twelve Tables." From Naphtali Lewis and Meyer Reinhold, eds. *Roman Civilization: Selected Readings*, vol I. New York: Columbia University Press, 1953. Copyright 1953 Columbia University Press, NY. Used by permission.

"Management of a Large Estate." Columella. From Naphtali Lewis and Meyer Reinhold, eds. *Roman Civilization: Selected Readings*, vol. II. New York: Columbia University Press, 1955. Copyright 1955 Columbia University Press, NY. Used by permission.

"Marriage, Adultery, and Prostitution." From S. P. Scott, trans., *The Civil Law*, Cincinnati: The Central Trust Co., 1932.

"Germany and Its Tribes." Tacitus. Edward P. Cheney, ed. and trans., *Translations and Reprints from the Original Sources of European History*. University of Pennsylvania Press, 1900.

"The Gospel of Bartholomew." From Edgar Hennecke, *New Testament Apocrypha*, ed. Wilhelm Schneemelcher, trans. R. M. L. Wilson. Philadelphia: Westminster Press, 1963.

"The Martyrdom of Saints Agape, Irene, and Chione." From Herbert Musurillo, ed. *The Acts of the Christian Martyrs*. (Oxford: Clarendon Press, 1972). Reprinted by permission of Oxford University Press.

"The Life of Saint Germanus." From *The Western Fathers*, ed. F. R. Hoare, Sheed and Ward, London and New York, 1954. Reprinted with permission of Sheed and Ward, Kansas City, MO.

"The Burgundian Code." Translated by Katherine Fisher Drew, University of Pennsylvania Press, 1949. Copyright © 1972 by the University of Pennsylvania Press.

"The Carolingian Capitulary Concerning Estates." From *Medieval Culture and Society*, ed. David Herlihy. (New York: Harper & Row, 1968). Copyright © David Herlihy. Reprinted by permission.

"Peasant Landholding." From Georges Duby, *Rural Economy and Country Life in the Medieval West*, translated by Cynthia Postan, University of South Carolina Press, 1968, and Edward Arnold Publishers. Reprinted by permission of University of South Carolina Press and Hodder & Stoughton Ltd.

"The Memoirs of Abbot Guibert of Nogent." Excerpts from *Self and Society in Medieval France: The Memoirs of Albert Guibert of Nogent*, edited by John F. Benton. Copyright © 1970 by John F. Benton. Reprinted by permission of HarperCollins Publishers.

"Marriage in Canon Law." From *The Records of Medieval Europe* by Carolly Erickson. Used by permission of Doubleday, a division of Bantam Doubleday Dell Publishing Group, Inc.

"Early Statutes of the Sorbonne." From *University Records and Life in the Middle Ages*, translated by Lynn Thorndyke. Columbia University Press, 1944 and 1972. Reprinted by permission of Columbia University Press.

"London Assize of Nuisance." From Helena M. Chew and William Kellaway, eds., *London Assizes of Nuisance, 1301–1431*. Copyright London Record Society, 1973. Reprinted by permission of London Record Society.

"Sentences against Heretics." From S. R. Maitland, *Facts and Documents Illustrative of the Heresy, Doctrine, and Rites of the Ancient Albigenses and Waldenses* (London: CJG and F. Rivington, 1832).

"The Annals of Ghent." From *The Annals of Ghent*, edited by Hilda Johnstone, 1951 (London: Thomas Nelson and Sons, Ltd., 1951). Reprinted by permission of Oxford University Press.

"The Black Death." Jean de Venette. From Richard A. Newhall, ed. *The Chronicle of Jean de Venette*, New York: Columbia University Press, 1953. Reprinted by permission of Columbia University Press.

"The Testament of Michele di Vanni Castellani (c. 1370)." From *The Society of Renaissance Florence: A Documentary Study* by Gene Brucker. Copyright © 1971 by Gene Brucker. Reprinted by permission of HarperCollins.

"How to Succeed in Business." An Anonymous Merchant. From *Social and Economic Foundations of the Italian Renaissance*, edited by Anthony Mohlo. John Wiley & Sons, New York, 1969. Reprinted by permission.

"The Goodman of Paris." From Eileen Power, ed. *The Goodman of Paris*. London, George Routledge, 1928.

"Florence: Catasto of 1427." From *The Society of Renaissance Florence: A Documentary Study* by Gene Brucker. Copyright © 1971 by Gene Brucker. Reprinted by permission of HarperCollins.

"On the Family." Leon Battista Alberti. Excerpt from *The Family in Renaissance Florence*, trans. Renee Watkins, from *I Libri della Famiglia* by Leon Battista Alberti, 1969, University of South Carolina Press. Reprinted by permission of Renee Watkins.

"The *Très Riches Heures* of Duc de Berry." Reprinted by permission of the Musée Condé, Chantilly, France.

"Articles of Peasants of Stühlingen and Lupfen." Excerpt from *Manifestations of Discontent in Germany on the Eve of the Reformation*, pp. 153–169, ed. and trans. by Gerald Strauss (Indiana University Press, 1971).

"On Marriage Matters." Martin Luther. Luther's Works, vol. 46. *The Christian in Society*, vol. 3, ed. Robert C. Shultz. General ed. Helmut T. Lehmann. Philadelphia: Fortress Press, 1967. Copyright © 1967 Fortress Press, by permission of Augsburg Fortress.

"Galateo: A Book of Manners." Giovanni della Casa. Excerpt from Giovanni della Casa, *Galateo*, translated by Konrad Eisenbichler & Kenneth R. Bartlett, 1986. Published by Dovehouse Editions, Inc. Second ed., 1989. 32 Glen Ave, Ottawa, Canada KIS 2Z7.

"Spanish Society in the Reign of Philip II." Gianfrancesco Morosoni. Excerpt from *The Pursuit of Power: Venetian Ambassador's Reports on Spain, Turkey, and France in the Age of Philip II, 1560–1600*, translated by James C. Davis. (New York, Evanston, and London.) English translation copyright © 1970 by James C. Davis. Reprinted by permission of HarperCollins Publishers.

"Life in Paris during the French Civil Wars." Pierre de L'Estoile. From Harry Lyman Ruellen, ed., *The Paris of Henry de Navarre as Seen by Pierre de L'Estoile. Selections from His Memoires—Journaux*, Harvard University Press, 1958. Reprinted by permission of Harvard University Press.

"The Miseries of War." Jacques Callot. Etchings from *Callot's Etchings*, edited by Howard Daniel, 1974 (New York: Dover Publications, Inc.). Reprinted by permission of the National Gallery of Art, Washington DC, Rosenwald Collection.

"The Witches of Huntington, Their Examinations and Confessions." 1646 pamphlet.

"The Trail of Diogo Henriques before the Portuguese Inquisition." Reprinted from *The Spanish Inquisition* by Cecil Roth, by permission of W. W. Norton & Co., Inc. All Rights Reserved, Norton Library Edition, published 1964.

"Edict Establishing the General Hospital for the Confining of the Poor Beggars of Paris." Excerpt from *The Century of Louis XIV* by Orest Ranum. Copyright © 1972 by Orest Ranum and Patricia Ranum. Reprinted by permission of HarperCollins Publishers.